Studies in Regional and Local History

General Editor Jane Whittle

Previous titles in this series
Founding Editor Nigel Goose

Volume 1: *A Hertfordshire Demesne of Westminster Abbey: Profits, productivity and weather* by Derek Vincent Stern (edited and with an introduction by Christopher Thornton)

Volume 2: *From Hellgill to Bridge End: Aspects of economic and social change in the Upper Eden Valley, 1840–95* by Margaret Shepherd

Volume 3: *Cambridge and its Economic Region, 1450–1560* by John S. Lee

Volume 4: *Cultural Transition in the Chilterns and Essex Region, 350 AD to 650 AD* by John T. Baker

Volume 5: *A Pleasing Prospect: Society and culture in eighteenth-century Colchester* by Shani D'Cruze

Volume 6: *Agriculture and Rural Society after the Black Death: Common themes and regional variations* by Ben Dodds and Richard Britnell

Volume 7: *A Lost Frontier Revealed: Regional separation in the East Midlands* by Alan Fox

Volume 8: *Land and Family: Trends and local variations in the peasant land market on the Winchester bishopric estates, 1263–1415* by John Mullan and Richard Britnell

Volume 9: *Out of the Hay and into the Hops: Hop cultivation in Wealden Kent and hop marketing in Southwark, 1744–2000* by Celia Cordle

Volume 10: *A Prospering Society: Wiltshire in the later Middle Ages* by John Hare

Volume 11: *Bread and Ale for the Brethren: The provisioning of Norwich Cathedral Priory, 1260–1536* by Philip Slavin

Volume 12: *Poor Relief and Community in Hadleigh, Suffolk, 1547–1600* by Marjorie Keniston McIntosh

Volume 13: *Rethinking Ancient Woodland: The archaeology and history of woods in Norfolk* by Gerry Barnes and Tom Williamson

Volume 14: *Custom and Commercialisation in English Rural Society: Revisiting Tawney and Postan* edited by J.P. Bowen and A.T. Brown

Volume 15: *The World of the Small Farmer: Tenure, profit and politics in the early modern Somerset Levels* by Patricia Croot

Volume 16: *Communities in Contrast: Doncaster and its rural hinterland, c.1830–1870* by Sarah Holland

Volume 17: *Peasant Perspectives on the Medieval Landscape: A study of three communities* by Susan Kilby

Volume 18: *Shaping the Past: Theme, time and place in local history – essays in honour of David Dymond* by Evelyn Lord and Nicholas R. Amor

Volume 19: *Lichfield and the Lands of St Chad: Creating community in early medieval Mercia* by Andrew Sargent

Volume 20: *Histories of People and Landscape: Essays on the Sheffield region in memory of David Hey* edited by R.W. Hoyle

Volume 21: *Managing for Posterity: The Norfolk gentry and their estates c.1450–1700* by Elizabeth Griffiths

Bricks of Victorian London

A social and economic history

Peter Hounsell

University of Hertfordshire Press
Studies in Regional and Local History

Volume 22

First published in Great Britain in 2022 by
University of Hertfordshire Press
College Lane
Hatfield
Hertfordshire
AL10 9AB
UK

© Peter Hounsell 2022

The right of Peter Hounsell to be identified as the author of this work
has been asserted by him in accordance with the Copyright, Designs
and Patents Act 1988.

All rights reserved. No part of this book may be reproduced or
utilised in any form or by any means, electronic or mechanical,
including photocopying, recording or by any information storage and
retrieval system, without permission in writing from the publisher.

British Library Cataloguing in Publication Data
A catalogue record for this book is available from the British Library

ISBN 978-1-912260-56-0 hardback
ISBN 978-1-912260-57-7 paperback

Design by Arthouse Publishing Solutions
Printed in Great Britain by Henry Ling Ltd

In memory of John Armstrong (1944–2017), mentor and friend

Contents

List of illustrations	viii
List of tables	x
Acknowledgements	xi
General Editor's preface	xiii
Introduction	1

Part I: Brickfields

1	A brick-built city: London brickmaking at the beginning of the nineteenth century	7
2	From clay pit to clamp: manufacturing the London stock brick	18
3	Finding the clay: landowners, brickmakers and the availability of land	37
4	'The rage for building': meeting demand for bricks in Victorian London	52
5	Brickfields in town and country	72

Part II: Brickmakers

6	Builders, brickmasters and speculators: brickmaking businesses and their owners	91
7	Land, machinery and labour: operating and financing the brickfield	104
8	The market for bricks: brickmakers, builders' merchants and customers	116
9	From brickfield to building site: delivering the bricks by road, rail and water	127

Part III: Brickies

10	'Hard and inappropriate labour': the brickies at work	151
11	'The perfection of untidiness, dirt and disease': the brickies at home	167
12	'Habits of intemperance': the brickies and the beershop	175
13	'Profane workmen': the brickies at prayer	188
14	Pug boys and barrow loaders: the children of the brickfields	195
15	'The great struggle': industrial disputes and trade unions in the brick industry	213

Part IV: An industry in decline

16	'The chief market is London': the challenge of the Fletton brick	237
17	Into the new century: stock brickmaking after 1900	245

Glossary	255
Bibliography	259
Index	273

Illustrations

Plates

1 Detail from Mylne's map of the geology and contours of London
2 Westminster from Chelsea Fields
3 Hammond Road brickfield, Southall
4 'London going out of town, or the March of Bricks and Mortar'
5 Brickwork in the Houses of Parliament
6 Metropolitan Railway, Baker Street station
7 English country brickworks
8 Stonefields brickfield, Islington
9 Map of Maynard's brickfield, Dawley
10 Kingsland Road brickfields
11 George Smeed
12 Garfield House, Sittingbourne
13 Unloading the barge, Lindsey Wharf, Chelsea
14 'Brickmakers', a family moulding gang
15 'The Brickmaker', a young woman pulling a crowding barrow

Figures

2.1	A chalk mill	20
2.2	Dodd's dustyard, Hoxton	24
2.3	Pug mill made in Sheffield	25
2.4	The layout of a moulding bench	25
2.5	Building a clamp, Edmonton	27
2.6	Belt-driven machinery on a Crayford brickfield	30
4.1	Indices of housebuilding in England and Wales, and London, 1856–1912	56
4.2	Greenwich Railway, Spa Road	59
4.3	Brick output 1785–1849	63
4.4	Brick output for England and Wales and London and the home counties 1816–49	65
5.1	Brick kilns	73
5.2	Brickmakers	73
5.3	Brickmaking districts in the London area in the nineteenth century	79
5.4	Brickmaking districts around the Thames Estuary, Swale and Medway	82
6.1	Gore Court, Sittingbourne	96
7.1	Advert for Bawden's brickmaking machinery	107
8.1	Advertisement for F. & G. Rosher, builders' merchants	120
9.1	Advertisement for Eastwoods, brickmakers and builder's merchants	129
9.2	Eastwoods' barge passing Greenwich Hospital	135
9.3	Brickmaking districts along the Grand Junction Canal in west Middlesex	138
9.4	Canal boat laden with bricks on the Grand Junction Canal	142
10.1	Crockett family at Starveall, West Drayton	165
10.2	Setters at a Crayford brickfield	166
11.1	The Visit to the Brickmaker's by 'Phiz' (Hablot Knight Browne)	168
11.2	Brickfield cottages at North Hyde, Heston	169
11.3	Smeed, Dean's houses at Murston	171
11.4	The Wooden Row, West Drayton	174
12.1	Brickmakers' Arms public house, Murston	180
13.1	Westbrook Memorial Hall, Heston	193
14.1	Heston National School	198
14.2	Children at work in a brickyard	205
14.3	Moulding gang at Edmonton	211
15.1	Brickmaking agreement 1883	216
15.2	Will Thorne, leader of the Gas Workers and General Labourers Union	222
16.1	London Brick Company yard at Fletton	241
17.1	Brickfields at Murston	250

Tables

3.1 Brick production at Findsbury Manor Farm, 1828–50	47
4.1 The growth in London's housing stock, 1801–1901	54
4.2 Estimated brick output by decade, 1820–86	67
4.3 Districts supplying bricks to London, *c.*1890	69
5.1 London brickfields visited by Ernest Dobson in the 1840s	78
5.2 Number of brickfields in counties surrounding London, 1860 and 1890	81
7.1 Costs of setting up a brickfield, 1899	110
7.2 Estimates of the costs of making 1000 bricks	110
8.1 Comparative costs of producing stock bricks in Middlesex and Kent	118

Acknowledgements

This book has been a long time in the making and so my thanks to people who have assisted me go back several decades to the time when I first began the research for my doctoral thesis. Above all my thanks go to the late Professor John Armstrong, my supervisor at Thames Valley University (now University of West London), to whom this book is dedicated, and my external supervisor Professor Martin Daunton (UCL and then Cambridge).

Much of the early research took place in the London Metropolitan Archives, and I am grateful for the assistance I received there, as well as at the National Archives, the British Library and the Kent Record Centre, and from archivists and local studies librarians at the City of Westminster and the London boroughs of Camden, Ealing, Hackney, Hillingdon, Hounslow and Islington.

A number of libraries and individuals have helped me in the search for illustrations at the local studies libraries at Bexley, Ealing, Enfield, Hillingdon, Hounslow, Islington and the Royal Borough of Kensington and Chelsea, at the London Metropolitan Archives and at the Science and Society Picture Library. I particularly appreciate the help of Andrew Mortlock at the London Brick Company's archive at King's Dyke brickworks, Allen Whitnell at Sittingbourne Museum and Tony Millatt at Mersea Museum. Matthew Goodhew, of Swale Borough Council, kindly arranged for me to see the portrait of George Smeed, which hangs in the Council Chamber in Sittingbourne. Mark Collins, the Estates Historian at the Houses of Parliament, made it possible for me to view the bricks in parts of the building not usually shown to visitors.

I have benefited greatly from my membership of the British Brick Society and the opportunity it has provided to go on visits to brickmakers near London who still make bricks by hand, particularly W.H. Collier at Marks Tey and H.G. Matthews at Chesham.

I have much enjoyed working with my friend Gary Marsh, a professional cartographer, who kindly drew the maps for this book as a retirement project. Dr Philip Woods kindly read an earlier draft of the text and gave me helpful comments and encouragement.

Jane Housham at UH Press saw enough in an early draft of this book to help me shape it into a version that could be published, and I am grateful to her and her colleague Sarah Elvins for seeing it through the press.

Finally, and most importantly, my family and friends have had to endure my enthusiasm for the history of brickmaking over the last three decades. My wife, Frances, herself a writer of local history, tolerated frequent discussions about my research, mostly with good humour, and has read several drafts of the book, as well as helping me compile the index.

Studies in Regional and Local History

General Editor's preface

The transformation of the British economy during the late eighteenth and nineteenth centuries was literally made of brick. Bricks were not only essential to urban expansion and the construction of factories and workshops, but to canals, railways and sewers. Yet the humble brick rarely features in histories of the period: it is hidden in plain sight. The production of bricks was not subject to the radical technological transformation experienced by iconic industries such as cotton or steel, but given it underpinned so many other transformations, it begs closer attention. This is what Peter Hounsell provides in this rich and detailed study of the brick industry in Victorian London. Like all the best local studies the book takes a multifaceted approach, combining the histories of business, technological change, landscape, architecture, labour, and many aspects of society. In doing so, it shows how all these approaches intersect in the lives of the men, women and children who worked in brickfields across London and the surrounding regions.

In common with many of the less glamorous industries of the nineteenth century, brick production was a messy combination of the old and the new. Most brick production took place in small, often ephemeral, businesses. These were set up by people from a wide range of backgrounds including builders, farmers, gentlemen and tradesmen. In common with agriculture, it relied on access to the right sort of land, and for much of the period it was seasonal. Clay was dug in the autumn and early winter, allowed to weather, and then moulded into bricks in late spring and summer. The winter workforce was only a tenth of that employed in the other half of the year. Brick-makers (known as brickies) worked in teams of six people, often including men, women and children from the same family. One adult male worker, the moulder, contracted with the brick-master and paid the other team members. In the 1860s up to half of the brickies working in these teams were children. Seasonality and fluctuations in the building trade made the work precarious and casual. Despite the fact they created the building block of some of the grandest architecture in London, brickies were lucky if their own housing was built of brick and had basic facilities such as cooking hearths. Yet brick-making was not immune to the wider changes of the period, with the 1870s marking transformations in both production technology and the organisation of labour. Steam and petrol replaced horses in providing power to mix the clay before moulding; improved methods of firing the bricks were introduced; and the moulding of bricks was gradually mechanised. In the same period legislation reduced the numbers of children and women employed, and workers began to organise in friendly societies and unions. By the end of the century however, bricks produced in the London region were being under-cut by Fletton bricks from near Peterborough. Fletton bricks, made of Lower Oxford Clay, were cheap to produce and created bricks that were ugly but very strong. The First World War spelled the end for the majority of brick producers in the London region.

Bricks of Victorian London provides many fascinating insights. London stock bricks were made not just from clay, dug out the brick fields, but of clay mixed with

Bricks of Victorian London

powdered chalk and ashes. Ashes were obtained from the dustmen who collected domestic refuse, around 80 per cent of which consisted of ash and clinker. The brickies sifted this material and used the rest to fire the bricks: an interesting example of recycling. Most nineteenth-century brick production used clay near the surface in areas with limited deposits. As a consequence, brick fields shifted over time but left in their wake traces of their existence: fields with a ground level inexplicably a few feet lower than the surrounding area, pubs named 'The Brickmaker's Arms', and numerous street and field names incorporating the element 'brick'. Finally, the book is particularly rich in evidence about the lives of workers. Brick-makers were much maligned by Victorian commentators as unruly, drunken, uneducated and irreligious. But often living outside more established communities, they were independent and ferociously hard-working, with their own work-practices and culture. These were the people who built London, alongside the investors, architects and builders who have more often gained the attention of historians.

Jane Whittle
Exeter, June 2022

Introduction

Brickmaking as an industry is less studied by historians than other sectors of the economy, but the expansion of the built environment of London during the nineteenth century surely reminds us of the importance of the construction industry and the materials on which it depended for the history of the capital.

There are some possible reasons for this neglect. Many brickmaking operations were quite small scale, and the size of the industry as a whole came not from a few dominant businesses but rather from the aggregation of many small units. A sense of this can be got from the number of times the label 'Brickfield' appears on nineteenth-century Ordnance Survey maps of the London area. Many of these businesses were short-lived and had little management infrastructure, and few of them have left much in the way of records, such as account books or sales ledgers. Their history is difficult to put together and has to be reconstructed from a range of sources. Small brickfields did not have many, if any, permanent buildings and there is a consequent lack of industrial archaeology to allow later generations to visualise the nature and scale of the work that took place on them. This contrasts, for example, with the solid bulk of cotton mills or warehouses, or the surviving chimneys and winding gear of mines. It was only at the end of the nineteenth century, when the larger businesses started to erect multi-chamber continuous kilns, that the skyline in brickmaking districts become dominated by groups of tall chimneys. Nevertheless, brickmaking was an industry that made an important contribution to the economy, employing thousands of people and making possible the rapid physical development of towns and cities in the nineteenth century, as well as the infrastructure of railways, canals and docks.

Despite apparent neglect, brickmaking is studied by some academic historians and a larger number of enthusiasts, and has its own special interest group in the British Brick Society. A handful of books provides a good introduction to bricks and brickmaking, and a number of regional studies have been published that carry detailed information about brickfields in particular areas.[1] However, relatively little has been written on the brick industry that supplied the London market, although Alan Cox's chapter 'Bricks to build a capital', in a volume about the building materials used in London after the fire of 1666, provides a succinct introduction to how and where they were made, how they were transported to London and where they were used.[2]

This book draws on that research and focuses on a shorter period than does Cox, roughly from 1800 to the First World War, but looks at the industry in more detail. It examines the different groups of people with an interest in brickmaking – landowners

---

1 J. Woodforde, *Bricks to build a house* (London, 1976); M. Hammond, *Bricks and brickmaking* (Aylesbury, 1981); C. Haynes, *Brick: a social history* (Cheltenham, 2019).

2 A. Cox, 'Bricks to build a capital', in H. Hobhouse and A. Saunders (eds), *Good and proper materials: the fabric of London since the Great Fire* (London, 1989), pp. 3–17.

1

Bricks of Victorian London

who had clay on their land, men and women who saw an opportunity to build a profitable business by exploiting that clay and the people who actually manufactured the bricks. This is set within an economic history framework examining supply and demand, the costs of manufacture and the way brickfields were financed.

The book is divided into four sections. In the first I consider how and why a brickmaking industry developed in the London area, and particularly how it expanded after the Great Fire; how the distinctive London stock brick was made; where the brickfields were located; and the demand and supply factors that affected the numbers of bricks that were produced. The section ends with a consideration of how manufacturers distributed the bricks from the production site to their customers.

The second section focuses on the businesses themselves and the people who ran them. It also provides some thoughts about the economics of the industry. Finally, it considers how bricks were sold and how a market for bricks developed.

Section three switches the focus to the people who actually made the bricks, known familiarly at the time as *brickies*. It examines their working lives, their homes and their habits. The workforce in nineteenth-century brickmaking was made up not only of men but also of large numbers of women and children, so a chapter looks at children's employment and how it was eventually controlled through the extension of the Factory Acts. A final chapter considers the attempts the brickies made to improve their pay and working conditions and how trade unions helped in achieving these aims.

The final section considers how the industry in the London area entered a long process of decline at the beginning of the twentieth century as a result of both the exhaustion of clay reserves and competition from brickmaking in other parts of the country, particularly the area around Peterborough.

The origins of this book go back several decades. I made my first tentative steps at researching London brickmaking in the 1970s, when I was interested in brickmaking in just a small area of West London near where I live: the village, now suburb, of Northolt in the present London Borough of Ealing. When I decided in the 1990s to work towards a doctorate in history I took the wider brickmaking area of west Middlesex as my subject – the area known in the nineteenth century as the 'Cowley district', from the village of that name near Uxbridge.[3]

Returning to brickmaking more recently, I have expanded the coverage in different ways: first geographically, to bring in brickmakers elsewhere in the London area and in the counties of Surrey, Essex and Kent who all supplied the London market with bricks; and secondly in terms of the people involved, both the owners and the men, women and children who worked for them. It is my hope, therefore, to have provided a rounded view of the industry during the nineteenth century.

But that is not all. I would like to think that this study will shed light on nineteenth-century economic and social life in a broader way. Although brickmaking is a distinctive industry it shares characteristics such as business structures, employment conditions, seasonality of employment and child labour with other parts of the Victorian economy. It also contributes to our understanding of the way that large cities such as London

---

3   P. Hounsell, 'Cowley stocks: brickmaking in West Middlesex from 1800', PhD thesis (Thames Valley University, 2000).

Introduction

interact with their hinterland and the interplay between the centre and the periphery. Brickmaking forms part of a larger network of trades and industries located on the outskirts of London – such as market gardening and dairying – that sustained the capital and allowed it to grow rapidly during the nineteenth century. There was always two-way traffic, particularly in the way that London imported food, building materials such as gravel, sand and cement, and other essentials, and in turn exported its waste materials. For example, hay came into the capital to feed the horses that provided the motive power of the capital, and the stable manure was returned to fertilise the fields on which the next crop of hay would be grown. In a similar way, the domestic refuse of London, particularly the residue from the ubiquitous coal fires, contributed the fuel to burn the bricks that were then used in the expansion of the built environment.

It is necessary to explain what this book does not attempt to do. It does not set out to document all the brickmaking firms that were active in the London area during the nineteenth century, so readers in search of a particular business or the brickmaking in a particular district may be disappointed. Other writers have done this for particular areas, as, for example, I did for the Cowley district, the Harper Smiths did for Acton and Pat Ryan for Essex.[4] I have drawn on their work, but my intention is different, that is to paint a more general picture of the industry in its different aspects.

Like many other industries, brickmaking has its own jargon. *Brickmaker* is a term that applies to both the person who physically made the bricks and the person who owned the brickfield. The latter were sometimes referred to as *brickmasters*, just as the former called themselves *brickies*, or in a more precise way *operative brickmakers*. The places where bricks were made were referred to both as *brickfields* and *brickworks*, the first reflecting that at the heart of any brickmaking operation was a piece of land with clay in it, the second used when a site had buildings and machinery. I have attempted to explain each new term as it is encountered in the text, but there is a glossary of terms at the back of the book for easy reference.

Lastly, I have used the units of measurement in use at the time rather than convert them into their modern decimal equivalents. So, throughout, area is delimited in acres, rods and perches and money is measured in pounds, shillings and pence. I have not generally attempted to give equivalent modern values for nineteenth-century prices; for readers keen to do that there are websites that provide conversions. However, one comparison might be instructive in comparing prices in the mid-nineteenth century with modern ones. Back then hand-made stock bricks sold for between 30s and 40s (£1.50 to £2) per thousand, while a modern hand-made stock brick costs about £2, or £2000 a thousand.[5]

---

4   A. and T. Harper Smith, *The Brickfields of Acton*, 2nd edn (Acton, 1991); P. Ryan, *Brick in Essex: the clayworking craftsmen and gazetteer of sites* (Chelmsford, 1999).

5   See, for example, <https://www.measuringworth.com/datasets/ukearncpi/> for a guide to earnings and retail prices, accessed 2 May 2022. Prices for a modern stock brick from <www.travisperkins.co.uk/product/building-materials/bricks-and-blocks>, accessed 21 December 2021.

Part I: Brickfields

Chapter 1

A brick-built city: London brickmaking at the beginning of the nineteenth century

The London region is said to be 'lamentably short of good quality building stone', and thus stone has always had to be brought from some distance into the city.[1] The sources closest and most accessible to London, but not necessarily the best, were Kentish ragstone and Reigate stone, and these were used as early as Roman times for buildings and the city walls. The Normans continued to use both for buildings such as the Tower of London, but also imported stone from Caen, in their homeland. After the Great Fire of 1666 Portland stone, transported by sea from Dorset, was widely used by Wren and other architects for their more prestigious commissions, of which St Paul's Cathedral is the most notable.[2] However, if stone continued to be used for churches and public buildings in the following centuries, brick became the common material for residential property in the squares and terraces of Georgian London. In the Regency and early Victorian period, however, the brickwork was sometimes obscured by a layer of stucco to meet the taste for evenly textured and coloured frontages.[3]

The origins of brickmaking are in the distant past, since clay has been used as a building material since prehistoric times. At its simplest river mud was applied to a wood or reed framework to create a wall; a more sophisticated method involved shaping wet clay into blocks and drying them in the sun.[4] The Romans are credited with introducing brick building into Britain, and evidence of their use of bricks survives from many sites across the country.[5] When the city of Londinium grew up on the north bank of the Thames suitable brick clay was readily available in the vicinity and evidence of Roman building is seen in surviving portions of the city walls, where tile courses as well as ragstone were used to face a rubble core.[6]

With the collapse of the Roman Empire in the west in the fifth century brickmaking in Britain fell into abeyance and the techniques were lost, but the many buildings that remained provided a ready source of materials for later builders. The Saxons and Normans recognised the structural potential of Roman clay products and employed

---

1 E. Robinson, 'Geology and building materials', in B. Cherry and N. Pevsner, *The buildings of England: London 3, north west* (London, 2002), pp. 91–3.

2 British Regional Geology, *London and the Thames Valley*, 4th edn, compiled by M.G. Sumbler (London, 1996), pp. 144–7.

3 R. Dixon and S. Muthesius, *Victorian Architecture*, 2nd edn (London, 1985), p. 16.

4 Woodforde, *Bricks*, pp. 19–34.

5 For the archaeological evidence for Roman bricks and tiles in Britain see G. Brodribb, *Roman brick and tile* (Far Thrupp, 1987).

6 J. Hall and R. Merrifield, *Roman London* (London, 1986), pp. 18, 28.

Bricks of Victorian London

them in a great many buildings, particularly in Essex, Kent and Sussex. There appears to have been a plentiful supply of reusable materials; at least a hundred Essex churches contain Roman bricks, which make their most extensive appearance in St Botolph's Priory, Colchester.[7] However, this process of reclamation could not continue indefinitely. The evidence from Essex buildings suggests that a point was reached in the twelfth century when stone came to be used for those structural elements for which salvaged bricks and tiles had previously been preferred. While this may have been a stylistic development, the change may mark the exhaustion of the reserves of undamaged earlier material.[8]

The first new bricks to be manufactured after the end of Roman occupation were produced in the twelfth century and are also seen in Essex, at Coggeshall Abbey. These were large bricks, so-called 'great bricks', and similar ones are found elsewhere in the eastern counties. It is possible that the expertise required to produce such bricks may have come through contacts with Cistercian houses on the continent, where the techniques of brickmaking had been preserved after the collapse of the Roman administration.[9]

During the thirteenth century great bricks were superseded by Flemish bricks, which had proportions similar to modern ones.[10] There is some debate as to whether this new style of brick was produced in England or on the continent, since it is difficult to be sure whether references to *flanderstiles* relate only to bricks imported from the Low Countries or also to bricks of a similar kind made locally. There are records of the shipment of bricks from abroad for particular building projects: over 100,000 Flemish bricks were used in 1283 for the curtain wall of the Tower of London; 114,000 bricks were brought from Calais for the royal palace at Sheen in 1422; and a further 40,000 were shipped for the rebuilding of Mercers' Hall. But, despite the sizeable quantities involved in these transactions, wholesale importation is thought to have been unlikely considering the ready availability of brickmaking clay in the counties closest to the continent as well as the cost of shipment, which, where it can be calculated, accounted for 60 per cent of the total bill.[11]

Certainly, by the fourteenth century indigenous brickmaking had been revived in England. In 1303 a municipal brickyard was established in Hull, and sometime later in the century a similar one operated at Beverley.[12] At the same time that imported bricks were being used at Sheen Palace, bricks were being made at Deptford for

---

7   J. Wight, *Brick building in England from the Middle Ages to 1550* (London, 1972), p. 21; P. Ryan, *Brick in Essex from the Roman Conquest to the Reformation* (Chelmsford, 1996), pp. 15–19.

8   Ryan, *Brick in Essex*, p. 20.

9   *Ibid.*, pp. 22, 43–4.

10   *Ibid.*, p. 31.

11   J. Schofield, *The building of London from the Conquest to the Great Fire* (London, 1984), p. 126; P. Nightingale, *A medieval mercantile community: the Grocers Company and the politics and trade of London, 1000–1485* (London, 1995), pp. 408–9, 413; T.P. Smith, *The medieval brickmaking industry in England, 1400–1450*, British Archaeological Reports British Series 138 (Oxford, 1985), pp. 23–5.

12   Smith, *Medieval brickmaking*, p. 27.

A brick-built city

repairs to London Bridge, although the craftsmen involved were probably Dutch.[13] Brickmakers from the near continent seem to have brought their skills into England, and many Dutch and German *brekemakers* have been identified working at sites in eastern England, where they encountered a familiar raw material.[14]

It was some time, however, before brick became a major building material in England, unlike in other northern European countries with which it had extensive trading links. The contrast can be explained by differences in economic geography, for while England is a small country with a complex geology, the north German plain is a large area where building stone is not readily available. Stone was a potential building material in many parts of England, as T.P. Smith puts it: 'Supplies of all grades of building stone were abundantly available in many parts of the country, and no part of England was so remote from those supplies that transport thereto was entirely unfeasible – at least so far as higher status buildings were concerned.'[15]

This may account for the relatively slow adoption of brick, but the late fifteenth century and the early part of the sixteenth century witnessed a first great age of English brickwork, when bricklayers were able to deploy a high standard of technical expertise and to develop imported details into an assured domestic style. The confident handling of the material is evident in major buildings such as Cambridge colleges, Hampton Court Palace, Lambeth Palace and Lincoln's Inn. John Leland recorded in the mid-sixteenth century that brick and tile were replacing timber and thatch in the London region, and brick became the fashionable material for country houses and even palaces.[16] During the course of the sixteenth century brick building was extended from the eastern counties to Hampshire, Berkshire and the counties around London; elsewhere geology still determined a different choice of building material.[17]

Even when buildings continued to be made mainly from less durable materials there were special applications for which brick was preferred. The constant danger of fire exercised the authorities and regulations requiring chimneys to be built of stone or brick were introduced in London in 1419.[18] A further boost to the use of brick in London came with an Ordinance of James I in 1607 which decreed that new buildings in the city and its suburbs should be built of brick or stone.[19] However, James's proud assertion that 'we found our citie and suburbs of London of stickes, and left them of bricke, being a substance farre more durable, safe from fire and beautiful and magnificent' was not borne out by subsequent events. In his grandson's reign much

---

13   Schofield, *The building of London*, p. 126.

14   J.E. Prentice, *The geology of construction materials* (London, 1990), pp. 163–4.

15   Smith, *Medieval brickmaking*, p. 4.

16   Wight, *Brick building*, pp. 136, 311–12, 314; N.J. Moore, 'Brick', in J. Blair and N. Ramsay (eds), *English medieval industries: craftsmen, techniques, products* (London, 1991), p. 216.

17   M. Airs, *The Tudor and Jacobean country house: a building history* (Far Thrupp, 1975), p. 115.

18   Wight, *Brick building*, pp. 65.

19   James I, *Proclamation touching new buildings and inmates 12 October 1607*, cited in L. Clarke, *Building capitalism: historical change and the labour process in the production of the built environment* (London, 1992), p. 48.

Bricks of Victorian London

of the City was destroyed in the Great Fire, when over 13,000 properties were lost. The enormous enterprise of rebuilding put great demands not only on the ranks of building craftsmen but also on the suppliers of building materials, which were required on a hitherto unknown scale.[20] The Act for the Rebuilding of the City of London of 1667 contained a series of building regulations that set the standards for the development of the streets and squares of the following century and, importantly, stipulated that all new buildings had to be constructed of brick or stone to guard against the future perils of fire.[21]

It is from this point that we can identify a significant and permanent brickmaking industry in the vicinity of London. The urgent need of bricks in the aftermath of the fire necessitated a rapid expansion of brickmaking capacity and encouraged speculators to enter the business in the hope of making a killing. Henry Tisdall was one of the more successful ones. He was given a licence to dig clay in Finsbury, paying a rent of £20 and a royalty of 1s on every thousand bricks made; he achieved an output of only 6400 bricks in the first season, but about 1.4 million in the next two years and a more impressive 2.7 million in 1669–70.[22]

A measure of the degree to which brick had become accepted as a major building material can be seen in the attempts to regulate its manufacture from the late fifteenth century onward. A statute of Edward IV in 1477 sought to standardise tile sizes, and there is earlier evidence from Essex that use of a standard mould was being enforced to reduce the irregularity of brick sizes.[23] Like most crafts, London brickmaking became subject to regulation by a City Company, though much later than many other trades and professions. Even then, the impetus came from the end users, the bricklayers, rather than the producers. The Tilers & Bricklayers Company was incorporated in 1568, and was given a monopoly of the supply of bricks and tiles and powers to regulate brick and tilemaking within an area of fifteen miles of the city.[24] This may suggest that many bricklayers and tilers were also manufacturers of the materials they used; however, it may have come about because the building craftsmen were better organised than the men who supplied them.

Despite the jurisdiction enjoyed by the Company, brickmaking remained a poorly regulated trade. The Company's records contain a few examples of brickmakers being bound as apprentices, but this kind of craft organisation never became strongly established. Indeed, a court case of 1615 confirmed that brickmaking was not

---

20 For the fire and its aftermath, see T.F. Reddaway, *The rebuilding of London after the Great Fire* (London, 1940), and S. Porter, *The Great Fire of London* (Stroud, 1996).

21 18 & 19 Charles II, c.2, *An act for the rebuilding of the city of London* (1667).

22 Other speculators, such as the diarist John Evelyn, got their fingers burnt. He lost £500 from an ill-considered venture into brickmaking. Porter, *Great Fire of London*, p. 125; T.P. Smith, '"Upon an adventure with others": John Evelyn and brickmaking after the Great Fire of London', *BBS Information*, 103 (April 2007), pp. 10–15.

23 Wight, *Brick building in England*, p. 28.

24 S. Inwood, *A history of London* (London, 1998), p. 106; W.G. Bell, *A short history of the Worshipful Company of Tylers and Bricklayers of the City of London* (London, 1938), pp. 18–19.

A brick-built city

included in the apprenticeship regulations of the Statute of Artificers of 1563, for it was said 'they are arts which require rather ability of body rather than skill'.[25] These apprenticeship clauses, in any case, were discontinued in a great many trades long before the Act itself was finally repealed in 1814.[26] A mid-eighteenth-century handbook on different trades appears to confirm this; the author equated a brick moulder with a journeyman, 'if they can properly be called so, who are paid by the master at so much a thousand'. He states that 'although they take no apprentices, they hire boys by the week, who learn the business as they grow up'.[27] Little had changed by the early nineteenth century, with moulders contracting with the owner to make bricks at a fixed piece rate and forming their own gangs, which included boys, who would learn the trade alongside the adults.

As brickmaking extended from the east coast to new parts of the country a variety of different types of brick came to be made, depending on the clays that were available. Clays are essentially weathered rocks that, when mixed with a suitable proportion of water, assume elastic qualities. They occur in many parts of Britain, but they are not uniform in composition and can occur in formations of varied geological ages. Nevertheless, 'as long as some small proportion of clay mineral is present, some kind of brick can be produced'.[28] Some clays were too hard to work by hand, and their exploitation had to await the invention of suitable machinery in the nineteenth and twentieth centuries. Most earlier brickmaking utilised superficial clays – that is, those near the surface of the soil – which were easily worked. By contrast, the economics of the modern industry require deep clay deposits that will support long-term investment and large-scale production, and this has caused manufacturers to abandon many previously used types of clay.[29] The discovery of the Lower Oxford clay, found beneath superficial deposits that were already being worked, revolutionised British brickmaking after 1880 – a development discussed in a later chapter.[30]

Brickmaking in the vicinity of London employed clays of the most recent geological age, the Pleistocene. These sedimentary clays are thought to be wind-blown loess deposits, containing only a small proportion of clay minerals but rich in silica, which vitrifies when fired and gives the yellow stock brick the durability for which it is renowned, surviving in the heavily polluted air of the nineteenth- and early twentieth-century city. These clays were referred to as *brickearth* and they supported

---

25 R.H. Tawney and E. Power (eds), *Tudor economic documents* (London, 1924), vol. 1, p. 382; E. Lipson, *The economic history of England*, vol. 3 (London, 1934), pp. 280–2.

26 Clarke, *Building capitalism*, p. 71; M.J. Daunton, *Progress and poverty: an economic and social history of Britain, 1700–1850* (Oxford, 1995), p. 275.

27 R. Campbell, *The London tradesman, being a compendious view of all the trades, professions, arts ... now practised in the cities of London and Westminster* [1747] (Newton Abbot, 1969), p. 169.

28 Prentice, *Geology*, p. 164.

29 *Ibid.*, p. 157.

30 J. Blunden, *The mineral resources of Britain* (London, 1975), pp. 151, 155.

Bricks of Victorian London

the major industry in Kent, Essex and Middlesex.[31] They should not be confused with the heavier London clay, which underlies the surface layers and contains a high proportion of smectite, which makes it liable to excessive shrinkage.[32] It is generally thought unsuitable for modern brickmaking, but one recent survey suggests that 'It was more widely used in the past; the vast numbers of bricks used to build the expanding London suburbs in the nineteenth century were the product of weathered London clay blended with street sweepings of grit and cinder.'[33]

Brickearth occurs on the alluvial terraces that border the present course of the River Thames; their presence is testament to changing water levels over geological time. Thus suitable material for hand brickmaking was found readily in the London area and experienced brickmakers would have been able to identify material appropriate for their needs. During the course of the nineteenth century, with the development of a more scientific understanding of geology, the occurrence of suitable brick clays could be more accurately predicted. The first comprehensive geological map of the London area, produced by R.W. Mylne in 1856, indicates the presence of extensive brickearth deposits (Plate 1).[34]

As the volume of brickmaking in the counties surrounding London expanded to meet the growing demand for bricks in the capital, so the best clays – the *malms* – were worked out, and brickmakers created artificial malms by mixing inferior clay with chalk and *breeze*, the ashes from coal fires, a technique that will be described in more detail later on. Judging the right proportions of the different ingredients required a level of expertise; brickmakers had to decide the potential of soils by eye and touch, drawing on their experience. By the mid-nineteenth century the chemical constituents had been identified, but the chemistry of brick clays is complex and a fuller understanding awaited more modern methods of analysis.[35]

It is thought that methods of brick manufacture changed little between the fifteenth century and the nineteenth. Early illustrations of brickmakers at work, such as the much reproduced plate from the *Netherlandische Bijbel* of 1425, purporting to illustrate the Jews making bricks in Egypt, show methods of manufacture similar to those described and illustrated in subsequent centuries.[36] In 1683 John Houghton

---

31 For a fuller explanation of the nature and qualities of brickearth see I. Smalley, 'London stock bricks: from Great Fire to Great Exhibition', *BBS Information*, 147 (March 2021), pp. 26–34, and I. Smalley, A. Assadi-Langroudi and G. Lill, 'Choice or chance: the virtues of London stock bricks for the construction of the Bazalgette sewer network in London c.1860–1880', *BBS Information*, 148 (September 2021), pp. 10–19.

32 Prentice, *Geology*, p. 164.

33 British Regional Geology, *London and the Thames Valley*, p. 140.

34 R.W. Mylne, *Map of the geology and contours of London and its environs 1856*, with an introduction by Eric Robinson, London Topographical Society no. 146 (London, 1993).

35 An example of the Victorian knowledge of clay chemistry can be seen in H. Chamberlain, 'The manufacture of bricks by machinery', *Journal of the Society of Arts*, 185/4 (6 June 1856), pp. 491–524. For a more modern description see P.S. Keeling, *The geology and minerology of brick clays* (London, 1963).

36 Woodforde, *Bricks*, p. 59; Wight, *Brick building*, p. 112.

A brick-built city

set out a description of contemporary brickmaking methods in a report to the sheriff of Bristol: he described the digging of the soil; the weathering of the clay over winter; its tempering in the spring; the use of a mould and a moulding bench with the board known as the *stock* – hence the description of this type of manufacture as stock brickmaking; the placing of the new bricks on a pallet; the transfer of the bricks to the hack ground for drying; and finally their burning in a kiln.[37] This method of manufacture remained the dominant one in the London area throughout the nineteenth century.

If in the fourteenth century some provincial towns had documented brickyards, it was probable that London, with its greater extent and scale of demand, would have supported a number of brickmakers on its outskirts. Brickmaking was more likely to be found on the east side of London and it was here that many industries developed, because the prevailing south-westerly winds kept the smoke out of the City. On the western side the City of Westminster, by contrast, became a residential and administrative centre. In the fifteenth century there were brickfields and limekilns on land belonging to the episcopal manor of Stepney, and there were several brickmakers in the Whitechapel area. John Stow described how in 1477–8 at the instruction of the mayor of London Moorfields had been 'searched for clay' to provide bricks to repair the City walls, and how a century later a large field in Spitalfields was 'broken up for clay to make bricks'.[38] Brick Lane had been so named as early as the mid-sixteenth century and was, according to Defoe, 'frequented chiefly by carts fetching bricks that way into White-chapel from brick kilns in those fields [Spitalfields] and had its name on that account'.[39] A number of sites where brickmaking was taking place are identified in the wake of the Great Fire, including Finsbury, Shoreditch, Red Lion Fields and Lamb's Conduit Fields.[40]

Following the rebuilding of the City after the Great Fire, housing development started in what would become the west end of London, and the owners of the great estates that dominated landholding – such as the Bedford or Grosvenor estates – began to make land available to speculative developers such as the financier Nicholas Barbon. He was, in the words of John Summerson, 'active all over London, building here a square, here a market, here a few streets or chambers for lawyers'.[41] An example of his work is Red Lion Square, dating from the 1680s. The first eighteenth-century building boom began after the Treaty of Utrecht in 1713 brought an end to a quarter of a century of continous warfare. The relative stability following the end of the war provided a favourable economic climate in which development could take

---

37 Woodforde, *Bricks*, pp. 58–60; Haynes, *Brick*, pp. 107–11.

38 K. McDonnell, *Medieval London suburbs* (London, 1978), pp. 122–3; J. Stow, *A survey of London reprinted from the text of 1603*, ed. C.L. Kingsford (Oxford, 1908), pp. 5–10, 163–75 <http://www.british-history.ac.uk/no-series/survey-of-london-stow/1603>, accessed 7 April 2021.

39 A.D. Mills, *Oxford dictionary of London place names* (Oxford, 2001), p. 29; D. Defoe, *A tour through the whole island of Great Britain*, abridged and edited by P.N. Furbank and W.R. Owens (London, 1991), p. 138.

40 E. McKellar, *The birth of modern London: the development and design of the city, 1660–1720* (Manchester, 1999), p. 74.

41 J. Summerson, *Georgian London*, rev. edn (Harmondsworth, 1978), p. 45.

Bricks of Victorian London

place.[42] Mayfair was laid out in spacious squares and neat terraces. Thereafter, speculative building continued throughout the century, but with periods of more or less intensive activity. Although the houses often had some ornamental stonework, they were essentially built of brick, making brick 'a vital component' for the builders of the period.[43]

The growth of new neighbourhoods created a demand for bricks that was largely met by the output of the local brickfields producing London stock bricks. At the end of the seventeenth century, when the 'Queen Anne' style predominated, the choice of architects was a red brick juxtaposed with white stonework, and the new ranges that Christopher Wren added to Hampton Court Palace around 1690 are among the finest examples of this style. On a smaller scale Wren rebuilt many London churches in brick with prominent stone quoins, creating a similar contrast of materials and colours.[44] However, in subsequent decades the fashion changed to something more muted. Isaac Ware had complained in the 1750s that 'the colour [of red brick] is fiery and disagreeable to the eye' and 'that there is something harsh in the transition from red brick to stone'. He thought that 'the grey stocks are to be judged best coloured when they have least of the yellow cast; for the nearer they come to the colour of stone ... the better'.[45] London stocks were in use for much of the Georgian period, and came in a range of colours, from a purplish shade to the grey that Ware advocated. Grey stocks were specified by the architect James Gibbs for St Peter's Church, Vere Street (just north of Oxford Street) in 1724, but the bricks actually used are largely a mixture of yellow and purple. Architectural fashion would change during the course of the century, but, as Alan Cox observes, because of the variety of shades 'the colour of the brick, on its own, does not provide a reliable method of dating buildings'. Nevertheless, in general terms, red or maroon bricks seem to have been preferred in the early decades of the eighteenth century, pale yellow or off-white in the middle decades and so-called malm bricks, with a more decided yellow colour, after 1770. In 1776 the agreement for the houses in Bedford Square stipulated that the bricks should be 'good grey stocks of uniform colour', but the bricks used were more yellow than grey.[46]

Although it is easy to see bricks in the houses of the Georgian period, even buildings that are otherwise clad in stone will have bricks in their construction.[47] The architectural impact of St Paul's Cathedral comes from Wren's use of Portland stone, but large quantities of bricks were used in largely hidden areas, including the vaulting

---

42   F.H.W. Sheppard (ed.), *Survey of London, vol. 39, The Grosvenor Estate in Mayfair, Part 1: General history* (London, 1977), p. 6.

43   A. Cox, 'A vital component: stock bricks in Georgian London', *Construction History*, 13 (1997), pp. 57–66.

44   J.W.P. Campbell, *Brick: a world history* (London, 2003), pp. 178–9.

45   I. Ware, *A complete body of architecture* (London, 1756), p. 61.

46   Cox, 'A vital component', pp. 58–9.

47   Crypts are often a good place to see brickwork in stone-clad buildings. Examples include St John, Smith Square (1728) or St Martin-in-the-Fields (1726).

A brick-built city

of the roof and in the crypt.[48] Bricks were also used in the churches built under the Fifty New Churches Act of 1711, including a number of fine buildings by Nicholas Hawksmoor, and the Commissioners responsible for the building programme took a keen interest in the quality of the bricks they were offered.[49]

Because of the prevalence of brickearth the demand for bricks in London during the eighteenth century could be met by the brickfields in the still rural areas surrounding the cities of London and Westminster and the inner suburbs, from which bricks could be delivered to the building site by horse and cart. Alternatively, they could be made on the building site itself, especially where the scale of building called for large numbers. The bricks for Wren's new ranges at Hampton Court were burnt on the grounds, but he bought bricks for Greenwich Hospital from a Mr Foe, later better known as the writer Daniel Defoe, at Tilbury in the 1690s.[50] Cavendish Square and Berkeley Square, from the 1720s and 1730s respectively, were built of bricks made on the spot and the garden in the middle of Russell Square is in a hollow created when clay was dug out for brickmaking around 1800.[51]

Brickmaking in the neighbourhood of residential areas was a continual irritant because of both the smoke that the kilns created and the passage of the heavy brick carts, which churned up road surfaces. Defoe had noted that 'Brick Lane ... was a deep dirty road' on account of the quantity of brick carts passing along it and, forty years later, Jonas Hanway complained of the way that Londoners had despoiled the outskirts of their city: 'We have taken pains to render its environs displeasing both to sight and smell. The chain of brick kilns that surround us, like the scars of the smallpox, makes us lament the ravages of beauty and the diminution of infant aliment.'[52] In a similar vein, but in verse, Charles Jenner lamented the northwards spread of the city, and with it the brickfields that supplied its growth: 'Where-ere around I cast my wand'ring eyes | Long burning rows of fetid bricks arise.'[53]

Brickfields established in areas further from the city probably developed mainly in response to local needs. In the sixteenth century there were, for example, tile kilns in Hampstead, at that time a separate village, and in 1665 there were brick clamps, an open kind of kiln, on Hampstead Heath.[54] John Yeoman, a visitor to Brentford in 1774, noted that the houses thereabouts were built of brick manufactured locally:

> The fields around the town are most of him [brick clay]. Dug out for clay they call it but it is sand and they mix it together In the fall of the year, Let it by all the

---

48 J.W.P. Campbell, *Building St Paul's* (London, 2008), pp. 100–2.

49 Summerson, *Georgian London*, pp. 84–97; M.H. Port (ed.), *The commission for building fifty new churches: the minute books 1711–27, a calendar*, London Record Society (London, 1986), p. 72.

50 Campbell, *Brick*, p. 179; F. Bastian, *Defoe's early life* (London, 1981), pp. 190–1.

51 Cox, 'A vital component', p. 62.

52 Defoe, *Tour*, p. 138; quoted in D. George, *London life in the eighteenth century* [1925] (Harmondsworth, 1965), p. 106.

53 Quoted in R. Porter, *London: a social history* (London, 1994), p. 94.

54 *Victoria County History. Middlesex, vol. 9: Hampstead and Paddington parishes*, ed. C.R. Elrington (London, 1989), p. 124.

Bricks of Victorian London

> winter before It will be fit to work. They don't burn them in kilns as we do here [in his native Hampshire], but they put them in a pile with Coal and Straw at the bottom with coal at every layer of bricks.[55]

We may draw two conclusions from his observations: first, that brickmaking was well established in the Brentford area at the time of writing, and that Brentford, with its Thames-side location, would have been in a position to supply other parts of London close to the river, rather than just a local market; and, secondly, that the method of stock brickmaking, with its seasonal routine of digging clay in the autumn and allowing it to weather over the winter, and its preference for clamp firing rather than the use of kilns, was well established.

London stock bricks provided the main element of the fabric of much of the domestic building of the eighteenth century, but in the fashionable squares and terraces there is usually some contrasting material. This might be stone, or the artificial Coade stone, a type of white terracotta that was in use in London in the 1770s. Bright red brick also makes a discreet appearance in the surrounds of windows, where gauged brickwork is often seen. Bricks are cut or rubbed to a particular shape and precisely measured or gauged to fit, for example, as part of a flat arch over a window. This treatment calls for a special type of brick, known as a rubber or cutter, which has a soft but uniform texture, enabling it to be cut with an axe or a saw and finished with rubbing stones, a time-consuming process that made rubbed and gauged brickwork twice as expensive as normal brickwork.[56] London stocks were unsuitable for such work, as a sandy loam is required to provide the right texture. It is thought that such bricks would have been sourced in Kent, Sussex or Berkshire, but some red bricks were manufactured in the London area from a stratum of soil that overlay the brickearth used to make regular stocks, and containing less lime. This allowed the red oxide in the clay to predominate when the bricks were fired. Unlike stock bricks, which were usually burnt in clamps, red bricks were usually fired in kilns. A number of bottle kilns, used for pottery and tiles as well as bricks, could be found at places around London in this period and later.[57]

In addition to London stocks, some use was made of bricks from further afield for prestigious projects. Just as Portland stone was shipped around the coast and up the Thames to central London, so it was possible to transport bricks by sea and river where the budget could absorb the additional costs. White bricks were transported from Suffolk, via the River Stour and down the east coast to the Thames estuary, to supply the style wanted by architects following the fashion started by Henry Holland at Brook's Club in 1776–8. Suffolk whites – made from a Gault clay – would remain popular in the nineteenth century.[58] Bricks like these made up only a small proportion of the bricks used in the city's buildings, however. For most of its needs, London relied

---

55 J. Yeoman, *Diary of the visits of John Yeoman to London in the years 1774 and 1777*, ed. M. Yearsley (London, 1934), p. 48. Spelling modernised.

56 Campbell, *Brick*, pp. 190–1.

57 Cox, 'A vital component', pp. 60–1.

58 Cox, 'Bricks to build a capital', p. 11.

A brick-built city

on a style of brickmaking, and a particular type of brick – the London stock – which, with some technical adaptations, would serve it for a further century and contribute to the distinctive appearance of its built environment.

Londoners venturing away from the centre of town would have encountered brickfields in what Henry Hunter termed the 'clay-pit zone', an intermediate area that was neither developed for housing nor still agricultural in character. This zone was not permanent, as it was inevitable that after a period of intensive exploitation the brickearth would be exhausted and the land revert to other uses. Hunter describes this process in agricultural terms, as if the bricks were themselves a crop that had been taken from the land:

> The brickearth is reckoned upon an average to run four feet in depth, and to yield one million of bricks per acre in each foot. The land is levelled after all the brick-earth is taken from it, and by the help of rubbish and manure is raised in its surface, though it still remains lower than the adjoining roads.[59]

Hunter's view is supported by Thomas Milne's land-use map of London and its environs published a decade earlier.[60] In some places, where brickmaking had been intensive, the process that Hunter described had already taken place, and there were fields at the beginning of the nineteenth century no longer in use for brickmaking, but whose prior use was clear to contemporaries because the ground level was lower than that in neighbouring fields.

This sense of an intermediate and impermanent zone on the edge of the city is nicely caught in the print *Westminster from Chelsea Fields*, published in 1838 (Plate 2). This view shows an area of disturbed ground dominated by a mound of earth and surmounted by a clay mill being turned by a horse. Rows of drying bricks are just visible in the middle distance, and beyond that are Westminster Abbey, the turrets of St John, Smith Square and the dome of St Paul's. As well as showing a brickfield on the edge of the built-up area, this print gives a good sense of the style of brickmaking that had developed during the century and a half since the Great Fire and which was the basis of the industry at the beginning of the nineteenth century. The way the London stock brick was made is the subject of the next chapter.

---

59   H. Hunter, *A history of London and its environs* (London, 1811), vol. 2, p. 3.

60   T. Milne, *Land use map of London and environs in 1800*, ed. G.B.G. Bull, London Topographical Society, nos 118 and 119 (London, 1975–6); G.B.G. Bull, 'T. Milne's land utilisation map of the London area in 1810', *Geographical Journal*, 122 (1956), pp. 25–30.

Chapter 2

From clay pit to clamp: manufacturing the London stock brick

At the beginning of the nineteenth century bricks were made by hand using techniques that, though perfected over time, had not changed significantly from those in use centuries earlier. Some suitable clay was dug out, worked into a malleable consistency and then moulded into the shape of a brick. The newly moulded 'green' bricks were allowed to dry in the open air and then fired until they were hard. Once cooled, they were sorted into different grades before being loaded into a wagon or barge for distribution. One important change had been the introduction of the *pug mill*, a device for mixing the clay prior to moulding, which came into general use in the later eighteenth century.[1]

There were regional differences in detail in these operations that derived partly from the different types of clay that were used and partly from tradition. There was a particular style of manufacture in the London area and this was adopted in the districts that in the nineteenth century were providing the capital with the grey or yellow 'stock' brick. This London mode of manufacture was described by Edward Dobson in his influential book *A rudimentary treatise on the manufacture of bricks and tiles*, first published in 1850, which has been drawn on by many modern writers.[2] It provides a detailed account of the processes involved, and its general accuracy is supported by descriptions of brick manufacture in professional journals and in government reports.[3] There is, however, a danger in assuming that all brickfields in the London area were using precisely the methods that Dobson describes. There were also some differences between the methods employed in London and Middlesex and those found in the Kent brickfields.

There was an annual cycle to the brickmaking process, which started with the digging out of clay during the late autumn and early winter. The moulding of bricks from this prepared clay took place during the late spring and summer of the following

---

1 Campbell, *Brick*, p. 206.
2 E. Dobson, *A rudimentary treatise on the manufacture of bricks and tiles* (London, 1850). Among the modern writers who use his descriptions and reproduce his illustrations area: Woodforde, *Bricks*; H. Hobhouse, *Thomas Cubitt: master builder* (London, 1978); Cox, 'Bricks to build a capital'.
3 Brickmaking techniques in the Cowley district were described by the owners of brickfields and their foreman, and by inspectors working for the Children's Employment Commission in the 1860s and the Factory and Workshops Commission in the 1870s: Children's Employment Commission (1862), 5th report of the Commissioners, with appendix, PP 1866, vol. 24, Report on brickfields by H.W. Lord and evidence, xxiv, pp. 135–8; Reports of the Inspector of Factories to her Majesty's Principal Secretary of State for the Home Department for the half year to 30 April 1877 (c.1794), PP 1877, vol. 56, p. 30. See also Chamberlain, 'The manufacture of bricks', p. 491f; H. Ward, 'Brickmaking', *Institution of Civil Engineers, Minutes of Proceedings* (1885–6, part iv), pp. 1–23.

From clay pit to clamp

year, when the weather was warmer and the days longer. It was deemed important that the clay should be allowed to weather over winter in order to ensure that it had the right consistency for hand moulding. To determine that this process was not skimped and the quality of bricks impaired as a result, this production cycle had been regulated from as far back as 1622, when a Royal Proclamation had stipulated that 'the first digging to be between Feasts of St Michael [29 September] and St Thomas the Apostle [21 December]' and 'that moulding to take place between Feast of the Annunciation of the Blessed Virgin Mary [25 March] and the last day of August'.[4] The same annual pattern, but with an adjustment in the dates, was included in an act of Parliament of 1726 that specified that 'earth or clay shall be dug, and turned at least once between 1 November and 1 February, and not made into bricks until after 1 March, and no bricks be made for sale except between 1 March and 29 September'.[5] However, later legislation relaxed these restrictions so that the earth might be dug at any time of the year, provided that it was turned once before it was made into bricks.[6] Nevertheless, the old pattern of digging clay in the autumn, weathering it over the winter and moulding bricks during the spring and summer seems to have prevailed in the London area throughout the nineteenth century.

Not all the soils that provided the raw material for brickmaking were the same. Even the clays employed across the south-east of England came from different geological formations and varied in their characteristics. Brickearth as it occurred in, say, Islington, Brentford, Yiewsley, Crayford, Shoeburyness or Sittingbourne may not have been the same, but, nonetheless, generally proved suitable for making a stock brick. A modern writer comments that:

> 'Brickearth' is an ancient term and is still widely used. It is also the cause of much confusion and imprecision in the scientific study of the loess deposits and brickmaking materials in Britain. The term was extensively used when the Geological Survey was mapping south-east England at the end of the nineteenth century. It referred to a loamy surficial and near-surficial deposit, often found in river valleys. It was not a precise scientific term, but at the time it was an adequate mapping term.[7]

Dobson, without the advantage of modern geological terminology, suggested that contemporary brickmakers would identify three categories of brickearth: strong clay, mild clay and malm. Malm, as we have seen, was thought to make the best-quality bricks, and this type of clay required no additives to make a suitably malleable

---

4   Charles I, *Proclamation for the due making and sizing of bricks* (1622).

5   12 George I c. 35, (1726) *An act to prevent abuses in making of bricks and tiles, and to ascertain the dimensions thereof, to prevent all unlawful combinations amongst any brickmakers or tile makers within 15 miles of the City of London in order to advance or enhance the price of bricks or tiles.*

6   10 George III c. 49, (1769–70) *An act for continuing and amending several acts for preventing abuses in making bricks.*

7   I. Smalley, 'The nature of brickearth and the location of early brick building in Britain', *BBS Information*, 41 (February 1986), p. 4.

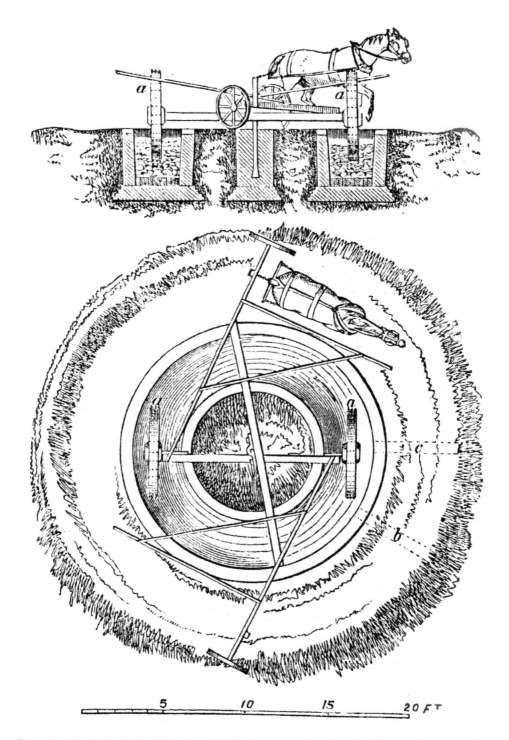

Figure 2.1. A chalk mill. An illustration to E. Dobson, *A rudimentary treatise on the manufacture of bricks and tiles* (1850).

From clay pit to clamp

material. Dobson argues that by the mid-nineteenth century such natural malms had become scarce, and so similar characteristics were created artificially, by the addition of ground chalk and ashes. This process was known as *malming*, the object being to produce an approximation to naturally occurring malms.[8]

The addition of chalk had three effects: it produced the characteristic yellow colour – the iron in the clay otherwise giving a reddish hue; it reduced contraction in the drying process, preventing cracking or distortion, and it also acted chemically, combining with the silica in the clay to produce a strong and hard-wearing brick.[9] Chalk was readily found in association with brickearth in Kent, where it was also used in the production of cement.[10] Middlesex brickfields did not have the same advantage, and chalk usually had to be brought from elsewhere. There was chalk at Harefield, right on the western border of the county, which was commercially exploited for cement production and supplied to some local brickmakers. There was also chalk extraction at Pinner in north-west London from the seventeenth century, and the underground mine was owned between 1830 and 1850 by Charles Blackwell, a well-known local brickmaker. Production on the site reached a peak in the mid-nineteenth century, but ceased about 1870. By this time chalk was cheaply available from open-cast chalk pits in the Thames Valley.[11] In other parts of the London area usable chalk was found on brickfields, but at a considerable distance below the surface. In 1817 a Plumstead brickmaker was extracting chalk and sand on his brickfield at a depth of eighty feet, working from a vertical shaft into a horizontal seam, when the shaft collapsed into itself. The workmen were buried and it took several days of heroic labour by military sappers to extricate the bodies.[12]

It was thought most effective to grind the chalk and, by adding water, to produce a slurry that could be easily mixed with the clay. As chalk mills, which consisted of a brick-lined pit with a central spindle that could be turned by a horse, were among the more permanent structures on the brickfield, their presence is often labelled on maps and plans. Dobson also described the use of a separate clay mill in which the creamy mixture from the chalk mill was mixed with the clay, but these do not appear on every site (Figure 2.1).[13]

In the Kent style of stock brickmaking the clay was mixed with chalk and water in a wash-mill and then piled up in 'wash backs', a type of wooden enclosure in which the washed clay was placed until it was needed. Washing the clay was a way of removing stones. It was then covered with ashes and left until the moulding season. In

---

8   Dobson, *Rudimentary treatise*, pp. 119–21.

9   *Ibid.*, pp. 121–2.

10   J.M. Preston, *Industrial Medway: an historical survey* (Maidstone, 1977), pp. 68–71.

11   D. Clements (ed.), *The geology of London*, Geologists' Association Guide No. 68 (London, 2010), pp. 15–38; the underground workings still exist: see R.W. Gallois, *A guide to the Pinner chalk mine*, 3rd edn (Hillingdon, 1998).

12   *Kentish Weekly Post or Canterbury Journal*, 11 April 1817.

13   Dobson shows the layout of the equipment on a brickfield: *Rudimentary treatise*, p. 124. Broad and Company used steam-powered clay and chalk mills at West Drayton in the 1890s. *British Clayworker*, October 1898, pp. 195–6.

Bricks of Victorian London

this arrangement each moulding bench, or berth, might have one or two washbacks, and each washback held enough clay mix for 300,000 to 400,000 bricks.[14]

The other ingredient added to the clay mixture was ashes, the residue of coal fires. The terms ashes and *breeze* were used fairly indiscriminately, but there was a distinction: breeze was the harder residue, similar to clinker; ash the finer and softer. The two were separated by screening with a sieve, and the finer material was mixed with the clay in a process known as *soiling* or *tempering*, while breeze was more likely to be used as fuel. The advantages of soiling may have been discovered by accident when, in the aftermath of the Great Fire, bricks were made from soil containing quantities of ash.[15]

The coarser residue was reserved as fuel for the clamps, either on its own or mixed with coal dust.[16] Large quantities of each were used – up to seven cwt of ashes and three cwt of breeze for every thousand bricks.[17] The addition of ashes to the clay mix had a two-fold objective: it both extended the clay as well as incorporating a certain amount of fuel within the brick itself. This helped to ensure that the brick burnt fully through when it was fired in a clamp, rather than in a more efficient kiln. There were, however, dangers in over-soiling, and the proportions had to be varied according to the 'strength' of the clay. A contemporary of Dobson, Joseph Lockwood, commented that 'Breeze or ashes constitute a very important element in the manufacture of bricks, for if carefully managed according to the quality of clay, it may be made to produce very effective results both with reference to colour and quality.' Lockwood suggested that typical proportions of raw materials were 65 per cent clay, 20 per cent breeze [in this case, probably ashes rather than cinders] and 15 per cent chalk on heavier clays, or 75 per cent clay, 15 per cent breeze and 10 per cent chalk on lighter soils. In some cases, a small quantity (2–5 per cent) of sand might be added.[18]

Sand was also needed to dust the moulds and moulding benches as the bricks were being made, to prevent the wet clay adhering. Sand had to be kept dry if it was to fulfil its purpose, so in some brickfields it was stored in 'sand houses'. In the absence of descriptions of what these looked like, we can only assume they were some sort of shed. On one Hackney brickfield in 1808 sand houses were set alight by a mentally unstable employee, suggesting timber construction, while on a Southall brickfield in the 1870s the sand houses were made of brick.[19] Supplies of sand were found in a number of places; sometimes it could be obtained near the

---

14   S.J. Twist, *Stock bricks of Swale* (Sittingbourne, 1984), p. 5. Washbacks were not often mentioned in descriptions of Middlesex brickfields.

15   Substances added to the clay mix were also known as 'Spanish', a term that seems to have come into use in the late seventeenth century. Porter, *The Great Fire*, p. 162; Cox, 'Bricks to build a capital', pp. 4–5.

16   Dobson, *Rudimentary treatise*, p. 122.

17   *British Clayworker*, December 1898, p. 250.

18   J. Lockwood, 'Bricks and brickmaking', *The Builder* (1845), p. 182.

19   They provided enough shelter that people were sometimes tempted to live in them. *Hampshire Chronicle*, 13 June 1808; a brickfield sale included 'the brick erections of 9 sand houses', *The Standard*, 19 November 1877.

From clay pit to clamp

brickfields, but, if not, it was readily brought by boat to brickfields that were adjacent to a canal or river.

Chalk, according to Dobson, was easily purchased at wharves in London for about 2s 10d per ton, while sand dug from the Thames near Woolwich was available at 2s per ton.[20] Ashes extracted from domestic refuse were delivered, mostly from the built-up central area of London, by barge or canal boat. They came in one of two states, either relatively clean or contaminated with vegetable matter, depending on whether the rubbish had already been sifted at the contractor's dustyard or was sent in its raw state. In the case of the latter the sifting took place at the brickfield.[21] This was a job that might be given to a child.[22]

There were financial benefits in the use of breeze as fuel even if it was inferior to coal. Coal was taxed in the London area by means of the Coal Duties, which were only finally abolished in 1889.[23] Because domestic fires did not burn very efficiently, the breeze recovered from domestic dustbins still had some calorific value. Mixed with some coal, breeze was, as noted, widely used for burning bricks in clamps.

A symbiotic relationship developed between brickmakers and dustmen. Contractors were employed by the London parish vestries to remove and dispose of the domestic refuse from their district. Since householders were dependent on coal fires for heating and cooking, ashes and clinker made up a large proportion of what they collected – as much as 80 per cent. The amount that brickmakers were willing to pay the dustmen for them at times covered the whole cost, and at other times subsidised the cost, of removal. A few dustmen became brickmakers in their own right, including Henry Dodd, the model for Dickens' Golden Dustman Noddy Boffin (in *Our Mutual Friend*). This practice of selling ashes to brickmakers continued well into the twentieth century, but with an increasing reliance on gas and electricity for cooking and heating the supply dwindled. It was only finally abandoned when the passing of the Clean Air Act in 1956 prohibited the domestic use of coal for heating in London, but some brickmakers continued to use what they had accumulated at their works for some years (Figure 2.2).[24]

Once the clay mixture had been allowed to stand and break down during the winter months it had to be thoroughly mixed to a consistency suitable for hand moulding. If the weather was dry at the beginning of the moulding season water might

---

20 Dobson, *Rudimentary treatise*, part 2, pp. 41–2.

21 For a description of the sifting process see J. Greenwood, 'Mr Dodd's dust yard', in *Journeys through London; or, byways of modern Babylon* (London, 1873), p. 64. On the relationship between dustmen and brickmakers see P. Hounsell, *London's rubbish: two centuries of dirt, dust and disease in the metropolis* (Stroud, 2013), pp. 16–17, 116–17; P. Hounsell, 'Spanish practices: dustbin rubbish and the London stock brick', *BBS Information*, 146 (October 2020), pp. 25–37.

22 J. Reed, 'Reminiscences of a Middlesex brickmaker', *Hayes and Harlington Local History Society Journal*, 79 (Spring 2009). And see below, chapter 14.

23 Hounsell, 'Spanish practices', p. 28.

24 It was claimed in the 1980s that the long-established Kent firm Smeed, Dean was still using old deposits of ashes, some of which had been brought from London by sailing barge a century earlier. Hounsell, 'Spanish practices', p. 31.

Bricks of Victorian London

Figure 2.2. Mr Dodd's dustyard at Hoxton. Illustration from J. Greenwood, *Journeys through London; or, byways of modern Babylon* (1873).

be added to produce malleability, and this became more necessary as the season went on. The mixing of the clay might be done simply by means of a shovel, but more usually in a pug mill. This was like a large barrel set on end with a vertical shaft passing through it to which were fitted a series of slanting blades; the action of these, in the manner of a food processor, broke up lumps and mixed the clay, the ashes and the chalk to a smooth consistency ready for the moulder. Usually, the raw clay was tipped into the top of the barrel and the 'pugged' clay extruded from a hole at the bottom. The shaft could be turned either by a horse or, later in the century, by steam power.[25] This simple but effective device was widely used; indeed, any brickmaker who did not employ a pug mill by the middle of the century would have been regarded as rather primitive (Figure 2.3).[26]

Bricks were made by a team usually of six people, which might include men, women and children, often drawn from the same family. The man who moulded the bricks, the *moulder*, was the leader of the team, or gang, and subcontracted with the owner of the brickfield to produce bricks at a given price. He then paid the other

---

25 Dobson, *Rudimentary treatise*, p. 125 (description), pp. 132–3 (illustrations).
26 This is implicit in the tone of Mr Laleham's report on methods in East Anglia in the 1870s: Reports of the Inspectors of Factories to her Majesty's Principal Secretary of State for the Home Department for the half year ending 31st October 1872, PP 1873, vol. 66, xix, p. 219; report of Sub-Inspector Henderson on brickmaking in West London: Reports of the Inspectors of Factories for the Half year ending 31st October 1876, PP 1877, xxiii, p. 30.

From clay pit to clamp

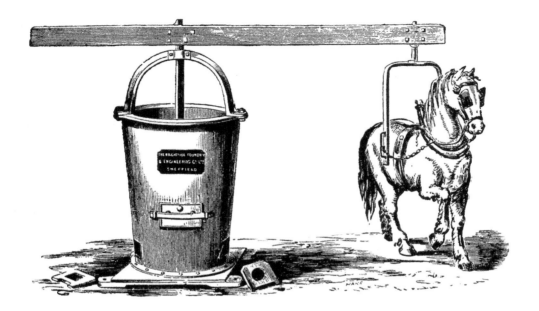

Figure 2.3. Pug mill made in Sheffield. Illustration from E. Bourry, *A treatise on ceramic industries: a complete manual for pottery, tile and brick manufacturers;* translated by A.B. Searle (1911).

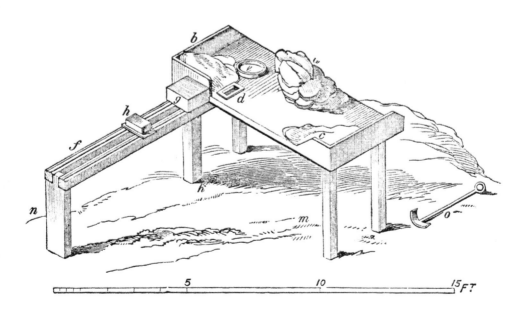

Figure 2.4. The layout of a moulding bench. Illustration from E. Dobson, *A rudimentary treatise on the manufacture of bricks and tiles* (1850).

Bricks of Victorian London

members of his team. The *temperer* was responsible for mixing the clay and loading the pug mill. The clay coming from the pug mill was collected by the *pug boy*, who broke off with a fork, also known in the trade as a *cuckle* or *cuckhold*, a piece of clay sufficient for three or four bricks, which he then carried to the moulding bench or *stool* (Figure 2.4). At the bench another member of the team, called sometimes the *clotmoulder*, or otherwise the *walk flatter*, shaped a piece of clay into a wedge and passed it to the moulder, who 'with a sharp jerk, flings the piece of clay ... into his mould', which had previously been sprinkled with sand.[27] The moulder cut off the excess clay flush to the top of the mould with piece of wood known as a *strike*. The base of the mould was the stock board (hence the name given to the type of brick made by this method), to which was attached a rectangular piece of wood that created the indentation on the underside of the brick, usually known as a *frog*.[28] The mould was larger than the size of the finished brick, as the newly made bricks lost moisture during the drying and firing processes and shrank to the required finished size.[29] Moulds were made of wood, sometimes reinforced with iron, and easily purchased from providers of agricultural equipment. All-steel moulds became available at the end of the century.

The freshly moulded brick, the *green brick*, was fragile and needed to be handled carefully to prevent it from going out of shape. The moulder placed it on a pallet board beside him, and it was the job of the next member of the gang, the *barrow loader*, to take the bricks one by one and transfer them to the long flat-bedded *hack barrow*. These barrows, which seem to have been of a fairly standard design, had a single wheel and accommodated either twenty-eight or thirty bricks in two rows.[30] Once full the barrows were wheeled by the *pusher-out* to the *hack ground*, or *hacks*, where they were unloaded and laid out in rows to dry, either in the open air or under some form of protection to keep off the rain. Dobson suggests that straw or reeds were used, but at some sites wooden hack covers protected the drying bricks. Hack covers appear in photographs from the end of the century and in descriptions of brickfield equipment. For example, 'three sets of nearly-new hack boards (about 1800 yards)' were included in the contents of a brickfield at North Hyde, Heston when it was sold in 1883.[31]

It is evident that brickfields often had large quantities of straw on site, as bedding for horses, to cover bricks when drying and to place between layers of bricks to prevent damage in transport. Straw was a potential fire hazard that could be ignited

---

27 Children's Employment Commission, 5th Report, PP 1866, p. 126. 'Stool' is a unit of measurement of a brickfield as well as the name for a moulding bench. They were also called 'berths' in Kent brickfields.

28 Dobson, *Rudimentary Treatise,* pp. 123–38. The general layout of a moulding bench is illustrated on p. 134.

29 By the mid-nineteenth century brick sizes had become generally standardised, although sometimes architects specified a different size to suit the particular decorative effect they wished to achieve.

30 Dobson, *Rudimentary treatise,* p. 136 (description), p. 137 (illustration).

31 *Ibid.,* p. 143; *Uxbridge Gazette & Middlesex & Bucks Observer,* 21 April 1883.

From clay pit to clamp

Figure 2.5. Building a clamp, Edmonton (c.1910). (London Borough of Enfield Local History Library)

either by men smoking at work or by sparks from steam engines.[32] A brickfield at Teynham in Kent was badly damaged when a spark ignited the thatched roof of one of the several sheds in which bricks were drying. Very quickly the fire took hold, resulting in damage to much of the site and to thousands of bricks.[33]

The length of time the bricks were left on the hack ground varied between three and six weeks, depending on the weather.[34] Midway through the period, when the bricks were partly dry, they were *scintled* or *skintled* – that is, turned at an angle to let air circulate around all the surfaces.[35] Once firm enough, and having shrunk in size by the evaporation of much of their water content, they were moved from the hack ground to the clamp or kiln (Figures 2.5 and Plate 3). In the London region clamps were widely used. The clamp was essentially a kiln without walls, where the bricks themselves provided the structure. They were built into a tower with a series of flue holes to allow a through draft. The clamp was built on a base of old, over-burnt bricks and was topped off with a layer of similar bricks. Breeze and coal dust were used to start the firing process. The construction of clamps was a skilled task, as it

---

32 *Morning Advertiser*, 1 September 1841.
33 *Morning Post*, 26 May 1888.
34 Dobson, *Rudimentary treatise*, p. 144.
35 *Ibid.*, p. 143.

Bricks of Victorian London

was necessary to ensure both stability in a structure that could incorporate as many as 100,000 bricks and the proper circulation of the hot gases.[36] A separate group of men, known as *setters* or *crowders*, built the clamps or loaded the kilns.[37] They used *crowding* barrows, of a different design to hack barrows, reflecting the greater resilience of the burnt bricks.[38]

It could take several weeks for a clamp to burn through, a fortnight being the minimum period.[39] Once the bricks had cooled sufficiently to be handled the clamp was carefully taken down and the bricks sorted. It was inherent in the way that a clamp was constructed that some bricks were more heavily burnt than others; over-burnt bricks were not offered for sale but reused as the basis for the next clamp. Some bricks, at the hottest part of the clamp, partially melted and were consequently misshapen, and termed *clinkers* or *burrs*; they were, Dobson tells us, 'sold by the cartload, for rockwork in gardens and similar purposes', including as decorative features in garden walls.[40] Some under-burnt bricks were sold as 'place bricks' – that is, they were thought suitable only for internal work. The remaining well-burnt bricks were divided into different categories, the distinctions between which are somewhat difficult to understand without examples to hand.[41]

Much of the traditional method of brickmaking survived through the nineteenth century, but was modified in a number of respects. A large number of patents were granted for processes involved in brickmaking, some to inventors, others to practising brickmakers. For example, the well-known London brickmaker William Rhodes secured two patents. One related to the way clamps were constructed, the aim being to reduce the damage to the bricks from rain; the other was the replacement of the ash derived from the domestic fires of the city with powdered coke, itself a by-product of the coal-gas industry.[42]

---

36   R.W. Brunskill, *Brick building in Britain* (London, 1990), p. 27.

37   A lengthy description of the construction of a clamp, including illustrations, is given in Dobson, *Rudimentary treatise*, pp. 144–54. For a photograph of a clamp on a Kent brickfield, see R.-H. Perks, *George Bargebrick Esq: the story of George Smeed, the brick and cement king* (Rainham, 1981), p. 29.

38   Perks, *George Bargebrick Esq*, pp. 24, 29 for photographs of crowding barrows in use.

39   Dobson, *Rudimentary treatise*, p. 154.

40   *Ibid.*, p. 153.

41   *Ibid.*, pp. 155–6. Dobson lists fifteen categories, while Willmott suggests that there were five or six. F.G. Willmott, *Bricks and brickies* (Rainham, 1972), p. 41. Modern bricks produced by traditional methods and fired in simple Scotch kilns still produce a variety of shades that are sorted before being sold. See, for example, the bricks produced by H.G. Matthews at Cheshunt. M. Chapman, 'Brick for a day: H.G. Matthews Brickworks, Bellingdon, near Chesham, Buckinghamshire', *BBS Information*, 142 (August 2019), pp. 39–46.

42   *The repertory of patent inventions and other discoveries and improvements in arts, manufactures and agriculture*, vol. I (London, 1825), pp. 275–6, patent granted to William Rhodes, of Hoxton, Middlesex, brickmaker, for an improvement in the construction of clamps for burning raw bricks, dated November 1824; *The repertory*, vol. XVI (London, 1833): Specification of the patent granted to William Rhodes of the Grange, Leyton, in the county of Essex, brickmaker, for an improved manufacture of bricks for building purposes, dated February 1833.

From clay pit to clamp

Technological changes in brickmaking took three forms. The first was the general application of steam or petrol engines across the brickfield, replacing horses. The second was improvements to the firing of bricks by the introduction of hot-air dryers and more efficient types of kiln. The third was the replacement of hand moulding by machines.

Early nineteenth-century brickfields were reliant on horse power. Illustrations of brickfields usually show a horse, forced to walk in a tight circle for hours each day, turning a clay or a pug mill. It is not clear from the available evidence whether a single horse worked all day or a relay team was involved; the former is likely, as descriptions of a brickmaker's working day indicate that there was an enforced lay-off at lunchtime while the horse was rested. Horses were also used to move clay or bricks around the brickfield in carts or on tramroads. Tramroads had a long history on industrial sites and found a ready application where heavy materials needed to be hauled across country to a canal or river. Using fairly simple technology, they were effective in raising the productivity of the horse.[43] Tramroads were employed extensively on brickfields, most often to move bricks from the manufacturing area to the dockside for loading into barges. They were also laid between the clay pit and the site where moulding took place, and this use increased as brickfields became larger and began to have fixed plant, such as engine houses and kilns. There were tramroads on Thomas Cubitt's mechanised brickfield at Burham in the 1850s.[44] Tramways are marked on many Ordnance Survey maps; for example, at South Shoebury in Essex Eastwoods had an extensive network of tramways linking the brickworks and the loading jetties, and at Southall in 1864 a tramway running under the railway linked a brickfield with the canal side.[45] Tramway rails and wagons appear in brickfield inventories. One at Northfleet had a 'tramway laid from the clamps to the wharf' in 1885; another at Althorne in Essex had one leading to a jetty on the River Crouch; and a third at Erith used one to connect to the North Kent Railway.[46] Tramway waggons and rails were part of the equipment of Lewisham Brickfields and Potteries in 1871, and of Heath Lane brickfields in Dartford in 1882.[47]

For linking brickfields to a canal or river, tramroads could be easier and cheaper to construct than docks. They were also more flexible, as a tramroad could be lifted and reused elsewhere. This was the thinking behind an extensive tramroad at Heston Farm. The farm was separated from the canal by an intervening property. The landlord, as owner of both, considered constructing a dock to link Heston Farm with the canal, costing up to £3000, but rejected this approach in

---

43 For the history of tramroads see 'Early iron railways', in J. Simmons and G. Biddle (eds), *The Oxford companion to British railway history* (Oxford, 1997), pp. 134–5; B. Baxter, *Stone blocks and iron rails* (London, 1966).

44 Hobhouse, *Thomas Cubitt*, p. 310.

45 Ryan, *Brick in Essex: the clayworking craftsmen*, p. 160. Excerpts from OS map, 1897; first edition OS map 6-inch map Southall/Heston, 1864. This map also shows several docks on the canal.

46 *Globe*, 25 November 1885; *Kentish Mercury*, 22 July 1876; *Globe*, 13 July 1874.

47 *Kentish Mercury*, 4 March 1871; *Daily Telegraph*, 14 February 1882.

Bricks of Victorian London

Figure 2.6. Belt-driven machinery on a Crayford brickfield. (London Borough of Bexley Local Studies and Archives Centre)

favour of a tramroad on the grounds of expense.[48] The tenant paid a way-leave for the use of it.[49]

With the widespread adoption of tramways on brickfields new skills were required to operate and maintain them; an advertisement in the 'Wanted' column of a newspaper in 1883 invited applications from 'good wheelwrights used to brickfield and tramway work' for a brickfield at Southend.[50]

Horses began to be phased out once portable steam or petrol engines were available and *horse keepers* were replaced by *engine drivers*, a job title that appears in census occupational descriptions from 1871.[51] Sales of brickfields also began to list

---

48 10 & 11 Victoria, Pr. c. 35 (1847), *Passingham estate act*. Copy at LMA Acc. 328/58; Ex parte Passingham estate act. Counsel M.J. Astley's opinion, 1846. LMA Acc. 328/54.

49 The way-leave was 1d per 1000 bricks and costs averaged £38 per year, implying that at least nine million bricks a year were being transported along the tramroad. Sale particulars North Hyde Farm and Depot estate 1871, LMA Acc. 328/105.

50 *Southend Standard*, 15 May 1883.

51 Examples from the 1871 census include William Lowe in Hayes, but on another brickfield in the same area James Trusler was a horsekeeper. James White, William Shaw, Thomas Smith and James Hetherington all are recorded as such at Southall and Alfred New at Northolt in 1881. Census Enumerator's Books, Hayes 1871; Southall, Northolt 1881.

From clay pit to clamp

engines as part of the machinery and equipment. Most of these engines were almost certainly stationary, and there are no specific mentions of steam locomotives being used in the counties around London (Figure 2.6). Machines allowed for larger-scale brickfield operations; as well as turning mills or hauling tramway wagons, engines could also be used to power pumps on larger brickfields where the clay source was at a considerable distance from the moulding area. The dug clay would be converted into a liquid state and pumped through pipes, then allowed to settle prior to moulding.[52] There are examples of this in Middlesex and Kent brickfields. On the Rutter brickfield at West Drayton in the 1890s clay was pumped 'in the form of a solution to be made with chalk' from the claypits.[53] A well pump and three slurry pumps were supplied to the Kent Co-operative Brickmaking Society Ltd near Teynham, so that the washed chalk and earth could be moved through iron pipes to the washbacks, a distance of about 450 yards.[54]

The second area of technological change occurred in the drying and firing of the bricks. Clamp burning remained the usual form of firing stock bricks through the nineteenth century, but improvements to kiln design led some Kent and Middlesex brickfields to introduce them. The simple Scotch kiln operated much like a clamp: it was filled with bricks, carefully stacked and fitted with flue holes to allow the hot gases to fill the space, and allowed to burn for several days. Like clamps, they were updraft kilns, whereby the heat was drawn through from bottom to top and the bricks at the bottom, nearest the heat source, were likely to be over-burnt. The alternative was the downdraft kiln, where heat is channelled to the top of the kiln and the exhaust gases are expelled from the bottom; the simplest kiln of this kind, generally known as a *beehive*, was introduced in the 1870s and 1880s.[55]

Once the bricks had cooled the kiln was unloaded and the process repeated; this was inevitably a discontinuous method. Newer designs of kiln were multi-chamber, which meant that one chamber could be loaded while another was firing, and then the output of the furnace switched from one to another. The best-known version of a multi-chamber kiln is the Hoffmann, named after its German inventor. Unlike a clamp or a Scotch kiln, the Hoffmann kiln was designed to burn continuously, sometimes for several years. A series of chambers was arranged around a central heat source, and the design allows the heat to be applied to one chamber at a time. So, while one chamber will be very hot and the ones either side heating up or cooling down, some chambers were cool enough to be unloaded and reloaded with green bricks.[56] Available from the 1850s on, kilns such as these involved greater capital investment, and were only likely to be needed on brickfields with a large output. They became

---

52 Pumps of this kind were described in the *Brick, Tile & Builders' Gazette*, 11 January 1887.

53 LMA Acc. 1386/382 Lease of brickfields by trustees of the estate of Francis de Burgh to D. and C. Rutter, 1895.

54 *British Clayworker*, May 1893, p. 32.

55 A patent for a kiln of this kind was granted to Thomas Minton in 1873. Campbell, *Brick*, p. 210.

56 The kiln was invented by Friedrich Eduard Hoffmann in the late 1850s. Early versions were circular, but to increase the capacity in 1870 the circle was stretched into an oval. They were really only suitable for brickfields making at least 2m bricks a year. Campbell, *Brick*, p. 212.

Bricks of Victorian London

more common at the end of the nineteenth century and in the early years of the twentieth. Smeed, Dean Ltd, a major Sittingbourne brickmaker, developed a red-brick plant in addition to its yellow stock production from 1906, and this utilised an 'Osman' continuous kiln, a development of the Hoffmann design.[57] The New Patent Brick Company's Northolt works included an eight-chamber kiln by 1901.[58]

Allied to the replacement of clamps with kilns was the introduction of hot-air driers for drying bricks in place of open-air hacks. These driers required the erection of buildings and a source of heat, often the waste heat from kilns. The advantage was the increased speed of drying, allowing the production cycle to be speeded up and making brickmaking in the winter months a possibility. A 'Wolff' drier was installed at Smeed, Dean's works at Murston, and a similar model at the New West End Brick & Joinery's works at Northolt.[59] Finally, in the twentieth century, drier and kiln could be combined: bricks on wagons would move from the drying floor through a tunnel kiln and emerge at the far end ready for sorting and sale, resulting, one would assume, in a lower level of damaged and misshapen bricks. Despite these innovations, however, many smaller brickfields persisted with the older technology into the twentieth century.[60]

The third and more difficult technological challenge was to replace hand moulding with machines that actually turned out the bricks, but the Victorians' appetite for mechanical invention and ingenuity resulted in a number of patented devices. The least elaborate of these machines were the presses that were designed to enable brickmakers to improve the surface finish and shape of hand-made bricks. Architects complained about the coarse texture of many hand-moulded bricks, which could arise from the imperfect mixing of the clay and from the ashes in the clay mix, which left cinder spots and pock marks where the cinder had burnt away completely. Moreover, in the polluted atmosphere of Victorian cities, smoother brick surfaces were more resistant to dirt. Hand-moulded bricks were sometimes misshapen and could lose their sharp edges when they were turned out of the mould.[61]

Pressed and polished bricks, however, were expensive, because of both the extra labour involved and the longer time spent drying in the hacks, but also, up to 1839, because they were subject to the excise duty at twice the rate of a standard brick. This did not prevent an enterprising Clerkenwell brickmaker, Samuel Roscoe

---

57 Perks, *George Bargebrick*, p. 45, and illustration on p. 70.

58 London Borough of Ealing, Local History Centre. Sale particulars New Patent Brick Company of London Ltd, 1901.

59 Advert for the Wolff Iron Clad Dryer, *British Clayworker* (March 1905), p. x.

60 Despite the installation of an automatic brick-making plant, forced dryers and a tunnel kiln 560 feet long in 1926 at one of the company's fields, clamps were still being built at another of Smeed, Dean's fields as late as 1928. Perks, *George Bargebrick*, pp. 53–4, 29.

61 Not all architects admired pressed bricks: George Gilbert Scott complained of their 'extreme smoothness' and William Butterfield, although he disliked London stock bricks, appreciated the rougher textures of other hand-made bricks. John Ruskin had an ideological objection to machine-made bricks, since, in his view, they obscured the human labour involved. K.A. Watt, 'Nineteenth-century brickmaking innovations in Britain: building and technological change', PhD thesis (Univ of York, 1990), pp. 87–8.

From clay pit to clamp

Bakewell, from devising a machine to impart the desirable polished surface. His patent brick press was in use before the reduction in the duty, and was installed in William Rhodes's Hackney brickfield.[62] However, it was found that even bricks produced by machines could be improved by surface pressing. The heavily mechanised Aylesford and Burham brickworks in the Medway employed them in the 1860s. 'If a special shape or particularly good surface is to be given to machine-made bricks they are pressed one by one in a hand machine, which is wheeled up and down the hacks. This press is worked by a man assisted by one or two boys.'[63] To the casual observer, this labour-intensive activity would seem to negate many of the benefits of mechanisation.

A further step was to experiment with equipment that replaced hand moulding by a mechanical action, and there were a great many patents granted for such machines. Some of these devices were still-born, perhaps never making it beyond the design stage, while others proved to be ineffective or unreliable. But a handful were successful and widely adopted. When visiting brickfields in London, Kent and Middlesex in the 1860s, W.H. Lord found only a few that were using machines at all, one of which was at the yard of J. & S. Williams in Shepherd's Bush. Here he was told that 'all our bricks are made by machines, five small and one large self-acting one, which delivers the bricks on to a patent barrow'.[64] All of these machines were of the Bawden type.

> In [this] kind of machine the clay needs no preparation but is taken from the surface to the machine. After being mixed with sand and ashes and a little water, it is shovelled into the pug mill and without being crushed by rollers, then passes out of the bottom into dies, which are sunk at intervals, two together, in a round iron table that revolves under the mill; each die is the size of the brick required. The two are filled at once, and deliver the bricks by raising them to the surface of the table after the full dies have left the mouth of the mill.[65]

The third type of machine was one that dispensed with a mould and instead extruded a column of clay that was cut by a series of wires into brick-sized pieces. Bricks made by such methods are usually known as *wire-cuts*. Widely taken up in the Midlands and North but less used in the southern counties of England, machines of this kind were to be found in some brickfields on the Medway. In these extrusion machines:

> The clay is brought up direct from the pit in barrows placed on a trolley which is drawn up an incline to a staging by the engine that drives the machine. In Slater's machine the clay is thence emptied into the pugmill and passes from that through rollers to be crushed; in the other [Bradley & Craven's], the position of the rollers and the pugmill are reversed; in either case it issues from the machine in a long bar or 'sheet'. This bar, as it is pushed out over narrow rollers is cut into

---

62 *Ibid.*, pp. 81–3.

63 Children's Employment Commission, 5th Report, PP 1866, p. 129.

64 *Ibid.*, p. 138.

65 *Ibid.*, p. 129.

bricks of proper thickness by wires fitted in a frame attached to the roller bed and worked by the hand. At some machines the sheet, after leaving the mouth-piece through the travelling rollers, falls as it is cut over a 'trap' roller and is placed at once by a boy on to the barrow. The bricks are then wheeled off and 'hacked up', 'skintled', set up aslant and edgeways, to dry them further, and finally 'crowded' and 'set' in the kilns, just as handmade bricks are.[66]

A Faversham brickmaker, making bricks by hand, gave his opinion as to why machines had been taken up in the Medway valley and not in the brickyards in his locality or at neighbouring Sittingbourne: it was down to the nature of the clay. In Burham and Aylesford they were using Gault clay, which produces a brick of an attractive creamy colour, but was harder to work. 'I do not think that machines would succeed for us, our dirt is too quick; but the gault which they use machines for down Burham way, would wear a man's arm off; that wants machinery.'[67]

When Thomas Cubitt switched production from London to his newly acquired site at Burham in 1852, the manufacturing process was as mechanised as the contemporary technology would allow, employing a type of machine that he had already used at his Thames Bank works. Thomas Ainslie, a brick and tile manufacturer of Alperton, Middlesex, patented his first machine in 1841, and from it developed an entire brickmaking system. His pug mill included rollers to crush lumps, and his machine worked on the extrusion method, but the brick was shaped by four rollers instead of being pressed through a die. His kilns had a complex system of interconnecting flues. Cubitt is known to have corresponded with the manufacturers of rival machines, but seemed content with Ainslie's models.[68] Following experiments he undertook in 1847, Cubitt concluded that a clamp-fired hand-made stock brick was more easily crushed than a machine-made and kiln-burnt one.[69]

The introduction of machines was designed to lower the manufacturing cost and to produce a superior brick, but there were disadvantages. The extrusion process produced a brick without a 'frog', which would be filled with mortar when the brick was laid, and its absence might cause bonding issues. Inevitably such bricks were also heavier than those with a frog. This problem was overcome by the introduction of bricks with perforations through them, into which mortar would enter, improving the strength of the bonding, and which also reduced their weight. One of the best known was Beart's Patent Gault brick, a premium-quality brick that was liked because of its colour. Produced by an intricate die, this wire-cut brick had twenty-one perforations.[70]

For brickmakers who invested heavily in machinery the capital outlay would be offset by employing fewer and less-skilled workers. While the machine replaced the

---

66   *Ibid.*, p. 129.

67   *Ibid.*, p. 145.

68   Hobhouse, *Thomas Cubitt*, pp. 310–14.

69   Watt, 'Nineteenth-century brickmaking inventions', p. 86 quoting a report in *The Builder* (1847), p. 537. The stock brick was crushed by a weight of 36 tons, whilst the machine brick survived a pressure of 60 tons.

70   Patents Nos 10636 (1845), 13275 (1850).

From clay pit to clamp

central part of the brickmaking process, the machine still needed to be fed with clay and the newly made bricks taken away to be hacked up. So, it was the walk flatter and the moulder who were in the most vulnerable positions, the more so as the moulder was the highest paid and most skilled worker in the brickfield. This challenged the traditional organisation of brickfield labour into subcontracted gangs.[71] According to Cubitt, his Ainslie machines were tended by three boys, and machine minding required no prior brickmaking experience.

> Our new process ... is so different to any-thing that brickmakers have done before that little good will be got by beginning with a person who has already worked at it. P.S. I should perhaps say that we have commenced in Kent, and Foremen only are brickmakers. We are doing all the work with the agricultural labourers of the place.[72]

Not surprisingly, the introduction of machines was opposed in some places. In Manchester in the 1860s there were Luddite-style incidents, sufficiently widespread and violent to prompt a Parliamentary Commission of Inquiry into the so-called 'atrocities'. There seems to have been far less opposition in southern England, and industrial action in the London area in the same period was not related to the introduction of machinery.[73] The surviving literature does not explain the wage structure in those yards that were mechanised, and when there were disputes about wage rates across the London brickfields in the 1880s and 1890s the discussion always seemed to be in the context of the traditional brickmaking gang. In the view of one writer the period of opposition to machinery passed and the introduction of machinery allowed the trade to grow and thus, further down the line, increased the number of workers employed in the industry rather than reducing it.

> The introduction of machinery into brickmaking was in many places attended with violent contests; the men who had hitherto had a monopoly in making the bricks by hand, having united in bands to prevent the use of machinery in the trade. We have not lately heard of any such insurrectionary movements, and trust they are at an end, leaving the conviction in this as in other cases that in the long-run machinery increases the number of hands to be employed ... there are still plenty of places in the Eastern Counties, where the machines have not penetrated, and probably never will; for in a small brickfield, the first expense would be too great; and the master brickmaker, who is generally the owner of a family, would prefer seeing the family doing the work which otherwise the machine would be doing.[74]

---

71 The gang system is described more detail in Chapter 10.

72 Hobhouse, *Thomas Cubitt*, p. 310.

73 For the 1860s 'atrocities' see R. Price, 'The other side of respectability: violence in the Manchester brickmaking trade 1859–1870', *Past & Present*, 66 (1975), pp. 110–32.

74 'Bricks and brickmakers', *Chamber's Journal of Popular Literature, Science and Arts*, 682 (3 July 1880), p. 429.

Bricks of Victorian London

Mechanisation altered the traditional rhythm of the brickmaking annual cycle, for when machines were installed in buildings rather than operating in the open manufacture continued year-round. A spokesman for a Crayford brickfield in the 1860s said 'Machinery is used by us in the winter, but not in the summer' and that during the former there was a two-shift system in operation, with the second shift starting at 6pm and ending at 5.30am. However, it is not stated which kind of machine was being used.[75]

Mechanisation went hand in hand with the shift to fewer and larger units of production, a process that will be explored in a later chapter. Firms operating on a bigger scale, and with good clay reserves, were in a better position to make capital investments and when operating efficiently were likely to benefit from economies of scale, with lower production costs than their smaller rivals.

Despite many instances of mechanisation, traditional stock brickmaking persisted in the London area well into the twentieth century. It is perhaps not surprising, therefore, that an architect, writing in 1896, still thought that London brickmaking was 'most antiquated' and one of the 'few forms that have survived the introduction of steam driven machinery'.[76]

---

75 No other references to a night shift have been found. Children's Employment Commission, 5th Report, PP 1866, p. 146.

76 H.G. Montgomery, 'Bricks and brickmaking', *Journal of the Society of Architects*, 3/6 (April 1896), p. 98.

Chapter 3

Finding the clay: landowners, brickmakers and the availability of land

Before they could start to make bricks prospective brickmakers had to choose a site on which to set up their works. Industrial location, particularly in the past, was determined by three main factors: the presence of raw materials; the availability of sources of power; and proximity to markets or to appropriate forms of transport. Bricks are heavy and bulky, with a low value-to-weight ratio, and finished bricks weigh less than the raw clay from which they are made. As a result, brickworks are nearly always sited close to the source of the main raw material.[1]

For much of the nineteenth century a brick manufacturing site was known as a *brickfield* – essentially a piece of land with brickearth in it. Clay-bearing land was acquired by purchase or via a lease. Purchase entailed an initial capital investment, whereas renting spread the costs over a number of years. Some brickmakers bought many acres of land, but generally there is no information about how much they paid for them. Records of tenancies survive in the archives, and provide better information about rented property. The willingness of landowners to make their land available for brickmaking was critical to the industry.

Landowners usually had options in the way they used their holdings, depending on the situation of their estates. Some, like the duke of Bedford, derived sizeable incomes from housing developments in London, such as Bloomsbury; others, like the marquess of Londonderry, derived substantial revenues from the mineral deposits, such as coal, beneath their land. Many owners, however, earned a large proportion of their income from farm rents.[2] Of the counties near London, Middlesex and Essex had no significant mineral deposits to exploit, but their proximity to the capital ensured that other options were available, including agriculture, brickmaking, gravel extraction and market gardening, for which brickearth also provided a fertile soil.[3] Kent, best known for its orchards and hops, also had chalk deposits for cement making and, in parts of the county, coal.

Where their land was close to a town or city, the lease or sale of land for residential development was financially attractive to landowners, especially when the outward edge of the built-up area began to press against their own property. Brickmaking to provide building materials for the new houses was also a good proposition. At the

---

1   Alfred Weber published his 'least cost location theory' in 1909. J. Bale, *The location of manufacturing industry*, 2nd edn (Harlow, 1981), pp. 46–53.

2   F.M.L. Thompson, *English landed society in the nineteenth century* (London, 1963), pp. 264–8.

3   M. Robbins, *A new survey of England: Middlesex* (London, 1953), pp. 32–3; L.G. Bennett, *The horticultural industry of Middlesex*, University of Reading, Department of Agricultural Economics Miscellaneous studies, 7 (Reading, 1952), pp. 17–18.

Bricks of Victorian London

beginning of the nineteenth century the Tyssen estate, the largest in Hackney and totalling about 600 acres, leased land to several brickmakers, including Thomas, Samuel and William Rhodes in 1806, and William and Thomas Rhodes in 1815, 1818 and 1822. Further leases were issued to Henry and John Lee in 1837, to Robert and William Webb in 1845 and to James and Alfred Stroud in 1865.[4] These brickfields were close to contemporary housing developments in which the estate also had an interest.

Further from the centre of London, where there was less demand for new housing, brickmaking continued throughout the nineteenth century within a largely agricultural environment. For example, in the area between Southall, eleven miles from the centre of London, and Uxbridge, four miles further west, which became known as the Cowley district, the choice was usually between some form of cultivation or brickmaking, and here the two were not incompatible.[5] The owners of established landed estates, taking a long view, were more likely to lease land than to sell it off, whereas the owners of smaller properties might choose to take a capital gain from its sale and invest the proceeds elsewhere.

Landowners might make their land available for brickmaking if they thought it offered a better return than agriculture. The presence of brick clay in a piece of land added a premium to its sale value; if let, the ground rents for agricultural land and brickfields were broadly similar, but landlords received additional payments in the form of royalties on the number of bricks made. The thinking that lay behind the licensing of land for brickmaking is rarely known, but there is one occasion where it is clearly stated. At Heston the trustees of Jonathan Passingham's will aimed to maximise the value of the estate for the benefit of the legatees, and to do so obtained a private act of parliament. This enabled them to grant brickmaking leases, because

> Farms called Heston Farm and North Hyde Farm contain brick and malm earth of considerable depth and excellent quality, and the same lands or some of them could be let to great advantage for the purpose of manufacturing bricks and other articles ... and by means of the monies to be derived from royalties and payments for brick and malm earth as aforesaid a sum will ultimately be produced sufficient for the purchase [of the neighbouring farm].[6]

Good archival records exist for landowners in the Cowley district, including landed families such as the Earls of Jersey in Heston and Southall; the de Burghs in Hillingdon and West Drayton; the de Salis family in Harlington; and the Shadwells in Northolt. Elsewhere aristocratic landowners such as the earl of Aylesford and Earl Thanet in

---

4   *Victoria County History. Middlesex, vol. 10: Hackney*, ed. T.F.T. Baker (London 1995), p. 75; London Borough of Hackney Archives D/F/RHO/3/2 1 October 1806; D/F/RHO/3/3 28 February 1815; M569 10 October 1818; M570 18 November 1822; M717 11 December 1837; M725 30 June 1845; M760 19 July 1865.

5   Robbins, *Middlesex*, pp. 353–5, 326.

6   7 & 8 Victoria, Pr.c. 22 (1844) Passingham Estate Act; LMA Acc. 397/11.

Finding the clay

Kent, Lady Mildmay in Islington and Lady Holland in Hammersmith all leased some land to brickmakers.[7] While in some parishes there was one dominant landowner, in others ownership was more diffuse. In the 1830s three owners at Grays in Essex, Thomas Theobald, John Jefferson and John Meeson, all leased land to brickmakers and cement makers, and the brickfields in Crayford on the other side of the Thames were leased from four different owners.[8]

As well as individual owners, corporate bodies such as the Church of England or the London livery companies also rented out land for brickmaking. The dean and chapter of Rochester cathedral was the largest landowner in Frindsbury, in the Medway valley, and by 1842 some forty-six acres, about one third of the total estate, were in use as brickfields.[9] In Hackney Thomas and William Rhodes and Henry and John Lee were tenants of St Thomas Hospital.[10] Later in the century the ecclesiastical commissioners managed land owned by the bishopric of Worcester in West Drayton and the bishop of London in Hammersmith.[11] Samuel Rhodes was a tenant of the Clothworkers Company in the 1830s, and the Goldsmiths Company's land in Acton was home to the first brickfield in the area in 1869.[12]

Enclosure could be a factor in opening up land for brickmaking, especially where previously there had been common fields still divided into strips. This process had been taking place since the seventeenth century, but enclosure by act of parliament was mainly concentrated in the period 1750 to 1819. It generally resulted in the consolidation of landholding into larger and less scattered units, bringing with it higher productivity and increased rents.[13] A parish such as Northolt in Middlesex was slow to be enclosed. Here brickmaking became centred on Tunlow Field, conveniently situated beside the canal but before enclosure in 1835 a common field, divided into strips, and consequently impractical to exploit for brickmaking. The first licences on this field were granted in 1834 and 1835.[14] A further complication found here was that this land was held on copyhold tenure – a form of manorial tenure that still survived in some places.[15]

---

7   Kent Archives and Local History Centre U234/L2; TNA IR29/17/298 Tithe award Rainham (1838); IR29/21/33 Tithe award Islington (1848); IR29/21/23 Hammersmith (1845) <http://thegenealogist.co.uk>, accessed 29 August 2021.

8   TNA IR29/12/145 Tithe award Grays Thurrock (1841); IR29/17/100 Tithe award Crayford (1839).

9   Preston, *Industrial Medway*, p. 52; A. Pearce and D. Long, *Chalk mining and associated industries of Frindsbury*, Kent Underground Research Group, Research Report 3 (1987), pp. 6–7.

10   TNA IR29/1219 Tithe award Hackney (1845).

11   See LMA DL/D/L/028/Ms12335. Colham Garden Manor: leases and an assignment of 149 acres of land in the parishes of Hillingdon and West Drayton and used as a brick field; DL/D/L/136/Ms12292. Fulham manor: leases and papers relating to several parcels of land used as brickfields in the parish of Hammersmith, Middlesex, 1875–1900.

12   TNA 29/21/33 Tithe award Islington (1848); Harper Smith, *Brickfields of Acton*, pp. 6–7.

13   Daunton, *Progress and poverty*, pp. 113–17.

14   Westminster Abbey Muniments (WAM) Northolt Court Roll; LMA Acc. 289/454.

15   Tenants paid an entry fine when they took over the land, and were subject to the jurisdiction of the manorial court. LMA Acc. 289/449 and 289/454.

Bricks of Victorian London

Both landlord and tenant needed to be confident that the soil in a particular field would be suitable for making bricks. They were looking for the presence of brickearth, but they also needed to know about its depth and its quality. Since there was no absolute certainty, until manufacturing started, about the quality of the brickearth, leases sometimes allowed for a system of arbitration if the soil was found not to be 'fair brickearth clay'.[16] In a notorious case one Kent clergyman was prosecuted for fraud when he misrepresented the quality of the clay in a field he had let, having shown a prospective tenant bricks allegedly made from it, but actually made from clay brought from elsewhere.[17]

The nature of the brickearth was important in terms of the profitability of a brickfield. Malm, as we have seen, was thought to be the best clay for brickmaking, requiring little in the way of additives to make a quality stock brick, but it could occur side by side with inferior brickearth. An eight-acre field in Hillingdon was said to contain 'a great depth of malm and common brickearth'.[18] Some soils might need screening to remove gravel or flints, or require the addition of ashes and chalk to make it malleable. Since purchasing these additives and transporting them to the brickfields inevitably increased production costs, the quality of the soil might influence the decision to exploit a particular field. One Northolt landowner, after commissioning a feasibility study of part of his estate, received a discouraging report from his agent to the effect that the clay was of inferior quality and would not offer a good return, as a 'full admixture of chalk and sand would be necessary'. The agent warned:

> In fact if the brickearth in your field had been of medium quality it would not have produced you any income at present because the building trade is not sufficiently flourishing to raise the price of bricks to such an amount as will pay the cost of making bricks from any clay which is not of decidedly superior quality.[19]

When the price of bricks was high the use of lower-quality clay might be justified in the same way that marginal land might be ploughed up when cereal prices were high.[20] However, with fluctuating demand for bricks and volatile prices, a risky proposition of this kind could rapidly become a liability to brickmaker and landlord alike.

As well as its quality, the depth of the brickearth was an important consideration, as it would determine the number of bricks that could be made from a particular parcel of land. The rule of thumb calculation was that an acre of brickearth could yield a million bricks for every foot depth of clay. With about four to five feet depth of clay an acre of land could keep a small brickmaker in material for at least a couple

---

16 E.g. lease of brickfield to James Hunt at Hillingdon 1842, LMA Acc. 1386/96.

17 'Serious charges against the Rev. W. English'. *East Kent, Faversham and Sittingbourne Gazette*, 25 February 1871.

18 *The Times*, 1 January 1887.

19 Letter from John Oakley to Lancelot Shadwell, 18 August 1857, LMA Acc. 289/192a.

20 This occurred during the French revolutionary wars. J.D. Chambers and G.E. Mingay, *The agricultural revolution, 1750–1880* (London, 1966), p. 117.

Finding the clay

of seasons.[21] The depth of clay varied from site to site, but in geological terms brickearth is regarded as a surficial deposit, only a few metres thick. The landowner could hazard a guess based on general experience of the neighbourhood, or adopt a more scientific approach. On part of the de Burgh estate in West Drayton a surveyor estimated that fields contained between four and a half feet and five feet of workable clay.[22] Trial borings on the land of Rudolph de Salis in Dawley in 1849 showed that the brickearth was mainly two to four feet in depth, but the maximum depth encountered was six feet nine inches, and its quality was 'in general very good'.[23] In some Hackney leases there was a stipulation that excavations should not be deeper than nine feet, but whether it was known that there was good brick clay at that depth remains unclear.[24] Sometimes the conditions of the lease could be varied if the brickearth proved not to be of sufficient depth to make its exploitation economic. One at Hayes in 1873 referred to 'fair average brickearth quality and where not less than two feet deep'.[25]

A surveyor's report of part of Philpott's Bridge farm, owned by Hubert de Burgh, suggested that the land was admirably suited for either agriculture or brickmaking on account of its containing 'fine loam and ... brickearth of considerable depth'. The farm brought in about £450 per annum as agricultural land, but if let for brickmaking could generate as much as £400 to £500 per acre, demonstrating the extra value to owners of licensing brickmaking on their land.[26]

Some brickmakers bought just enough land for a few years' production, while others built up extensive holdings that provided clay reserves for decades. These freehold purchases required an upfront capital investment but resulted in lower ongoing revenue costs. In the 1840s James and William Scott owned just over 100 acres in Hammersmith.[27] The Southall Brick Company owned 76 acres in 1858.[28] Thomas Cubitt bought the freehold of 189 acres of land at Burham in Kent, and George Smeed eventually owned as much as two and a half square miles (1600 acres) of land in and around Sittingbourne.[29] Of course, the initial cost could be spread over several years by means of a mortgage. The Acton Brickworks, of around twelve acres, was purchased in 1878 by James and Alfred Stroud in this way.[30]

---

21 J. Middleton, *View of the agriculture of Middlesex*, 2nd edn (London, 1807), p. 25.

22 Report by William Thompson to Messrs Palmer, Bull and Fry, 26 November 1875, LMA Acc. 1386/262.

23 The National Archives (TNA) RAIL 830/94.

24 Lease of land for brickmaking from Tyssen to T. and W. Rhodes, 10 October 1818. London Borough of Hackney Archives M569.

25 LMA Acc. 538/1st Dep/42/15.

26 Valuation of an estate in the parish of Hillingdon ... the property of Hubert de Burgh, 1832. LMA Acc. 742/105.

27 TNA IR/29/21/23 Tithe award Hammersmith (1845).

28 TNA BT41/638/3491.

29 Hobhouse, *Thomas Cubitt*, p. 310; Perks, *George Bargebrick*, p. 7.

30 All the other brickfields in Acton at this period were leased. Harper Smith, *Brickfields of Acton*, pp. 22, 54.

Bricks of Victorian London

Many prospective brickmakers might have insufficient capital to purchase a brickfield, so would look to lease the land, hoping that they could generate sufficient revenue to pay the recurrent costs of rent and royalties. It is understandable that smaller firms would take this route, but it was also true of some larger operators as well: for example, the brickfields of James Day Burchett & Son in the 1890s, totalling 138 acres, were all leased from a number of different owners.[31] Some brickmakers worked both freehold and leasehold land. Odell Ltd had 44 acres of freehold land, but a much larger acreage of leasehold land, some 167 acres.[32]

Unless they proposed to undertake brickmaking in their own right, owners who wanted to exploit the clay reserves on their land needed to find tenants. One way to do this was to advertise in the newspapers. This example is typical:

> Superior Cowley Brickearth. To be let. 20–30 acres of superior brickearth near West Drayton, Middlesex traversed by the Grand Junction Canal and brickfields can be opened without any large outlay of capital, as there are already considerable buildings erected on part of the ground.[33]

On the other hand, prospective tenants could approach landowners in areas of known brick clay, particularly if other brickmakers were already at work there, or they could advertise in the 'Wanted' columns. This Fulham brickmaker was looking for a new brickfield with sales in the London market in mind:

> Wanted to rent or purchase: from 5 to 10 acres of land, containing earth suitable for brickmaking. Must be within 5 miles of London, or close to waterside in the Cowley or Kent brickmaking districts. Mr. J. Johnson, Moore Park Brickworks, Fulham, S.W.[34]

As well as a source of clay, brickmakers needed other raw materials, particularly chalk, ashes, sand and water. A source of water on or near a brickfield was essential. Of one Cowley brickfield it was said that 'a constant stream of water flows through the land', while a brickfield in Streatham was said to have 'clay of a very superior quality and coloured with marl, and running water of great abundance'.[35] At the end of the century it was possible that brickmakers could depend on piped water, rather than wells or streams; in Acton in 1895 one brickfield had its water supplied over the eighty-acre site by vulcanised rubber pipes connected to the mains of the Grand Junction Waterworks Company.[36]

Equally important for a brickmaker was access to a transport node in order to get the product to market. One landlord offered 'a field adjoining a navigable canal two

---

31   TNA BT31/6615/46552.

32   TNA BT31/5649/39405.

33   *The Times*, 17 September 1853.

34   *The Builder*, 28 July 1860.

35   *Ibid.*, 14 February 1852, 15 March 1845.

36   *Acton Gazette*, 16 June 1894.

Finding the clay

miles from a station on the Great Western Railway' in west Middlesex, and, as we have seen, another brickfield in the vicinity was also served by the canal.[37]

This advertisement for a piece of land tried to tempt a prospective client by covering all the bases:

> To brickmakers and builders. To be let on lease or otherwise, from 10 to 50 acres of land, containing brickearth 20 feet in depth, with a supply of chalk in the same field; water 30ft from the surface. The above is situated half a mile from Gravesend, Kent, approached by good roads, and close to the line of the intended North Kent Railway.[38]

For landlords the financial return from brickmaking came from two sources: rents and royalties. Rents charged to brickmakers were generally in line with prevailing agricultural rents, but at the higher end of the range. The rents landowners could expect from farmers depended on a number of factors – the prices of agricultural products, farmers' demand for land and the state of the economy as a whole. However, when farmers enjoyed increased profitability from a rise in prices for their products, landowners might not always benefit, if the land was let on long leases. They also had to make allowances for farmers who found that falling prices for produce left them unable to meet rents that had been agreed when prices were higher. This was reflected in the length of leases. Tenants benefited from long leases that allowed them to enjoy the returns on their investment over time. But during the Napoleonic Wars long leases became less popular. Landlords were reluctant to grant them in a time of inflation, and in the post-war years falling prices discouraged tenants from taking on long-term commitments.[39] A shift to shorter leases provided more flexibility for landowners but made tenants more vulnerable to rent rises.[40] To achieve the increased rents of the 'High Farming' era of the middle of the century landowners often had to invest in improvements, such as land drainage (often using clay pipes), new farm buildings or enclosure.[41] Agricultural rents themselves varied according to the quality of the soil and the use to which the land was put.[42] Land laid to permanent grass was more valuable than arable land, reflecting the greater profitability of dairy farming or hay growing. The difference in value between the two at Frogmoor Farm, Hayes, in

---

37 *The Builder*, 21 February 1852; *The Times*, 17 September 1853.

38 *Ibid.*, 11 January 1845.

39 M.E. Turner, J.V. Beckett and B. Afton, *Agricultural rent in England, 1690–1914* (Cambridge, 1997), pp. 11, 68.

40 Chambers and Mingay, *The agricultural revolution*, p. 129; Daunton, *Progress and poverty*, pp. 53–4.

41 Chambers and Mingay, *The agricultural revolution*, p. 167; B.A. Holderness, 'Agriculture 1770–1860', in C.H. Feinstein and S. Pollard (eds), *Studies in capital formation in the United Kingdom, 1750–1920* (Oxford, 1988), pp. 11–27.

42 Rents on these Middlesex estates were much higher than the national average, as provided by Turner *et al.*, *Agricultural rent in England*. This reflects two factors: (a) the paucity of readily available data from Middlesex and (b) the impact of the proximity of the metropolis on the use and value of land.

Bricks of Victorian London

1838 was as much as 20 per cent.[43] In 1858, when agricultural land in Northolt was being let at between 25s and 40s per acre, a brickmaking lease also valued the land at 40s.[44] A large parcel of land in Aylesford went for about 63s an acre on a very long lease in 1881, but even higher rates of £5 an acre had been achieved in Shoreditch in 1839 and Harlington in 1853.[45]

As landowners were theoretically in a position to make strategic decisions to maximise their incomes, we might expect there to be a correlation between the level of agricultural rents and landowners' interest in brickmaking, since it would be logical to favour the latter when the returns from farming were poor. If shorter leases for farmers had become common, it is perhaps strange that the term of leases given to brickmakers were often quite long. Fourteen- or twenty-one-year terms were quite common, which meant that they spanned the usual trade cycle of nine years, and were usually for longer periods than farming tenancies. Exceptionally, land was let for thirty or even forty years.[46] We may suggest that landowners anticipated that, following a single agreement with a brickmaker, all the brickearth in their land would be exhausted, accomplishing that one-time opportunity to profit from it. Of course, the brickearth might be exhausted before the end of the lease, so some leases had a termination clause, allowing the brickmaker to surrender the lease early, and shorter leases were given where it was known that the amount of remaining brickearth in the field was limited. In one case a brickfield was held on a rolling one-year tenancy.[47]

Occasionally leases provided for the land to be surrendered piecemeal as the brickearth was worked out. An 1854 lease specified that the land on a forty-nine-acre brickfield could be returned in blocks of two acres, while one to D. & C. Rutter in 1895 allowed land to be surrendered in parcels of at least an acre, either when the brickearth was exhausted or if there was found to be less than three feet depth of workable clay.[48] One brickmaker was not required to pay the royalty once the brickearth was used up but had to continue to pay the ground rent for the full term.[49]

The larger part of a landlord's income came from the royalty paid on the number of bricks made, expressed as a sum per thousand. An 1864 lease of about thirty-eight acres at Dawley charged an annual rent of £154 – roughly £4 an acre – but the anticipated royalty payments over the same period were in the region of £400.[50] An 1877 lease in Hammersmith set the annual royalty at £750, compared with a rent of only £51; the royalty

---

43   Values were 30s, 25s and 20s per acre for the arable fields, but 40s, 30s and 25s for meadows. LMA Acc. 180/211.

44   LMA Acc. 289/194; WAM N.107.

45   Kent Archives and Local History Centre U234/L2; LMA Acc. 969/63; London Borough of Hackney Archives M721.

46   De Salis estate, Dawley. Lease of land to John Rutty and George Verey. LMA Acc. 969/62; De Burgh estate. Lease of land at West Drayton to Samuel Pocock. LMA Acc. 1386/101.

47   Agreement between Earl of Jersey and F.C. Reed for land at Southall. LMA Acc. 405/Bundle 1.

48   LMA Acc. 969/64a; Acc. 1386/382.

49   LMA Acc. 405/1.

50   This equates to 2s 0d per thousand on a make of four million bricks. Lease from Shackle to White and Stacey. LMA Acc. 538/2nd deposit/3517.

Finding the clay

equates to 2s 6d per thousand bricks on an output of six million.[51] Royalty rates varied widely, the range extending from 1s 3d (Hillingdon 1855) to 2s 6d (Southall 1898) and even 3s 3d (Hackney 1865). These rates did not increase consistently throughout the century, so other factors must explain the variation, such as the prevailing market price for bricks, the length of the lease and the rent being charged. One landlord set the royalty for one tenant at 2s 6d in 1849, but a year later charged Samuel Pocock only 1s 3d; in this case the land involved was 100 acres and the term of the lease was forty years. Here, one assumes, the landlord was looking for a steady income over a long period.[52]

To ensure an adequate return the landowner usually stipulated the expected level of production, expressed as either a fixed monetary payment or a minimum output of bricks. Placing such conditions in a lease tilted the balance of the agreement in favour of the landowner, and the tenant was squeezed if demand flagged or prices fell, although he could usually average out under-production in one year with greater production in another. James Hunt's lease of land at Heston in 1844 stipulated that he should make two million bricks per season; if that figure was not reached, the royalty payment on that number was still payable, but Hunt could make more bricks in subsequent years without additional payment, the aim being to produce an average of two million per annum.[53] Leases, despite their length in some cases, did not contain a mechanism by which royalty rates could be varied if circumstances changed, but landowners benefited from greater royalties when market conditions encouraged brickmakers to increase production. However, a clause in another Heston lease suggests a sensitivity to the fluctuating demand for bricks, since the minimum output of one million bricks could be reduced if, on 25 March in any year, just at the beginning of the moulding season, half a million bricks 'remain on the ground' – that is, unsold. In that case the minimum output was to be halved.[54] A clause such as this, however, is unusual.

Minimum quantities ranged from 1.5 million (Heston, 1845) to six million (Hillingdon, 1882), guaranteeing a payment of £150 and £450 respectively.[55] The minimum quantity might also be expressed as a cash sum, such as £337 10s, the equivalent of three million bricks at 2s 3d per 1000 (Southall, 1878). Production in excess of this was charged at a rate per thousand.[56] Occasionally there was a differential royalty, with production greater than the prescribed minimum being charged at a lower rate. One lease stipulated a minimum of four million bricks at 1s 9d a thousand, but production in excess of five million was charged at only 1s 6d (Dawley 1854).[57] In another case the royalty increased from year to year, assuming a steady growth in production, although the underlying rate per thousand remained the same.[58] It is difficult to know whether these royalty levels

---

51 Lease of land by Ecclesiastical Commissioners to Williams and Wallington, 1 March 1877. LMA DL/D/L/136/MS12292.
52 LMA Acc. 1386/101.
53 LMA Acc. 328/47.
54 LMA Acc. 328/43.
55 LMA Acc. 328/51; DL/D/L/028/Ms12335.
56 LMA Acc. 1103/006.
57 LMA Acc. 969/64a.
58 LMA Acc. 405/1.

Bricks of Victorian London

were consistently achieved or whether landowners took action when tenants fell short of their agreements, as it is only rarely that the quantity of bricks actually produced is known. In one case, Thomas Watson, a tenant on the Osterley estate, was expected to pay £250 in 1899, £375 in 1900 and £500 in the following year, but his actual production would have generated royalties of no more than £296, £264 and £299.[59]

Unusually, royalties on the Tyssen Estate in Hackney in the early years of the nineteenth century were expressed as a fixed sum to be paid over the term of the lease. For Thomas and William Rhodes in 1822 the royalty payment was set at £3200 over a thirty-one-year period, and similar arrangements were included in leases of 1806, 1815 and 1818.[60]

As royalties were charged on the quantity of bricks made, there had to be a mechanism by which the landlords' agents could check the accuracy of the returns the brickmakers made to the estate office. An element of trust must have been involved, and if there were cases of fraudulent reporting they do not seem to have reached the courts. Landowners always reserved the right to enter the premises to check that the terms of the lease were being met. Up to 1850, while an excise duty on bricks was in force, leases specifically refer to the number of bricks assessed for the tax as the basis of the assessment for royalties.[61] The Excise Duty had an allowance of 10 per cent for wastage – that is, bricks spoiled in the drying and firing stages which could not be sold – and an allowance such as this was sometimes perpetuated after the repeal of the tax.[62]

Landowners might take professional advice about the financial returns they could expect. In 1849 the de Salis family were advised that the brickearth on their land at Dawley was sufficient to make 83 million bricks at a rate of about three million per annum. At a royalty rate of 2s 3d this could yield the estate a steady income of £337 per annum in addition to the ground rent.[63] Unfortunately, it is usually difficult to gauge the returns owners actually received, but there is useful information about the De Burgh estate in Hillingdon and West Drayton between 1856 and 1871. During this sixteen-year period there was a general upward trend in the income from rents. In the years when the rents and royalties can be separately identified, the receipts from brickmakers were as high as 46 per cent of the estate's total income in 1856 and 59 per cent in 1861. However, by 1871 royalties from the remaining two brickmakers brought in only 6 per cent.[64]

For Manor Farm, Frindsbury, owned by the dean and chapter of Rochester cathedral, output figures are available from 1828 to 1850, from which we can estimate the probable royalty income (Table 3.1). Production varied from year to year, but it was

---

59   *Ibid.*

60   London Borough of Hackney Archives M570; D/F/RHO/3/2; D/F/RHO/3/3; M569.

61   Lease of brickfield at Hackney to William Rhodes 5 October 1839. London Borough of Hackney Archives M721; Lease of brickfield at Hillingdon to James Hunt 5 January 1842 LMA Acc. 1386/96. For the way the Duty was assessed see chapter 4.

62   See Samuel Pocock's leases from the Ecclesiastical Commissioners in Hillingdon in 1875 and 1882. LMA DL/D/L/028/Ms12335.

63   TNA RAIL 830/93–5.

64   £593 rental and royalties out of a total estate income of £712 (1856), £1099 rental and royalties out of £1227 (1861), £221 out of £3526 (1871). LMA Acc. 1386/385.

Finding the clay

Table 3.1
Brick production at Frindsbury Manor Farm, 1828–50.

Output and calculated royalty income (based on a royalty rate of 1s 6d per 1000 bricks)

	Output	Royalty
1828	1,962,700	£147
1829	1,088,832	£82
1830	3,928,250	£295
1831	3,369,785	£253
1832	3,361,825	£252
1833	1,689,200	£127
1834	2,852,100	£214
1835	8,959,000	£672
1836	8,730,335	£655
1837	9,294,875	£697
1838	6,906,100	£518
1839	8,260,050	£620
1840	11,314,000	£849
1841	10,326,500	£774
1842	11,218,900	£841
1843	10,613,000	£796
1844	14,071,000	£1,055
1845	10,504,300	£788
1846	6,732,839	£505
1847	2,652,000	£199
1848	2,314,000	£174
1849	2,365,000	£177
1850	2,413,324	£181
Total	144,927,915	£10,870

Source: Preston, *Industrial Medway*, p. 53.

significantly higher in the decade after 1835, when Henry Everest took on a contract to make eight million bricks. The peak year was 1844, when the royalty income would have topped £1000, and when Manor Farm was said to be contributing 1 per cent of the national brick output.[65]

---

65   Preston, *Industrial Medway*, pp. 52–4.

Bricks of Victorian London

Leases were sometimes assigned by one brickmaker to another, usually as a result of the bankruptcy of the original lessee. Examples of such transfers include Thomas Maynard's purchase in 1873 of the lease of a brickfield at Dawley from the liquidator following the bankruptcy of John Rutty, and the acquisition in 1886 by Broad and Harris of the brickfields of Samuel Pocock in Hillingdon, again as the result of insolvency.[66]

Occasionally land occupied by brickmakers was still held by manorial tenure. In such cases the lord of the manor had a financial interest in activities undertaken by his copyhold tenants, and would need to license any brickmaking. The Ecclesiastical Commissioners challenged Hubert de Burgh's right to license brickmaking on land that he had leased to Samuel Pocock, and required them to pay a shared royalty of 7½d per 1000 bricks.[67] Having been once bitten, de Burgh agreed to grant a lease to another brickmaker only once the land had been enfranchised.[68] In other cases, Thomas Shackle was required to pay a royalty of 2d per thousand to the manor of Hayes, and a Mr Norton paid the same rate to the manor of Northolt.[69]

The returns from brickmaking could help compensate landowners when their agricultural incomes were falling, as well as providing a transition from arable farming to meadow or pasture or to building development. The biggest challenge came during the 'Great Depression' of the 1870s and 1880s, when there was a fall in rents that lasted until 1914.[70] However, the depression affected other sectors of the economy, including construction, and the brick industry also experienced low demand and reduced output.

As brickearth became worked out, landowners might be willing to allow the gravel that often underlay it to be exploited, either by an existing brickmaker or by a new tenant. There was a steady demand for gravel for roadmaking and for other civil engineering purposes, and London vestries awarded annual contracts for its supply. A number of contractors regularly bid for these contracts; some sourced gravel from the Thames estuary, others from west Middlesex.[71] Messrs Studds won a tender to supply gravel to Paddington Vestry in 1857; forty years later the supplier was Odell & Company Ltd. Both firms were also brickmakers. Samuel Pocock was able to sustain a contract with Marylebone Vestry for 1859–60 from the material dug out – nearly 20,000 tons – while extending the dock on his West Drayton brickfield.[72] London

---

66 Maynard was a brick merchant based at Paddington basin. Broad and Harris were also based there. LMA Acc. 969/66 and DL/D/L/028/Ms12335.

67 LMA Acc.1386/102.

68 LMA Acc. 1386/108. Enfranchisement effectively changed the land from copyhold to freehold, at a price. The Copyhold Act of 1852 allowed tenants to demand enfranchisement. The remaining copyhold tenures were converted into freehold following the Law of Real Property Act 1922.

69 LMA Acc. 180/181–182; He paid £24 15s 10d for the 1835 and 1836 seasons. LMA Acc. 289/457.

70 P.J. Perry, *British farming in the Great Depression 1870–1914: an historical geography* (London, 1974), p. 107.

71 City of Westminster Archives Paddington Vestry. Minutes 13 March 1857; Works Committee 22 December 1899.

72 TNA RAIL 830/93–95.

Finding the clay

vestries also tendered contracts for flints, which were found on some brickmaking sites; Henry Dodd supplied Shoreditch vestry with gravel, sand and flints, the last from Kent.[73] In 1904 100,000 cubic yards of flints were shipped out of Milton Creek, near Sittingbourne.[74]

Royalties on gravel extraction were charged either on the weight or volume of gravel extracted, or on the acreage of land being worked. George Gibson paid the Osterley estate royalties of 7d per cubic yard on the gravel removed, while on an old brickfield at Hillingdon in 1853 Messrs Studds were charged £110 per acre. The firm seems to have worked the land steadily, paying £110 in 1858, £220 in 1859 and £110 in 1860.[75]

Brickmaking and gravel extraction offered a short-term advantage to the landowner, as the opportunity could be enjoyed only once. Both activities were destructive of the land and conditioned how it might be used in the future. Gravel pits left large holes in the ground that flooded, and worked-out sites are often given over to recreational use, as at Little Britain in the Colne Valley. Others have been infilled and reclaimed. Brickmaking, with only a few feet of earth removed, did not preclude a subsequent agricultural use, if the process was managed carefully. In Hammersmith in the 1840s a number of old brickfields were described as 'reclaimed' and put to arable. The topsoil, which had been removed before clay digging, was put back and manure applied. There were, however, conflicting opinions about whether land treated in this way could be as fertile as before. Middleton was optimistic: 'The brickfields lie close to the town, where manure is to be had in any quantity; and as the carriage costs are but little, they are repeatedly dressed, by which means they soon recover their former fertility.'[76] Another writer, half a century later, was not so easily convinced: 'It is manifest that there must be a deterioration of the land, though the manure conveyed from London as back carriage by the canal boats in some measure replaces the natural by the introduction of artificial fertility.'[77] Yet some land at North Hyde, Heston, which had been in use as a brickfield for twenty-five years, was said to have 'been levelled and restored to its original agricultural uses', and surveyor William Heron claimed of a farm in Hillingdon that 'some fields that have been dug out have now as fine crops as any in the country'.[78]

It was inevitable that the digging out of the brickearth would lower the level of the ground and could interfere with drainage, leaving the land liable to waterlogging. The problem was made more acute by poor management:

---

73 Shoreditch Vestry, *Report of the Medical Officer of Health for the parish of St Leonard Shoreditch* (London, 1878).

74 Perks, *George Bargebrick*, p. 45.

75 LMA Acc. 405/3; LMA Acc. 1386/99–100; LMA Acc. 1386/385; City of Westminster Archives Paddington Vestry. Minutes 2 March 1858.

76 *Ibid.*, p. 26.

77 J.C. Clutterbuck, 'The farming of Middlesex', *Journal of the Royal Agricultural Society of England*, 2nd series, 5 (1869), p. 8.

78 Sale particulars, North Hyde Farm and Depot estate. LMA Acc. 328/105; LMA Acc. 742/105.

Bricks of Victorian London

> There is generally difficulty in getting the brickmakers and gravel diggers to level the mounds occasioned by their works, and in leaving the soil dry; in a very few instances they have even sunk the surface so much, as to occasion ponds of small extent. The best remedy for this, and other matters of like nature, would be for the owner of the soil or his agent to make the most especial agreements or leases; and afterwards to give such attention as would secure the covenants being duly executed.[79]

Landowners often adopted this approach, and introduced covenants into their leases. They followed a standard pattern. Prior to digging the brickearth, the top soil was to be carefully removed (a process known as *uncallowing*), put aside and replaced at the end of the lease.[80] The depth of top soil to be removed is occasionally specified: in one case it was at least eighteen inches.[81] Existing watercourses and drainage were to be preserved. Joseph Bennett's lease of Tunlow Field in Northolt in 1847 contains provisions to avoid waterlogging; he should

> dig for brickearth and level the said field as aforesaid as to preserve a sufficient fall for spring or surface water from west side to east side and shall and will during the said term use his and their best means and endeavours to make and secure ... a sufficient and proper drainage by means of proper ditches and other watercourses ... .[82]

Despite stipulations that water was not to be left standing, reports of drowning incidents on brickfields suggest that flooded clay pits were common.[83] Brickmaking in one part of Northolt left a pond of over an acre in extent, which was a considerable nuisance.[84] Other covenants relate to the maintenance of hedges and ditches.

Not everyone observed the terms of their lease. One landlord was forced to remind his tenants that they had not returned the land to the condition required in their lease, and 'in order to prevent litigation' he asked them to appoint an arbiter with whom he could negotiate the necessary remedial measures.[85]

Leases did not usually specify the replacement of the excavated brickearth by other material, such as manure or rubbish, although, as we have seen, the ready availability of both in the London area suggests they may well have been used. They could be easily shipped by canal or river to many brickfields. For example, land at

---

79 Middleton, *View*, p. 24.

80 E.g. Pocock's lease at Hillingdon in 1855. LMA Acc. 1386/101; Daniel Rutter's leases at North Hyde in 1864. LMA Acc. 328/60. For a manorial licence see Thomas Shackle's from the Manor of Hayes in 1848. LMA Acc. 180/182.

81 Lease by Earl of Jersey to Paul Mecklenburg, 1890 LMA Acc. 405/7.

82 WAM N.107.

83 See Chapter 5.

84 Valuation Office, Field Book, Northolt. TNA IR58/29130/Schedule No. 107.

85 This occurred at the end of a 21-year lease in 1862. The landlord was Thomas Shackle, the tenants Heron and Rutter. LMA Acc. 538/2nd dep/3501.

Finding the clay

Southall in the 1840s was said to have been 'well manured with stable dung procured from London'. Street sweepings, containing a high proportion of horse dung, was another cheap commodity near the capital.[86]

By the end of the century landowners such as the earls of Jersey, owner of the Osterley estate, were aware of the potential of their land on the edges of towns such as Southall for housing development. Now the presence of brickearth might be a factor in making the land attractive to prospective developers. A sale in 1919 included a twenty-eight-acre field containing 'a bed of brickearth, which has been partly worked, giving the advantage to the purchaser of space for immediate development with material for making bricks while the prepared land is being covered [i.e. with houses]'.[87]

Some conclusions may be drawn about brickmaking's relationship to land. Brickmaking could offer a useful source of income for landowners, either from the higher value of the land if sold or from rents and royalties if they let it out. Brickmaking, however, was not the primary source of income for many landowners, certainly not in the long term, and in areas that were distant from the built-up area of London it existed within a continuing agricultural environment. It offered a one-off opportunity for landowners to profit from their land's potential, and occupied a transitional place between other types of land use.

---

86   H. Tremenheere, 'Agricultural and educational statistics of several parishes in the county of Middlesex', *Journal of the Statistical Society of London*, VI (May 1843), p. 122; F.W. Crees, *The life story of F.W. Crees*, ed. C.H. Keene (Ealing, 1979), p. 5.

87   London Borough of Ealing, Local History Centre. Sale particulars, Osterley Estate, 6 June 1919.

Chapter 4

'The rage for building':
meeting demand for bricks in Victorian London

In the early decades of the nineteenth century London seemed to be growing at an unprecedented rate, and new suburbs were springing up on every side.

> The rage for building fills every pleasant outlet with bricks, mortar, rubbish, and eternal scaffold poles, which whether you walk East, West, North or South seems to be running after you. We heard a gentleman say, the other day, that he was sure a resident of the suburbs could scarcely lie down after dinner, and take a nap, without finding when he awoke, that a new row of buildings had started up since he closed his eyes.[1]

For the novelist Wilkie Collins the builders were like the great invaders of old, such as Alexander or Napoleon, 'triumphantly bricklaying beauty wherever they go!' To keep up with such a pace of development Collins would have us believe that 'bricks were called for in such quantities, and seized on in such haste, half-baked from the kilns, that they set the carts on fire, and had to be cooled in pails of water before they could be erected into walls'.[2]

The best-known visual representation of this phenomenon, George Cruikshank's 1829 engraving *London going out of town or, the March of Bricks and Mortar*, shows a shower of bricks colonising rural areas outside the city. Like Collins' military analogy, Cruikshank draws on the idea of barbarian hordes rampaging across the countryside (Plate 4). Bricks became symbols of a seemingly unstoppable tide of development.[3] As the city continued to expand, more and more bricks were needed for houses and for the new types of residential building that appeared during the nineteenth century, such as blocks of flats. Apartment blocks for the poor, such as the Peabody buildings, caustically dismissed by novelist George Gissing as 'terrible barracks ... millions of tons of brute brick and mortar', shared with the mansion flats of the wealthy a difference in scale to what had gone before. Architects endeavoured to deal with the monotony of large expanses of walling by using contrasted bands of different coloured bricks.[4]

---

1 Entry for 'Park' in J. Elmes, *General and bibliographical dictionary of the fine arts* (London, 1826).

2 W. Collins, *Hide and seek* [1854] (Oxford, 1993), pp. 26–7.

3 George Cruikshank was living in Clerkenwell when he created his famous cartoon and observed the building developments going on around him. P. Temple (ed.), *Survey of London, vol. 47. Northern Clerkenwell & Pentonville* (London, 2008), pp. 188, 228.

4 G. Gissing, *The Netherworld* [1889] (Oxford, 1999), p. 274 quoted in R. Dennis, *Cities in modernity: representations and productions of metropolitan space, 1840–1930* (Cambridge, 2008), p. 228. Peabody buildings, for example, use yellow London stocks and pale cream gault bricks.

'The rage for building'

Other new types of building called for different construction materials. Metal and glass offered opportunities to produce a lightness and transparency impossible with brick and stone, and were used to great effect in railway train sheds and pre-eminently in the building housing the Great Exhibition of 1851, the Crystal Palace. Yet even in buildings which displayed a more modernist aesthetic there was usually a need for brickwork somewhere in the structure.

In the first half of the nineteenth century many public buildings continued to be built in the neo-classical style and be faced with stone, such as the National Gallery (1838), the Royal Exchange (1844) and the British Museum (1847). By this time, however, a new architectural style was becoming fashionable – the Gothic revival. This gained popularity following the construction of the new Houses of Parliament, after its predecessor had been destroyed by fire in 1834. It was stipulated that the new building should follow either Gothic or Elizabethan precedents, and Charles Barry, the winner of the competition to design it, chose a perpendicular style that sat easily alongside the adjacent Westminster Abbey.[5] As well as becoming one of London's most distinctive landmarks, the resulting building 'established Gothic as the national style, took it away from the eccentric and made it official'.[6]

Construction in the Gothic revival style did not depend on a single form of building material. While the medieval buildings from which it drew its inspiration were mostly of stone, brick had begun to be used in the fifteenth and sixteenth centuries. Moreover, the continental travels of many architects brought them into contact with styles of medieval building that were less common in the British Isles, such as the imposing brick-built town halls of Belgium. It became acceptable to use brick for the exteriors of major buildings and churches, and architects such as William Butterfield used polychrome brickwork enthusiastically in, for example, All Saints, Margaret Street. Polychromatism required architects to specify bricks from several different sources, often at a distance from London.

The Gothic revival style was also applied to commercial buildings, for which there were no medieval counterparts, and finds its apogee in St Pancras station and the Midland Grand hotel. Another clay-based material that became widely used for the exterior of buildings was terracotta, which, like brick, came in a number of different shades and can be seen on the facades of the Prudential Insurance building, the Natural History Museum and the Albert Hall.[7]

Even when buildings were outwardly built of stone there were often substantial quantities of brick concealed behind the façade. A great deal of attention was paid to finding a suitable stone for the exterior of the new Houses of Parliament, which came from a quarry in Yorkshire, but the bricks used in the building came from much closer to

---

5   C. Shenton, *Mr Barry's war: rebuilding the Houses of Parliament after the Great Fire of 1834* (Oxford, 2016), p. 115.

6   R. Furneaux Jordan, quoted by A. Fredericksen in 'Parliament's genus loci: the politics of place after the 1834 fire', in C. and J. Riding (eds), *The houses of parliament: history, art and architecture* (London, 2000), p. 105.

7   For the use of terracotta, see M. Stratton, *The terracotta revival: building innovation and the image of the industrial city in Britain and North America* (London, 1993).

Bricks of Victorian London

home (Plate 5).[8] *The Builder* reported in 1847 that 'The interior parts of the walls are of hard burnt Cowley stocks, exclusively from the fields of Mr Westbrook of Heston, which are admitted to be the best manufactured of any that are made for the London Market.'[9]

The architect George Street was an enthusiast for brickwork and wrote an influential book, *Brick and marble in the Middle Ages*, in 1855. One of his major commissions was the Royal Courts of Justice, which has been described as 'the last great national monument built in the Gothic style'.[10] This building shows two different faces. The main elevation on the Strand is clothed in Portland stone, with towers and turrets, but on the Bell Yard side the much simpler rear elevation is largely of brick.[11]

Table 4.1
The growth in London's housing stock, 1801–1901.

Increase in the number of houses in London between decennial censuses 1801–1901	
1801–11	24,903
1811–21	32,208
1821–31	47,686
1831–41	27,264
1841–51	48,616
1851–61	53,173
1861–71	76,321
1871–81	73,932
1881–91	60,857
1891–1901	24,835

Source: LCC *Statistical Abstract for London* (1901), Vol. IV, tables 1, 2, 3; LCC *Statistical Abstract for London* (1911–21), tables 1, 2, 3.

So how might we measure the growth in demand for bricks that all this new building generated?[12] One method is to look at the increase in London's housing stock across the nineteenth century, as counted in the decennial censuses (Table 4.1). There was a fourfold increase in the number of houses in London, from 142,042 in 1801 to 611,837 in 1901, but the growth rate varies from decade to decade. Cruickshank's perception of a rush of building in the 1820s is reflected in the figures for that decade, certainly as compared with those that preceded and followed it. The rate of growth also slows in the

---

8   24 million bricks were said to have been used in the still-incomplete building by 1853. *London: what to see and how to see it* (London, 1853), p. 71.

9   *The Builder*, 17 April 1847.

10   Dixon and Muthesius, *Victorian Architecture*, pp. 170–2.

11   The 35 million red bricks used in the building came from Hampshire. J. Beckett, 'The Chandlers Ford brickworks 1860–1915', *BBS Information*, 145 (May 2020), pp. 11–12.

12   For a more detailed discussion of demand indicators see Hounsell, 'Cowley Stocks', pp. 39–70.

'The rage for building'

1880s. The low figure for the 1890s is a reflection of the shift of building activity from inner London to the outer London suburbs, which are not included in the London figures.

The censuses also record the number of houses in the process of being built. For example, in the inner London districts in 1851 some 4815 houses were under construction; as roughly 30,000 bricks were required for a modest house, that represents a need for some 144 million bricks that year.[13]

Another method of determining the number of residential properties being built in the last quarter of the century is an examination of the returns of the Inhabited House Duty. From these the increase in the number of houses from one year to the next can be calculated. The number of houses subject to the tax in London rose from 479,000 to 756,000 between 1875 and 1910, and there was a larger increase from 370,000 to 984,000 in the counties of Essex, Hertfordshire, Kent, Middlesex and Surrey. The peak year in this series was 1898–9, when the housing stock in London grew by 17,000 units and that of the home counties by 32,000. Using the same multiplier as before, this amounts to a demand for about 1470 million bricks in the greater London area.[14]

Unsurprisingly, the rate of growth was not constant. The demand for bricks for housebuilding in 1898–9 was double that for the previous year, and the highest of the century. This is because speculative house building is thought to follow a cyclical pattern, moving from expansion to recession and back again. Boom conditions lead to 'overheating', a situation where there are shortages of labour, capital and stock, and prices rise as a consequence. Once costs reach a certain point a brake is put on further investment and a recession occurs in which there is falling output, reduced profits, rising unemployment and an eventual stabilisation of prices. This then provides the platform for a further upswing.[15] There are also longer swings across the economy as a whole.[16]

These periodic fluctuations from 1855 to the outbreak of the First World War are observable in the indices of housebuilding compiled by economic historians for England and Wales, and for London alone. Graphically both series show peaks in the late 1870s and around 1900, and between them a deep trough which has its lowest point in 1890 (Figure 4.1).[17] Because of the significance of London in the national picture, the fit between the London picture and the national one is a tight one, albeit slightly offset by a year or two.[18]

---

13   E. Cheshire, 'Results of the Census of Great Britain in 1851 … ', _Journal of the Statistical Society of London_, 17/1 (March 1854), pp. 45–72.

14   B. Thomas, _Migration and urban development_ (London, 1972), pp. 45–58.

15   R. Price, _Masters, unions and men: work control in building and the rise of labour, 1830–1914_ (London, 1980), p. 99.

16   R. Lloyd-Jones and M.J. Lewis, _British industrial capitalism since the Industrial Revolution_ (London, 1998).

17   J.P. Lewis, _Building cycles and Britain's growth_ (London, 1965); for London indices see E.W. Cooney, 'Capital exports and investment in building in Britain and the USA, 1856–1914', _Economica_, new series, xvi/64 (1949), pp. 347–54 and J.C. Spensley, 'Urban housing problems', _Journal of the Royal Statistical Society_, lxxxi (1918), pp. 161–210.

18   This is not the case for other cities. R. Rodger, _Housing in urban Britain, 1780–1914_ (Cambridge, 1989), p. 17, figure 1.

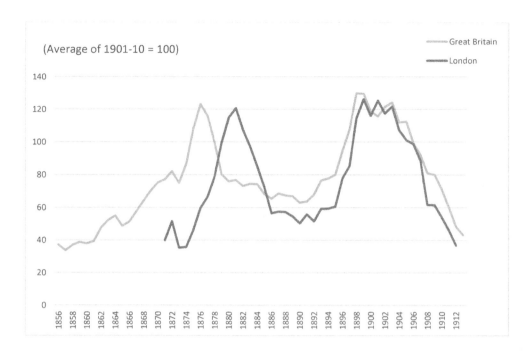

Figure 4.1. Indices of housebuilding in England and Wales, and London, 1856–1912. Lewis, *Building cycles and Britain's growth* (1965); Spensley, 'Urban housing problems' (1918).

Press reports provide corroborating evidence of these fluctuations and we can say with some confidence that the period from 1850 to the late 1870s was a good one for brickmakers. By contrast, the trough between the peaks of 1878 and 1900, the so-called Great Depression, with a collapse in the volume of housebuilding, posed a significant challenge to the industry, unless there was a compensating growth in non-residential building.[19] For London especially, the 1880s were regarded as a crisis decade. The building industry remained slack and particularly hard winters brought outdoor work to a halt, with much unemployment and homelessness.[20]

The economy began to improve from the mid-1890s and housebuilding picked up, creating a peak in demand in 1898. In that year a commentator estimated that the demand for bricks in the London area had now reached 1000 million a year, and enthused that

---

19   W.A. Lewis, *Growth and fluctuations, 1870–1913* (London, 1978), p. 51; later historians have not always agreed with that title; see S.B. Saul, *The myth of the Great Depression, 1873–1896* (London, 1969).
20   A.J. Drummond, 'Cold winters at Kew Observatory, 1783–1942', *Quarterly Journal of the Royal Meteorological Society*, 69 (1943), p. 23; G. Stedman Jones, *Outcast London: a study of the relationship between classes in Victorian society* (Harmondsworth, 1984), pp. 281–2, 296–9.

'The rage for building'

> Possibly at no time in the history of the brickmaking industry has there been such a large and steady demand in London for bricks … . The enormous amount of railway and engineering works that have been arranged for the present year, quite outside the ordinary demand from building houses, which is increasing very rapidly, seems to promise that 1898 will be one of the best years that the brickmaker in London has ever experienced.

This high level of demand was reflected in the price of London stocks, which rose from 24s to 40s 6d per thousand in a matter of two years.[21] However, from that high point there was a dramatic fall down to the First World War. In 1913 activity in the housebuilding market was at its lowest level since 1862.[22] This volatility in the market was recognised at the time. Would-be brickmakers were cautioned that 'Whenever the time comes that brickmakers cannot supply demands, new yards are built – often more than the market justifies; so that none in the business can realise a fair profit. Too much competition means low prices.'[23]

We have seen how we might estimate the level of demand for bricks for housebuilding, but it is more difficult to assess the requirements for other types of construction, including that of business premises, such as offices and factories; churches; and public buildings, such as town halls, theatres, concert halls, museums and art galleries. However, what marked out the nineteenth century from its predecessors was the number of major infrastructure projects, especially docks, canals and railways. These schemes called for bricks in much greater quantities than did house building, but the demand from each of these sectors was concentrated in particular parts of the century, with periods of great activity followed by slacker ones. For many of these civil engineering projects the quality of the bricks was more critical than it was for most domestic structures.

The earliest of these periods was the development of the canal network. Canal building was intense in the 1790s, and it was during the so-called 'Canal Mania' that the Grand Junction Canal was promoted. It was designed to link the Midlands with the Thames, crossing Middlesex on its way to Brentford and Paddington. The Regent's Canal, completed in 1820, connected with it at Paddington, and provided a waterway around the north of London, reaching the Thames at Limehouse. Canal companies needed bricks for locks, docks, tunnels, aqueducts and buildings such as warehouses and toll-houses. In the construction phase of the Grand Junction the canal company had its own brickworks at Alperton that produced a surplus above what was required for its own needs, which it sold to London builders.[24]

---

21 *Builders' Merchant*, March 1898.

22 This period is explored in S.B. Saul, 'Housebuilding in England, 1890–1914', *Economic History Review*, 2nd series, xv (1962), p. 122.

23 *Brick, Tile & Builders' Gazette*, 9 August 1887.

24 A.H. Faulkner, *The Grand Junction Canal*, 2nd edn (Rickmansworth, 1993), p. 53; for the canal company's own brickmaking at Alperton see TNA RAIL 830/51 Dividend Book for the Grand Junction Canal Company 1802–41.

Bricks of Victorian London

Although the number of bricks needed by the canals was considerable, it was exceeded by that required for the expansion of the London docks, especially between 1800 and 1830. New facilities were needed at the end of the eighteenth century to receive the growing volumes of goods arriving from overseas and new docks were promoted by companies that held monopoly rights in certain trades. The first was the West India Dock, occupying some sixty acres and opened in 1803, followed by the London Dock two years later and the East India Dock in 1806. The Baltic, Norway, East Country and Commercial Docks were built within the next few years. A further group was opened in the 1820s, including St Katherine's Dock, and by 1830 London possessed docks covering 170 acres, which had cost something in the region of £7 million to construct. After this, the sector was quiet for the following five decades, until the congestion of these docks caused the opening of new docks at Tilbury in 1886.[25] The first warehouses at the West India dock used over two million bricks, and such was the scale of building in the docks that in 1800 a contract for 40 million bricks was let.[26]

The railway age began with the opening of the Liverpool and Manchester Railway in 1830, and was followed by the first boom in construction in the late 1830s and 1840s, the period of the so-called 'railway mania'. In 1847–8 over 1000 miles of new railways were built. With the housing market flat and trade generally depressed, railway building dominated the construction activity of the decade. A further peak in construction occurred in the early 1860s, when over 600 miles were added in a year. Around 1870, once the main trunk network had been completed, construction dropped back to less than 400 miles a year and then hovered around the 200-mile mark for the rest of the century.[27]

The first railway to be built in London was the London & Greenwich in 1836, with its terminus at London Bridge (Figure 4.2). Compared with other pioneering lines this was short in length, only three and a half miles, but it is notable for being built almost entirely on a single viaduct of 878 arches, constructed from 60 million London stock bricks.[28] The main trunk routes came into London shortly afterwards, including the Great Western Railway. Its approach to its terminus at Paddington was mostly on the level, but for many other railways tunnels or lengthy viaducts were necessary. Viaducts, of course, have the most visible impact on the landscape.[29]

On its way into Euston the London & Birmingham Railway had to construct a major tunnel at Primrose Hill, a crossing over the Regent's Canal and a cutting through high retaining walls.[30] The disturbances caused by the building of the line on its

---

25 G. Jackson, 'Ports', in D. Aldcroft and M. Freeman (eds), *Transport in the Industrial Revolution* (Manchester, 1983), pp. 202–3.

26 S. Porter (ed.), *Survey of London, vol. 43. Poplar, Blackwall and the Isle of Dogs* (London, 1994), p. 254.

27 B.R. Mitchell, *British historical statistics* (Cambridge, 1988), p. 541; C. Wolmar, *Fire & steam: how the railways transformed Britain* (London, 2008), pp. 86–8.

28 Campbell, *Brick*, p. 215; M. Darby, *Early railway prints, from the collection of Mr and Mrs M.G. Powell* (London, 1974), pp. 22–3; Wolmar, *Fire and steam*, pp. 58–9.

29 It did require a viaduct, the Wharncliffe viaduct, across the Brent Valley between Hanwell and Southall. Campbell, *Brick*, p. 203.

30 S. Taylor (ed.), *The moving metropolis: a history of London's transport since 1800* (London, 2001), p. 41; J.T. Coppock and H.C. Prince (eds), *Greater London* (London, 1964), p. 60.

'The rage for building'

Figure 4.2. Greenwich Railway, Spa Road. Engraving. (London Picture Library/London Metropolitan Archives)

approach into central London was the subject of one of Dickens' most vivid pieces of descriptive writing, in *Dombey and Son*.[31] The Great Northern Railway's route into King's Cross also had to be tunnelled under the northern heights and the Regent's Canal.[32] The approach of the Midland railway into St Pancras was particularly difficult for the contractor; it involved digging a tunnel of a mile and a quarter lined with some 30 million bricks, excavating deep cuttings and using a further 60 million bricks to construct the arches that raised the platforms above the level of the Euston Road and created the extensive warehouses now a feature of the rebuilt modern station.[33]

The world's first underground railway, a stretch of the Metropolitan Railway between Paddington and Farringdon, was opened in 1863. Built on the cut and cover principle, and following existing streets where possible, this again required considerable quantities of bricks for the tunnels themselves, for retaining walls and for the station buildings (Plate 6). The Metropolitan District Railway's line from South Kensington to Westminster followed in 1868. Gloucester Road station, one of the best-preserved station buildings of this period, is built of yellow stock bricks.[34]

---

31 C. Dickens, *Dombey and Son* (London, 1847), chapter 6 quoted in Coppock and Prince, *Greater London*, pp. 109–10.
32 Coppock and Prince, *Greater London*, p. 115.
33 *Ibid.*, p. 128.
34 Taylor, *The moving metropolis*, pp. 54–69; C.E. Lee, *The District Line* (London, 1973), pp. 8–10.

Bricks of Victorian London

Aside from the railways, there were other major construction projects. The Thames Tunnel was one of the most spectacular engineering works of the first half of the century. Built to the design of Marc Isambard Brunel, with the assistance of his better-known son, it took seventeen years to complete. It consisted of a double tunnel that required around 7.5 million bricks for the linings.[35] Many miles of brick sewers were constructed prior to 1855 by the various Commissions of Sewers, but the scale of these undertakings was dwarfed by Bazalgette's London-wide scheme of 1858–75. This 'work of no common magnitude' cost £4.1 million and comprised 1300 miles of sewers that absorbed 318 million bricks and 670,000 cubic metres of concrete. From the point of view of the market for bricks in the London area, this huge quantity of bricks was needed within a main construction phase of only six years.[36]

Demand from the various sectors of the construction industry varied across the nineteenth century. Broadly speaking, canal building was at its peak in the 1790s; dock schemes in the 1800s; residential developments in the 1820s; railways in the 1840s; and industrial, commercial and public buildings in the 1850s.[37] The contributions of each of these sectors to the total demand for building construction and the way that the balance shifted from one decade to another affected the nature as well as the volume of demand for bricks.

Contractors for large-scale schemes often found it convenient to make their own bricks close to the building site, especially if transport would otherwise form a significant part of the total cost. Many projects were close to a source of suitable clay, given its widespread distribution in the London area. Tunnels, particularly, could be lined with bricks made from the excavated clay. During the building of the Metropolitan District Railway's southern extension in the 1860s the contractors opened a brickworks said to have been able to produce 500,000 bricks a week. One of these contractors, Waring Brothers, also had a brickworks at Old Ford to supply its needs when constructing the Midland Railway into St Pancras in the same decade.[38]

Housebuilding was different. Some developers, such as Thomas Cubitt, the creator of Belgravia and other London districts, had sizeable brickmaking activities of their own, but most houses erected in nineteenth-century London were put up in groups of twos and threes by small firms or individual craftsmen.[39] They would not have found it convenient to make bricks on site or to operate their own brickyards

---

35 P. Clements, *Marc Isambard Brunel* (London, 1970), p. 102.

36 S. Halliday, *The Great Stink of London: Sir Joseph Bazalgette and the cleansing of the Victorian metropolis* (Stroud, 1999), p. 77; J.W. Bazalgette, 'On the main drainage of London …', paper read to the Institution of Civil Engineers (14 March 1865).

37 C.H. Feinstein, 'Capital formation in Great Britain', in P. Mathias and M.M. Postan (eds), *The Cambridge economic history of Europe, vol. VII: the industrial economies: capital, labour and enterprise* (Cambridge, 1978), p. 41.

38 *Daily Telegraph*, 24 August 1866; *Observer*, 21 July 1867.

39 During the period 1840–70 80 per cent of building firms in London built six houses or fewer. H. J. Dyos, 'Speculative builders and developers of Victorian London', *Victorian Studies*, XI (1968), pp. 659–60.

'The rage for building'

to satisfy their modest needs. They would depend on brick merchants, or purchase direct from manufacturers.

The demand for bricks could be met from three possible sources: secondhand material from demolished buildings; imports from the near continent; and domestic production. Secondhand bricks came on the market in fairly large quantities as a result of metropolitan improvement schemes, such as the building of the early underground railways, whose cut and cover technique often required the demolition of property, or street improvements where new streets were cut through existing built-up areas. These projects created a demand for bricks for new buildings, but the site clearance made available a supply of old bricks as well. They were usually sold at auction, and sales were advertised in trade journals such as *The Builder*. In 1850 300,000 old bricks were offered for sale following the demolition of properties in Wheeler Street, Spitalfields as part of improvements that created Commercial Street.[40] In May 1860 work on the Metropolitan Railway resulted in the sale of half a million stock bricks from a row of houses in the Marylebone Road. A million bricks came on the market with the demolition of the old Chelsea waterworks the same year.[41] Even as late as 1894, 1.5 million bricks were sold at a third of the cost of new ones following the demolition of sixty-six houses in Bermondsey by the London, Brighton and South Coast Railway.[42] It is possible that, at times when large quantities of reclaimed bricks were available, demand for new bricks may have been reduced or their selling price might have been driven down. What is not clear is whether secondhand stocks would have been reused in exterior work, or whether they substituted for the cheaper place bricks often used for interior walls.

Bricks were imported at various times, and there was a particular concern towards the end of the century about cheap imports from the continent. In 1890 imports were made because the strike-affected Kent industry was unable to meet demand, and in 1898 because demand was very high. It was said that 'enormous quantities of bricks are being imported from France, Belgium and even Italy to meet the requirements of this country', including 12,557 tons of bricks sent from Dunkerque to ports in south-east England.[43] Despite this, there is little evidence that foreign bricks contributed regularly to the total required over the whole century. There were, however, fears about the threat they posed to the domestic industry, especially if they could be produced more cheaply, because of either a more benign tax regime or more efficient methods of production. There were some strange and, seemingly, short-lived attempts to import bricks from much further away than the near continent. A cargo of 15,000 bricks was landed at Liverpool from China in 1846, and in 1876 it was reported that bricks from Japan had been allowed into the country duty-free and placed on the London market, where they were 'instantly bought up'. The bricks were acknowledged

---

40   *The Builder*, 17 August 1850; for Commercial Street see F.H.W. Sheppard (ed.), *Survey of London, vol. 27. Spitalfields and Mile End* (London, 1957), pp. 256–64.

41   *The Builder*, 5 May and 17 May 1860.

42   *South London Press*, 24 February 1894.

43   *Essex Standard*, 11 November 1899; *Huddersfield Chronicle*, 23 May 1899. For the 1890 strike see chapter 15.

Bricks of Victorian London

to be of excellent quality, and London builders were said to be willing to place large orders for future supplies, but this was probably no more than a one-off experiment.[44]

The majority of new bricks used in London were sourced in or near the capital. If there was a good match between the pattern of demand and supply, this should be apparent in both the overall growth in brick output over the century and in periodic fluctuations. The brick industry had to respond to a range of different kinds of need, from a few thousand bricks to many millions. The modern brick industry in the United Kingdom is dominated by a handful of large manufacturers, but in the early nineteenth century the industry was made up of many small suppliers, some of whom produced only two or three million bricks a year. There was always a place for such small firms, but only larger businesses were able to service the demands made by big contracts. One of the first of these came with the construction of the West India Dock. Once it became apparent that the bricks could not be made on site, as originally intended, it became necessary to quickly source 40 million bricks from elsewhere. These came from several brickmakers, but principally from William Trimmer, who barged consignments up the Thames from Brentford, and John Fentiman of Kennington, who supplied 22 million.[45] By the 1840s large contracts were becoming common and a few companies were able to capitalise on their ability to supply bricks of consistent quality in the quantities required. Pre-eminent among these was Sittingbourne brickmaker George Smeed, whose bricks were used for several dock schemes, the Great Exhibition buildings in 1851, King's Cross station and the first phase of the Underground Railway.[46]

Attempts to correlate brick demand and supply are hampered by a lack of consistent data on brick production, as the government saw no need to collect data about the output of the brickmaking sector until the beginning of the twentieth century. However, from 1785 to 1849 there are output statistics from the Brick Excise Duty. William Pitt's government, in need of funds at the end of the American War of Independence, decided to levy a duty on building materials, including stone, slates, tiles and bricks. The tax was introduced at 2s 6d per thousand bricks and was raised in stages to its highest level of 5s 10d in 1805. An allowance of 10 per cent was made to cover losses from damage or bad weather.[47]

The Excise Department's published figures are thought to be a reasonably reliable indicator of output, since the mechanics of collecting the tax – which was assessed on the bricks in their newly moulded state on the brickfield – made it quite difficult

---

44   Japan had been exporting to the USA, but their bricks faced a 20 per cent import duty. It was said that the proposal to export to Britain was made at the instigation of a young Japanese who had been sent to be educated in England at the Japanese government's expense. *The Standard*, 3 September 1846. *Star (Guernsey)*, 22 April 1876; *Morning Post*, 19 April 1876.

45   Porter, *Survey of London, vol. 43*, pp. 254–5.

46   Perks, *George Bargebrick*, p. 49.

47   24 George III, c. 24 (1785) *An Act for granting to his Majesty certain rates and duties upon bricks and tiles made in Great Britain and for laying additional duties upon tiles imported into the same*; Brunskill, *Brick building in Britain*, pp. 192–3. The first rise to 4s was in 1794, the second to 5s in 1796. N. Nail, 'Brick and tiles taxes revisited', *BBS Information*, 67 (March 1996), pp. 11–13.

'The rage for building'

Figure 4.3. Brick output 1785–1849 (in millions). Shannon, 'Bricks – a trade index, 1785–1849' (1934).

to evade.[48] An excise officer had to visit each brickfield at least five times a fortnight and 'on each survey he must show the date and minute of his visit, the numbers of moulders at work, the particular flat or hack on which the bricks etc. are laid ... and the number of bricks in the height of each hack'.[49]

Owners of brickfields were also expected to submit returns every six weeks. In view of the number of brickfields and the number of inspectors required to carry out such frequent inspections, the Commissioners of the Excise came to the conclusion in the 1830s that the expenditure incurred in collecting the tax must be disproportionate to its yield.[50] Nevertheless, the duty remained in force until 1850, so for sixty-five years totals of brick production and the duty collected are available. During that period national output rose dramatically from 358 million to 1462 million, an increase of 308 per cent at an average annual growth rate of 4.74 per cent (Figure 4.3).[51] However, as we have come to expect, within this overall upward trend there was a series of quite marked peaks and troughs, and the highest output occurred in 1847, when 2000 million bricks were made. If brick output is viewed in the light of demographic trends,

---

48 H.A. Shannon, 'Bricks – a trade index, 1785–1849', *Economica*, 1/3 (1934); reprinted in E.M. Carus-Wilson (ed.), *Essays in Economic History*, vol. 3 (London, 1962), p. 188.
49 Eighteenth report of the Commissioners of Inquiry into the Excise establishment, Bricks, PP 1836, vol. 26, p. 8.
50 *Ibid.*, p. 6. They disputed the Excise Department's figures, which put collection costs at only 11s for each of the 5711 businesses, compared with an average tax yield of £70.
51 Shannon, 'Bricks – a trade index', pp. 200–1 (Table A).

Bricks of Victorian London

then for the period 1786–1816 the increases in brick output largely kept pace with population growth, but for the period 1817–1849 brick output was increasing faster than population by a factor of a third. This suggests that a greater proportion of brick output was then being used in non-domestic construction.[52]

Separate figures are also available for the duty collected at the London office for 1816–49 and for fifty local offices from 1829 to 1849.[53] These local offices included Uxbridge, which returned figures for the Cowley district, as well as parts of Hertfordshire, Bedfordshire and Buckinghamshire; Surrey, whose area included Brentford on the Middlesex side of the Thames; Essex; and Rochester, which handled the brickyards near the River Medway. The London office, responsible for collecting the duty in the central area, included major brickmaking districts such as Islington and Hackney.[54] Output from London brickyards increased from about 25 million in 1816 to 85 million in 1849 – about 4 per cent of national output in the first year and 6 per cent in the last. In the boom years of 1818–25, however, London contributed closer to 10 per cent of national production. The peak year was 1825, when output was 231 million, after which production fell away sharply. From a low point of only 60 million in 1835 output increased steadily again, but the highest level reached before the abolition of the tax was only 115 million in 1847.[55]

The total output of the four collection centres in the home counties rose over twenty years from 185 million to 259 million, with a peak year in 1846 (a year earlier than London), when 430 million bricks were produced (Figure 4.4).[56] As can be seen from the graph, the overall growth in production masks wide fluctuations corresponding to peaks and troughs in the building cycle – what one economic historian has described as 'the spasmodic outbursts of activity and subsequent stagnation common to all construction trades'.[57]

Despite the growth in brick output during the period when the excise duty was in force, suggesting that the tax did not have a restraining effect on production, there were calls for its abolition or for a lowering of the rate.[58] In 1830 Henry Parnell, in an influential book, *On financial reform*, argued for the repeal of the taxes on building materials and other domestic manufactures and their replacement with taxes on property and income, because 'the duty on bricks and tiles falls heavily on industry' and retarded the growth of the national economy.[59] Certainly it had forced up construction

---

52   *Ibid.*, p. 192.

53   *Ibid.*, pp. 192–5.

54   Not all of the bricks produced in Kent, Essex and Surrey would have been used in the London area, but it is not possible to distinguish between areas in these counties that were close to London and those that were not. Eighteenth report, Bricks, PP 1836, pp. 463–4.

55   A.K. Cairncross and B. Weber, 'Fluctuations in building in Great Britain, 1785–1849', reprinted in E.M. Carus-Wilson (ed.), *Essays in Economic History*, vol. 3 (London, 1962), p. 333 (Table A).

56   *Ibid.*, pp. 318–32.

57   Shannon, 'Bricks – a trade index', p. 190.

58   T.P. Smith, 'The brick tax and its effects', *BBS Information*, 57 (November 1992), pp. 4–11; 58 (February 1993), pp. 14–19; 63 (October 1994), pp. 4–13.

59   H. Parnell, *On financial reform*, 3rd edn (London, 1831), p. 23.

'The rage for building'

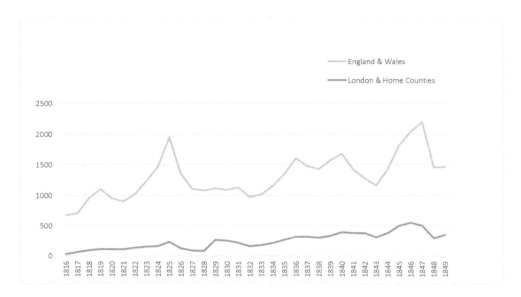

Figure 4.4. Brick output for England and Wales, and London and the home counties, 1816–1849 (in millions). Cairncross and Weber, 'Fluctuations in building in Great Britain, 1785–1849' (1956); Shannon, 'Bricks – a trade index, 1785–1849' (1934).

costs, as the cost of brickwork had risen from £7 15s to £12 a rod.[60] Brickmakers argued that the high tax rate made the domestic product uncompetitive with bricks produced abroad, such as in Germany, where they were not taxed and cost only 15s a thousand compared with 35s in Britain.[61] The tax accounted for nearly 20 per cent of brickmakers' costs; one brickmaker, whose business failed in 1831, had sold bricks to the value of £6493 over the previous five years, but had paid £1350 in duty.[62]

With a few exceptions the rate of tax was the same for all qualities of bricks, and this proved particularly severe for the producers of the cheaper grades, such as the place bricks used in interior work. It encouraged manufacturers to release substandard bricks on to the market, since if losses to damage at the works exceeded the 10 per cent wastage allowance they would otherwise be paying tax on bricks they could not sell.[63]

Although the taxes on slates and tiles were removed in 1831 and 1832 respectively there was a reluctance to do the same for bricks. Giving evidence to a parliamentary enquiry in 1835, James Trimmer, described as 'proprietor ... of one of the largest brickworks in the neighbourhood of London', asked why the duty remained on bricks when it had been removed from other building materials. Fellow London brickmakers Stephen

---

60 'Report of a delegation to the Board of Health. Evidence of Mr Godwin, architect', *The Builder*, 2 February 1850, p. 56. A rod of brickwork is about 4500 bricks.
61 *Ibid.*, evidence of Mr Lindley.
62 TNA B3/2572 Bankruptcy hearings against Henry Hickman, 19 Edgware Road 1831.
63 Eighteenth report, Bricks, PP 1836, p. 171.

Bricks of Victorian London

Bird and William Rhodes complained that those paying the duty to the London office were expected to pay at a greater frequency than those reporting to provincial offices. Moreover, they were at a further disadvantage because of their use of clamps rather than kilns. Bricks burnt in clamps took a longer time to get to market and thus extended the time between the assessment of the bricks for tax in their green state and their eventual sale, requiring access to more working capital.[64] Nothing positive came from this enquiry as far as the brickmakers were concerned and the tax remained in force for a further fifteen years.

Finally, in 1850 the Chancellor of the Exchequer announced that the duty was to be abolished. Welcome though that was, there was now a need to manage the transitional period, because some brickmakers held unsold stock on which the duty had already been paid and would be put at a considerable disadvantage trying to sell them against newly made bricks on which duty was not being levied. Following a meeting with a deputation of brickmakers, the Chancellor decided to make the repeal of the duty immediate, but agreed to a drawback of 50 per cent on stock in hand. He also extended the drawback to those manufacturers who had recently entered into contracts at the old prices.[65]

The repeal of the tax on bricks had two effects. The anticipated fall in prices occurred within a few weeks, taking five or six shillings off the price of stocks; Ward & Co., a Bankside merchant, had offered Cowley stocks at 35s in March 1850, but under the headline 'Duty off bricks' reduced the price to 29s in May.[66] Strangely, however, Henry Dodd, who also advertised regularly that year, held his prices at their January level right through the summer.[67] The lifting of the tax was good for business. There was a buoyant market for bricks, as demand was rising quite steeply at the end of the 1840s. Demand, however, soon pushed prices up again. Shortages of bricks and increasing prices often occurred in the early months of the year, when stock levels were low and the new season's production not yet available. A newspaper article in April 1852 noted that the previous year's stock was nearly exhausted and that consequently 36s to 40s per thousand was being asked, a price some 15 per cent higher than a few years before, when the brick excise duty had still been in force.[68]

After 1850, with no tax to collect, the government ceased to measure brick output until the early twentieth century, when it started to systematically measure economic activity through the Census of Production. The first one was in 1907, when the total quantity of bricks produced in the United Kingdom by a workforce of 69,592 was 4,794,739,000, with a gross value of £8,324,000.[69] If output increased at a steady

---

64 *Ibid.*, pp. 170–7.

65 The delegation included some familiar names: Heron and Rutter, Bennett, Bird, Hunt, Rutty, Rhodes, Everest and Pocock. *The Builder*, 23 March 1850, p. 136 and 30 March 1850, p. 149.

66 *Ibid.*, 2 March 1850; 11 May 1850.

67 *Ibid.*, 5 January 1850; 17 August 1850; 28 September 1850. By August Dodd should have had new supplies of bricks on which the duty had not been levied.

68 *Daily News*, 9 April 1852.

69 Census of Production. Final Report on the 1st Census of Production of the United Kingdom, 1907, PP 1912–13, vol. 109, p. 746. The Census of Production Act of 1906 was introduced by the chancellor of the exchequer, David Lloyd George. The data was collected by questionnaires sent to businesses.

'The rage for building'

Table 4.2
Estimated brick output by decade, 1820–86.

Estimates of brick output 1820–86	
1820–30	1,210m
1830–40	1,330m
1840–50	1,662m
1850–60	1,884m
1860–70	2,070m
1870–80	2,490m
1880–86	3,000m

Source: Brick & Tile Gazette, 11 May 1886.

rate over this fifty-year interval, the growth rate was roughly 45 per cent per decade. In 1886 an anonymous contributor to the trade press estimated the average annual output for each decade between the 1820s and the time of writing (Table 4.2). These decade averages also suggest a steady upward trend in brick production, but they smooth out peaks and troughs in output characteristic of the building cycle and observable in the years when the brick duty was in force. It is likely that they continued in the period between 1850 and 1907, for which we do not have systematic output statistics. To understand these we must rely on estimates made by people at the time and on anecdotal reports about the state of trade in different years.

The only fairly scientific surveys were those undertaken by Robert Hunt, keeper of mining records at the Geological Survey, in the 1850s. In 1855 he came up with a figure for national production of 1800 million.[70] In 1858 he conducted another survey across Great Britain and recorded the names, and sometimes the output, of the brickmakers who responded to his questionnaire. He published a county-by-county estimate of production and the market value of the bricks produced. The total for Great Britain he put at 2,503,004,600 bricks with a value of £2,911,960. This suggested that, a decade after the lifting of the tax, output had already increased by 71 per cent; this significant rise of about 100 million a year might seem to confirm contemporary opinion that the excise duty had acted as a brake on brick production.[71]

In the following decade a number of brickmakers in London, Middlesex and Kent, but not in Essex, were interviewed by H.W. Lord, an inspector for the Children's Employment Commission. As a result, there is more detailed information about the brick industry at this period than for many others. One Southall brickmaker Mr Tildesley

---

70 R. Hunt, *Mining records: mineral statistics of the United Kingdom of Great Britain and Ireland for the year 1855,* Memoir of the Geological Society of Great Britain and the Museum of Practical Geology (London, 1856), p. 99.

71 Watt, 'Nineteenth-century brickmaking inventions', p. 158.

Bricks of Victorian London

estimated that there were about 250 stools, or gangs, at work in the Cowley district, thirty of them on his own field. Based on the output of one local firm, whose nineteen stools each produced about 690,000 bricks, the whole area had the potential to make around 170 million bricks a year.[72] It is difficult to gauge the level of output from the brickmakers at Shepherd's Bush, Stoke Newington and Peckham also interviewed by Lord, but it is likely that they were eclipsed in scale by the large businesses in Kent. The Burham Brick and Cement Company claimed to employ 577 people, and Mr Smeed at Sittingbourne around 500, working some fifty stools. Based on these numbers, Smeed's output could have been about 37 million bricks per annum.[73] Two brickmakers at Crayford each employed over 300 people.[74]

The industry achieved this increase in production in three ways: by increasing the number of brickfields, by enlarging the capacity of brickmaking operations and by expanding geographically into new areas. In the absence of official statistics it is possible only to roughly estimate the increase in the number of businesses over the second half of the century, but by counting the entries in trade directories from *c.*1860 and from the 1890s it would seem that the number of businesses in the four counties surrounding London increased by over 25 per cent. Middlesex had the smallest number of brickfields and the lowest level of growth of the four counties.[75]

Alongside the increase in the number of firms, there was a growth in the size of business units. Large manufacturers, owning brickfields in more than one area, began to dominate the industry towards the end of the century: Broad & Co in the Cowley district; Smeed, Dean, and Wills & Packham in the Sittingbourne area; Rutters in Middlesex and Essex; and Eastwoods in Kent, Middlesex and Essex.

When Hunt published figures for brick output in 1858 he estimated that the four counties around London supplied 328.25 million bricks, 13 per cent of the national output, with Middlesex, which also included most of London north of the Thames, contributing 107.5 million.[76] In 1892 it was thought that about 800 million bricks were being supplied to London from a number of different brickmaking districts, but by then the Medway and Swale yards were the dominant players in the London market, although London brickfields still made a significant contribution to the total. Brickmakers further from London, and delivering bricks by rail, were also having an impact. These figures, however, by their nature, appear to be rough and ready estimates, and can provide only a guide to the relative importance of each of the districts (Table 4.3).[77] The decline of brickmaking in Middlesex came about for two reasons. First, some brickfields, like those in Hackney, which had been active in

---

72 Children's Employment Commission, 5th Report, PP 1866, p. 137.

73 A brickmaking gang, or stool, was capable of producing between 750,000 and 1 million bricks in a season.

74 Children's Employment Commission, 5th Report, PP 1866, pp. 141–2, 145–6.

75 *Kelly's Directories* – Surrey (1855), Kent, Essex and Middlesex (1862); Kent, Surrey (1891), Essex, Middlesex (1894).

76 R. Hunt, *Mineral statistics of the United Kingdom of Great Britain and Ireland, being part two for 1858,* Memoirs of the Geological Society of Great Britain (London, 1860), pp. 15–16.

77 *British Clayworker,* November 1892.

'The rage for building'

Table 4.3
Districts supplying bricks to London, *c.*1890.

Estimate of the origin of bricks supplied to London c.1890 (in millions)	
Sittingbourne yards (Kent/Medway)	250m
London yards	150m
Peterborough and Great Northern yards	100m
Shoeburyness and Sheerness yards (Essex)	100m
Cowley and Grand Junction Canal yards	100m
Great Eastern Railway yards	100m
Total	800m

Source: *British Clayworker*, November 1892.

the early decades of the century, had been absorbed into the capital's built-up area; and, secondly, other brickfields had now been closed as the brickearth was worked out.

Brickmakers always had to negotiate the cyclical fluctuations that characterised the building industry, and they did this by increasing or reducing production. When demand was slack the owners might mothball a brickfield for a year or cut output by working fewer stools and employing fewer workers, something that was relatively easy to do as workers were only contracted for the season. There was usually a reserve pool of labour that could be drawn on when needed. At the same time, owners tried to maintain their profit margins by reducing wages.

When bricks were in heavy demand brickmakers could cash in, as shortages resulted in higher prices while production costs would not rise to the same extent. However, high prices for bricks often prompted the workers who made the bricks to look to increase their wages, or at least return them to levels they had previously enjoyed. This was particularly so during the deep depression that occurred in the 1880s, when a want of new building projects caused prices to fall. Stocks that had been selling for 40s per 1000 in July 1885 and 42s 6d in December of that year fetched 31s in February 1886 and only 25s a month later. These prices prevailed for the remainder of the year and throughout the following one.[78] Faced with diminishing returns, manufacturers reduced the rate they paid to moulders for each thousand bricks from 4s 8d to 4s 2d in 1884, and imposed a further cut of 2d in 1886.[79] These reductions in wage rates would come back to haunt the trade when conditions began to improve, provoking the trade union action of the following years.[80]

---

78 *Brick & Tile Gazette*, 15 July 1885; 8 December 1885; 9 February 1886; 9 March 1886; 12 July 1887; 13 December 1887.

79 *Brick, Tile & Potteries Journal*, 9 June 1891.

80 For these labour disputes, see chapter 15.

Bricks of Victorian London

Supply was also dependant to some extent on the weather. As much of the work in a traditional stock brickfield was done in the open air, wet summers could prevent the men working, and this inevitably reduced productivity. Moreover, rain could damage the bricks once they had been made and before they had been fired. In 1879 brickmakers from the London area, meeting towards the end of the season, complained that poor weather had resulted in a fall in output of as much as a third and that they had sustained significant losses as a result. For Mr Richardson, at Vauxhall, the same number of stools at work in his field had produced only 16 million bricks compared with 25 million the previous year, with a higher than usual proportion of inferior ones.[81]

Cuts in production sometimes had unexpected consequences. As we have already noted, brickmakers depended on ashes and breeze extracted from domestic rubbish as a source of fuel, and if brickmakers reduced production they needed less ashes, leaving rubbish contractors with the problem of disposing of this material. In 1855 it was reported that dust contractors were reluctant to take up contracts for rubbish collection, and this hesitation was attributed to 'a stoppage in brickmaking, and the lull in trade'.[82] In 1885 rubbish was beginning to accumulate at the London refuse wharves as 'a consequence of the great depression in the brickmaking trade'.[83]

Finally, demand for yellow stock bricks was subject to changing architectural fashion in the latter part of the nineteenth century. Stock bricks were generally of a fairly rough texture, but now the demand was for smoother bricks, which were most likely to be produced by extrusion methods. It was said that 'Stock bricks are under a cloud. A new generation of architects and engineers has arisen who will not have them, preferring machine-made bricks.'[84]

The Gothic style, dominant for decades, began to be displaced by the Queen Anne revival style. This had been growing in popularity since 1862, when William Makepeace Thackeray had a house built for himself in Kensington, and it found a wider expression with buildings designed by Richard Norman Shaw, especially those at Bedford Park in the 1880s. For this style red bricks were required, and these could not be made by the traditional methods employed in the London area.[85]

Even when buildings did not fully embrace the new style, it became common for buildings to have street frontages in red bricks, while yellow stocks were relegated to the side and rear elevations. As a result, some brickmakers in the London area did start to make red bricks; the East Acton Brick Works was producing 'red bricks, dark or light' by the 1880s, and in 1892 the company made only red bricks during the strike that affected the whole neighbourhood. The red brick makers, presumably employed on different terms to their colleagues, took no part in the strike and remained at work.[86]

---

81 'The brickmaking trade', *Daily News*, 5 September 1879.

82 *The Builder*, 14 April 1855.

83 Mr A. Allen, Surveyor to the Vestry of St Luke's, Shoreditch, *The Builder*, 12 January 1886.

84 *British Clayworker*, April 1894, p. 9.

85 Dixon and Muthesius, *Victorian Architecture*, pp. 26–7, 65–8; Cox, 'Bricks', p. 14; Ward, 'Brickmaking', p. 7.

86 Harper Smith, *Brickfields of Acton*, pp. 52–3; *Acton Gazette*, 23 April 1892.

'The rage for building'

Broad & Company were also producing red wire cuts at their Southall works in the late 1890s.[87] Greater capital investment – primarily in erecting kilns – was required for manufacturing red bricks, and larger firms were in a better position to provide this.[88]

By the end of the nineteenth century the demand for bricks in the capital was being met from a variety of places in the home counties, with Kent pre-eminent, and in increasing quantities by rail from more distant brickfields in the Midlands. The firms supplying the market had become larger, and some had brickfields in more than one district. They were dependent on efficient means of transport to bring their products to market. These are subjects that are considered in the following chapters.

---

87 *West Middlesex Gazette*, 12 February 1898.
88 This view is proposed by Perks, *George Bargebrick*, p. 45.

Chapter 5

Brickfields in town and country

A brickfield fulfils two requirements: it is a source of the clay itself and it also provides a space to manufacture, dry and fire the bricks. Raw clay, being heavy and bulky, is hardly ever transported far from the clay pit to the point of production. There were rare exceptions to this general rule, one of which was the barging of clay to Thomas Cubitt's Thameside works in 1852. Cubitt made bricks at a number of sites to supply his estate developments, but at this point suffered a shortage of suitable clay, as his original sources were becoming worked out.[1]

Since in the London region clay suitable for brickmaking is easily found, brickfields were established in many parts of London and Middlesex, in Buckinghamshire and in several places in Surrey, Kent and Essex. Ordnance Survey maps from the mid-nineteenth century are dotted with the legend 'brickfield', 'brickworks' or 'brick yard' and sometimes with 'chalk mill' or 'clay mill', all indicating the presence of brickmaking activity.

The distinction between a *brickfield* and a *brickworks* will tend to be based on the presence, or otherwise, of substantial buildings on the site. The former may have no buildings, and the one semi-permanent structure often labelled on maps is the 'chalk mill'. Most of the other structures were temporary in nature; benches for the moulders to work at and perhaps a hut as an office for the foreman or clerk. In addition, there were rows of bricks drying in the hacks and the clamps in which the bricks were burnt. It is easy to see why a brickfield operating in this way would leave little mark on the landscape, at least as far as the cartographer and the industrial archaeologist are concerned. A *brickworks*, by contrast, will usually include a series of buildings – sheds and kilns being the most likely – and the term was more often used later in the nineteenth century, when production units had become larger and a degree of mechanisation had occurred.

Photographs of late nineteenth-century brickworks are dominated by the tall chimneys of the kilns. There are fewer illustrations of what an early nineteenth-century brickfield looked like. W.H. Pyne's three engravings with the title *Brick Kilns* (1823) include a general view of a brickfield, with, in the foreground, crowding barrows and a cart being loaded with bricks (Figure 5.1). In the background a labourer is wheeling clay in a navvy barrow from the claypit to a clay or chalk mill, which is being turned by a horse. The same artist's *Brick Makers* (1802) is a sheet of three picturesque views of brick moulding taking place: gangs of men, women and children are working under roughhewn shelters. In the middle image a woman is placing a brick on a pallet board and a young girl is transferring the bricks one by one on to a hack barrow (Figure 5.2). This is clearly an artistically contrived scene, but useful nonetheless.[2]

---

1   Hobhouse, *Thomas Cubitt*, p. 291.

2   W.H. Pyne, *Microcosm; or, a picturesque delineation of the arts, agriculture, and manufactures of Great Britain*, 2 vols (London, 1808); *Brick Kilns* is from *Artistic and picturesque groups for the embellishment of landscape, in a series of above 1,000 subjects* (London, 1817).

Brickfields in town and country

Figure 5.1. 'Brick Kilns', from W.H. Pyne, *Artistic and picturesque groups for the embellishment of landscape, in a series of above 1,000 subjects* (1817).

Figure 5.2. 'Brickmakers', from W.H. Pyne, *Microcosm; or, a picturesque delineation of the arts, agriculture, and manufactures of Great Britain* (1808).

The painting *An English country brickworks* (c.1840), attributed to Nicholas Condy, provides a view of a brickfield in a rural setting (Plate 7). We can see all the expected elements of a brickfield of the period – a horse turning a mill, the moulders at their benches, the bricks being laid out in the hacks and, on the right, a clamp being built. This contrasts with the drawing of brickmaking on the Stonefields estate in Islington, with its view across the brickfield to Liverpool Road and the imposing outline of the workhouse in the background (Plate 8). This is a small-scale operation, with a single moulder at work and a pug mill in the foreground. The ground beyond the hacks has evidently been dug up to provide the clay.

Not many plans of brickfields seem to have been made, but one does survive for Thomas Maynard's Harlington operation, showing a substantial site with, in addition to the two chalk mills, eight dwelling houses, a public house, a barn and stables, a cart shed and an engine house (Plate 9). There is also a dock connecting to the canal

Bricks of Victorian London

and unloading platforms beside the canal. The area being dug for clay is indicated, and the 'kiln ground' is likely to be the site where the clamps were built, conveniently close to the canal. The substantial parcel of agricultural land and orchard is either reserved as a future source of brickearth or an area from which the brickearth had already been extracted.[3]

It is possible to categorise brickfields into three types: temporary ones for a single building project; ones that were an integral part of a housing development; and independent ones that existed to satisfy the general needs of the building trade. Temporary brickfields were useful, particularly for major infrastructure projects such as docks and railways, especially when the construction site was at some distance from other sources of bricks and where the number of bricks required was substantial. The Copenhagen Tunnel that brought the Great Northern Railway's lines into King's Cross station was built by Pearce and Smith in 1849–50, and their men converted the clay they dug out into the bricks with which the tunnel was lined. They used methods that were different from those of the usual London brickmaking, perhaps in order to speed up production. The clay was neither weathered nor tempered, but ground with steam-powered rollers rather than mixed in a pug mill. The bricks were dried under cover on a heated floor and kiln-fired. They were said to be of an 'irregular reddish-brown colour' and of 'fair average quality'. The first batches of bricks had been made without the addition of ashes, but they proved brittle and apt to crack in the kiln.[4] During the construction of the Penge tunnel under Sydenham Hill for the London, Chatham and Dover Railway brickworks were established at either end of the tunnel to supply the 33 million bricks with which it was lined.[5] Bricks were made on site for the Royal Victoria Dock at Plaistow by the contractors, Peto, Betts and Brassey.[6]

Brickfields were opened for some large building complexes as well. George Myers, who won the contract for Colney Hatch Asylum, made ten million bricks using the clay dug out for the foundations.[7] In the 1870s land was leased for a brickfield next to the site of the as-yet-unbuilt Wormwood Scrubs prison in Hammersmith. Convict labour put up the buildings and manufactured the yellow stock bricks from which it is mainly constructed.[8] This followed a similar exercise at Chatham dockyard, whose extension in the 1860s had also been constructed by convicts, who had made around 110 million bricks by 1875. The bricks were machine-made of clay from the site, mixed with gault clay from Burham on the Medway, sand from Aylesford and a small quantity

---

3   Maynard's brickfield at Dawley. LMA Acc. 969/69. The plan is undated, but from other evidence it is likely to be from the 1870s.

4   Bricks could otherwise take more than six months to be made, from the first digging of the clay in the autumn to moulding in summer the following year. Woodforde, *Bricks*, p. 131; Dobson, *Rudimentary treatise*, pp. 45–6.

5   A. Gray, *The London, Chatham and Dover Railway* (Rainham, 1984), p. 54.

6   The brickfield was rated by Barking vestry at £76 in 1853. J.E. Oxley, *Barking vestry minutes and other parish documents* (Colchester, 1955), pp. 53–4.

7   P. Spencer-Silver, *Pugin's builder: the life and work of George Myers* (Hull, 1993), p. 89.

8   Ecclesiastical Commissioners to Directors of Convict Prisons. Lease of land at Hammersmith, 7 August 1879. LMA DL/D/L/136/MS12292.

Brickfields in town and country

of ash from the shipyard's boilers. They were dried in covered hacks that extended in many parallel rows for a total of eight and a half miles, then burnt in Scotch kilns.[9]

Another example of brickmaking for a single project took place in the Middlesex village of Greenford. William Perkin, credited with the discovery of mauve, the first artificial dye, set up a factory to manufacture it there on a site beside the Grand Junction Canal.[10] As Greenford at this time was a village of fewer than 1000 people, there was not otherwise any large-scale demand for bricks. In 1857 Perkin's builder father quickly constructed the factory, which over time grew into a sizeable complex. In 1865 Greenford had a twenty-acre brickfield that we may reasonably suppose was established just to supply the requirements of the factory, and then ceased to be needed. By 1872 the land had reverted to a hay meadow.[11]

The same approach could also work on smaller-scale projects. For the construction of the Marylebone New Cemetery in 1805–6 the local vestry employed Thomas Wheatley, a brickmaker from Wapping in East London, to dig the foundations for the chapel and other buildings and the footings for the boundary walls. He was then required 'upon, from and out of the said new intended burial ground' to manufacture one million 'hard sound and well burnt grey stock bricks'.[12]

The second type of brickfield came into existence as part of a residential development in which a stretch of agricultural land was transformed into part of the built-up area. To do this, developers acquired plots of either leasehold or freehold land, laid out roads and built houses, or sublet individual plots to small builders. Part of the land would be reserved for brick manufacture until the estate was nearing completion, at which point the brickfield was itself built over. This process occurred with James Leroux's development of Brill Farm and the surrounding area in Somers Town towards the end of the eighteenth century. As much as forty acres of land was devoted to clay extraction, enough for 120 million bricks and 4000 houses. In the first decade 300 houses were built, implying the consumption of some two million bricks annually.[13]

Thomas Cubitt, one of the larger developers of the first half of the nineteenth century, made bricks on his new estates wherever possible, an exception being the Bedford estate in Bloomsbury, where the landowner prohibited any excavation except for foundations. Despite initial impressions that the land on which his developments in Belgravia were built was unsuitable for a housing estate, Cubitt,

> on examining the strata, found them to consist of gravel and clay of inconsiderable depth; the clay he removed and burnt into bricks, and by building

---

9   *Illustrated London News*, 20 April 1867, pp. 385–6. The article carried an engraving of the rows of hacks.

10   L.E. Morris, 'The genius of Perkin: story of his discovery and the courageous venture by which he founded the coal-tar dyestuffs industry', *The Dyer and Textile Printer*, CXV (1956), p. 754.

11   *The Builder*, 8 July 1865; *Post Office Directory of the Six Home Counties* (1870); *The Times*, 13 September 1871; LMA Acc. 1261/46 (1872).

12   He was paid £1 10s per thousand for stock bricks and £1 6s for place bricks. City of Westminster Archives D Misc. 69B/1.

13   Clarke, *Building capitalism*, pp. 129–38.

Bricks of Victorian London

> on the substratum of gravel, he converted this spot to one of the most healthy [the area had been known as a clayey swamp] to the immense advantage of the ground landlord and the whole metropolis.

The better drainage on gravel meant that the houses would be less likely to suffer from damp. Once some of the new houses were occupied, he moved his brickfield to waste land south of the Grosvenor Canal.[14] Cubitt also had brickfields in Clapham, but the largest was in the Caledonian Road. He also supplied bricks to the many builders who subcontracted to build houses on these new developments.[15]

For the builder, being able to make bricks near their building site made practical and economic sense, but it came with disadvantages. The residents of the new properties might well be pleased with the houses into which they had moved, but less welcoming of the brickfield on their doorstep, from which the bricks used to build those houses had been sourced. At its worst, the process was liable to create a 'chaotic district of half-formed streets and full-developed brick-fields', as the novelist Margaret Oliphant described it.[16]

The third type of brickfields was those established to meet general needs, rather than linked to a particular development. They were more likely to have a longer life and to acquire a semi-permanent character, sometimes operating for decades. Brickfields that supplied London's growing needs in the nineteenth century were located both on the fringes of the built-up area and further afield, in those parts of the home counties where transport links made it economically viable to convey bricks to the capital. The spread of the built-up area, and increasing building density within it, finally engulfed the brickfields nearer to the centre and forced production farther out.

However, London grew not only from the centre outwards: a more complex and uneven pattern of development took place, with villages and towns on the outskirts themselves expanding until they joined up with outward development from the centre, sometimes leaving pockets of open land. So, in the 1890s there was a thriving brickmaking industry in the west London areas of Acton, Willesden and Shepherd's Bush, supplying the needs of the neighbouring districts before these areas became part of the continuous development of the outer suburbs.[17]

Brickfields had been a familiar, but not always welcome, presence in London for centuries. At the beginning of the nineteenth century Henry Hunter observed that, in what he termed the 'clay-pit zone', 'The face of the land is deformed by the multitude of clay pits from which is dug the brick-earth used in the kilns that smoke all around London to the great annoyance of the neighbouring inhabitants.'[18]

At this period the frontier separating the built-up area from farmland and the historic villages on the north side of the capital was the New Road linking Paddington in the west

---

14 Hobhouse, *Thomas Cubitt*, p. 307.

15 *Ibid.*, p. 308.

16 M. Oliphant, *The rector and the doctor's family* [1863] (London, 1986), p. 39.

17 For Acton brickfields, see Harper Smith, *Brickfields of Acton*.

18 Hunter, *A history of London*, vol. 2, p. 3.

Brickfields in town and country

with Clerkenwell and the City in the east.[19] Originally designed to bypass the crowded centre of London, it would later mark the southernmost point that railways coming into London from the north were allowed to penetrate, with Marylebone, Euston, St Pancras and King's Cross stations all positioned along it. In the decades after the Napoleonic wars the area north of the New Road would see extensive housing development, with a consequent need for brickfields. At the western end they were opened up for John Nash's development of Regent's Park and on an 1804 map of the neighbouring parish of St Pancras eight brickfields are identifiable.[20] Further east, Hunter noted of Islington that 'many bricks are made in the part adjoining to Hackney parish', and of Hackney itself 'that large quantities of bricks are made, particularly about Kingsland'. It is in these areas that the most brickmakers are identified in the commercial directories of the period.[21]

In Hackney, by the beginning of the nineteenth century, there were already worked-out fields whose prior use was evident only because 'the surface is lowered from four to ten feet (average five) by the earth having been dug out and manufactured into bricks, over an extent of 1,000 acres or more'.[22] These worked-out fields had 'been put again into a state of cultivation; and with the assistance of manure, are little less productive than in their original state'.[23] Hackney still had 170 acres of brickfields in *c*.1805.[24] The same was true of neighbouring Islington, where the land that had not been developed 'during the present rage of building' had been converted into brickfields or used as pasture by the dairy farmers who supplied the city with milk.[25] As these brickfields began to be worked out, the land was often incorporated into new housing estates by men such as William Rhodes, a major brickmaker and developer.[26]

There was still much brickmaking activity in this area at mid-century. When Ernest Dobson was researching his book about brickmaking during the late 1840s he visited a dozen brickfields in the area (Table 5.1).[27] Areas to the west of London also had significant concentrations of brickmaking. The Trimmer family were well established in the early years of the century at Brentford, near Kew Bridge. In nearby Hammersmith in the 1830s, some 215 acres of land were in use as brickfields and although by the 1840s this had reduced to 114 acres it still represented 23 per cent of the total area of the parish. Brickmaking, observed one contemporary, was the most extensive

---

19 It is now the Marylebone, Euston, Pentonville and City Roads.

20 H.C. Prince, 'North-west London 1814–1863', in J.T. Coppock and H.C. Prince, *Greater London* (London, 1964), pp. 101, 88.

21 Hunter, *A history of London*, pp. 77, 79; *Pigot and Co.'s London and provincial new commercial directory*, 1822–3.

22 Middleton, *View*, p. 23.

23 D. Lysons, *The environs of London: Volume 2, county of Middlesex* (London, 1795), pp. 451.

24 D. Lysons, *The environs of London, Part 1*, 2nd edn (London, 1811), p. 294.

25 D. Hughson, *London, being an accurate history and description of the British metropolis and its neighbourhood ...* (London, 1805–9), vol. 6, p. 375.

26 He secured a building lease in 1821 covering 150 acres from which the district known as de Beauvoir Town was created. *Victoria County History. Middlesex, vol. 10: Hackney*, ed. T.F.T. Baker (London, 1995), pp. 33–5.

27 Dobson, *Rudimentary treatise*, part 2, p. 41.

Bricks of Victorian London

Table 5.1
London brickfields visited by Ernest Dobson in the 1840s.

Brickmaker	Address	Modern London borough
Ambler	Balls Pond Road Canonbury	Islington
Basset	Camden Town	Camden
Cubitt	Caledonian Road	Islington
Dodd	New North Road Hoxton	Hackney
Lee & Sons	Upper Clapton	Hackney
Plowman	Finchley	Barnet
Pocock	Caledonian Fields	Islington
Randell	Maiden Lane, Camden Town	Camden
James Rhodes	Shepherd & Shepherdess Fields, Hoxton and Maiden Lane	Hackney & Westminster
Thomas & William Rhodes	Balls Pond Road	Islington
Stroud	Canonbury	Islington
Webb	Stoke Newington	Hackney

Source: Dobson, *Rudimentary treatise* (London, 1851), Part 2, p. 41.

manufacture in the area, and 'the quantity of bricks that have been made in this parish within the last 30 years is incalculable'.[28]

In addition, there were brickfields in the Notting Dale district of North Kensington, in the shanty town known as the Potteries, whose most visible, and olfactory, occupation was the fattening of pigs. Alongside that activity 11 per cent of the male heads of households in 1851 were engaged in working the adjacent brickfield. Employment here dropped in later decades, and the application of the Nuisance Acts drove out the piggeries by 1872. By then the brickmakers may have moved to Shepherd's Bush. However, a map of 1888 still has an open space marked as 'Brick Fields'.[29]

Fifteen years after Dobson's enquiries, the inspectors for the Children's Employment Commission visited several brickfields in and around London and reported on a handful in London: J. & S. Williams at Shepherd's Bush, Messrs Stroud and Mr Gasclin, both at Stoke Newington, and Messrs Eastwood at Queens Road, Peckham.[30]

As the presence of clay suitable for making bricks was widespread in the London area it is not surprising that brickfields were located in many districts at various times

---

28   P.D. Whiting, *A history of Hammersmith, based upon that of Thomas Faulkner in 1839* (Hammersmith, 1965), pp. 89, 125.

29   The area was later known for its laundries. P.E. Malcolmson, 'Getting a living in the slums of Victorian Kensington', *London Journal*, 1 (1975), pp. 36–7; *Bacon's new large-scale Ordnance Atlas of London and Suburbs* (London, 1888).

30   Children's Employment Commission, 5th Report, PP 1866, pp. 138–40.

Brickfields in town and country

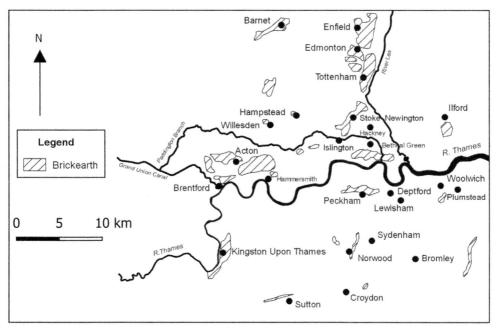

Figure 5.3. Brickmaking districts in the London area in the nineteenth century.

in the nineteenth century, although perhaps not on the same scale as at Hackney or Hammersmith. Within the modern area of Greater London they were to be found at mid-century at Islington, Tottenham, Camden Town, Stoke Newington, Hammersmith, Harrow, Limehouse, Hampstead, Barnet, Edmonton, Clapton, Bethnal Green and Ilford, north of the river; and, south of the river, at Sydenham, Bromley, New Cross, Lewisham, Plumstead, Deptford, Brixton, Croydon, Peckham, Woolwich, Kingston, Lower Norwood and Sutton (Figure 5.3).[31] Many of these would eventually disappear under the bricks that they had once produced, but a pronouncement in 1886 that 'brickmaking in the immediate vicinity of London has almost ceased', while reflecting a trend exacerbated by the Great Depression, was premature.[32]

Over time brickmaking in urban areas became less and less acceptable. Although conveniently sited to meet the needs of local builders, brickfields were a nuisance to local residents. Kilns or clamps, but especially the latter, created unpleasant smoke and provoked protests about smells and damage to health that prompted local vestries to invoke their powers under the nuisance acts.[33] In 1863 the General Board

---

31　Hunt, *Mineral statistics*, pp. 40–2 (Surrey), pp. 42–4 (Kent), pp. 44–5 (Middlesex). *Post Office Directory of Essex, Hertfordshire, Kent and Middlesex*, 1855.
32　*Brick & Tile Gazette*, 20 April 1886.
33　The Smoke Nuisance Abatement (Metropolis) Act 1853 had a rather restricted remit, but a series of Nuisance Removal Acts, starting in 1846, could be used against businesses that produced offensive smells. Hounsell, *London's rubbish*, p. 43.

Bricks of Victorian London

of Health instructed the Enfield Local Board that they could treat brick burning as an offensive manufacture within the terms of the 1848 Public Health Act.[34] Similar complaints persisted right through the nineteenth century. In 1885 Hampstead Vestry took out an injunction against Mr Ellt in Fleet Road, who was told that he must cease burning bricks because of the 'sickening and disagreeable emanations'.[35] In a much reported case, Chiswick Local Board took action in 1890 against a brickmaker at Stamford Brook whose operations had upset the residents of nearby Bedford Park, prompting a prediction that 'the outcry against clamp burning in brickyards near London suburbs ... will probably drive the trade eventually into more rural spots ... or compel an alteration in the method of manufacture'.[36] Indeed, in the same year the London County Council passed a byelaw designed to prevent brick, tile and similar burning being carried on in ways that caused a nuisance.[37]

The situation was complicated by the failure of smoke to observe local authority boundaries. In 1894 Kensington Vestry took action against three brickmakers in Wood Lane, Shepherd's Bush, in the neighbouring parish of Hammersmith, prompting a magistrate to accuse that vestry of neglect. Its Medical Officer protested that he received few complaints from local residents, and that he did 'not at all believe that the brick-makers of Wood Lane have ever caused any nuisance to the inhabitants of Kensington from the burning of bricks'. There was a broader issue relating to the practice of the wealthier London vestries of exporting their refuse to poorer ones for processing, and its subsequent use by brickmakers. The nuisance caused in Hammersmith came mainly from the presence of ashes and house refuse deposited by Kensington Vestry.[38]

The Ecclesiastical Commissioners, who owned a large tract of undeveloped land to the south of Wormwood Scrubs, sought to mitigate the nuisance from the presence of rough dust on their lessees' brickfields through restrictive covenants. Their tenants in Wood Lane could tip unsifted refuse only on the parts of the brickfield furthest from the road, within a small area, and only in the winter months. The rough dust could be used only for the purpose of making bricks, and they had to 'burn, bury or destroy the softcore and all the offensive matter' within forty-eight hours after it had been sifted.[39]

While brickmaking in areas close to London continued under increasing restrictions, there had already been a shift in the main centres of production, so that by the end of the nineteenth century the majority of the bricks needed by the capital's builders came from further afield (Table 5.2). According to one industry observer, 'As far as I know, stock bricks were originally made in Middlesex, near Cowley, whence

---

34   Enfield Archives C1 Enfield Local Board of Health Minute Book 1 (1850–5), p. 257 Letter from General Board of Health to Enfield Local Board dated 4 June 1863; 11 & 12 Victoria c. 63 (1848) *An act for promoting the public health* (The Public Health Act 1848).

35   Hampstead Vestry MOH Report for the Year 1885–6, pp. 40–1.

36   *Brick, Tile & Potteries Journal*, 8 July 1890, pp. 2–3, 7; *British Clayworker*, February 1893, p. 218.

37   *Brick, Tile & Potteries Journal*, 11 November 1890, p. 1.

38   Hammersmith Vestry, MOH report for 1894, pp. 203–4.

39   LMA DL/D/L/136/MS12292. Ecclesiastical Commissioners to Edward Collins, licence to deposit rough dust on land in the Parish of Hammersmith 9 March 1877.

Brickfields in town and country

Table 5.2
Number of brickfields in counties surrounding London, 1860 and 1890.

	1860	1890	Increase (%)
Essex	67	87	29.8
Kent	123	154	25.2
Middlesex	37	39	5.4
Surrey	53	76	43.4
Total	280	356	27.1

Source: *Kelly's Directories*: Essex 1862 and 1894; Kent 1862 and 1891; Middlesex 1862 and 1894; Surrey 1855 and 1891.

is derived the name "Cowley stocks"; then they were made in Kent, particularly in the neighbourhood of Sittingbourne; and latterly in Essex.'[40] In the Cowley district brickmaking took place within a largely rural environment, alluded to by John Galsworthy in one of his Forsyte novels: 'Fleur went on to Paddington [en route to Maidenhead]. Through the carriage the air of the brick-kilns of West Drayton and late hayfields fanned her still flushed cheeks.'[41] Taking a train from Paddington towards Bristol on a summer day, with the window down, the traveller would be confronted by the sight and smoke of the brickfields as well as the sweeter smell of the mown hay in the western outskirts of London. These brickfields predated the building of the railway and early guidebooks to the Great Western Railway advised travellers, in more prosaic terms than Galsworthy's, of what they could expect to see as their train gathered speed out of Paddington. This is from 1852:

> After leaving Southall the Railway crosses, within half-a-mile of each other, both the Paddington Canal and the Grand Junction Canal, near the latter of which it runs nearly to the Drayton Station, thirteen miles from the London terminus; and near here, on the north more particularly, we may notice extensive brickfields, which furnish a large portion of the supply for the new buildings going on at the north-western end of the metropolis.[42]

The Cowley district takes its name from the village of Cowley, just to the south of Uxbridge, where brickmaking was established shortly after the opening of the canal in the 1790s. By 1818 it was observed that:

---

40 *British Clayworker*, April 1894, p. 9.

41 J. Galsworthy, *To Let* (London, 1921), Chapter 8.

42 G. Measom, *The illustrated guide to the Great Western Railway* [1852] (1985), p. 17. The Paddington Canal referred to is the Paddington arm of the Grand Junction Canal, opened in 1801. For a fuller description of the canal and its role in Middlesex brickmaking, see chapter 9.

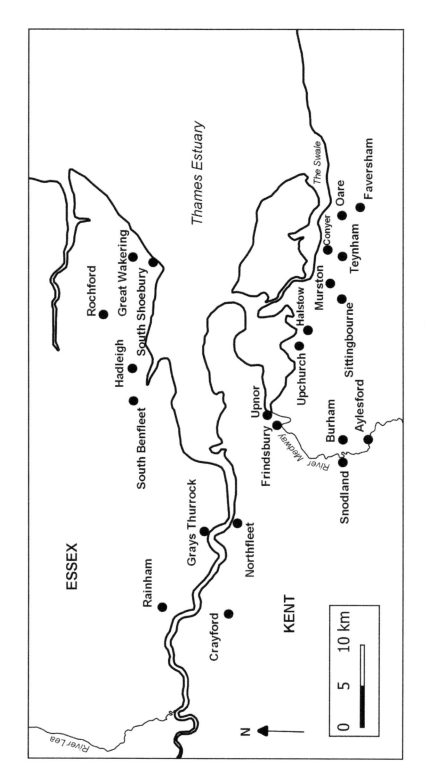

Figure 5.4. Brickmaking districts around the Thames Estuary, Swale and Medway.

Brickfields in town and country

> The neighbourhood of Uxbridge is remarkable for very extensive brickfields, in which several hundred persons are employed ... The brick-earth extends for several miles through the parishes of Hillingdon, Cowley and West Drayton and has been a source of great emolument to the proprietors. Some portions of the land have been known to sell as high as between £500 and £600 per acre.[43]

Some of these brickfields were owned by men who had been, or continued to be, brickmakers in areas closer to the centre of the city, and now saw the opportunity to expand into new areas as their older brickfields became worked out or were taken over for housing development. Larger acreages would be available to rent or purchase, land values were likely to be lower and clamp burning was more easily tolerated than in more densely populated areas. Thomas and William Rhodes of Islington took on the lease of a thirty-five-acre brickfield at Dawley in 1853 and James and Abraham Stroud of Stoke Newington established themselves in Hillingdon in 1838 and in Southall by the 1860s.[44] At that point Stroud's Southall brickfield was larger than their one in Stoke Newington.[45]

Brickfields further from the capital began to take over the role previously fulfilled by the brickfields in the inner suburbs. Brickmaking was already established by the 1820s at sites with good access to river transport such as Crayford, on the Kent bank of the Thames, and Grays and Thurrock on the Essex side. It was said of Grays that 'the making of bricks is carried on here extensively, and they are forwarded to London in barges kept solely for that purpose' and of Little Thurrock that 'the inhabitants are principally employed in the making of bricks'.[46] Finally, the reach of the London market extended to a number of sites near the Swale, in the Sittingbourne and Faversham area, at the mouth of the Medway and along the river itself, so by 1890 this part of Kent was the largest supplier of yellow stock bricks (Figure 5.4).[47]

The amount of land being worked for clay at any one time was often quite small in relation to the overall acreage of a brickfield, so the owner or tenant needed to find productive uses for the remainder. As a result, parts of brickfields continued to be used for agricultural or horticultural purposes, which would provide an additional source of income for the owner. This co-existence of brickmaking and agriculture is depicted in a watercolour of the Kingsland Road area around 1830: the land to the left of the path is clearly in use for brickmaking, while that on the right has growing crops, which might be potatoes (Plate 10).[48] Brickmakers cultivated the land themselves or let others use it for grazing or for a hay crop. The New Patent Brick Company allowed Northolt farmer F.W. Crees to 'use without payment for mowing and grazing purposes

---

43 G. Redford and T.C. Riches, *The history of the ancient town of Uxbridge: being a reprint of the original edition published in 1818* (London, 1885), p. 75.

44 LMA Acc. 969/63.

45 Children's Employment Commission, 5th Report, PP 1866, pp. 135, 139.

46 *Pigot and Co.'s London and Provincial Directory*, 1826–7.

47 See Table 4.3.

48 LMA SC/PZ/HK/01/019 Watercolour attributed to C.H. Matthews. It is thought that the figure walking along the path is the brickmaker William Rhodes. The words *Fox going home to his dinner* are written on the margin of the picture in pencil.

Bricks of Victorian London

… such part of the land as has not yet been used for brickmaking purposes'.[49] In 1885, when taking over an existing brickfield in West Drayton, Broad, Harris & Co. agreed with the landlord 'to bring the worked out part of the brickfield into good cultivation while continuing their brickmaking on the remainder', and as late as 1935 these conditions were still being adhered to and 'the whole of the land, except that actually in use for brickmaking, is now in agricultural occupation'.[50]

Produce from brickfields came up at auction. In summer 1851 Heron & Rutter sold growing crops of wheat at their brickfield at Yiewsley, and sixty-four acres of corn, oats and barley at Heston and Hayes.[51] As late as 1909, D. & C. Rutter sold from their field at West Drayton 'Three ricks of hay, small stack of oats with the straw and an old stack of ditto with ditto. Also, a growing crop of up-to-date and other potatoes on about three acres.'[52]

*

Although busy places when the brickmakers were hard at work in the summer months, at other times brickfields were extensive unsupervised open spaces. They do not seem to have been adequately fenced and were regularly invaded. In the daytime children played on them, and at night they fulfilled a number of different functions, some innocent, some less so. Within the built-up areas of town they were a kind of liminal space, not subject to formal control, and thus posed 'problems of urban order'.[53]

Residents in certain parts of the capital came across brickfields, but, even if they did not do so directly, there were frequent newspaper reports describing incidents taking place on them. They were full of hazards, with uneven ground, flooded clay pits and smoking clamps, and inevitably accidents happened. The saddest involved the deaths of homeless people by asphyxiation and of children by drowning.

Homeless people were attracted by the warmth of burning clamps, which were usually left unattended at night. Sleeping on or beside a clamp, initially comforting on a chilly night, was a risky business, and many were overcome and asphyxiated by carbon dioxide and carbon monoxide fumes. Once drowsy they could also be badly burnt. This report tells a story that was all too common:

> On Saturday Mr Baker held an inquest at The Bull, Haggerstone Road on the body of William Butler, aged 18. James Morsey, clerk to Mr Rhodes, brickmaker, said he was walking across the fields at six o'clock that morning, when he saw the deceased lying apparently asleep upon a pile of bricks then in process of

---

49 London Borough of Ealing, Local History Centre Sale particulars, New Patent Brick Company of London Ltd, 1901.

50 Church of England Record Centre ECE/7/1/7583/1. Letter from Messrs Clutton to Pringle 29 July 1885; ECE/7/1/7583/4. Letter Messrs Clutton to Ecclesiastical Commissioners, 23 July 1935.

51 *Windsor and Eton Express*, 19 July 1851.

52 *Ealing Gazette and West Middlesex Observer*, 23 October 1909.

53 D. Churchill, *Crime control and everyday life in the Victorian City: the police and the public* (Oxford, 2018), p. 106.

Brickfields in town and country

burning; witness, knowing the deadly nature of the vapour, ran immediately to remove him, but found him quite dead. Upon examining him he found his right arm and shoulder severely burnt. He thought the deceased had laid on the bricks the previous night on account of their warmth, and that he had been overcome by the fumes. Mr Pickering, surgeon, said the death had been caused by suffocation. Verdict, accidental death.[54]

Although unregulated spaces where the homeless and destitute might expect to remain undisturbed, brickfields seem to have been patrolled by the Metropolitan Police, who were quickly on the scene of some incidents. In August 1841 a constable crossing Cubitt's brickfields in Chelsea discovered 'three wretched-looking Poles' lying on some straw in the open air.

> A Polish interpreter who attended, explained to the Magistrate that the defendants were poor persons, who had within the last three months come to England from France. The first of them had obtained some casual employment in the Docks; the second was a Dutch slipper-maker, at which he was able to earn only two shillings per week; and the third was a dresser of hare skins worn on the chest by consumptive persons. They had gone to sleep in the brickfields, not conceiving there was any harm in it.[55]

It was said that this brickfield had been invaded a number of times by 'foreigners' and that, 'as such persons were in the habit of smoking', there was a danger that this might cause a fire in the straw that was widely used about the brickfield. This remark may be a sign of prejudice against immigrants, rather than the expression of a real threat presented by their presence on a brickfield. Cubitt, though, was inclined to be generous, and forgave them. The defendants were discharged.[56]

A mass invasion of a brickfield could cause damage to the drying bricks laid out in the hacks. A bizarre incident occurred in 1823 when patrons of the White Conduit House, in Barnsbury, rushed on to a neighbouring brickfield to view the spectacle of a passing balloon, trampling on the hacks, knocking over the clamps and causing £150 of damage.[57]

The lack of supervision of brickfields made them attractive places to hide, to engage in criminal behaviour or to dump bodies. Four boys who died of asphyxiation on another of Mr Rhodes' brickfields in Maiden Lane, St Pancras, in 1842 had absconded from the local workhouse.[58] In 1856 two boys were found living on a Hackney brickfield, where they had constructed a cave for themselves, complete with cooking facilities, and from this base had been raiding local orchards and hen coops

---

54   *The Era*, 8 October 1843.

55   It is interesting that the police were able to acquire the services of a Polish interpreter, a more difficult task then than in contemporary London. *Morning Advertiser*, 1 September 1841.

56   *Ibid.*

57   *Oxford University and City Herald*, 23 August 1823.

58   *Morning Post*, 2 September 1842.

Bricks of Victorian London

for supplies.[59] In 1906 the police broke up an illegal gambling session on a brickfield in Hendon.[60] Bodies were often discovered, some of them murder victims. In August 1813 a man was found in a pool at Battle Bridge; in March 1824 another, identified as a tailor, was found in a clay pit in Bethnal Green.[61]

Probably the strangest case of all occurred on another brickfield in Bethnal Green. In 1826 it became the base for a rampaging gang of thieves – as many as 500 or 600 persons if newspaper reports are to be believed – that terrorised the area for several weeks that summer. They stole from homes and shops, attacked drovers on their way to Smithfield Market and made off with the cattle, and violently assaulted and robbed people on the streets. They used the heat from the clamps to 'cook whatever meat and potatoes they plunder from the various shops in the neighbourhood'. Strangely, reports do not mention any subsequent impact on the operation of the brickfield. Such was the seriousness of the problem, however, that the local magistrates had to appeal to the home secretary, Robert Peel, for assistance. The problem was eventually brought under control, with a number of the young men being apprehended, tried and convicted.[62]

People seem to have taken short cuts through brickfields. After dark this was not always safe, though, especially as the brickfield might be the haunt of men sleeping rough or congregating for criminal purposes. Almost inevitably there were cases where girls and women were attacked and raped. A 14-year-old girl was set upon by two men on Rydon's brickfield in the Balls Pond Road on a September evening in 1862 between 8pm and 9pm. In March 1876 a woman taking a familiar route across Waring's brickfield in Southall was confronted by a group of men, dragged into a sand house and gang raped.[63] In 1844 William Bladen, a mat maker, was charged with raping Mary Cook. The two had been members of a party attending Sadler's Wells Theatre, after which they separated and went towards their respective homes. When Mary was passing across the brickfields, Bladen overtook her, pulled her some yards from the path and, as the newspaper reported, 'effected his purpose'. She did not report the assault until two days later and, as was often the case, the jury acquitted the alleged rapist.[64]

Death by drowning was all too common. Although the flooded clay pits in the London area were not likely to be very deep, it is possible to drown in a few feet of water, especially in the case of children. A boy aged seven, truanting from school, fell off a raft at Williamson's brickfield in Willesden and, despite several adults being present, little attempt was made to save him, to the incredulity and disgust of the coroner.[65] On Mr Collis's brickfield in Croydon there were two drownings in fourteen months. In the first case a boy decided to bathe in a pond, but couldn't swim and

---

59 *Press (London)*, 13 September 1856.

60 *Hendon and Finchley Times*, 17 August 1906.

61 *Hampshire Chronicle*, 2 August 1813; *Kentish Weekly Post or Canterbury Journal*, 2 March 1824.

62 *The Times*, 19 September 1826, p. 3; *Observer*, 24 September 1826; *The Times*, 28 October 1826.

63 *North London News*, 6 September 1862; *Middlesex Chronicle*, 4 March 1876.

64 *Lloyd's Weekly Newspaper*, 10 March 1844.

65 *Middlesex Gazette*, 1 October 1898; *Hackney and Kingsland Gazette*, 28 September 1898.

Brickfields in town and country

found himself out of his depth. The owner subsequently put warning signs around the pond, but this did not prevent another boy falling from a raft and drowning the following summer.[66] It was not only water that was a danger to children. A group of them was buried while they were searching for 'little treasures' in a heap of ashes on a Plumstead brickfield, and two died.[67]

Brickfields also have their place in scientific history. During the nineteenth century palaeontology and geology developed as scientific disciplines and brickfields featured quite often in the discovery of fossilised remains and Neolithic tools.[68] As early as 1806 a mammoth's skull with tusks of 'enormous length' was unearthed in a brickfield at Kingsland, and a range of bones and teeth was found at Trimmer's field at Brentford in 1826.[69] Individual collectors began to visit brickfields on the lookout for discoveries and field trips were organised by members of the Geologists' Association and other bodies to sites across London.[70] The brickfields at Ilford were especially rich in remains, but many other sites across the region produced interesting finds.[71]

*

At the end of the lease, or when the brickearth had been exhausted, there were a number of options for the land, depending on the location. A brickfield on the edge of a built-up area would probably be developed for housing, but in other places the land would normally revert to an agricultural use and remain that way for decades. Although clay extraction would be expected to have diminished the quality of the land, it might provide the potential for new uses.

Some old brickfields became public open spaces. The thirty-six-acre Minet country park in Hayes incorporates some old brickfields, as does Victoria Park in Hackney, opened in 1848. Of the redundant brickfields of East Acton one became part of Wormholt Park, while an existing residential development was extended over another.[72] There is a Cranham Brickfields open space in Havering, and a Brickfields Meadow in Croydon.

Some old brickfields were destined for a less salubrious use as rubbish tips, especially when gravel extraction had also taken place. With the reduction of brickmaking at the end of the nineteenth century the demand for ashes and breeze

---

66 *Croydon Guardian and Surrey County Gazette*, 14 June 1879, 28 August 1880.

67 *Daily Telegraph*, 15 June 1871, p. 2.

68 C. Juby, 'London before London: reconstructing the Palaeolithic landscape', PhD thesis (Royal Holloway College, 2011); B. Maddox, *Reading the rocks: how Victorian geologists discovered the secret of life* (London, 2017).

69 R. Owen, *A history of British fossil mammals and birds* (London, 1846), p. 246; *British Press*, 1 April 1826.

70 E.g. *Proceedings of the Geologists' Association*, 14 (1895–6), p. 188; 18 (1903–4), p. 409.

71 *Essex Naturalist*, 2 (1888), p. 53.

72 N.W. Walford, 'Bringing historical British population census records into the twenty-first century: a method for geocoding households and individuals at their early twentieth century addresses', *Population, Space and Place* <https://doi.org.10.1002/psp2227>, accessed 12 October 2021.

Bricks of Victorian London

dried up, leaving dust contractors with the problem of how to dispose of the rubbish they collected. Much of it was buried in landfill sites, and old gravel pits were often used for this purpose. As gravel digging in the Cowley district continued well into the twentieth century firms such as William & Joseph Studds, Thomas Clayton and William Boyer used the deep excavations they had caused to deposit London's rubbish.[73]

Small short-lived brickfields, once worked out, left little trace of their existence, except for the lowered level of the ground. However, those in long-term production had an impact on the local environment, creating small settlements of cottages, beershops and mission halls that often survived the demise of the brickfield and were absorbed into the townscape.

---

73   City of Westminster Archives. Paddington Vestry works committee. Minutes January 1896.

Part II: Brickmakers

Chapter 6

Builders, brickmasters and speculators: brickmaking businesses and their owners

The owner of a business was often referred to as a 'brickmaker', but this is a confusing term, as employees were also known as brickmakers. In the later part of the nineteenth century the increasing use of the term 'brickmaster' made the distinction clearer. This chapter is concerned with who these brickmasters were and how their businesses were organised.

It would be difficult to identify all the brickmakers who supplied bricks to the London market during the course of the nineteenth century, but the number runs into several hundred. In 1845 there were 239 brickmaking businesses listed in a trade directory covering the six home counties of Essex, Kent, Middlesex, Surrey, Sussex and Hertfordshire. Many of these were located too far from London to have been supplying the metropolitan market; a rough estimate suggests that more than sixty might have been sending their bricks to the capital. However, cross-checking directory entries with other sources suggests that trade directories under-report the number of brickmakers, as not all of them chose to advertise, and thus provide only an indication of the number of active businesses at any one time. It requires diligent checking of a range of source material to put together comprehensive lists of brickfields and brickmakers, so, for example, it is possible to identify from estate records and Ordnance Survey maps more brickfields than there are brickmakers listed in directories.[1] This is not something that is attempted here.

The size and character of brickmaking operations changed during the course of the nineteenth century, with increased levels of capital investment, mainly in machinery. Brickmaking, despite its particular characteristics, was subject to many of the same pressures as other businesses, such as fluctuations in demand and cash flow problems. Again, like the owners of many small businesses, brickmakers were at risk from bankruptcy, as their regular appearance in the pages of the *London Gazette* testifies. Thomas Burton of Hillingdon in 1830, Charles Hancock, also of Hillingdon, in 1833, Thomas Stevens of Northfleet in Kent in 1843, William White of Bethnal Green in 1846 and Arden Hinkley of Sittingbourne in 1871 are just a few bankruptcies selected at random from the *Gazette*.[2]

Two important changes occurred at the middle of the century. The first was that bricks ceased to be taxed, removing one of the checks to the growth of the industry.

---

1   Pat Ryan has published a detailed gazetteer of the sites and their owners and identified around 120 brickfields. An 1896 trade directory records 87 brickmakers. Ryan, *Brick in Essex*, p. 41. For brickworks and owners in the Acton area see Harper Smith, *Brickfields of Acton*; for the Cowley district see Hounsell, 'Cowley stocks'.

2   *London Gazette*, 18 June 1830; 28 October 1834; 31 March 1843; 13 November 1846; 10 March1871.

Bricks of Victorian London

The second was that a new form of business organisation became possible, the limited company, which reduced the liability of the owner and spread the financial risk. Prior to this, brickmaking businesses were owned by individuals or by partnerships, usually of two or three people.

There was no one kind of man, or woman, who went into the brick trade. Some had grown up in the business, others were new to it; some started as builders or developers, others as farmers; some may have started as brick moulders, others were gentlemen entrepreneurs. It is difficult to know what the route into brickmaking was for an Edward Westbrook, a Samuel Tildesley or a Daniel Rutter, whose names appear in brickmaking leases in the 1840s. Unlike other trades, there was no formal apprenticeship route into brickmaking and, although there are a few instances of men working their way up and eventually owning their own brickfield, it is most likely that a number of brickmakers were men with some capital to invest who chose to try brickmaking. It was possible to start in a small way with a few acres of land, employing a dozen workers and making a million or two bricks, and build up the business from there. Owners could always acquire the necessary expertise by employing an experienced foreman or manager to direct the day-to-day operations.

Building or contracting was one route into brickmaking. Many builders, particularly before there was a fully developed market for bricks, might choose to make their own, as the amount of equipment and capital required was modest. Some were large-scale operators, such as the Rhodes family and Thomas Cubitt, but smaller builders also took up brickmaking, such as the Rigby brothers, Joseph and Charles, builders and contractors operating from 22 Holywell Street, Westminster; Peter Pearse, a builder from Holborn; and Thomas Watson, a builder and contractor in Southall – all had brickfields in the Cowley district.[3] William Willett of Kensington, Williams & Wallington of Shepherd's Bush and William Cooke of West Kensington were builders or contractors who leased brickfields in Shepherd's Bush.[4] James Hunt and Joseph Bennett of Horseferry Road, Westminster, seem to have specialised in constructing sewers, as they were awarded contracts worth £20,000 with the Westminster Sewers Commission in 1826. These required them to 'perform brickwork with sound well-burnt stock bricks' conforming to a sample provided by the Commissioners. In the 1840s Hunt and Bennett separately rented brickfields in Hillingdon and Northolt respectively.[5] Robert and Edward Curtis were builders in West Ham in the 1840s and family members successfully took on a range of related activities as brickmakers, surveyors and estate agents. Robert Curtis bought the manor of Vange Hall, near Southend-on-Sea, part of which he turned in a brickfield.[6] Stephen Watkins, of Portland Town, Regent's Park, was a builder too, leaving a number of unfinished houses when his business folded in

---

3 . LMA Acc. 969/64a; Acc. 405/Bundle 1.

4 LMA DL/D/L/136/MS12292.

5 LMA Acc. 328/47; WAM N. 107; LMA WCS 330.

6 W. White, *History, gazetteer and directory of the county of Essex* (Sheffield, 1848), p. 242; 'West Ham industries', in *Victoria County History. Essex, vol. 6: Becontree hundred now within the London Boroughs of Newham, Waltham Forest and Redbridge*, ed. W.R. Powell (London, 1973), pp. 76–89.

Builders, brickmasters and speculators

1827.[7] Henry de Bruno Austin may more properly be thought of as an estate developer rather than a builder, as he was responsible for the layout of a large part of West Ealing in the early 1860s. Like Watkins, he went bankrupt before many of the houses were completed. Both the plans for his estate and the size of his brickfield reveal considerable ambition: in 1865 he was in possession of a thirty-four-acre brickfield in Hayes on which stood thirteen cottages known as Austin's Row.[8] Perhaps the most surprising example of contractor turned brickmaker, however, is the architect John Nash. When he was employed by the Office of Works in rebuilding Buckingham Palace in the 1820s he was criticised for selling his own bricks and cement to the tradesmen he employed, and these bricks may have come from a brickfield he leased in Southall in 1826.[9]

Occasionally this process could work in the opposite direction, with a brickmaker diversifying into building or estate development. Stephen Bird, a brickmaker in Kensington, successfully worked his sixteen-acre brickfield for decades, but started to build on it in 1861, when he was in his eighties.[10]

Farmers were another group who might decide to try their hands at brickmaking, once they became aware of the potential of the land they occupied. Some may have been drawn into brickmaking after making their own clay drainage tiles to improve their soil. Inventors, such as Robert Beart, developed tilemaking machines simple enough to be operated by farm labourers. Some farmers, therefore, found brickmaking was an opportunity to put agricultural land to a more lucrative use, and combined the two activities. The Rhodes family in Hackney had been graziers before they started brickmaking. Edward and Thomas Shackle were farmers who combined brickmaking with husbandry in Hayes. William Hinds was described as a farmer and brickmaker at Heston in the 1820s, as was William Valder at Cowley in 1845.[11]

People from a range of commercial backgrounds came to brickmaking, too. Ralph Ratcliff seems to have been a butcher before taking up brickmaking in Southall.[12] Thomas Morgan was a hatter in the City who tried his hand at brickmaking in Hayes, unsuccessfully as it turned out.[13] On a larger scale, George Smeed, whose firm became the biggest producer of London stock bricks after mid-century, had started out shipping goods from Kent up the Thames and around the coasts, and barge

---

7   TNA B3/5292.

8   P. Hounsell, *Ealing and Hanwell past* (London, 1991), pp. 64–5; London Borough of Hillingdon, Museum and Archives Service. Hayes Valuation 1865.

9   J. Mordaunt Crook and M.H. Port (eds), *The History of the King's Works, vol. VI: 1782–1851* (London, 1973), p. 139; *Victoria County History. Middlesex, vol. 4: Harmondsworth, Hayes, Norwood with Southall, Hillingdon with Uxbridge, Ickenham, Northolt, Perivale, Ruislip, Edgware, Harrow with Pinner*, ed. T.F.T. Baker (London, 1971), p. 47.

10   He died in 1865. F.H.W. Sheppard (ed.), *Survey of London, vol. 37. North Kensington* (London, 1973), p. 79.

11   LMA Acc. 180/181–182; *Pigot & Co.'s London and Provincial Directory*, 1828/9; *Post Office Directory of the Six Home Counties*, 1845.

12   *Post Office Directory of the Six Home Counties*, 1845; LMA Acc. 538/2nd dep/1452.

13   *London Gazette*, 3 September 1830.

Bricks of Victorian London

building and ownership always formed an important aspect of his business, earning him the soubriquet George Bargebrick.[14] John Minter, who went into partnership with Samuel Tildesley in Heston and Gravehurst in Kent, had been born in Faversham but became established as a linen draper in Notting Hill in the 1860s. He married his partner's daughter and later ran a brickfield at Southall in his own right in the 1880s.[15] Both men seem to have prospered in the business, at least for a time, moving to nice homes in the western suburbs. At the time of his death in 1877 Tildesley was living at Beaconsfield House in Hanwell, having previously lived at Castlebar Park, Ealing. His son-in-law was living at Hughenden House in Ealing in the 1870s, and at Cippenham Lodge, Southall, at the time of his bankruptcy in 1883.[16]

Strange combinations of occupations were possible: Edward Eades was described as grocer and cheesemonger, farmer, brickmaker and auctioneer at Wimbledon in 1847.[17] But possibly the most unusual background for a brickmaker was that of Paul Mecklenburg. He had been born in Germany and trained as a watchmaker, jeweller and optician in Switzerland and Spain before arriving in England and becoming a naturalised British citizen. He opened a jeweller's shop in Hounslow, but in the 1880s gave up this business and went into partnership with his father-in-law, operating brickfields in Scrattage, Lampton and Southall under the title of Brown & Mecklenburg.[18]

Finally, there are those entrepreneurs who became involved in brickmaking but who, unlike working brickmakers, presented themselves as gentlemen rather than tradesmen. It would be good to know more about the background of Samuel Pocock. He was described as a 'gentleman' and lived at various addresses: Russell Square (1855), Ealing (1859), Duke Street and Adelphi, both in Westminster (1870). He went bankrupt in 1871, but was in business again by 1875, only to became bankrupt again in 1884.[19] Harry Burr, who took a lease on a brickfield in Aylesford in 1881, was also described as a 'gentleman' and had an address in Waterloo Place, Pall Mall, in central London.[20] Brickmaking seems to have been the kind of business to which people with some disposable income were attracted, in the hope, presumably, of making a handsome return. Advertisements for brickfields were sometimes pitched to attract such people – 'to Capitalists and brickmakers' was the headline of one in 1881.[21] It is difficult to know how successful an investment such ventures were. When limited liability became available from the 1850s there was the possibility of taking up shares in a company, with a lower level of risk.

---

14 Perks, *George Bargebrick*, p. 5.

15 LMA Acc. 328/59; *Post Office Directory of the Building Trades*, 1870; *Kelly's Trades Directory Middlesex*, 1882.

16 For information about the Tildesley and Minter families see <www.theminters.co.uk>, accessed 10 January 2022.

17 He had obviously failed in at least one of these, as he was bankrupt in 1847. *Morning Advertiser*, 10 June 1847.

18 *Middlesex Chronicle*, 10 July 1920; LMA Acc. 506/37; Acc. 405/bundle 7.

19 LMA Acc. 1386/101,102; Acc. 538/2nd Dep/1312, 1315; DL/D/L/028/Ms12335.

20 Kent Archives and Local History Centre U234/L2.

21 *Daily Telegraph*, 24 June 1881.

Builders, brickmasters and speculators

Once established, successful brickmakers could look to expand by acquiring more land, either once the brickearth in the first field began to run out or when a lease was coming to an end. New brickfields could be close by, if land was available, but they could be elsewhere across the London region. For brickmakers working near the centre of London the option of looking outside the metropolitan area, where there was less pressure on space and land values were lower, was attractive. So the industry expanded in rural Middlesex, the Thames estuary and the Medway, all of which had good transport links to central London. If brickmakers were already equipped with their own wharves in central London there was a ready-made supply route for the products of their new brickfield. Henry Dodd, whom we have already encountered, had his base at the City Wharf, Hoxton on the Regent's Canal, but in the 1860s he was also making bricks in a field in Yeading (Hayes, Middlesex) capable of producing about 15 million bricks per annum.[22]

Success in business allowed some brickmakers to become wealthy, buy landed property, take on the trappings of a gentleman and assume positions of authority in the community. By 1838 Daniel Rutter was styled as a gentleman and resident at Montague House, Uxbridge Common.[23] In 1861 he was living with his family and several servants at Parkfield, Hillingdon Heath, and was a Justice of the Peace in Uxbridge.[24] John Minter was at times a churchwarden, a Guardian of the Poor, a charity trustee and a member of a Highways Board and then of a Local Board.[25] Paul Mecklenburg was a member of the Heston School Board and the Heston & Isleworth Local Board.[26]

Such was the success of the business interests of George Smeed that he was said to be one of the wealthiest men in the county (Plate 11). He lived at Gore Court, Sittingbourne, in Kent, a grand mansion in the ante-bellum style (Figure 6.1). He was a Justice of the Peace and left £160,000 in his will. A fellow Sittingbourne brickmaker, Daniel Wills, of Wills & Packham, built himself a fine town house, Garfield House, in nearby Park Road, complete with a tower from where, it was said, he could keep an eye on his barges entering and leaving Milton Creek (Plate 12). Henry Dodd, the 'Golden Dustman', was able to retire to a country house at Rotherfield. He left £100,000 in his will, making him, like George Smeed, the equivalent of a modern multi-millionaire.[27]

George Furness's early career was as a railway and public works contractor in England, Italy and as far away as Odessa, and he was awarded contracts as part of the London sewage scheme in the 1860s. He lived at Roundwood House in Willesden. When house building started in earnest in the neighbourhood, he formed the Willesden Brick & Tile Company, which produced red bricks as well as stocks,

---

22   Greenwood, *'Mr Dodd's dust-yard'*, pp. 64–71; London Borough of Hillingdon, Museum and Archives Service. Hayes Valuation, 1865. The output is calculated from the number of stools at work on the field.

23   *Pigot & Co.'s London and Provincial Directory*, 1838; LMA Acc. 1386/97.

24   *Uxbridge & West Drayton Gazette*, 3 December 1867.

25   Obituary in *West Middlesex Gazette*, 15 March 1902.

26   *Uxbridge & West Drayton Gazette*, 24 January 1891.

27   Perks, *George Bargebrick*, op. cit., p. 9; P. Hounsell, 'Henry Dodd', in *Oxford dictionary of national biography* (Oxford, 2004) <www.doi.org/10.1093/ref:odnb/66457>, accessed 4 May 2022.

Bricks of Victorian London

Figure 6.1. Gore Court, Sittingbourne, the home of George Smeed. (Sittingbourne Museum)

ornamental earthenware, roof tiles, drain pipes and glazed bricks. The company was a major employer in the area and stayed in business until 1937. As a successful businessman, Furness found himself at the heart of local affairs. He served on the Local Board, which he chaired for six years, and on the school board, and was a churchwarden and a Guardian of the Poor.[28]

Partnerships were a common form of business organisation throughout the century, but carried a risk, as they left the partners with unlimited liability for any debts incurred by the firm.[29] They were found at all levels of commerce, banking and manufacture. Importantly, many partnerships were between members of the same family and such instances of 'family capitalism' meant that the success of the business determined the financial well-being of the whole family.[30] Brickmaking followed the national pattern with many partnerships, often family-based. Daniel and Charles Rutter were in partnership together and the firm continued under the name D. & C. Rutter but was later operated by Frederick, Algernon and Edward, Daniel's

---

28 *London Evening Standard,* 3 December 1863; *Kilburn Times,* 11 January 1889; Census 1881 Kilburn; <https://en.wikipedia.org/wiki/george_furness>, accessed 3 November 2021.
29 M.W. Kirby and M.B. Rose (eds), *Business and enterprise in modern Britain: from the eighteenth to twentieth century* (London, 1994), pp. 64–6.
30 Daunton, *Progress and poverty,* p. 246.

Builders, brickmasters and speculators

sons.[31] Other family partnerships included William and Joseph Studds (Hillingdon), Thomas and William Rhodes (Dawley) and Joseph and Charles Rigby (Dawley), all operating in the 1850s.[32] Partners might become attached to the family through marriage, as we have seen with Tildesley and Minter and Mecklenburg and Brown. Similarly, George Hambrook Dean married George Smeed's eldest daughter and later they consolidated their interests in Smeed, Dean and Company Ltd.[33]

Partnerships had a specific basis and were executed via a partnership agreement. A few examples of these agreements survive. John William Warner of Acton and James Omans of Southall, both describing themselves as brickmakers, arranged to work Stroud's brickfield in Acton under the name of John Warner and Company in 1894. The partners had equal shares in the business, whose assets included the tenancy of the brickfield, plant and equipment, and cash in the bank. The partnership was initially for five years and the agreement stipulated the amount that each partner was entitled to draw in cash each week, respectively 45s and 35s; four years later the sums were increased to £6 10s and £3 5s, suggesting that the business was successful. The brickfield, however, closed the following year.[34]

The alternative to partnership was some form of limited liability company, but the ability to form such companies had been restricted by the Bubble Act of 1720, passed in the wake of the South Sea Company's collapse. As a result, until 1855 limited liability had to be sanctioned by legislation or a royal charter, restricting its application to major enterprises such as banks and overseas trading companies, and eventually to canal and railway companies.[35] Companies like these were exceptional and for most firms the partnership proved very adaptable to the changing needs of business. Partnerships could be extended as necessary and, if additional resources were required, new partners could be brought in to provide extra capital, technical expertise or managerial control.[36]

Limited companies were formed for a variety of reasons. Struggling businesses could be shored up with a fresh injection of capital and the removal of the dangers of unlimited liability. Conversely, a company might be formed to allow a prospering business to expand or to invest in new plant and equipment. Others were completely new ventures, and some look highly speculative, in the sense that they were heavily capitalised and designed to exploit a newly patented method of manufacture that might not live up to its promise. Two early companies were formed under the provisions of the Joint Stock Companies Act of 1844. The Patent Waterproof & Common Brick & Tile Company was capitalised at £100,000, a large amount for the period. The patentee

---

31 LMA Acc. 1386/382.

32 LMA Acc. 1386/99; Acc. 969/63, 64a.

33 Perks, *George Bargebrick*, p. 7.

34 The details were entered on a pre-printed form, which assumes that most of the terms were standard ones, with a space for particular clauses. London Borough of Ealing, Local History Centre Partnership agreements, 1894, 1898. Harper Smith, *Brickfields of Acton*, p. 54.

35 Daunton, *Progress and poverty*, p. 286.

36 Kirby and Rose, *Business and enterprise*, p. 65.

Bricks of Victorian London

was said to have won a gold medal at the Great Exhibition in 1851.[37] The London Patent Brick Company Ltd called a first annual general meeting in 1854 and had its first stock of bricks for sale in 1855. The company had offices in the City, but the manufacturing site was at Northolt, beside the Grand Junction Canal.[38] It probably reregistered under the 1855 Act, as a newspaper commented that a 'large majority of these companies are simply joint stock companies, re-entered under the new act, to give their shareholders the advantage of limited liability'.[39] By 1859, however, it was in trouble, and was wound up that year. Unfortunately, from the information available, it is often difficult to judge the performance of individual businesses and determine why they failed.[40] The use of patent methods in brickmaking is discussed in more detail in Chapter 8.

Limited companies were easier to set up after the passing of the Limited Liability Act in 1855, which provided a legislative framework for their registration and monitoring.[41] In the following decades a number of brickmaking companies were formed.[42] Many were active in the Cowley, Kent and Essex areas before 1900, and the articles of association and other documents survive for some of them. Examples include the Southall Brick Company Ltd (formed in 1858), William Mead & Co Ltd (1887), Hewett's Brick and Tile Company (1889) and the East Acton Brickworks and Estates Ltd (1888), all operating to the west of London; Eastwood and Co Ltd, operating in Middlesex, Kent and Essex; and Smeed, Dean and Co. Ltd (1875) in the Sittingbourne area. The Willesden Brick and Tile Co Ltd was in production by 1877.

Many of these businesses are technically known as 'conversions': that is, businesses that were already in existence as partnerships, rather than completely new ventures. Although the earliest of these companies dates from 1858, most were formed later in the century, reflecting the overall growth in the number of registrations in each decade following the passing of the 1855 Act. It was only in the 1880s that there was a significant decline in the use of the partnership in favour of the limited company, and it was only in some industrial sectors, such as shipping, iron and steel, and cotton, that the newer form of organisation made a sizeable impact.[43]

The removal of the brick excise duty, followed five years later by the more ready availability of limited liability status, provided an impetus to the industry. There is

---

37 *Sun*, 1 July 1853; Watt, 'Nineteenth-century brickmaking inventions', p. 173.

38 *Express*, 5 October 1854; *Morning Advertiser*, 8 November 1855.

39 *Sun*, 13 November 1856.

40 *Morning Advertiser*, 25 March 1859; the best source of information on companies comes from TNA BT31 and BT41 series, but these relate to companies that were wound up either voluntarily or as compulsorily by their creditors.

41 18 & 19 Victoria c. 133 (1855) *An act for limiting the liability of members of certain joint stock companies* (The Limited Liability Act); P.L. Cottrell, *Industrial finance 1830–1914: the finance and organisation of English manufacturing industry* (London, 1980), p. 52.

42 Shannon identified 181 brick, tile and cement companies formed between 1866 and 1874, and 289 formed between 1874 and 1883. H.A. Shannon, 'The limited companies of 1866–1883', *Economic History Review*, 4/3 (1932), pp. 290–316.

43 P.L. Payne, *British entrepreneurship in the nineteenth century* (London, 1974), p. 19; Kirby and Rose, *Business and enterprise*, p. 68.

Builders, brickmasters and speculators

evidence of new businesses starting up and taking advantage of the new provisions. Two early enterprises in the Cowley district were the Southall Brick Company and the Cowley Brick Company. The former, registered in 1858, was built upon an existing partnership, but was unusual because the partners were not significant shareholders in the new company. The company's stated object was 'the granting of periodical loans to Henry Hobbs and George Tilley of Southall, Middlesex, brickmakers', these loans to be secured by a mortgage on the seventy-six-acre brickfield, its plant and the three million bricks in stock. Earlier in the year of incorporation advances totalling £16,800 had been made to Hobbs and Tilley, who for their part undertook to produce 20 million bricks per annum for seven years, an output that was capable of providing work for between 160 and 190 people during the moulding season.[44] With this output Hobbs and Tilley could have generated a gross income of some £30,000 per annum, making it easily possible to service the interest payments on the mortgages, initially £769 per annum. However, the company was dissolved before 1860, following the bankruptcy of Hobbs and Tilley with debts of £53,000. They attributed the failure of the undertaking to strike action by their workmen.[45]

The Cowley Brick Company Ltd, formed a decade later in 1869, was, by contrast, a completely new enterprise, with local investors and a modest £8000 in share capital. The principal shareholders were Edward Hilliard, of Cowley House, and his relative G.T. Hilliard, while the company secretary, Herbert Barlee, and the brickfield foreman, Thomas Hall, held a nominal two shares. Sadly, there is little information about the company's progress until it was voluntarily wound up in 1880, having ceased to trade. Following the closure of the company Barlee continued to operate on his own account, appearing in trade directories as a brickmaker until the turn of the century.[46]

Smeed, Dean & Co. Ltd was formed in 1875 with £140,000 in share capital and three shareholders: George Smeed, the founder of the business, and now 64 years old, his son-in-law George Hambrook Dean, and the works foreman John Andrews. A historian of the company argues that incorporation and strong leadership by these three individuals enabled the business to survive the depression that affected the brick trade in the 1880s and to remain a successful company well into the twentieth century.[47]

William Mead & Co Ltd, registered in 1887, lasted twenty-seven years, but was not exclusively a brickmaking operation. Mead worked as a dustman with wharves at Paddington, as a farmer at Shredding Green, Iver, and as a brickmaker and gravel and sand merchant at Iver and Acton Vale. The company had a nominal capital of £50,000 and brought together Mead's disparate business interests. The firm was a private one and the shareholders were all family members, with the exception of the company secretary. We might surmise that the intention behind the firm's formation

---

44 TNA BT41/638/3491; RAIL 830/93–95.

45 *London Evening Standard,* 12 November 1859; TNA BT41/638/3491; its relationship to a similarly named company, secretary William Savage in 1876, is not clear. *Post Office Directory of the Building Trades,* 1870; *Kelly's London Suburban Directory,* 1876; *The London Gazette,* 17 January 1860.

46 TNA BT31/1458/4374; *Kelly's Directory of Middlesex,* 1886, 1890, 1899.

47 Perks, *George Bargebrick,* p. 37.

Bricks of Victorian London

was to provide a secure future income for William Mead, who by 1901 was living in retirement in Bournemouth.[48]

The dissolution of one company was often followed by the creation of a new one. Hewett's Brick & Tile Company Ltd, established in 1889, is an example of this. Capitalised at only £5000, it lasted five years. George Hewett purchased the lease of Durden brickfield in Southall from Henry Odell, who had taken on the fifteen-acre field six years earlier, and Odell had shares in the new company.[49] The company was wound up voluntarily in 1894 and in the same year Hewett became managing director of the Southall Brick & Terracotta Co. Ltd, working the same Durden field.[50] The new company only lasted two years.[51]

By the 1890s the industry was increasingly dominated by larger and more highly capitalised businesses. In this respect it conformed to a trend observable in many sectors of British industry, yet the average paid-up capital of all companies in 1914 was less than £40,000.[52] So, as elsewhere, there was still room in brickmaking for the smaller producer, either as a partnership or a private company. James Day Burchett Ltd was registered in 1896 with capital of only £5000 and grew out of operations at various locations in west Middlesex that went back to at least 1842 with Ann Burchett at Heston.[53] The company acquired sites at Cowley, Dawley and Isleworth, worked some itself and leased others. The company's office, unusually, was neither in the City nor close to the brickfields, but near Ealing Broadway station, suggesting that Ealing, then a rapidly developing suburb, was an important market for its products. The company had ceased trading by 1903.[54]

One way a company could develop was through vertical integration. Firms such as Eastwoods, Odell Ltd and Broad & Co Ltd combined brickmaking and the sale of building materials. Eastwoods was a builders' merchant founded early in the nineteenth century with premises at Belvedere wharf in Lambeth and elsewhere in London. In the 1880s it merged with five brickmaking firms – E.F. Quilter of Suffolk, J.E. Butcher of Frindsbury, Josiah Jackson of Shoebury, Charles Richardson of Vauxhall and John Woods of Singlewell. Prior to this, Eastwoods had secured the exclusive right to sell Butcher's output in the London market, and this merger appears to have been a further step towards ensuring a guaranteed supply of bricks for its business. Eastwood & Co Ltd, when reconstructed in 1902, had share capital of £400,000.[55]

Both Odell and Broads started out as partnerships and looked to achieve integration of their manufacturing and selling interests. Henry Odell made bricks in west Middlesex and traded in building materials as Odell & Son at Paddington basin. With

---

48   TNA BT31/3958/25112.

49   TNA BT31/5649/39405.

50   TNA BT31/4424/28789.

51   TNA BT31/5866/41193.

52   A.E. Musson, *The growth of British industry* (London, 1978), pp. 247–8.

53   TNA BT31/6615/46552; *British Clayworker*, February 1896; LMA Acc. 328/18.

54   It was dissolved in 1904; TNA BT31/6615/46552.

55   Willmott, *Bricks and brickies*, pp. 1–2; Kent Archives and Local History Centre U1531/B8; TNA BT31/16870/74567.

Builders, brickmasters and speculators

nominal capital of £75,000, the new company united the two component businesses and became one of the largest brickmaking concerns in the Cowley district, with some 200 acres of leasehold and freehold land, a number of workmen's cottages and a fleet of boats.[56] Despite this apparently dominant position, the company had a troubled history and in 1895 was put into receivership by the Grand Junction Canal Company, from whom it rented its wharves. The assets of the company were put up for auction by order of the Court of Chancery.[57] A new company, Odell and Co. Ltd, was formed in 1897, but the family had no interest in the new enterprise, the main investor being Thomas Clayton, also based at Paddington basin. The company became Thomas Clayton (Paddington) Ltd in 1910.[58]

Broad and Co. Ltd started as a partnership between Clements Burgess Broad and George Harris. Born in 1852, Broad worked first on the railways before taking up a position with the Paddington-based builders' merchant Charles Richardson in 1872. Eight years later he started on his own account at South Wharf Road, Paddington, and entered into a partnership with Harris, who was working in his father's building firm.[59] Their brickmaking interests started when they acquired Pocock's fields at Hillingdon and West Drayton in 1884.[60] The brickmaking business was known as Broad, Harris and Co. and included in the partnership the farmer Joseph Gregory.[61] In 1896 the two arms of the business – the builder's merchant operating from the wharf at Paddington, railway depots at Finchley Road and the LNWR goods yard, and their brickfield operations – came together in Broad & Co. Ltd. Capitalised at £50,000, the new company also had shares in two other manufacturers, Gibbs and Canning, a leading terracotta manufacturer in Staffordshire, and the Southchurch Brickfields Co. Ltd. Harris and his son Arthur managed the brickfields in west Middlesex. In 1898 the twenty-two stools at West Drayton were each producing 35,000 bricks per week by traditional methods, with little use of machinery.[62] Hit by the downturn in demand at the end of the century, the company was reconstructed in 1901, with Broad retiring the following year.[63] The brickworks at Southall were sold at a loss, but the company retained its fields at West Drayton until the 1930s.[64]

The strong market for building materials that resulted from the house building boom of the late 1890s may have been the incentive for the businessmen who established the New Patent Brick Company of London Ltd in 1896. Without, apparently, any experience in the trade, the investors purchased a local licence to the Invicta brickmaking machine, patented in 1891 by two Australians, and then bought

---

56   TNA BT31/5649/39405.

57   *Southall-Norwood Gazette*, 13 July 1895.

58   *British Clayworker*, April 1898, p. 32; Faulkner, *The Grand Junction Canal*, p. 183.

59   City of Westminster Archives unidentified newspaper cutting, *c.*1974.

60   LMA DL/D/L/028/Ms12335.

61   LMA Acc. 1214/1340.

62   *British Clayworker*, October 1898, pp. 195–6.

63   TNA BT31/6681/46980.

64   City of Westminster Archives unidentified newspaper cutting, *c.*1974.

Bricks of Victorian London

a former brickfield beside the canal at Northolt.[65] There were nineteen shareholders at the company's formation, increasing to twenty-seven by 1901, several of the new shareholders being Germans resident in England. Despite an injection of funds in 1899, the company did not prosper and was liquidated in 1903. The Invicta company itself was no more successful.[66]

Other organisations also made bricks as an adjunct to their main activities. We have already encountered the brickmaking operations of the Grand Junction Canal Company at Alperton and those of HM prisons.[67] London County Council also found itself operating a brickfield. When it acquired the site for the Norbury housing estate in 1900 it inherited an existing brickfield and a mound of dug clay. The council took over the business using direct labour, but the early results were of poor quality; visitors to the site found bricks that 'crumble to the touch', and the majority of the five million bricks made in the first two seasons were fit only for hardcore. Critics pointed to the fact that there was a commercial brickfield nearby that could have provided the council's requirements. Nevertheless, despite complaints of mismanagement and the waste of ratepayers' money, the council continued to invest in the brickfield. By 1906 the first cottages built from the council's bricks had been completed, and by the following year some 11 million bricks had been made, the council having by then invested £21,000 in the operation. Some bricks were also used on another of the council's housing estates, at Totterden in Tooting.[68]

Lastly, a brickfield became part of the Salvation Army's Hadleigh Colony in Essex. At the end of a decade marked by economic gloom, William Booth published proposals for tackling unemployment in his book *In darkest England, and the way out* in 1890. He proposed setting up colonies in the countryside to take in the unemployed of the cities. The Salvation Army purchased 900 acres of farmland at Hadleigh in Essex and, although the work that the colony provided was primarily agriculture, there was also a brickfield. Using secondhand equipment, and blessed with good clay reserves and sand on site, the brickworks produced up to 20,000 bricks a week, generating an income as well as providing a social benefit to the workers. With a tramway connection to a wharf on the Thames, the colony was able to sell its output into the London market. Following a visit to the colony in 1892, the *British Clayworker* reported:

> The way out of darkest England is to be by the brickfield. The crowd of woebegones who have retired to that charming country seat known as Hadleigh are many of them perforce turning their serious attention to the ancient craft of brickmaking ... . After six months of colony life, the attenuated, miserable being

---

65 Patent No. 2071 (1891) for 'an improved dry press brickmaking machine'.

66 TNA BT31/6946/48889 New Patent Brick Company of London Ltd; TNA BT31/6016/42484 Invicta Patent Brick Manufacturing Co Ltd; London Borough of Ealing, Local History Centre Sales particulars, New Patent Brick Company, 1901.

67 See above chapter 5.

68 *Globe*, 30 November 1904; *Croydon Guardian and Surrey County Gazette*, 18 February 1905, 26 January 1907; *Islington Gazette*, 20 December 1905; *South London Press*, 2 June 1906.

Builders, brickmasters and speculators

who had scarce strength enough to crawl becomes a straight-backed muscular man, who dares look the world in the face, and who does a hard day's work with cheerfulness and alacrity.[69]

Hadleigh Farm is still owned by the Salvation Army, but bricks are no longer made there.

Brickmaking could be a lucrative business if managed well, but was subject to fluctuations in demand throughout the nineteenth century. Commercial decisions made when demand was rising could easily result in losses when there was a downturn in the building cycle. While some brickmakers managed to create long-term profitability, for others brickmaking was an unsuccessful speculation ending in insolvency. The next chapter looks at the issues involved in setting up and sustaining a brickmaking business.

---

69 Stedman Jones, *Outcast London*, pp. 311–12; 'In darkest England – making bricks at the SA Farm Colony Essex', *British* Clayworker, October 1892, p. 148; Ryan, *Brick in Essex*, p. 115.

Chapter 7

Land, machinery and labour: operating and financing the brickfield

Brickfield owners all faced financial challenges in establishing themselves and maintaining their businesses as going concerns. The three main types of expenditure they incurred related to the clay from which their bricks were made, the machinery that was used in their manufacture and the wages of the workforce.

The starting point was the acquisition by lease or purchase of some clay-bearing land. We may assume that word of mouth among the fraternity directed men to new sites, but, as we have seen, landowners often advertised land for use as brickfields, such as the following:

> Brickearth in Kent. – to be let at a royalty. 10 acres of brickearth, close to a navigable creek, which is free of all charges, also near a station on the London, Chatham & Dover Railway. Apply A.B., Post office, Sittingbourne.[1]

Some prospective brickmakers, instead of just scanning the 'For Sale' columns, made their needs known in the 'Wanted' section, as in this case:

> Brickearth. Any person having land containing good brickearth situated within twenty miles of London, and near the River or canal, may hear of a purchaser by addressing a letter to W.S. at the office of *The Builder*.[2]

These examples relate to the sale of unworked land, but there was also a market for established brickworks, which came on the market usually because the existing owner had failed, died or decided to retire. Such sales might include an existing stock of bricks. The brickfield could be bought as a going concern or the bricks and equipment sold off in lots, enabling the purchase of secondhand plant at a reduced price. As we have seen, Broad & Harris were able in 1884 to acquire the extensive brickfield of Samuel Pocock in West Drayton following his bankruptcy.

Depending on their experience, the new owners might need to take on a manager or foreman to run the business, which is what may be happening in this case:

> Wanted, a brickfield, with or without plant, neighbourhood of London preferred. Also, a thoroughly competent man to take over management of same. Apply J. L. 88/89 Great Prescott Street, Goodman's Field E.[3]

---

1   *The Builder*, 6 May 1865.
2   *Ibid.*, 20 December 1845.
3   *Ibid.*, 1 July 1865.

Land, machinery and labour

As many brickfields were bought and sold each year, there was a steady supply of foremen and managers on the lookout for new positions. This notice appeared in a 'Situations wanted' column:

> A practical brick manufacturer who has had the management of yellow stock brickfields in the Cowley district, for several years past, seeks an appointment as manager; good commercial experience; capable organizer of work and managing of men; good accountant and salesman. F.R. c/o *British Clayworker*.[4]

Access to this sort of professional expertise was important for new entrants in the industry. For much of the nineteenth century brickmaking methods were based on custom and practice, and skills passed on from one brickmaker to another. An experienced brickmaker could presumably determine the quality of the clay by rubbing it through his fingers. By the 1880s, however, the chemistry of brick clays and the firing process were better understood and brickmaking could be operated on a more scientific and less rule-of-thumb basis. Now, in response to an enquiry about what constituted good brick clay, the editor of the *Brick, Tile & Builders' Gazette* could state confidently that 'a good brick earth should contain 20 per cent – 30 per cent of alumina, and from 50 per cent – 60 per cent silica, the remainder consisting of lime, carbonate of magnesia, oxide of iron, water etc'.[5]

In the 1890s a professional body, the Institute of Clayworkers, was formed in association with the *British Clayworker* journal, and operated a technical department to provide advice to its members. There were also consultants. Acton brickmakers Messrs Cullis Bros said they could help with 'clays, kiln building, machinery in general, and the laying out of yards to the best advantage', and W.T. Curry, styling himself a 'brickwork expert', offered services including advice on production methods and equipment, the testing of clays, arbitrations, valuations and the modernisation of old yards. In addition, by virtue of his 'large clientele' he could facilitate the purchase of existing yards and the formation of limited companies.[6]

The principal capital outlay facing a new brickmaker was for the land on which the brickfield was situated. This was a one-off cost if he bought the freehold, but if its purchase was funded through a mortgage there was a recurring interest charge. On leased land the rent was a twice-yearly charge, and a royalty would also need to be paid each year. Some idea of the value and cost of land can be gauged from the assets of a firm such as Odell Ltd towards the end of the century. Their freehold land was valued at £8000 (£180 an acre), the 167 acres of leasehold land at £4000 (£24 an acre).[7] The Invicta company paid £5030 for thirty-four acres of land at Northolt in 1895, at £148 an acre, and much of the purchase price was met by a mortgage of £3300.[8] In 1867 Matthew Newman bought twenty-six acres of land with brickmaking

---

4   *British Clayworker*, September 1896.
5   *Brick, Tile & Builders' Gazette*, 14 September 1886.
6   *Builders' Merchant*, October 1898.
7   TNA BT31/5649/39405. Its estimated assets were £50,000, including the freehold and leasehold land.
8   TNA BT31/6016/42484.

Bricks of Victorian London

in mind, and paid £3120 (£120 an acre).[9] The Southall Brickmaking Company's land was mortgaged for the large sum of £16,800 in 1858, leaving it with mortgage repayments of £769 per year.[10] We have looked at the rental charges for leased land in an earlier chapter.

Having acquired his field, a brickmaker needed to purchase plant and machinery because, although the actual moulding of the bricks was subcontracted out, the owner remained responsible for supplying equipment. Inventories from brickfield sales provide a good idea of what was required. Equipment included navvy barrows (for moving clay to the pug mill), off-bearing barrows (for moving bricks to the hacks) and crowding barrows (for carrying the dried bricks to and from the clamps or kilns). There would be moulding stools (benches) and the moulds themselves. Pug mills were another piece of equipment in universal use. These items could be bought new or picked up secondhand from brickfield sales. In an 1873 sale a pug mill went for £1, eight crowding barrows for a total of £1 15s and 100 pallets and three brick moulds for 5s.[11]

In brickmaking districts there were dealers selling basic tools and equipment, much of it quite simple in construction. They also supplied the tools used in agriculture. Illustrations suggest that off-bearing and crowding barrows changed little in design over time, and local smiths and wheelwrights would have been capable of making them. More complex machinery could be had from specialist firms. Ironfounders George Stacey & Sons of Uxbridge supplied 'steam engines and boilers, pumps, wash mills, chalk mills and pug mills, elevators and all the machinery of brickmaking', according to their advertisements. E.P. Bastin & Company offered similar products from their works at West Drayton, including driving gear, different kinds of mill and a full range of specialist barrows. Bastin's was a sufficiently large company to exhibit at the Agricultural and Building Trades exhibition of 1886.[12] There were eight brick and tile machine makers listed in the *London Post Office Directory* in 1882, and a further five brick mould makers, one of which was the sole agent for Smeed, Dean's patent steel mould.[13] Specialist firm Joseph Jopling, in Moorgate, was a frequent advertiser in the mid-1880s, selling off-bearing barrows for £1 3s 6d, crowding barrows for £1, navvy barrows for 10s and steel moulds and stocks for 8s 6d. Jopling was also the London agent for a range of brickmaking machinery.[14]

Although a number of patented brickmaking machines became available from the middle of the nineteenth century they were never universally adopted, some brickmakers relying on hand moulding and clamp firing up to the end of the century,

---

9   London Borough of Hillingdon, Museum and Archives Service Minet Estate Papers, N477.

10 TNA BT41/638/3491. This contrasts with the probable rent of about £230, which would have been paid for leasehold land.

11 Kent Archives and Local History Centre U55/SP/691 Sale particulars Wickham Brick Fields, Strood, Kent for Mr William Wood 3 December 1873.

12 *Marvel and Middlesex Register*, 1 January 1876, p. 1; *The Builder*, 20 March 1886; *Brick & Tile Gazette*, 20 April 1886.

13 *Post Office London Directory*, 1883, part 3, p. 1462.

14 *Brick, Tile & Builders' Gazette*, 13 July 1886.

Land, machinery and labour

Figure 7.1. Advert for Bawden's brickmaking machinery (*The Builder*, 14 January 1865).

even in the larger brickfields, such as those of Broad and Company.[15] At the time it was said that London brickmakers were backward in their methods and indifferent to the use of machinery and that hand-made stocks were inferior to machine-made bricks. As a result, they were gifting market share to more progressive manufacturers outside the capital.[16] Nevertheless, as we have seen, there is evidence of the use of brickmaking machines, such as Bawden's, in some yards from the 1860s onwards (Figure 7.1).[17]

Most brickfields employed some machinery, and steam or petrol engines were widely in use to power pug mills, clay mills or pumps. The contents of the Rose Farm

---

15 LMA Acc. 1386/382; 'Stock bricks for the London market, and how they are made', an article about Broad and Co., *British Clayworker*, October 1898, pp. 195–6.

16 A paper given by H. Chamberlain and the following discussion set out the opposing viewpoints. Chamberlain, 'The manufacture of bricks by machinery', pp. 491–524.

17 See chapter 2. Bawden claimed that its machine was 'the best and cheapest in the world. Its simplicity and capability surprise everyone. Must be seen at work to be appreciated.' *The Builder*, 20 May 1865. For the adoption of Bawden machines by Smythe and Williams see Children's Employment Commission, 5th Report, PP 1866, pp. 137–8.

Bricks of Victorian London

brickfield, Isleworth, in 1896 did not include moulding machinery, but did feature steam engines:

> Pallet boards, mould stocks, running plates, pug mills, elevators, wash mills, pumps, sand, tempering, off bearing and crowding barrows, 4 kilns and boards, 10,000 hack caps, six brick carts, harness etc, blacksmith's, wheelwright's shop, office furniture. 8hp portable engine (Clayton & Shuttleworth), 8hp portable steam engine (Barton & Stearn), high pressure horizontal steam engine (Hallbrook & Co).[18]

Brickmaking machines were available from a number of specialist manufacturers. John Ainslie operated from Alperton in Middlesex for some years and prospective customers could view his machines at the works, at the company's offices in Piccadilly and at the Polytechnic Institution, Regent Street.[19] Many of these engineering companies, however, such as Bradley & Craven of Wakefield or Whittaker of Accrington, were located in the north of England. They exhibited at the major trade shows, advertised widely in the trade press and operated through local agents such as Jopling, who acted for W. Foster & Co Ltd of Lincoln, Thomas Hill & Sons of Manchester and John Whitehead & Co of Preston. In addition to brickmaking machines, other equipment was needed on larger brickfields. Zadig & Co., which had a London office, specialised in portable railway track and wagons.[20] Taylor & Neate of Rochester introduced its powerful clay pump in 1886 and installed it in Smeed, Dean's brickfield at Murston.[21] Brickmakers could also acquire plant of continental European or American manufacture through local agents, and trade journals carried articles about foreign brickfields and innovations in production methods.

Purchasing machinery and steam engines and erecting sheds meant significant capital expenditure for the proprietor of a brickworks, but it is often difficult to know what the costs were in relation to the turnover of the business, as the account books of brickmaking businesses rarely survive. Cubitt expended £54,000 in purchasing the land and equipping his Burham works.[22] Hopefully, this kind of expenditure would be offset by lower labour costs.

To be in a position steadily to recoup that kind of investment argued for stable market conditions, but these could not be relied on because of fluctuating demand. For many brickmakers it proved easier to regulate costs by varying the quantity of bricks made, the size of the labour force employed to make them and the rate of wages paid, rather than risk having idle or underused capital equipment on which interest payments might continue to be made. In the 1880s prices fell and manufacturers reacted by cutting the piece rates paid to the moulding gangs. This was hardly likely to be welcomed by the workmen, but they seem to have accepted the necessity of

---

18   *British Clayworker*, September 1896.
19   *The Builder*, 1 May 1847; Hobhouse, *Thomas Cubitt*, p. 213.
20   *British Clayworker*, December 1896.
21   *Brick, Tile & Builders' Gazette*, 19 November 1886, 11 January 1887.
22   Hobhouse, *Thomas Cubitt*, p. 315.

Land, machinery and labour

the reduction, while the effect of wage cuts was mitigated by a general fall in the cost of living of over 30 per cent between 1873 and 1896.[23] By contrast, when in the 1890s demand began to grow and price levels rose, the workmen began to press for a return to the old wage levels. In those conditions, then, the introduction of labour-saving machinery would have seemed more attractive, especially for some of the new limited companies, which were more highly capitalised than their predecessors.

So, what were the costs of such plant and equipment? Unfortunately, only a few advertisements carried prices, but there are some examples. We have seen the prices Jopling charged for the basic equipment. At the other end of the technological scale a nearly new Clayton steam-powered brickmaking machine together with a pair of crushing rollers was offered for £230 in 1860. Bawden's moulding machines cost £55 for the smaller model and £80 for the larger.[24]

Once the land had been acquired, the scale of any additional capital outlay depended on the size of the proposed workings and the degree of mechanisation that was envisaged. At a minimum level a brickfield could be operated with one clay mill plus a pug mill for each of the moulding stools. These were the biggest expense; in contrast, the tools of the moulding gangs – a number of shovels, buckets and sieves – cost only a few pounds. In the 1899 edition of his treatise on brickmaking Dobson estimated the costs of setting up a stock-brick operation using traditional methods, without kilns, steam power or any substantial buildings.[25] The combined cost of equipping a basic brickfield with one moulding stool was in the region of £90, with six stools about £125. The breakdown of costs is shown in Table 7.1.

He also estimated the running costs of this small brickfield – including wages, rents, royalties and rates – at £1 1s 10d per thousand bricks, with the largest single element in these costs being the wages of the moulding gangs, which accounted for 25 per cent of the total. At a time when London stocks were selling at £2 a thousand (the price in 1898), the gross income from one stool making 750,000 bricks a year would be around £1500, and the profit £680.[26]

Other writers estimated the cost of brickmaking at different times during the course of the nineteenth century: Middleton in 1805, Dobson in 1850, Ward in 1885 and Dobson again in 1899.[27] They calculated the total cost at £1 7s 0d, £1 5s 0d, (both including Excise duty at 5s 10d per thousand) £1 0s 4d and £1 1s 10d respectively. Each, regrettably, produced their costings in slightly different ways. However, if the

---

23 Lewis, *Growth and fluctuations*, pp. 69–70.

24 *The Builder*, 28 July 1860, 28 May 1865.

25 Dobson, *Rudimentary treatise* (1899), p. 161. The lack of machinery seems anachronistic, given that many brickmakers had by then invested in tramways, steam engines, pumps and pipework. However, manual methods persisted in some Kent brickyards into the 1920s and in the Cowley district until the 1950s. Perks, *George Bargebrick*, p. 29; London Borough of Hillingdon, Museum and Archives Service MF23; *Hayes Gazette*, 29 September 1950.

26 Dobson's *Rudimentary Treatise* (1899), p. 162. There is a similar table in the first edition of 1850. Prices had varied little between the two editions.

27 Middleton, *View*, p. 7; Ward, 'Brickmaking', p. 23; Dobson, *Rudimentary Treatise* (1850), part II, p. 44, (1899), p. 162.

Bricks of Victorian London

Table 7.1
Costs of setting up a brickfield, 1899.

	Cost (£ s d)	Total costs (£ s d)
For each brickfield		
Chalk and clay mills	£60–70	
Pug mill	£12	
Cuckold	5s 6d	£82 6s 0d
For each moulding team		
Moulding stool	£1 1s 0d	
Mould	10s 6d	
3 sets of pallets @ 26 in each set, 9s per set	£1 7s 0d	
3 off-bearing barrows @ £1–0s-0d each	£3 0s 0d	£5 18s 6d
Total		**£89 4s 6d**

Source: Dobson, *Rudimentary Treatise* (London, 1899), p. 161.

Table 7.2
Estimates of the costs of making 1000 bricks.

Category	Cost per 1000 bricks			
	Middleton 1807	*Dobson 1850**	*Ward 1885*	*Dobson 1899*
Raw materials: ashes, chalk, sand and clay (costs of clay are the royalty of *c*.2s 6d paid on each 1000 bricks)	7s 6d (34% of total costs)	7s 2¼d (29% of total costs)	7s 0d (34% of total costs)	6s 4d (29% of total costs)
Labour: brickearth, moulding, hacking, setting and loading	8s 0d (36%)	9s 0d (36%)	9s 6d (47%)	9s 4d (43%)
Equipment: implements, cost of horse, cover boards, interest on capital	-	-	2s 0d (10%)	2s 2d (10%)
General business expenses: preparing hacks, making roads, materials for buildings, coal and wood, office expenses, rent of field, bad debts and superintendence of the business	6s 6d (30%)	8s 9¾d (35%)	1s 10d (9%)	4s 0d (18%)
Total	**£1 2s 0d**	**£1 5s 0d**	**£1 0s 4d**	**£1 1s 10d**

Note: * Dobson's 1850 calculation includes Brick Excise Duty at 5s 10d or 23% of the total cost.
Sources: Middleton, *View*, pp. 23–6; Dobson, *Rudimentary treatise* (1850), p. 44; Ward, 'Brickmaking', p. 23; Dobson, *Rudimentary treatise* (1899), p. 162.

Land, machinery and labour

different elements are grouped into broad categories the costs are attributable as shown in Table 7.2.

From these figures it can be seen that for a modestly equipped brick business in the London area only about 10 per cent of the costs related to the use of plant and equipment and the largest proportion, between a third and a half of the total, represented labour costs. Raw materials consistently made up a further third. Brickmakers, working in this way, required relatively little fixed capital to set up a brickfield, but had to have access to enough working capital to pay for raw materials and wages in the early part of the season, until an income began to come in from the sale of the current year's make. As James Trimmer put it, 'If [a brickmaker] can get a piece of ground he can go to work, and it is not like some other trades that large buildings must be erected; but a man to go into the brick trade with any advantage must have a considerable capital certainly.'[28] This was particularly important while the Excise Duty was still in place, as the duty was assessed on the bricks in the hacks, not on the subsequent sales. As a result the owner might be paying the tax several months before he was able to sell the bricks, creating a cash-flow issue.[29]

Having survived the first year, in the following winters the lower wage costs could be met from the sales of the stock of bricks remaining on the field at the end of the summer. One of the techniques that worked to the owner's advantage was the custom of holding back 4d or 6d per 1000 bricks from the weekly wage of the moulding gang and paying it at the end of the season. The ostensible purpose was to provide funds at the end of the season to help the labourers through the close season, but it also helped the owner with an early-season cash shortfall. The holdback is discussed in more detail below (see p. 214).

It may be instructive to compare these estimates with the actual costs of a Hayes brickmaker in the 1820s, albeit an ultimately unsuccessful one. The expenses of Henry Hickman's operation over a five-year period totalled £8649, of which the largest element was labour (46 per cent), followed by the cost of ashes and breeze (17 per cent) and Excise Duty (16 per cent). He paid tax on 4.5 million bricks (out of total make of 5.1 million, with the 10 per cent allowance for waste). The cost of land was only a small element in the overall costs, with rent at £20 a year and royalties of about £70 per annum. He invested little in equipment, which was valued at only £50. If these figures can be taken at their face value Hickman's manufacturing costs were 33s 7d per 1000 bricks, when the prevailing sale price was only 36s for stocks or 26s for place bricks. However, it appears that Hickman was able to sell his bricks at only 29s and 18s respectively, generating an income of £6493 6s 5d and a net loss of over £2000, thus explaining his insolvency.[30]

In addition to rents and royalties, brickmakers were also liable for rates – highway rates, poor rates and sometimes rates under the Lighting and Watching Act of 1833.

---

28 Eighteenth report, Bricks, PP 1836, p. 8.

29 *Ibid.*

30 Hickman rented his land from Heron and Rutter, who were his largest creditors. He purchased his ashes from Stapleton, a well-known London dust contractor. TNA B3/2572; *Taylor's Builders' Price Book*, 1825, 1830.

Bricks of Victorian London

The rateable value upon which they were levied was a reflection of the rental value of the property. Rates were a contentious issue for brickmakers, and disputes occurred over whether the rateable value of a brickfield should be the same as an equivalent area of agricultural land or whether an additional element should be added to reflect the greater revenue generated by brickmaking. The formula that rating authorities came up with was to add an additional amount based on the number of bricks made or the potential capacity of the brickfield.

So, in Heston in 1868, the highway rate book records the number of moulding stools on the brickfield as part of the assessment. Samuel Tildesley's brickfield, together with house, wharf, workshops, stables, twenty-three cottages and fourteen moulding stools, had a rateable value of £749 10s, and Rutter's brickfield, with twenty-five moulding stools and eleven cottages, was rated at £1324 10s, which meant they paid rates of £12 10s and £22 respectively. In the same year the rateable value of the two properties for the poor rate was put at £696 10s (on thirteen stools) and £1684 (on twenty-seven stools). In a later rate book the calculation of the rateable value becomes clearer and there is a consistency across the valuations of the brickfields. Thomas Hiscock, who had two fields, each with one stool on it, was assessed at £34 for each stool. Rutter's twelve stools were similarly assessed at £34 each, a total of £408.[31]

This method of poor rate assessment was contested in the 1840s by brickmakers in Middlesex and Kent. A group in Heston, led by Edward Westbrook, challenged the parish's calculation, taking their case first to the Quarter Sessions, which upheld the parish's position, and then to appeal. Previously the land had been assessed as agricultural land, but now the Overseers of the Poor had calculated the number of bricks made. Westbrook held just over twenty acres of land, from two different landlords, with rents at £2 or £3 an acre. The rateable value was set at £362 10s so, with a rate at 1s 6d in the pound, he was charged £27 3s 9d. A similar appeal was made by Henry Everest of Frindsbury, on the Medway. It is clear that the parish authorities here had made a decision to take advantage of the amount of brickmaking occurring in their area to bring in a bigger income. Both cases were considered together by the Court of Queen's Bench in 1847, the judgement of which supported the parish authorities.[32]

Another case that reached the Queen's Bench was brought by the overseers and parish council of Crayford in 1897 against Rutters under the provisions of the Watching and Lighting Act 1833. This act, designed to cover some of the costs of policing, made a distinction between domestic and industrial property, which needed more supervision by the police, and agricultural land, which needed less, and a higher and lower level of rate was set accordingly. The parish argued that because the brickfield contained some buildings, including an engine house, wash mills, the clamps and a hard standing where the bricks were dried, it should be rated as buildings not as land, to which Rutter objected. In this case the court accepted the brickmaker's position and ruled that a brickfield should be rated as land.[33]

---

31 London Borough of Hounslow archives. Heston Highway rate book 1868; Heston Poor Rate book 1868; Heston Highway rate book 1872.

32 *The Law Journal Reports for the Year 1847*, XVI (1847), pp. 87–96.

33 *The Times*, 19 March 1897, p. 14.

Land, machinery and labour

In order to start and maintain their business proprietors would need access to funds. Family members might provide capital, and some men, who had been successful in other spheres of business, became involved in brickmaking through marriage. Alternatively, owners could look for partners who had spare capital to invest. In 1860 a brickmaker advertised either for a purchaser for his brickfield or for a partner to join him in the business, suggesting an investment of £5000, of which half was to be paid in the first three months of their association in the expectation of making and selling 15 million bricks. These would fetch at least £2 per thousand and provide a turnover of £30,000 per annum. However, for many small-scale brickfields, capital investment on this level would not have been required.[34]

Two types of financing were required for a business: short-term loans provided working capital and helped with cash flow, while long-term ones facilitated company growth and enabled the purchase of plant and equipment. Cash flow was a particular issue in the first year of operation, as there was a nine-month lead time before the first batch of bricks was ready for sale. For this reason, the minimum royalty in some brickfield leases was sometimes set lower for the first year of occupancy. For example, in their lease of a brickfield in Hammersmith in 1875 Thomas Bell and Matthew Scott were to pay a fixed royalty of £250 in the first year and thereafter £500.[35]

Bricks were supplied to customers either for cash or on credit. Since company sales ledgers generally do not survive, there are only occasional glimpses of the sales process. In this case Herbert Barlee, the manager of the Cowley Brick Company, received a letter asking for the prices of bricks. These were given and then Barlee received an order:

> Sir, in reply to yours of yesterday, I will thank you to send to Battersea Wharf, one barge of stocks, say about 30,000, at 28s, cash at a month [i.e. on 30 days credit]. At the same time, I beg to hand you [a] reference, Mr C. Zencraft, iron and stone merchant, 42 Kings Road, Asylum Road, Old Kent Road, S.E.

Although Barlee took up the reference before sending any goods, and then sent two barges with bricks, he was the victim of an elaborate scam and the company did not get paid. The gang involved were subsequently apprehended and were convicted of fraud.[36]

Brickmakers were often paid in bills of exchange, which were redeemable at a period up to three months ahead, effectively providing the customer with three months' credit. The holders of such bills could wait for their money, use them to pay one of their own creditors or cash them in at a discount house at less than their full value (say £98 on a bill with a value of £100).[37] Henry Hickman, whose unprofitable activities led to his bankruptcy, owed a number of people for advances made against bills, and

---

34   *The Builder*, 25 August 1860.

35   LMA DL/D/L/136/MS12292 Lease of land at Hammersmith to Messrs Bell and Scott 4 March 1875.

36   Old Bailey Proceedings Online: (t18710918–630) Trial of Daniel Feiler for deception 18 September 1871 <https://www.oldbaileyonline.org/browse.jsp?name=18710918>, accessed 4 May 2022.

37   The process is explained in Daunton, *Progress and poverty*, pp. 248–9.

Bricks of Victorian London

one of the creditors of Stephen Watkins was the scavenging firm of William Townsend, which had presumably supplied ashes, in the sum of £185 on bills of exchange.[38]

Short-term loans were available from a number of sources. Banks could give assistance in the form of overdrafts or loans, and landowners or builders' merchants might extend credit.[39] Landowners could also provide assistance by allowing arrears on the payment of rent and royalties, especially in the case of the latter when the number of bricks made had been reduced by a wet summer. Leases often included a clause that allowed the minimum number on which royalties were to be paid to be averaged out across a series of seasons to account for such eventualities. In some of the rentals in the Cowley district landowners seem to have received no royalties from some brickmakers in particular years.[40]

When brickmakers needed access to longer-term investment the most usual means was self-financing: ploughing back the profits of the business. This would be especially important for young businesses and for many companies that remained small and family-owned. Established businesses, with proven track records, could more easily draw on external sources of capital. The role of banks in providing this sort of capital has been the subject of debate. On the one hand, it has been argued that banks were generally reluctant to lend money to industrial concerns, but, on the other, the apparent failure to support manufacturing seemed to result from a lack of demand, which itself stems from the habit of self-financing. Of the 327 private banks nationally in 1850 most had a local focus. They operated as credit banks, rather than investment banks, but they could provide some long- and medium-term loans.[41] Uxbridge's main bank, Hull, Smith & Company, played a part in financing local industry, including brickmaking; for example, it advanced Samuel Pocock £1500 for discounted bills of exchange.[42]

Mortgages were a much-used form of extended investment where land or property were involved and there are a number of examples of mortgages being secured on brickfields. Hull, Smith converted some of Pocock's debt to them into a mortgage and at the time of his bankruptcy he owed the bank nearly £800.[43] Mortgages were provided by individuals as well as banks, and solicitors played an important role in putting investors in touch with those seeking funds. Joshua Knight of Baltic Wharf Pimlico advanced £4100 to Matthew Scott in 1876 secured on his brickfield at Wood Lane, Hammersmith. After a series of sales, Knight received the sum of £9943. The new owners of this brickfield then took out a new mortgage of £8000 at 5 per cent interest.[44] This method of financing was also used by limited companies; in 1909

---

38   TNA B3/2572; B3/5292.

39   Such practices occurred in a number of other industries, but there are no specific examples of such credit being given to brickmakers. Kirby and Rose, *Business and enterprise*, p. 93f.

40   LMA Acc. 328/47; Acc. 1386/384.

41   The issues are discussed in M. Collins, *Banks and industrial finance in Britain 1800–1939* (London, 1991), pp. 19, 22.

42   LMA Acc. 538/2nd dep/1312.

43   LMA Acc. 538/2nd dep/1316.

44   LMA DL/D/L/136/MS12292.

Land, machinery and labour

Coles, Shadbolt and Co. Ltd was advanced £4000 by the London & County Bank against their freehold property at Harefield, but two further mortgages the same year came from private individuals. Thomas Maynard received a loan of £500, secured on his leasehold property at Harlington with interest payable at 5 per cent, from a James Fishwick of Westmoreland in 1868. Maynard later purchased the lease of another brickfield from the receivers for the sum of £1500.[45] As we have seen, Henry Hobbs and George Tilley received mortgage advances of over £16,000 before the formation of the Southall Brick Company.

Limited companies could also secure funds by the issue of shares, but it is clear that many brickmaking firms were essentially private in character and did not want to extend ownership beyond the circle of the original subscribers. This was a problem faced by many private companies in the late nineteenth century, but there were ways of avoiding the difficulty. When firms went public only debentures or preference stock were offered for sale, the family retaining the equity.[46] The New Patent Brick Company increased its capital with the issue of £5000 in preference shares in 1899. Henry Marks, the principal shareholder in the firm of Cullis, Phillips, provided the company with £2420 in 1903, and Silcock & Co., a 'company that does not issue an invitation to the public to subscribe to its shares' issued in 1907 eleven debentures of £100 bearing interest of 6 per cent.[47] In 1885 the Northfleet & Swanscombe Brickfields Co. Ltd issued 678 first mortgage debenture bonds of £10 each, with interest as high as 10 per cent.[48]

Brickmaking could be a profitable business and many men made a success of it, but the numbers of bankruptcies suggests that things could go badly wrong. Failures could result from bad luck – poor choice of site, difficult market conditions or bad weather – or inadequate management.

Once a brickmaker had a stock of bricks ready for sale, how did he go about marketing and selling his product? This is a question we turn to in the next chapter.

---

45 LMA Acc. 969/68; Acc. 969/66.

46 J. Armstrong and S. Jones, *Business documents: their origins, sources and uses in historical research* (London, 1987), pp. 21–2.

47 TNA BT31/6946/48889; BT31/7216/51033; BT31/10958/83222.

48 *Globe*, 25 November 1885.

Chapter 8

The market for bricks:
brickmakers, builders' merchants and customers

Bricks, once made, had to be sold, so how did brickmakers go about it, and what was the nature of competition in the London area? Producing what was a basic building product, how could brickmakers ensure that their bricks made an impression in a crowded market?

As a general rule, to acquire a competitive advantage over its rivals a business can adopt one of two basic strategies: it can manufacture a product similar to those of other companies but, through greater efficiency or by accepting a lower profit margin, sell it at a lower price (competition by price); or it can make a superior or distinctive product that will be easily recognised in the market place and be specifically sought by customers (differentiation).[1]

Both approaches were employed in the nineteenth-century business world, but overt price competition was often avoided because it could be self-destructive and quickly eat into profitability. With basic commodities, firms could not escape the pressure to charge the going market price and commercial advantage was, therefore, best sought by reducing costs rather than by lowering prices.[2] In such cases, differentiation was largely irrelevant, whereas elsewhere, in the consumer goods sector, it proved useful, especially where it could be supported by advertising, for instance in the cases of the early household brands, such as Bass, Beecham and Lipton.[3]

Do these forms of competition relate to the manufacture and sale of bricks? In the early part of the nineteenth century it would seem that this industrial sector was too immature for notions of competitive strategy to have much meaning. When bricks were made by builders at the building site market conditions did not prevail; when bricks were purchased from a local brickfield competition was restricted by the cost of transport. Even if there was a competitor in the neighbourhood the product of one brickmaker was unlikely to differ sufficiently from that of another to allow a customer to exercise a choice. Even when purchasing through a merchant, builders were usually selecting a generic product, although there were some exceptions to the general rule.

However, there was scope for some differentiation in the bricks on sale in London for two reasons: one was the availability of bricks of different colours and textures from elsewhere in the country, and the other was the entry into the market of patented bricks. Many areas of the country had clay suitable for making bricks, but these clays differed in their composition and the resulting bricks varied in colour, texture and strength. The Victorian delight in polychrome brickwork meant that bricks of different

---

1   M.E. Porter, *The competitive advantage of nations* (London, 1990), p. 37.
2   Kirby and Rose, *Business and enterprise*, pp. 215–16.
3   *Ibid.*, pp. 217–19; W.H. Fraser, *The coming of the mass market 1850–1914* (London, 1981), p. 146.

The market for bricks

colours were prized for their decorative qualities. For example, Reading developed a grey brick by adding rock salt during the burning; S. & E. Collier's version was known as Waterloo Silver Greys.[4] We have already noted the fashion for white bricks from Suffolk. Particular bricks might also be sought after for other characteristics, such as compressive strength, and Staffordshire blues were valued for their use in engineering applications. The hard red shiny Accrington NORI bricks were made of pressed shale and were noted for their resistance to atmospheric pollution and grime.[5] NORI is not an acronym; it is merely IRON spelt backwards.

During the course of the nineteenth century stock bricks available to buy in London began to be produced in a number of new areas, particularly in the Cowley district of west Middlesex, in northern Kent and in southern Essex. They were a generic product, made from similar clay using similar methods, but nevertheless the number of brickmakers and the availability of cheap canal or river transport created a competitive environment. There were undoubtedly some variations in quality between the products of different producers, but the sale price would have been broadly similar. However, there were some variables in the costs that manufacturers incurred, such as the rent and royalty payments on the brickearth they leased, their moulders' pay and the costs of some of the other raw materials they used. Bricks from Cowley makers were said to have been more expensive to produce than those from Kent and Essex brickfields, putting them at a competitive disadvantage. This difference was shown in a table of comparative costs that appeared in a trade journal in 1887, suggesting that production costs in the Cowley district were just over a shilling a thousand more than in Kent as a result of higher labour costs in Middlesex because of its proximity to London and the more ready availability of chalk in Kent (Table 8.1).[6] To remain competitive, Cowley makers had to decide whether to settle for a smaller profit margin.

The next generation of manufacturers, who began supplying bricks by rail from sites north of the city, did not pose a significant threat to the stock brickmaker as long as they only produced relatively small quantities of speciality bricks, which were chosen either for their appearance or for their extra strength or durability. Once, however, the brickmakers of the Peterborough area had perfected the Fletton brick London's brickmakers faced a considerable challenge and by the early 1890s the market for bricks in London had changed fundamentally. The development of the Fletton brick is discussed in chapter 16.[7]

There is little evidence of overt competition between individual stock brickmakers on price. Contemporary reports make it clear that prices fluctuated in line with the level of demand. Within the prevailing trade price, brickmakers and merchants were probably willing to offer discounts according to the quantities required and the nature of the delivery arrangements. Many advertisements do not carry prices, suggesting

---

4   S. Muthesius, *The English terraced house* (London, 1982), p. 210.

5   R.W. Brunskill and A. Clifton-Taylor, *English brickwork* (London, 1977), p. 67.

6   *Brick, Tile & Builders' Gazette*, 11 January 1887, p. 194.

7   *British Clayworker*, April 1893, pp. 18–19; R. Hillier, *Clay that burns: a history of the Fletton Brick industry* (London, 1981).

Bricks of Victorian London

Table 8.1

Comparative costs of producing stock bricks in the Cowley district, Middlesex, and at Sittingbourne, Kent, 1887.

Per 1000 bricks	Cowley/Southall	Sittingbourne
Ashes and breeze and wheeling on	2s 9d	2s 6d
Chalk	1s 6d	9d
Engine etc pugging including fuel and stores	9d	1s
Foreman	7d	6d
Moulding	4s 10d	4s 6d
Sand	9d	6d
Setting	2s 1d	2s
Skintling	3d	3d
Sorting	1s	9d
Washing and wheeling earth	1s 4d	1s 6d
Waste	9d	1s
Wear and tear, tools and plant, including wash caps and boards	1s 3d	1s 6d
Rent, rates and taxes	6d	6d
Royalty	2s	2s
Total	**20s 4d**	**19s 3d**

Source: *Brick, Tile & Builders' Gazette*, 11 January 1887, p. 194.

that market prices were known to potential customers and that bargaining around that figure was possible.

Brickmakers reduced their prices under certain circumstances. A common instance was when they had a large quantity of bricks on their hands that they needed to dispose of quickly, either to improve cash flow or to clear unsold stock off the brickfield to make space before the start of the new season. In 1860, for example, an advertisement appeared in *The Builder* offering '120,000 very sound place bricks, within half a mile of the Paddington Canal' near Uxbridge, and in the same issue a Hammersmith brickmaker had on offer 100,000 bricks for cash.[8] In neither case was there an indication of price. There were inevitably dangers if bricks were sold at too low a price, and Robert Dove's financial difficulties, culminating in bankruptcy in 1829, were caused or compounded by the sale in 1826–7 of over three million bricks at a loss of £1310 and smaller losses in 1829 occasioned by selling bricks at barely half their cost price.[9]

Auction sales of bricks on a brickfield were not uncommon. Sales took place for different reasons: sometimes to generate cash flow, but on other occasions because of the closure of the brickfield as a result of bankruptcy, retirement or the end of a lease. In

8   *The Builder*, 12 May 1860.
9   TNA B3/1447 Bankruptcy of Robert Dove.

The market for bricks

May 1860 400,000 good stock and place bricks, 'assorted and arranged in convenient lots', were put up for auction at a brickfield in Russia Lane, Victoria Park.[10] This sale was evidently only partially successful, since some weeks later bricks from the same site were being offered at prices a third below the prevailing rates.[11] In 1875 E.P. Newman auctioned five million bricks produced on the fields of Waring Brothers at Southall. Twenty years later the same auctioneer sold two million bricks on behalf of Messrs Burchett & Son.[12] An auction in Ealing in October 1855 involved 500,000 bricks sold in more than fifty lots of varying quantities. From the catalogue it is clear that the bricks were still in clamps and it is specified that the top and bottom courses would not be sold, as they were generally overburnt. The customers were all local builders and the largest purchaser secured nineteen lots for a total of £139 4s, for which he paid a deposit of £28 on the day, the rest to be paid before delivery. The price paid for some of the lots was as low as 20s per thousand for stocks and less than 16s for the lower-quality *grizzels*.[13] We also know what the bricks fetched at a sale in 1861 at the Bell Brick Field, at Orpington in Kent, which was closing down at the end of the lease. In total 130,000 bricks were sold, mostly in lots of 5000. Stock bricks went for 30s a thousand and place bricks for 20s.[14] The prevailing prices in the early 1860s were nearer £2 a thousand for stocks and £1 15s for place bricks.[15]

We don't know if customers were able to distinguish between the stock bricks produced in one part of the London area or another, or between individual makers in the same district. Builders' merchants such as F. Rosher and Charles Richardson in the 1860s and 1870s advertised their bricks as Cowley and Kent bricks, and did not specify individual makers (Figure 8.1). Eastwoods, on the other hand, had an exclusive agency for several Kent brickmakers, among them Messrs Butcher of Halstow and Otterham, and also supplied yellow and pale malm cutters and facing bricks by Edward Ashenden of Sittingbourne.[16] However, the products of familiar Cowley manufacturers such as Pocock, Rutter and Tildesley did not appear in the advertisements of London brick merchants, nor did they place any of their own. From the 1880s, however, with the vertical integration that had taken place in the industry, some builders' merchants could promote their own bricks: an Eastwoods' advertisement in 1884 lists its brickfields at West Drayton and Sittingbourne.[17] Bricks with makers' names or initials on the frogs do not seem to survive for Cowley makers, but they do for the larger Kent makers, such as the Burham Brick and Cement Works (BBCW), Wills & Packham (WP) and Smeed, Dean (SD).[18]

---

10   *The Builder*, 12 May 1860.

11   Stocks were at 28s rather than 34s; place bricks at 18s rather than 27s. *The Builder*, 16 June 1860.

12   *The Builder*, 10 July 1875; in the case of Burchett it was presumably to clear the remainder of the previous year's make at the start of the new season. *Middlesex Chronicle*, 6 April 1895.

13   LMA Acc. 469/1. Sale of bricks by auction at Ealing 8 October 1855. *Grizzels*, like place bricks, were used for inside work.

14   Kent Archives and Local History Centre U2725/B2/291. Sale of bricks, Bell Brick Field.

15   *Laxton's Builders' Price Book*, 1860 and 1862.

16   *The Builder*, 5 May 1860.

17   *Laxton's Builders' Price Book*, 1884, p. 71.

18   For makers' marks, see 'Old bricks – a history at your feet; a celebration of old named bricks', a website created by Chris Smalley. <www.brocross.com/bricks>, accessed 5 October 2021.

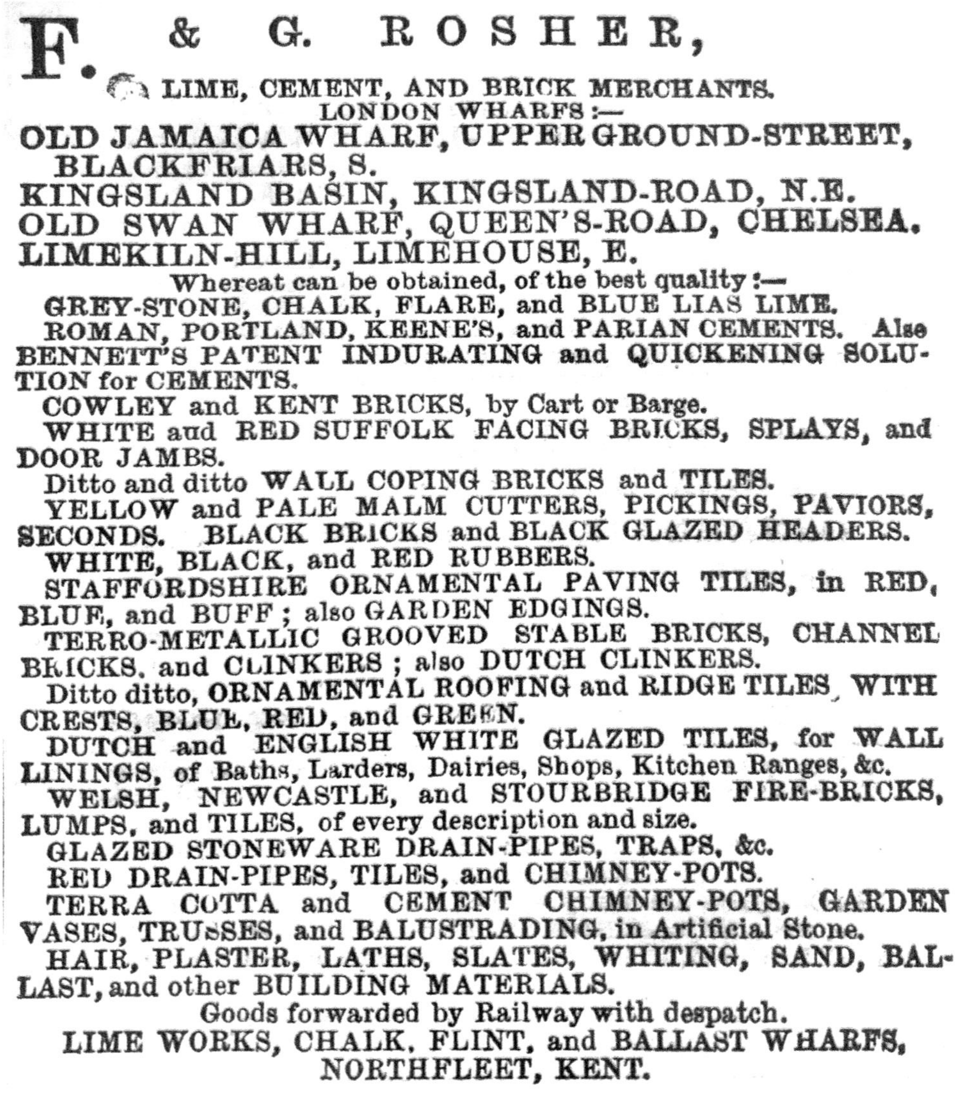

Bricks of Victorian London

F. & G. ROSHER,

LIME, CEMENT, AND BRICK MERCHANTS.

LONDON WHARFS :—

OLD JAMAICA WHARF, UPPER GROUND-STREET, BLACKFRIARS, S.

KINGSLAND BASIN, KINGSLAND-ROAD, N.E.

OLD SWAN WHARF, QUEEN'S-ROAD, CHELSEA.

LIMEKILN-HILL, LIMEHOUSE, E.

Whereat can be obtained, of the best quality :—

GREY-STONE, CHALK, FLARE, and BLUE LIAS LIME.

ROMAN, PORTLAND, KEENE'S, and PARIAN CEMENTS. Also BENNETT'S PATENT INDURATING and QUICKENING SOLUTION for CEMENTS.

COWLEY and KENT BRICKS, by Cart or Barge.

WHITE and RED SUFFOLK FACING BRICKS, SPLAYS, and DOOR JAMBS.

Ditto and ditto WALL COPING BRICKS and TILES.

YELLOW and PALE MALM CUTTERS, PICKINGS, PAVIORS, SECONDS. BLACK BRICKS and BLACK GLAZED HEADERS.

WHITE, BLACK, and RED RUBBERS.

STAFFORDSHIRE ORNAMENTAL PAVING TILES, in RED, BLUE, and BUFF ; also GARDEN EDGINGS.

TERRO-METALLIC GROOVED STABLE BRICKS, CHANNEL BRICKS. and CLINKERS ; also DUTCH CLINKERS.

Ditto ditto, ORNAMENTAL ROOFING and RIDGE TILES, WITH CRESTS, BLUE, RED, and GREEN.

DUTCH and ENGLISH WHITE GLAZED TILES, for WALL LININGS, of Baths, Larders, Dairies, Shops, Kitchen Ranges, &c.

WELSH, NEWCASTLE, and STOURBRIDGE FIRE-BRICKS, LUMPS, and TILES, of every description and size.

GLAZED STONEWARE DRAIN-PIPES, TRAPS, &c.

RED DRAIN-PIPES, TILES, and CHIMNEY-POTS.

TERRA COTTA and CEMENT CHIMNEY-POTS, GARDEN VASES, TRUSSES, and BALUSTRADING, in Artificial Stone.

HAIR, PLASTER, LATHS, SLATES, WHITING, SAND, BALLAST, and other BUILDING MATERIALS.

Goods forwarded by Railway with despatch.

LIME WORKS, CHALK, FLINT, and BALLAST WHARFS, NORTHFLEET, KENT.

Figure 8.1. Advert for F. & G. Rosher, builders' merchants (*The Builder*, 7 January 1865).

Since all these companies were producing a similar product, what distinguished the named firms from the rest may have been largely an issue of scale, as it would be difficult to promote your brickfield if the output was only one or two million per annum, but much easier if it was ten or twenty. A firm like Smeed, Dean became known for its ability to supply large quantities of bricks for important building projects, and seem to have gained a reputation for reliability and consistency. However, it is difficult to know whether a premium price was asked for them.

An effective way to develop a brand identity was to patent a production method. Patents were an important way of identifying a product, especially before the Trade

The market for bricks

Marks and Designs Act of 1875 made it possible to register a trade mark. A number of these patented bricks were sold in the capital but there were few, if any, actually being produced in the London area. For example, it was claimed that Ingram's Patent Solid Bricks had twice the compressive strength of a standard Staffordshire blue brick.[19] Another successful patented brick was the Beart perforated gault brick, made by Robert Beart himself at Arlesey in Bedfordshire, but also licensed to other brickmakers.[20] Architects sometimes specified them: builders intending to build on a housing development in Kensington in the 1870s were required to use Ipswich, Suffolk, Gault or Beart's Patent bricks, all of which would have provided a paler look than yellow stocks.[21] Beart's product was readily identifiable not only by its colour and texture – there were other types of gault brick – but by the perforations that reduced the weight of the brick. It attracted a premium price. This may suggest that yellow stocks occupied the bottom end of the market, a view illustrated by the building of the Albert Hall: the main walls were constructed of picked Cowley stocks, no maker recorded, hidden behind a façade of red bricks supplied by William Cawte of Fareham, and with terracotta decoration by Gibbs & Canning.[22] However, it seems likely that the finer grades of London stocks, especially the paler shades, were acceptable alternatives to the Suffolk whites or gault bricks that were sometimes specified.[23]

The challenge for the stock brickmaker was to produce bricks of a consistent quality and colour, since clamp burning resulted in bricks of varying colours and degrees of hardness. The contemporary literature suggests that bricks from the clamps were sorted by quality, with the best stocks at one end of the spectrum and fused overburnt bricks, suitable only for garden walls or as hardcore, at the other.[24] As well as variations in quality, there were also variations in colour, from a pale grey, often highly prized, to a more acid yellow. For many projects the natural variation caused by clamp burning was perfectly acceptable. This variation in colour is immediately apparent on viewing Victorian buildings. What we don't know is exactly how the brick merchants operated. Were bricks always sorted by the manufacturer at the yard into their many categories, or shipped unsorted to the merchant and separated on arrival? Were batches of bricks from individual makers kept separate, or mixed together by grade and colour?[25]

---

19 *The Builder*, 5 May 1860.

20 P. Hounsell, 'Robert Beart', in *Oxford dictionary of national biography* (Oxford, 2004) <https://doi.org/10.1093/ref:odnb/48801>, accessed 4 May 2022.

21 H. Hobhouse (ed.), *Survey of London, vol. 42. Southern Kensington: Kensington Square to Earls Court* (London, 1986), p. 170.

22 F.H.W. Sheppard (ed.), *Survey of London, vol. 38. South Kensington museums area* (London, 1975), p. 189.

23 Cox, 'Bricks to build a capital', p. 11.

24 Dobson identifies fourteen qualities of stock bricks, with *malms* being the finest and *burrs* or *clinkers* the worst. Dobson, *Rudimentary treatise* (1899), pp. 155–6.

25 With modern hand brickmaking, bricks coming out of a Scotch kiln or a clamp vary in colour, and to satisfy the needs of the customer they are sorted into bricks of similar shades or sold as mixed shades where a natural variety is desirable.

Bricks of Victorian London

In most cases it is difficult to link the bricks produced at a particular brickfield with the projects in which they were used, as sales ledgers rarely survive. There are only a few occasions where we can be certain. As we have seen, bricks produced by Edward Westbrook at Heston were selected in 1847 for the interior walls of the new palace of Westminster because of their high quality.[26] Northolt's bricks were said to have been of superior quality and were employed in the construction of London's sewers.[27] We know more about the brickmaker Smeed, Dean, which supplied, inter alia, bricks for King's Cross station, the Crystal Palace, a number of docks and the first underground railway.[28]

The stock brickmakers were in competition with each other, but not ruthlessly so – rather the opposite. At times, particularly when market conditions were difficult or in the face of concerted trade union activity, they were inclined to work together. This is seen most clearly in the district-wide setting of the wages paid to moulding gangs or sale prices. An association of masters in the Cowley district was in existence by 1887 and many familiar figures were members. At a meeting in October that year James Stroud presided and Mr Harris (of Broad, Harris) was the secretary. Mr Wragge (the chairman of Eastwoods), Mr Burchett and Mr Mecklenburgh were all present. On this occasion the firms agreed on a concerted attempt to raise prices. The Cowley masters also suggested that the owners in Kent should form their own association so that they could work with them to discuss trade matters.[29] This resulted in the formation of the Kent & Essex Stock Brickmasters' Association, which was prominent in the strikes of the 1890s.[30] Despite their earlier importance, in 1900 a trade correspondent could suggest that the Cowley industry

> presents a striking illustration of the immense loss to the manufactures of a district, through the lack of an effective trade combination. In the old days it was an accepted fact that Cowley stocks always sold at two or three shillings per thousand above Kent stocks; but the Cowley markets [presumably the author meant 'London' markets] have for some time past seen Kent bricks selling for two or three shillings above the price realised for Cowley bricks – an object lesson which, it is hoped, will have some effect in emphasising the advantages of combination.[31]

Brickmakers did not, however, embark on the kind of horizontal mergers or combinations that were seen in other sectors of the economy, such as cement production, in the period 1890–1905.[32] The formation of Eastwoods, discussed earlier, is the main exception to this rule.

---

26 *The Builder*, 17 April 1847.

27 J. Thorne, *Handbook to the environs of London* (London, 1876), article on Northolt.

28 Perks, *George Bargebrick*, p. 9.

29 *Brick, Tile & Builders' Gazette*, 10 May 1887, 9 October 1888.

30 *British Clayworker*, October 1900, p. 251; June 1892, p. 58; the strikes are considered in chapter 15.

31 *British Clayworker*, January 1900, p. 311.

32 The Associated Portland Cement Manufacturers, a combination of twenty-seven firms formed in 1900, was by 1919 the thirteenth largest company in the United Kingdom. D.J. Jeremy, *A business history of Britain, 1900–1990s* (Oxford, 1998), pp. 200–2.

The market for bricks

Labour costs varied little as wage rates were customarily fixed across the district at the start of each season. However, there were occasions when the system was undermined by individual owners. It seems they made verbal agreements with their moulders that they would consider an increase in wages if one was proposed elsewhere in the same district, or so the men alleged. The failure subsequently to honour such an understanding was at the heart of a dispute between Samuel Pocock and some of his moulders in 1876, which resulted in a strike and a subsequent court case brought by the employer for breach of contract. The men's demands for an increase had been occasioned by a rise paid by a Slough brickmaker. The Cowley masters resisted a rise of 6d per thousand to match this and denied that such a mechanism existed to vary the contract price. The issue was put to the arbitration of a group of four men and four employers, but the outcome was not reported.[33]

Two general points arise from this case. First, manufacturers collectively agreed the rate for moulders in their district, and did not anticipate one of their number paying over the odds. This further implies that there was no need to offer a differential over their rivals' rates in order to recruit workers because there was always an available pool of labour. The fact that one of the moulders in the Pocock case, William Warner, had been an employee of the same firm for twelve years suggests a degree of loyalty to an employer.[34] Secondly, as we have seen, because labour costs comprised a large proportion of the overall manufacturing costs, owners would be determined to keep moulding rates as low as possible to maintain their profit margins.

There were several ways in which bricks were sold to customers. At the simplest level, the manufacturer could sell direct at the brickfield gate and the customer could take away the bricks with his own transport or have them delivered. Some brickmakers placed advertisements in trade journals or newspapers. Newspaper advertising grew considerably in the early part of the nineteenth century but up to 1848 was subject to excise duty. Advertising generally was also responsive to movements in the business cycle and there were obvious peaks in 1825 and 1847.[35] Trade journals, however, were not subject to the duty and brickmakers could make use of outlets such as *The Builder*, which carried advertisements for bricks soon after its launch in 1843.[36] Henry Dodd advertised regularly in 1850, and encouraged prospective buyers to visit his brickfield 'only a quarter of an hour's walk from the City'. There they could view bricks that were 'sound, well burnt and unusually free from defects', which could be delivered within two miles of the brickfield at no additional cost.[37] In 1860 a Mr Browning offered stocks and place bricks from his Widmore brickfields in Bromley, which could be loaded on trucks at Bromley station on the Mid-Kent railway.[38] Mr Johnson advertised, under the banner '*Bricks! Bricks! Bricks!*', stock bricks from his brickfields at Fulham

---

33 *Marvel and Middlesex Register*, 18 May 1876.

34 *Ibid.*

35 T.R. Nevett, *Advertising in Britain: a history* (London, 1982), pp. 26, 29.

36 *Ibid.*, p. 43.

37 *The Builder*, 5 January 1850.

38 *Ibid.*, 12 May 1860.

Bricks of Victorian London

and Finchley Road.[39] Henry Kyezor of Hounslow advertised, with a similar headline, for several months in 1870.[40]

As well as 'for sale' notices from brickmakers and auctioneers, there were also 'wanted' advertisements. In 1821 an auctioneer placed a request for '100,000 well burnt gray stocks', but the project for which they were needed was not specified.[41] A few years later another agent in the City was in the market for 200,000 bricks delivered by river, and proposing to pay for half in a month, the rest in two.[42] More strangely, an architect advertised for bricks 'in any quantity' to be delivered to Westminster, Pimlico or Paddington.[43] Another agent in Spitalfields sought 200,000 bricks 'to consist of best stocks and half-and-halves, about an equal quantity of each', to be delivered near the Regent's Canal east of the City.[44] In 1860 a Dalston builder or agent was in the market for 325,000 stock bricks to be delivered to Hounslow Barracks.[45] Further research is needed to provide conclusive evidence, but it may be that these types of sale became less common later in the century as the number of builders' merchants grew and there was more vertical integration in the sector. In a later case a 'wanted' advertisement for cement and bricks gives the impression that this came from a business intending to operate as a builders' merchant and seeking to set up its supply chains.[46]

The building industry in the nineteenth century experienced a number of changes, one of which was the appearance of the general contracting firm, providing all the disciplines of building work previously supplied separately by carpenters, bricklayers and plumbers. These large firms were a response to two developments. The first was the increasing size of building contracts, not only for major civil engineering projects but also for public institutions such as workhouses, asylums and hospitals.[47] The second was the change in the method of awarding contracts, particularly for government buildings. By the early nineteenth century competitive tendering had been adopted and it was found more efficient to contract for whole buildings rather than make separate agreements for each trade. By mid-century *contracting in gross* was in widespread use and encouraged the development of multi-disciplinary firms.[48]

These major contractors, of which Thomas Cubitt is the best known and documented, set up their own works to provide materials and fabricate many of the components used in their projects.[49] Among other large firms were those of George

---

39   *Ibid.*, 20 May 1865.

40   *Ibid.*, 2 June 1870.

41   *The Times*, 30 April 1821, p. 1.

42   *Ibid.*, 5 June 1824, p. 1.

43   *Ibid.*, 2 November 1844, p. 10.

44   *Ibid.*, 27 February 1846, p. 1.

45   *The Builder*, 18 August 1860.

46   *The Times*, 6 December 1882.

47   One of the earliest such contractors was Alexander Copland, who employed 700 men at the end of the eighteenth century. Copland had earned over £1 million building barracks. C. Powell, *The British building industry since 1800: an economic history*, 2nd edn (London, 1996), pp. 18–19, 31.

48   *Ibid.*, p. 28.

49   Hobhouse, *Thomas Cubitt*, Chapter 14, pp. 281f.

The market for bricks

Myers, who had workshops at Ordnance Wharf, near Westminster Bridge, and probably a brickfield in Ealing in the 1850s; and Holland & Hannen, who operated a brickfield in Southall in the 1860s.[50]

These large operators were in the minority, and most builders bought the bricks they needed direct from the manufacturer or through an intermediary such as a builders' merchant, who would also supply a range of aggregates, ironmongery and sanitary goods. Brickmakers outside London often appointed agencies in the city. Agencies developed first in the stone trade because it had always been necessary to bring stone from some distance to the capital, so it made commercial sense for the quarry owner to appoint agents to take orders and arrange the local distribution. A number of such agencies were in operation by 1850. The Devon Haytor Granite company's depot was on the Regent's Canal in Mile End, and Luard Beedham & Co., which imported French stone from Falaise and Caen, had wharves on the Thames and Regent's Canal and at Paddington Basin.[51] In terms of clay products, firebricks were the first to be sold by agents in London, because there was no suitable clay for this kind of brick in the vicinity of London. They were brought from Stourbridge, Newcastle and Wales by William Ward of Honduras Wharf, Bankside, in 1845, and he also sold a variety of other building materials; keen to expand his product range, he solicited the business of 'country brickmakers wishing to introduce their bricks, white facings and others, in the London market [who were invited to] send samples and prices for cash'.[52] Similar agencies were set up for bricks and terracotta brought to London by railway after 1850. The Great Northern goods yard at King's Cross housed agencies for a number of firms; in addition to Robert Beart's, other companies with offices there included brickmaker William Dennis and Sons, also based at Arlesey in Bedfordshire, and terracotta manufacturer Joseph Cliff & Son of Leeds.[53]

Builders' merchants became important intermediaries in the supply chain between the manufacturer of materials and the builder, especially to service the needs of small building firms. If a builder bought from a brickmaker only a mile away the bricks were delivered by the cartload. When that brickmaker was ten or more miles away and consigning his bricks by the boatload of 20,000–30,000 bricks along the canal, or even larger quantities by Thames barge, there was a place for an intervening wholesale function. There was a large increase in the number of builders' merchants during the course of the nineteenth century. By 1870 there were 100 firms nationally and in 1910 there were 1300, the largest of which had outlets in three or four cities.[54] In London a number of merchants were operating in mid-century. Charles Richardson, at Vauxhall and Paddington Basin, John & William Eastwood, at Belvedere Road, Lambeth, and Messrs Rosher & Co, with depots at Blackfriars, Millbank, Kingsland Basin on the Regent's Canal and Limehouse, were all advertising Kent, Essex and Cowley stocks.

---

50 Spencer-Silver, *Pugin's builder*, pp. 82, 89. The brickfield, let on a twenty-one-year lease from 1858, was worked out by 1875 and reverted to agricultural use. LMA Acc. 506/15; 405/1.
51 *The Builder*, 23 February 1850.
52 *Ibid.*, 2 August 1845.
53 *Post Office London Directory*, 1863, 1882.
54 Powell, *British building industry*, p. 87.

Bricks of Victorian London

Messrs W. & T.N. Gladdish maintained depots at Belvedere Road, Lambeth, Wharf Road, City Road, Pratts Wharf, St Pancras and Danvers Wharf, Chelsea.[55] Some London merchants positioned themselves to handle materials brought by rail as well as water: Peters Bros had depots at Upper Ground Street, Lambeth, Paddington Basin and the Bricklayers Arms station, Old Kent Road.[56]

Several Cowley brickmakers found it convenient to have a London depot through which to channel their products, and the inland port that grew up at Paddington Basin became an important centre for building materials. In 1870 there were four brick and tile merchants located there, and some merchants also became manufacturers in their own right, such as Odell & Co., Broad & Co. and William Mead.[57] Coles, Shadbolt combined the manufacture of bricks and cement with a wholesale business. Their works were at Harefield, just north of Uxbridge, and they had depots in London, Middlesex and elsewhere in the country. Some idea of the range of suppliers that a firm like this bought from can be inferred from a list of its creditors when the company was reorganised in 1904. Over 200 businesses were owed a total of over £7000, including a number of brick, gravel and cement firms, among them the Arlesey Brick Company, Broad & Co. Ltd, two Fletton producers, B.J. Forder & Son Ltd and the London Brick Company, and several Cowley brickmakers.[58]

Stock bricks remained a basic building product, and largely generic in character, but there were variations in quality and appearance. Many smaller brickmakers merely contributed their few million bricks to the stocks of the merchants and wholesalers, but the larger and longer-established firms were able to build up a reputation for consistent quality and to create a brand identity in the market. There is not the evidence to support an investigation into whether variations in the quality of the product affected the price that customers were willing to pay, but it could have been a contributory factor in understanding why some firms succeeded and others failed, if their costs were similar. As in business generally, success or failure resulted from the decisions made by the owner and the skill with which he, or she, ran the firm.

---

55 *Marchant and Co's Builders and Building Trades' Directory*, 1857.

56 *Post Office Directory of the Building Trades*, 1870.

57 *Ibid.*

58 TNA BT31/10743/81437.

Chapter 9

From brickfield to building site: delivering the bricks by road, rail and water

Brickmakers supplying the London market relied on good transport links to their fields in order to bring in raw materials and to distribute the finished goods. Once bricks were ready for sale, purchasers had a choice of collecting them from the brickfield or having them delivered to the building site. For short distances this would be by horse and cart; otherwise, the bricks could be consigned by rail or water transport to a convenient wharf or goods yard.

Bricks are an awkward cargo, with a low value-to-weight ratio. They are brittle and easily chipped and so require careful handling to prevent damage. Because of their shape they demand systematic stacking to optimise the use of space in wagons and boats. For those reasons, in the days before palletisation, loading bricks was a necessarily labour-intensive activity. It was said that, when loading barges, bricks were thrown five at a time by someone standing on the jetty to another man in the hold of the boat, a process that had to be repeated at the other end of the journey.[1] Time taken loading and unloading made up a considerable part of every journey.

To keep costs down it was sensible to manufacture bricks as near to the place where they would be used as possible, but, despite this, there was always a greater movement of bricks and other building materials than might be expected. Stone on sale in London during the 1850s and 1860s included Yorkshire paving, Bath stone, Devon granite and Bangor slates.[2] In 1852 Thomas Cubitt brought 2463 barge loads of Purbeck stone, Penryhn slates and Sunderland glass to his Thameside works, and sent finished materials from there to Shoreham and the Isle of Wight.[3] As we have seen, Suffolk white bricks, shipped via the River Stour and the Thames, were used in London from the eighteenth century onwards.[4] After 1850 competition was provided by the growing railway network, which expanded the market radius of brickfields with no easy access to water. The Midland Railway conveyed Gripper's Nottingham bricks, which were used for the exterior of St Pancras Station, creating a symbolic link with the area that the railway served.[5] Beart's patented bricks, produced at Arlesey on

---

1   Perks, *George Bargebrick*, p. 31.
2   *The Builder*, 23 February 1850; 25 August 1860.
3   For the building of Kemp Town and Osborne House, respectively. Hobhouse, *Thomas Cubitt*, pp. 290–1.
4   Suffolk whites remained popular in the nineteenth century. Pale grey stock bricks were seen as an acceptable alternative. Cox, 'Bricks to build a capital', p. 11; in the 1890s stocks sold for £2 per thousand and Suffolk white for £4 5s. *Laxton's Builders' Price Book*, 1893, p. 50.
5   J. Simmons, *St Pancras Station*, 2nd edn (London, 2012), pp. 57–9.

Bricks of Victorian London

the Great Northern Railway, became widely available in north London.[6] Fletton bricks, produced near Peterborough, became serious competitors of London stocks in the 1890s.[7] Bricks were also imported from continental Europe when demand exceeded local availability, such as during the building booms of the 1890s and the 1920s.[8]

The fashion for polychrome brickwork encouraged the use of bricks from different sources. For instance, the architect William Butterfield used London stocks, Staffordshire blues and Suffolk reds at St Augustine's Church, South Kensington.[9] By the 1860s the larger builders' merchants in London provided bricks in a range of colours and styles. The Eastwoods' advertisement shown in Figure 9.1 is not untypical.

The distance that bricks could economically be moved – the so-called 'market radius' of the brickfield – usually depended on the nature of the bricks involved. As freight charges were determined by weight rather than value, the transport costs of higher-priced bricks were more easily absorbed. For journeys of only a few miles, and for small quantities, horse and cart was practical, but for greater distances water-borne transport was more economic. As a result, the main bulk carriage of bricks into London for the later decades of the nineteenth century was by river barge or canal boat.

For brickmakers it was important to consider the available means of transport when acquiring a brickfield and so it is not surprising that advertisements often mentioned the available transport facilities. Having access to more than one means of delivery allowed a brickfield to serve a wider market. In 1865 a brickfield between Hayes and West Drayton was 'near two stations on the Great Western Railway and about ¼ mile from a wharf on the Grand Junction Canal'.[10]

Even short road trips in the capital were not without problems because of toll charges. Most main roads had been incorporated into turnpike trusts during the eighteenth century and, whatever the benefits in terms of the upkeep of the surface, they hampered the easy movement of goods. Tolls added as much as 6d per 1000 to the cost of bricks delivered in many parts of London. Although tolls were removed from some roads, including Oxford Street, Edgware Road and the New Road in 1830, nonetheless in the 1850s Henry Dodd calculated that about half the bricks he supplied from his north London brickfields were still incurring them. Toll charges also had a more insidious impact. Where a delivery route required the payment of a toll the requisite cash would be given to the carters, but they often took an alternative route that evaded the toll, allowing them to pocket the money. This both increased the time taken to make deliveries because the toll-free route was usually more circuitous and also caused significant wear and tear to side roads, which had not been built to sustain such heavy traffic as fully laden brick carts.[11]

---

6   Bedfordshire Archives Z41/A2/1/1, Minutes of Bearts's Patent Brick Company 1853–57.

7   H. Paar and A. Gray, *The life and times of the Great Eastern Railway, 1839–1922* (Welwyn Garden City, 1991), p. 45.

8   See chapter 17.

9   Cox, 'Bricks to build a capital', p. 14; Dixon and Muthesius, *Victorian architecture*, pp. 15, 205–6.

10   *The Builder*, 8 July 1865.

11   Inwood, *A history of London*, p. 545. Report from the Select Committee on Metropolitan Communications, PP 1854–5, vol. 10, p. 186. Tolls were abolished completely in 1872.

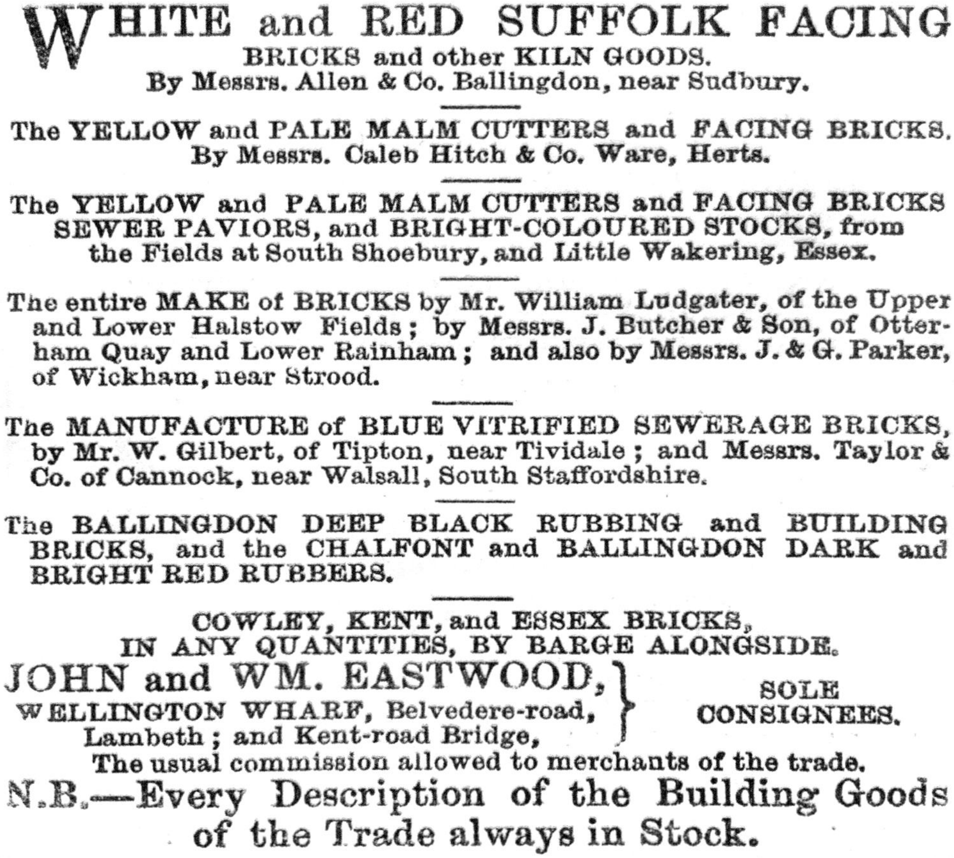

From brickfield to building site

WHITE and RED SUFFOLK FACING
BRICKS and other KILN GOODS.
By Messrs. Allen & Co. Ballingdon, near Sudbury.

The YELLOW and PALE MALM CUTTERS and FACING BRICKS.
By Messrs. Caleb Hitch & Co. Ware, Herts.

The YELLOW and PALE MALM CUTTERS and FACING BRICKS
SEWER PAVIORS, and BRIGHT-COLOURED STOCKS, from
the Fields at South Shoebury, and Little Wakering, Essex.

The entire MAKE of BRICKS by Mr. William Ludgater, of the Upper
and Lower Halstow Fields; by Messrs. J. Butcher & Son, of Otterham Quay and Lower Rainham; and also by Messrs. J. & G. Parker,
of Wickham, near Strood.

The MANUFACTURE of BLUE VITRIFIED SEWERAGE BRICKS,
by Mr. W. Gilbert, of Tipton, near Tividale; and Messrs. Taylor &
Co. of Cannock, near Walsall, South Staffordshire.

The BALLINGDON DEEP BLACK RUBBING and BUILDING
BRICKS, and the CHALFONT and BALLINGDON DARK and
BRIGHT RED RUBBERS.

COWLEY, KENT, and ESSEX BRICKS,
IN ANY QUANTITIES, BY BARGE ALONGSIDE.

JOHN and WM. EASTWOOD,
WELLINGTON WHARF, Belvedere-road,
Lambeth; and Kent-road Bridge,

SOLE CONSIGNEES.

The usual commission allowed to merchants of the trade.

N.B.—Every Description of the Building Goods of the Trade always in Stock.

Figure 9.1. Advert for Eastwoods, brickmakers and builders' merchants (*The Builder*, 22 April 1865).

London brick manufacturers felt that this put them at a disadvantage compared with those with access to water transport and complained to a parliamentary enquiry about their difficulty:

> The water conveyance ruins us. The Commissioners of the Metropolitan Roads have put a very great addition of toll on the carriage of bricks. We used to draw 4,000 bricks for 4d a day at Ball's Pond Road. and now it is 3s [a load] or 9d per thousand ... . Makers of bricks, at a short distance from London, who send in by water carriage, ruin us with the heavy turnpike tolls.[12]

---

12   Evidence of William Rhodes, 4 March 1835. Eighteenth report, Bricks, PP 1836, p. 25.

Bricks of Victorian London

The writer was presumably referring to cargoes on the Thames, rather than on the canals, which would also have been subject to toll charges. Not surprisingly, transport charges accounted for a significant proportion of the final selling price of a brick. In the 1850s bricks doubled in cost, it was thought, at a distance of sixty miles from the brickyard.[13] Builders' price books regularly quoted costs for carting bricks, which reveal that the cost of the first mile, which included loading and unloading, was much greater than that for subsequent miles, in a ratio of 4:1 (4s as against 1s in 1856).[14] By the 1890s these prices had risen to 5s and 1s 6d respectively and remained the same despite fluctuations in the selling price of bricks.[15] This meant that transporting a thousand bricks a distance of five miles added 8s to their price in the 1850s and 11s in the 1890s. Beyond a certain point, then, the costs of carting became uneconomic, especially if the carter could not cover the distance within a working day, requiring an overnight stay. Water or rail transport was more cost effective.

Nevertheless, even if the main part of a journey was by other means, nearly every delivery involved an element of carting, from a wharf or railhead to the building site. Each transhipment was demanding in labour and time and involved the risk of damage as well as providing opportunities for theft. When in 1838 contractors Grissell & Peto were building part of the Great Western Railway at Westbourne Green they sourced their bricks from Stroud's brickfield at Cowley. They were brought along the canal to the Paddington wharf of John Curnock, who delivered the bricks to the building site. Two years later a consignment of bricks required for a sewer, also at Westbourne Green, were shipped from Heron & Rutter's brickfield at Cowley to George Skuse's wharf at Paddington. He was paid 3d per thousand bricks for the wharfage, 9d for the unloading and 2s 6d for carriage to the site.[16] Bricks sent by rail also needed to be unloaded from wagons at a station goods yard and carted to site; for example, in 1899 bricks for Lord's Cricket ground were unloaded at Highbury sidings on the Great Northern Railway and carted from there to St John's Wood.[17]

Most brickfields had some local trade. In the 1880s and 1890s deliveries to the developing suburbs of west London would have been made from brickmakers in the neighbouring areas of Southall, Hayes, Acton, Shepherd's Bush and Willesden. Information about such local deliveries is limited and, depressingly, usually comes from police reports about traffic accidents or the mistreatment of horses. In 1883 a carter working for Southall brickmaker Mr Rowe was charged with causing an obstruction while making a delivery in Ealing and another carter in his employ was summoned for cruelty to his horse in the same month.[18]

---

13 Brunskill, *Brick building in Britain*, p. 35.

14 *Laxton's Builders' Price Book*, 1856.

15 *Ibid.*, annual editions 1890–9.

16 Old Bailey Proceedings Online: (t18380514–1272) Trial of Thomas Sidwell, 1838 <https://www.oldbaileyonline.org/browse.jsp?div=t18380514-1272>, accessed 4 May 2022; (t18400817–2128) Trial of Geoge Skuse, 1840 <https://www.oldbaileyonline.org/browse.jsp?name=18400817>, accessed 4 May 2022.

17 *Morning Post,* 1 February 1899.

18 *Uxbridge Gazette & Middlesex and Bucks Observer,* 17 February 1883.

From brickfield to building site

Most brickmakers owned a few delivery carts and could also call on local jobbing cartmen as necessary.[19] Even a small business in Notting Hill working two stools owned three 500-brick capacity carts and two lighter ones.[20] Horses formed part of a brickmaker's stock in trade. When James Rhodes gave up brickmaking in 1841, he put up for sale twenty cart horses and an unspecified number of brick and rubbish carts.[21] Messrs Rutter sold '20 powerful young and strong cart horses, out for constant work in their brickfields' in 1864.[22] Later in the century Eastwoods, brickmakers and builders' merchant, had stabling for the 150 horses employed in their deliveries.[23] Horses were a valuable asset, costing between £20 and £35 to buy, and their upkeep was also expensive.[24] A jobbing horse cost 12s 7½d a week in hay and oats in the 1890s, and the purchase of feed could account for as much as 40 per cent of the cost of any carrying operation.[25] In 1831 brickmaker Henry Hickman reckoned the cost of the upkeep of his horses in total at 21s a week, and the wages of the man who looked after them at 24s.[26]

The use of horses to move material around the brickfield or to turn pug or chalk mills for part of the week and then to make deliveries could result in horses becoming overworked. In her campaigning novel about the ill treatment of horses, *Black Beauty*, Anna Sewell describes an encounter with a brick cart stuck in the mud because of its heavy load:

> It was a sad sight. There were the two horses straining and struggling with all their might to drag the cart out, but they could not move it; the sweat streamed from their legs and flanks, their sides heaved, and every muscle was strained, while the man, fiercely pulling at the head of the fore horse, swore and lashed most brutally.[27]

While this is fiction, it reflects cases of mistreatment, some of which reached the courts. In 1876 a cart delivering bricks from Henry Kyezor's Hounslow brickfield to Kingston was stopped by a policeman concerned about the condition of the horse, which had been used to move ashes around the brickfield on weekdays and then engaged in making deliveries on the Saturday.[28] The Society for the Prevention of Cruelty to Animals, founded

---

19   Several brick carters, or carmen, appear in the census. Census Enumerator's Book, Southall 1881.

20   *Morning Advertiser*, 8 March 1862.

21   *Ibid.*, 8 November 1841.

22   *The Times*, 2 September 1864, p. 12.

23   Preston, *Industrial Medway*, p. 93; although it is not stated, these stables were probably at the firm's Belvedere depot, at Lambeth.

24   These are the prices given for cab horses: see T. May, *Gondolas to growlers: the history of the London horse cab* (Stroud, 1995), pp. 52–4.

25   T.C. Barker and D. Gerhold, *The rise and rise of road transport, 1700–1990* (Cambridge, 1993), p. 17; J. Tilling, *Kings of the highway* (London, 1957), p. 47.

26   TNA B3/2572.

27   A. Sewell, *Black Beauty* (1877), chapter 20.

28   This was during the close season for moulding. *Middlesex Chronicle*, 12 February 1876. The distance to Kingston was about eight miles.

Bricks of Victorian London

in 1824, also undertook prosecutions.[29] In 1857 three brickmakers were summoned to Greenwich Police Court after one of its inspectors had discovered pug mills being turned by horses in 'a most shocking state' with wounds particularly to the shoulders. The brickmakers were all issued fines, which the owner of the brickfield paid.[30]

Horses and carts continued to be used throughout the nineteenth century and into the early decades of the twentieth, but by 1900 mechanised road transport was becoming available. In that year a steam traction engine was in use near Palmer's Green station, towing three trucks of bricks from the London Brick Company's brickfield, and Smeed, Dean also used them to move bricks from the works to their railway sidings.[31]

For longer distances, transport by river or canal constituted the principal means of moving bricks into the capital. For Kent brickmakers there was an established trading route between London and the Medway towns, with cargoes of timber, corn, hops, paper, coal and lime.[32] Bricks were usually carried in spritsail barges, developed from vessels originally designed to carry agricultural produce. About 80ft long, with a square section to facilitate loading difficult cargoes, they could carry 70 to 100 tons, giving them a capacity of up to 50,000 bricks. Hundreds of these barges, sometimes known as *brickies*, were employed in the Kent and Essex trades by companies such as Smeed, Dean, Rutters, Wills & Packham and Eastwoods.

Eastwoods' advertisement (Figure 9.1) identified stock bricks from a number of individual makers in Kent and Essex whose brickfields were located along the Thames estuary, the River Medway and the Swale.[33] The Swale, the stretch of water between the mainland of north Kent and the Isle of Sheppey, connects at its western end with the mouth of the River Medway, and from it a number of creeks served brickfields at Conyer, Oare and Milton. Lower Halstow and Upchurch are on the Medway estuary, while Burham, Snodland, Aylesford and Frindsbury are on the river itself, which was navigable as far as Maidstone for vessels drawing up to seven feet. The route to central London required barges to leave the Medway at Sheerness, around the Isle of Grain, before entering the Thames.

On the north bank of the Thames the Essex villages of Wakering and Shoebury, near Southend-on Sea, also became an important brickmaking district. The Benfleet creek provided access to the Thames for brickfields at South Benfleet and Hadleigh. Nearer London brickmaking took place at Grays, on the Essex side of the river, and at places such as Northfleet, Swanscombe and Crayford, on the southern side.[34]

Barges were crewed by two men – the master and the mate – who were paid on a piece rate. The crew of a spritsail barge sailing from Kent to central London could

---

29 The SPCA was granted the 'Royal' appellation in 1840. H. Velten, *Beastly London: a history of animals in the city* (London, 2013), pp. 11, 67–8; P. Atkins (ed.), *Animal cities: beastly urban histories* (London, 2016), p. 103.

30 *Kentish Mercury*, 27 June 1857.

31 *Middlesex Gazette*, 10 March 1900; see illustration in Perks, *George Bargebrick*, p. 56.

32 E.J. March, *Spritsail barges of the Thames and Medway* [1948] (London, 1970), p. 23.

33 *The Builder*, 22 April 1865.

34 Cox, 'Bricks to build a capital', p. 11; A. Hann *et al.*, *The Medway valley: a Kent landscape transformed* (Bognor Regis, 2009), pp. 23–52.

From brickfield to building site

earn up to 3s per 1000 bricks.[35] A few bargees have left records of their careers in the brick trade. Isaac Baker made his first trip in 1886 in the *George & Ellen*, a thirty-nine-ton boat with a capacity of 32,000 bricks, operated by Eastwoods. For the trip from Halstow to Putney he was paid 1s 6d per 1000 bricks. Later, as master of the thirty-six-ton *Dabchick*, he was paid 29s to carry 29,000 bricks to the River Lea up Bow Creek. In his youth he had taken barges up the Thames to the Limehouse Cut, from which boats could enter the Regent's Canal (Plate 13).[36]

When barges had to pass under the many bridges of central London their crews had to lower the sails and take down the masts. Men known as *hufflers* were employed to assist barge crews in negotiating the bridges; they operated from little sailing dinghies and positioned themselves where boats might need assistance. An extra 6d per 1000 might be paid to crews for working under the bridges, to compensate for the extra length of the journey and for the payment to hufflers.[37] Other challenges presented themselves when working up the canals. Trips on the Regent's Canal might involve a passage through the Maida Hill tunnel, which had been built without a towpath, necessitating legging the barge for a quarter of a mile, with the assistance of a man stationed at the mouth of the tunnel for this purpose, who was paid 1s. This was not required for the other tunnel at Islington, which similarly had been built without a towpath, but was later fitted with a steam engine to draw barges through.[38] When conveying sand from Kent or Essex to the Cowley brickfields, the crew of eighty-five-ton barges had to negotiate the first lock at Brentford on the Grand Junction canal and then unload their cargo into smaller boats for the onward journey.[39]

Barges, once unloaded, required a return cargo. This would often be the domestic rubbish on which brickmakers depended for their supplies of ashes and breeze. Where the rubbish had been already sifted on the dust wharf, the cargo of ashes would be relatively inoffensive, but still very dusty, as a contemporary noted: 'Many barges are slipping by, among which, we select the *Alice* of Rochester. She is laden with ashes for the brickmakers down on the Medway, and the cindery fluff covers everything, and the grit makes its way even to the inmost recesses of our lunch ...'[40]

Cargoes of unsifted refuse, on the other hand, were considered a dangerous freight because of the fear of spontaneous combustion. This rarely if ever happened, but barges on their way down the river would be accompanied by swarms of flies.[41]

Working the spritsail barges required considerable skill. When fully laden, barges sat very low in the water, with only a few inches' freeboard, which could be problematic in rough weather. While working in and out of shallow creeks, careful observance of the tides was required to avoid running aground. Sittingbourne's Milton

---

35   H. Benham, *Down tops'l: the story of the East coast sailing barges*, 2nd edn (London, 1971), p. 141.

36   March, *Spritsail barges*, pp. 25–7.

37   Benham, *Down tops'l*, p. 141.

38   March, *Spritsail barges*, pp. 25–7; Anon., 'Through London by canal', *Harper's New Monthly Magazine*, 1885 (reprinted by British Waterways Board, 1977), p. 10.

39   March, *Spritsail barges*, pp. 26–7.

40   Anon.,'Through London by canal', p. 11.

41   Willmott, *Bricks and brickies*, p. 21.

Bricks of Victorian London

Creek was particularly busy with boats laden with bricks or cement, and as many as forty might leave on the same tide.[42] The Thames was a congested waterway, and so, inevitably, collisions occurred. In 1883 the Smeed, Dean barge *Ruth* was run down by a steamboat, fortunately without loss of life. In 1889 the same owner lost *Providence*, which had to be broken up after being hit by another boat.[43] The barge *Empress*, belonging to John Hudson of Sittingbourne, was sunk in the Swale in 1878 with 40,000 bricks on board.[44]

Although, as a non-perishable commodity, bricks did not depend on speed of delivery, nevertheless the late arrival of a consignment could have an economic impact on the customer. Slow journeys also limited the earning power of the crews, so there was an incentive to make as quick a journey as conditions allowed, and some of the barges made smart passages. For example, in June 1899 the forty-four-tonner *Kate Emily* left Rochester on a Sunday morning at 10am with 36,000 bricks, reached Woolwich at 7pm and, when the tide turned, was taken in tow by a tug, reaching Richmond on Monday morning.[45]

The larger brickmaking concerns owned sizeable fleets. In the 1830s and 1840s George Smeed bought a number of vessels and by 1869 the business owned sixty barges and other craft. He continued to add to his fleet with boats built in his own yard, starting with *The Three Sisters* in 1845, and by the purchase of secondhand boats at auction.[46] Neighbouring brickmakers, such as Wills & Packham, also owned and built barges. Rutter's developed a distinctive type of craft, the *pitch-piners*, taking their name from the timber of which they were made, which were built at Crayford, on the south bank of the Thames. The original *pitch-piners* carried 35,000 bricks, and later vessels could accommodate 40,000 bricks.[47] By 1914 Eastwoods had built up a fleet of forty-four boats, some of which were able to work up the Regent's, the Grand Junction and the Surrey Canals, and had many wharves in central London and as far upstream as Mortlake, Teddington and Weybridge.[48] The barges of these large companies were a familiar sight on the Thames, and flying their company flags was a source of advertising for their owners: Eastwoods had the wording 'Eastwoods Brickmakers' in large letters on their sails (Figure 9.2).[49]

With so many boats involved in the trade, dozens of barge-building yards were established along the creeks and inlets off the Medway and the Thames. Around Milton Creek, off the Swale, there were some eighteen yards and 400 barges were completed from the nineteenth century onwards.[50]

---

42 March, *Spritsail barges*, p. 25.

43 Perks, *George Bargebrick*, p. 35.

44 *Illustrated Police News*, 17 August 1878.

45 March, *Spritsail barges*, pp. 29–30.

46 Perks, *George Bargebrick*, pp. 15–23.

47 Benham, *Down tops'l*, pp. 139–40.

48 Willmott, *Bricks and brickies*, pp. 2, 45–8, 67.

49 March, *Spritsail barges*, pp. 21–2.

50 'Ship and barge building on Milton Creek', <www.sittingbourne-museum.co.uk>, accessed 20 September 2021.

From brickfield to building site

Figure 9.2. Eastwoods' barge passing Greenwich Hospital. (Mersea Museum/Ron Green)

Older boats were often preferred in the brick trade, once they were past being used for better types of work. Secondhand barges came up regularly at auction. In 1858 four sailing barges 'from a leading firm in the brick trade' were auctioned at Crayford.[51] In June 1878 the topsail barge *Marion*, with a capacity of 40,000 bricks, was sold at Sittingbourne.[52] George Smeed paid between £100 and £200 each for eight barges he purchased in 1869, and in 1871 he acquired several barges once owned by Henry Everest.[53] In addition to purchase, barges could be hired for £72 per year in 1883.[54] A brickmaker inserted a 'wanted' advertisement for six barges for the brick and flint trade in 1876.[55] Brickmakers who did not own their own boats were able to call on the carrying companies, such as Goldsmiths of Grays, founded in 1848, which was the largest operator of Thames barges prior to the First World War.[56]

The brickmaker and rubbish contractor Henry Dodd, whom we have encountered several times already, has an interesting place in the history of the spritsail barge. He

---

51 *The Times*, 16 April 1858, p. 2.
52 *East Kent Gazette*, 8 June 1877.
53 Perks, *George Bargebrick*, p. 23.
54 March, *Spritsail barges*, p. 26.
55 *East Kent Gazette*, 9 September 1876.
56 'Grays Thurrock', in *Victoria County History. Essex, vol. 8: Chafford and Harlow hundreds, including Brentwood, Harlow and Thurrock*, ed. W.R. Powell (London, 1983), p. 45.

Bricks of Victorian London

conceived of the idea of a sailing match for Thames barges with the aim of improving their construction and sailing qualities. The first race took place in 1863, and was won by Dodd's own boat, *W.H.D.* Dodd left money in his will to ensure that races took place after his death and barge sailing matches continue to the present day.[57]

Away from the Thames, brickmakers in places such as Hackney or Walthamstow had access to the Regent's Canal or the River Lea, on which there were docks where bricks could be loaded and unloaded. A brickfield that William Rhodes leased in Hackney in 1843 was on the banks of the Regent's Canal. In 1865 the Stroud family leased a brickfield at Upper Clapton, adjoining the River Lea, which already had a sizeable dock or 'cut' from the river into it.[58]

Canals had the advantage over rivers of being deliberately constructed to connect places for economic reasons. Although a few canals had been built in earlier centuries, canal-building in England started in earnest in the mid-1700s, with the most intensive period of construction in the early 1790s, during the so-called Canal Mania. This was in response to a rapid rise in foreign trade that depended on efficient transport links between ports and inland manufacturing sites.[59]

Promoted in this period of heightened interest, the ninety-three-mile-long Grand Junction Canal proved to be one of the most successful. It was designed to shorten the existing route between Birmingham and London by over a hundred miles and was originally built to connect with the Thames at Brentford. However, as traffic began to build up the company realised the benefit of a more direct route into London, avoiding the use of the river and the series of locks that had to be negotiated to reach it.[60] This was achieved by building a branch from Bull's Bridge, Hayes, north and then east to Paddington, still on the edge of the built-up area of London, which opened in 1801. Following a contour line, thus removing the need for any locks, the so-called 'Long Level' extends between Paddington and the Cowley lock at Uxbridge. With a fourteen-foot profile, allowing the use of wide boats, and the absence of locks, the Paddington branch became by far the most important and successful of all the Grand Junction's extensions.[61] As early as 1810 more London-bound trade travelled along the Paddington arm than used the main line via the Thames.[62]

Although the canal had been built to facilitate the movement of manufactured goods from the Midlands to London, the Grand Junction Canal's biggest contribution, especially after the railways captured many of the more valuable commodities, was in moving high bulk, low dispersion cargoes, such as foodstuffs, fuel and building

---

57   March, *Spritsail barges*, pp. 82–3.

58   London Borough of Hackney Archives M724 Lease from Middleton to Rhodes 28 September 1843; M760 Lease from Tyssen Amherst to J.M. and A.W. Stroud 19 July 1865.

59   B.F. Duckham, 'Canals and river navigation', in D. Aldcroft and M. Freeman (eds), *Transport in the Industrial Revolution* (Manchester, 1983), pp. 101–8.

60   *Ibid.*, p. 108; Faulkner, *The Grand Junction Canal*, pp. 1–2.

61   Faulkner, *The Grand Junction Canal*, p. 49.

62   113,220 tons as against 78,476 tons. C. Hadfield, *The canals of the East Midlands* (Newton Abbot, 1966), p. 119.

From brickfield to building site

materials.[63] By mid-century over 75 per cent of the traffic on the Grand Junction was local rather than through trade.[64] Boats carrying bricks would have been a regular sight on the lower reaches of the canal. Traditional narrow boats carried about forty tons of cargo, about 13,000 bricks, but wide boats could hold between 26,000 and 30,000.[65] A brickfield with an output of 15 million units a year would have generated 500 or more boatloads.

The terminus at Paddington quickly became a busy inland port, and by 1807 there were 'already deposits for wood, timber, coal, lime, coke, ashes, bricks, tiles, manure and many other things'.[66] In these early years, bricks were the most important inwards cargo.[67] There were depots for several brickmakers and builders' merchants, such as Charles Richardson. Moreover, the connection made with the Regent's Canal at Paddington meant that boats could work further east across north London to wharves on that canal. Another major builders' merchant, Frederick Rosher and Co., had a number of wharves across London, including one at Kingsland Basin on the Regent's Canal. Cowley brickmakers James & Alfred Stroud had a depot at De Beauvoir wharf, off Kingsland Road.[68] Paddington's exports included many waste products from the city, such as rubbish and manure, and these continued as staple traffics into the twentieth century.[69]

Many brickmakers on the west side of London were dependent on the Grand Junction Canal and it is possible that the brickmaking potential of the land was appreciated only as the bed of the canal was being dug, as Middleton proposed: 'The cut shewed the soil to be a most fertile loam of from one to five feet in depth, on loamy, flinty gravel, six or eight feet; then leaden coloured clay ... . Bricks are everywhere ready (being made near the sides of the canal) for supplying its own needs.'[70] Very soon brickfields were opened up on both sides of the canal between Uxbridge and Heston along the main arm of the canal and along the lower end of the Paddington arm (Figure 9.3). Bricks could be offloaded at building sites adjacent to the canal. One observer travelling on the Regent's Canal in 1885 encountered: 'a little fleet of monkey-boats, deep down in the water with bricks and sand, which they are here unloading for these brand-new suburbs of Kensal New Town and Queen's Park'.[71]

Cowley brickmakers were also able to make deliveries to wharves on the Thames via Brentford, presumably the route used by Edward Westbrook to convey bricks from his Heston brickfield for the rebuilding of the palace of Westminster. Information about

---

63 G.W. Crompton, 'Canals and the industrial revolution', *Journal of Transport History*, 14/2 (1993), p. 97; Duckham, 'Canals and river navigation', pp. 97, 132.

64 Faulkner, *The Grand Junction Canal*, p. 123.

65 330 stock bricks weighed one ton and a thousand bricks, therefore, weighed over three. *Spon's Architects, builders and contractors pocket book ... 1880*, p. 21.

66 Middleton, *View*, p. 533.

67 Faulkner, *The Grand Junction Canal*, pp. 53–4.

68 *Post Office London Trades and Professional Directory*, 1870.

69 Hounsell, *London's rubbish*, pp. 46, 120.

70 Middleton, *View*, pp. 531–2.

71 Anon., 'Through London by canal', p. 7.

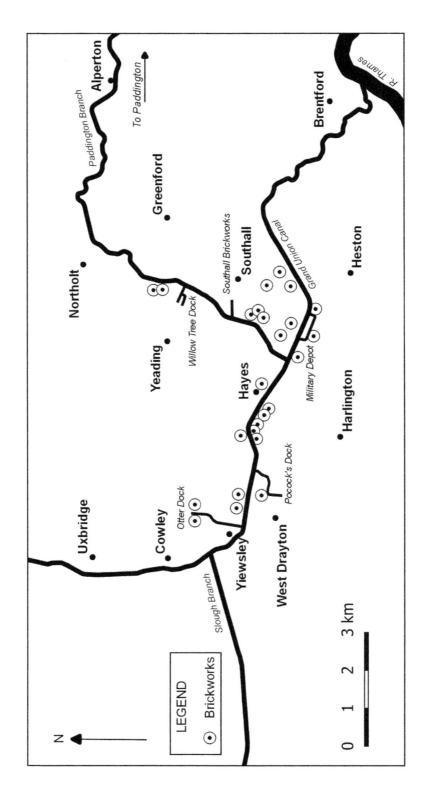

Figure 9.3. Brickmaking districts along the Grand Junction Canal in west Middlesex.

From brickfield to building site

such deliveries is scant, but in 1871 the Cowley Brick Company is known to have sent several consignments to Battersea wharf, Cherry Garden Stairs, Bermondsey and Lindsey wharf, Chelsea.[72]

Canal boats relied on horsepower for propulsion. A single horse pulling a canal boat was much more productive than a horse pulling a cart, and was able to move as much as fifty tons.[73] Like spritsail barges, canal boats had a crew of two: one to steer the boat, the other to lead the horse. Some crews and their families had no permanent homes and lived in cramped quarters onboard.[74] Like their counterparts on the Thames, older boats were used for carrying bricks, once they were past their best. The unsavoury nature of the return cargoes of rubbish or manure meant living conditions on brick boats were worse than on other canal boats, and a cause of concern to factory inspectors.[75]

At the brickfield it was necessary to have easy access to the canal for loading boats. The simplest way was across the towpath, a practice sanctioned by the canal company, subject to the fence beside the canal being replaced and kept in repair.[76] The second method was a wharf on the canal itself and, where the brickfield was a large one, there could be a long frontage. As the Grand Junction Canal was wide, boats tied up at the wharf were unlikely to impede through traffic.[77] The third option was to create a private dock – usually known as a 'cut' – from the canal itself into the brickfield.[78] As many as twenty purpose-built docks were cut on the stretch of canal that transected the Cowley district and some of these were of considerable length, with side branches.[79]

Since access to the canal was an important consideration for brickmakers, their leases usually specified if there was an existing dock or cut. Daniel Rutter's lease of land in West Drayton in 1862 provided for the use of both a dock and a 350ft frontage onto the canal itself.[80] Another lease from the same owner in 1849 also included access to a cut, but here the tenant was required to keep the dock itself, and the

---

72 These orders for bricks were all part of an elaborate fraud. Old Bailey Proceedings Online: (t18710918–630) Trial of Daniel Feiler for deception 18 September 1871 <https://www.oldbaileyonline.org/browse.jsp?name=18710918>, accessed 4 May 2022.

73 Crompton, 'Canals and the industrial revolution' p. 93.

74 H. Hanson, *The canal boatmen, 1760–1914* (Gloucester, 1984), p. 94.

75 *Ibid.*, p. 132; families were still living on refuse boats in the 1920s; see W. Freer, *Women and children of the Cut* (Nottingham, 1995), pp. 66–8.

76 Mr Pope of Hillingdon obtained such permission in December 1804. TNA RAIL 830/41. Grand Junction Canal Company. General Committee Minute Book 1802–5, p. 442.

77 The New Patent Brick Company had the use of a wharf wall of 250 feet at Northolt and an option on a further 305 feet, but also had a dock of 380 feet. London Borough of Ealing, Local History Centre Sale Particulars, New Patent Brick Company of London, 28 November 1902.

78 Maynard's brickfield at Harlington had a 'dock and stage for the unloading of ashes, clinker and for loading brick and gravel', and a 'stage for loading bricks and gravel into boats' and 'unloading platforms for ashes, chalk etc.' LMA Acc. 969/69 Plan of Maynard's brickfield at Harlington.

79 Faulkner, *Grand Junction Canal*, p. 149 (includes a map of the docks).

80 LMA Acc. 1386/105.

Bricks of Victorian London

bridge that took the towpath over the dock entrance, in good repair.[81] Access to wharves on rivers were selling points for brickfields in other districts as well, such as on the River Lea in Hackney or the Medway.[82]

If a dock did not already exist then the brickmaker might be allowed to construct one. Samuel Pocock's forty-year lease of land at Hillingdon in 1855 allowed him to make whatever docks he required, but at his own expense.[83] When Peter Pearse leased land on the Osterley estate in Southall he had permission to excavate a dock, but, unusually, the landlord specified the size and location of it.[84] In these cases the brickmakers seem to have borne the entire cost, but when de Salis let land at Dawley to the Rhodes brothers in 1853 he encouraged the brickmakers to construct a dock and agreed that 'on completion of a lay-up dock ... to the satisfaction of the lessors they, the said lessors, will pay to or allow to the said lessees out of the first year's royalty the sum of £50 for and towards the making of such lay-up dock'.[85]

Construction of docks also required the permission of the canal company, which owned the banks and the towpath. This took the form of a licence for a term of years and a nominal sum for access. There were further complications when the dock was to be on the side of the canal that carried the towpath. In the period before powered boats, bridges had to be built over dock entrances sufficiently high to permit the passage of boats, but not too steep to cause difficulties for the horses walking over them. Cuts had to be carefully constructed, particularly to ensure that there was no leakage that could drain water from the canal, since maintaining water levels was always a major concern.[86] In addition, there was a need to ensure the upkeep of dock entrances and bridges. If the users of the dock were not liable for any repairs the responsibility rested with the ground landlord.[87]

As clay was exhausted the currently worked part of the brickfield generally became located farther from the canal or river, so brickmakers had to decide how to secure continued access, since to be economically viable manufacturing sites had to be within what has been termed 'a narrow corridor of superior locational space'.[88] This was achieved in one of three ways: building a tramroad to connect the dock with the brickworks; pumping clay from the distant clay pit to a working area near the canal; or

---

81   LMA Acc. 1386/98.

82   For example, on the River Lea at Upper Clapton in 1865 (London Borough of Hackney Archives M760) or Aylesford on the Medway in 1881 (Kent Archives and Local History Centre U234/L2).

83   LMA Acc. 1386/101.

84   LMA Acc. 405/1 Lease to Peter Pearse, 1859; lease to Thomas Jacobs, 1879. However, there is no evidence that the dock was constructed.

85   LMA Acc. 969/63.

86   Licences to Thomas Shackle, 1825; to Southall Brick Company, 1859; to John Jay, 1854 and subsequently to Henry Dodd, 1860. Canal & River Trust (previously British Waterways, Hemel Hempstead, Estates Division Deeds) BW99/10/3/1 Shackle 1825. A few such dock entrances remain, including that over Lyon's dock in Greenford.

87   Canal & River Trust Correspondence file. Dutton's dock, West Drayton.

88   G. Turnbull, 'Canals, coal and regional growth during the industrial revolution', *Economic History Review*, 2nd series, XL/4 (1987), p. 544.

From brickfield to building site

extending an existing dock. The use of tramroads and slurry pumps has been discussed earlier. Extending a cut was neither a cheap nor an easy process, although some of the costs could be offset by the sale of the gravel that was dug out. Many brickmakers chose to do this, and some docks were extended several times and reached considerable lengths. In the West Drayton area Pocock's dock extended to 1120 yards by 1893, while nearby Otter dock had several branches and was 1845 yards long.[89]

Like their counterparts on the Thames, many Cowley brickmakers owned their own boats. In the early days of the canal only a few boats can be positively identified as carrying bricks. A fifty-six-ton boat registered to George Watkins of Brentford was 'employed in the brick trade', and Ralph Dodd had a thirty-four-ton boat 'principally employed in the brick trade to and from Paddington'. Trimmer of Brentford owned at least two boats, one of them a wide one of seventy tons that may have worked on the Thames as well.[90] One of the boats of general carrier Thomas Homer, who owned more than twenty craft, was 'at present [1806] in the employ of Mr Samuel White, Brentford, in the brick trade to and from Paddington'.[91] Messrs Bird of Hammersmith registered their first thirty-four-ton boat in 1818.[92]

Many early brickmaking businesses were not large enough to justify the costs of owning their own boats and so hired boats as required. As firms became larger after 1850 it made economic sense for their owners to operate their own boats, since this reduced transaction costs, but required production levels to be sufficient to keep the boats, and their crews, busy. Heron & Co of Hillingdon had a number of boats, including the thirty-eight-ton *Emily* and the thirty-nine-ton *Frederick*; D. & C. Rutter, also of Hillingdon, the *Algernon*. Francis Newell of Southall owned two forty-tonners, one unnamed, the other the *Susan*; James, John and Isaac Nutman of Northolt the *Isaac*; James Stacy of Cowley the *Catherine*; and Henry Austin of Hayes the *Confidence*. J. & A. Stroud's confidently named boats *Express* and *Lightning*, both of thirty-eight tons, would probably have been used to serve their Southall brickfield. Henry Dodd, at Eagle wharf on the Regent's canal, had several boats, including the thirty-seven-ton *Sun* and the seventy-eight-ton *Brick*.[93] Both Rutters and Eastwoods operated canal boats at the turn of the century, as well as Thames barges.[94] Brick merchants also owned their own boats. Charles Richardson of Paddington registered a thirty-nine-ton boat *The Kent*; his competitor, Rosher, the ninety-one-ton *Harry & Edward* (Figure 9.4).[95]

---

89 Faulkner, *Grand Junction Canal*, p. 202; TNA RAIL 830/93–95. These documents contain the transcripts of the hearing of Pocock v. GJCC in Chancery 1877.

90 Canal & River Trust, BW99/6/5. GJCC Gauge Books, entry nos 1330, 825, 603. Gauging canal boats was a method of ascertaining the weight of cargo carried by measuring the craft's freeboard, and a register entry was maintained for each boat active on the canal. Copies of the register were held at each major junction on the canal. Only the early register entries indicate the kind of cargo carried.

91 *Ibid.*, nos 625, 674.

92 *Ibid.*, no. 2187.

93 *Ibid.*, nos 8409, 8697, 8168, 8186, 8423, 8480, 8482, 8167, 9026, 9081, 8182, 8422, 9001, 9095, 8655.

94 Canal & River Trust, BW99. GJCC Brentford Toll Book 1901; Willmott, *Bricks and brickies*, pp. 45–8.

95 Canal & River Trust, BW99/6/5. GJCC Gauge Books, entries nos 8409, 8697.

Bricks of Victorian London

Figure 9.4. Canal boat laden with bricks on the Grand Junction Canal. (C. Herridge)

Company boats were also used to carry raw materials such as sand to the brickfields. In October 1897, for example, two of Broad's boats brought a total of 107 tons of sand to Dawley via Brentford, and in April 1901 Eastwoods, Odell, Rutters and the East Acton Brick Company all had boats bringing sand to their sites in west Middlesex.[96]

Some independently owned boats, the so-called 'number-ones', were employed to transport bricks, but by the 1870s, as a factory inspector commented, 'few of the barges on the canal are owned by the men who navigate them. They are either in the hands of the canal company, brick manufacturers or contractors.'[97] One exception to this general trend was W.H. King, whose family owned a pair of boats, usually worked together. King's diary entries for March and April 1895 record that the boats were working between the brick and cement works of Coles, Shadbolt at Harefield and their depot on the Regent's Canal at King's Cross.[98] Another individual owner may have been Richard Sivers, a native of Northolt, whose boat *Prudence* was tied up there on Census Day 1881 with a fifty-ton cargo of bricks.[99]

Unlike boats on the river, canal boats were subject to a toll payable to the canal company. Tolls were levied per ton mile and generally tapered down as mileage increased. The rates were established by the act of parliament that enabled the construction of the canal, but there was a common practice of allowing discounts,

---

96 Canal & River Trust, BW99. GJCC Brentford Toll Books, 1897 and 1901.
97 Factory Inspector Henderson, writing specifically about the Grand Junction Canal between Rickmansworth and Paddington. Factory and Workshops Acts Commission, Report of the commissioners appointed to inquire into the working of the Factory and Workshops Act, Vol. II – Minutes of evidence (c.1443), PP 1876, vol. 30, Appendix C, vol. xxix, p. 129.
98 Canal & River Trust. Diary of W.H. King; Hanson, *The canal boatmen*, pp. 114–15.
99 Census Enumerator's Book, Northolt 1881.

From brickfield to building site

known as drawbacks, to encourage certain trades on particular stretches of the canal. The rate for bricks established by the Grand Junction Canal Act of 1793 was ½d per ton mile (1½d per 1000 bricks), but this was increased by a series of further acts.[100] Reductions took place in the face of railway competition from the 1840s onwards, and in 1851 the rate for bricks was 10d per ton for the journey from any brickfield south of Uxbridge to Paddington.[101] However, in 1860 and 1866 there were rises resulting in a maximum toll of 1s 2d a ton.[102] Samuel Pocock, who was making 15–20 million bricks in the 1870s, calculated that he was paying the canal company £3000 a year in tolls.[103]

Like their Kent and Essex counterparts on the Thames, canal boats bringing bricks into London returned with cargoes of ashes collected from the refuse wharves at Paddington.[104] This symbiotic relationship was established early in the life of the canal. In 1804 the canal company agreed to a drawback on 'all ashes carried from Paddington to the brickfields at Norwood and North Hyde for the purposes of brickmaking'.[105] In 1815 it proposed 'to regulate the tonnage of bricks, breeze and ashes to induce persons conveying such articles to carry them to Paddington in preference to Brentford', again by offering a drawback, presumably to encourage the removal of waste materials from the centre of London.[106] Even in 1904, when Middlesex brickmaking was in decline, 104,467 tons of bricks were carried to Paddington, while a total of 635,961 tons of waste materials went in the other direction, much of it now dumped in worked-out brickfields or gravel pits.[107]

For most of the century canal boats were hauled by horses, but steam-powered boats started to be used from the mid-1870s and Odell owned one such steam 'tug' in 1893. It became common to work two boats together, with a powered boat towing an unpowered 'butty'. The major carrier Fellows, Morton & Clayton, having used steam-powered boats since 1886, began to experiment with oil engines before the First World War.[108]

The costs of canal transport were principally the expense of buying or hiring boats, horses and their upkeep, the wages of boatmen and their assistants and the tolls payable to canal companies. Canal boats cost somewhere in the range between £80 and £150, and in 1874 secondhand boats were fetching from £10 to £31.[109] Odell's fleet was valued at £2000, a smallish element of the overall assets of the firm, which totalled £50,000.[110]

---

100 Faulkner, *Grand Junction Canal*, pp. 5, 74.

101 TNA RAIL 830/44 GJCC, General Committee Minute Book 1828–58.

102 TNA RAIL 830/45 GJCC, General Committee Minute Book 1858–1924.

103 Pocock v. GJCC High Court, Chancery Division. TNA RAIL 830/93.

104 Hounsell, *London's rubbish*, pp. 46–7.

105 TNA RAIL 830/41 GJCC General Committee minutes, 8 May 1804.

106 *Ibid.*, 1 June 1804; TNA RAIL 830/43 GJCC General Committee Minute Book, 15 June 1815.

107 That is the equivalent of over 9000 journeys. Faulkner, *Grand Junction Canal*, p. 195.

108 C.P. and C.R. Weaver, *Steam on canals* (Newton Abbot, 1983), chapter 'The steam narrow boat'.

109 Prices relate to 1808 and 1856 respectively. Hanson, *Canal boatmen*, pp. 105, 107; TNA RAIL 830/50 GJCC Traffic Committee 1875–7. 19 July 1876; 9 August 1876.

110 TNA BT31/5649/39405.

Bricks of Victorian London

In the 1870s boatmen in the brick trade were among the lowest paid on the canal: some received a fixed rate of 18s per week, others were paid by the freight carried and could earn more, but at the risk of a less regular income.[111] In 1863 George Gale was paid 3s 6d per thousand to move 12,000 bricks (one boatload presumably) from Bulls Bridge to Watford and H. Roberts 3s a thousand for a similar load to the same destination from West Drayton.[112]

Railways provided an alternative form of transport from the 1840s. They did not necessarily attract established traffic in bulky commodities such as bricks away from rivers and canals, but they enabled the exploitation of brickfields that were not served easily by either. Many stock brick manufacturers supplying the London market had access to navigable water, but this was not the case for brickfields nationally, especially in the Midlands, so railways played a significant part in their distribution networks.[113] Robert Beart and Joseph Cliff both had brickworks near the Great Northern's main line, which enabled them to set up distribution hubs at King's Cross.[114] Brickmakers inevitably had an interest in the construction of new railway lines if this enabled them to open up new markets for their products. One of the promoters of the Nottingham suburban railway in 1885 was Edward Gripper, and a siding was built into his brickyard.[115] Railway companies themselves had a large requirement for bricks, both during the construction of lines and also generally for new station buildings and repairs. The London & North Western Railway had its own brickworks at Crewe, producing at one time more than six million bricks a year.[116]

Railways also opened up new markets to brickmakers whose existing trade was by water. The East Kent Railway (later the London, Chatham & Dover (LCDR)) served the brickmaking districts of Faversham, Sittingbourne and Teynham, and also towns in the Medway valley. These districts were attractive on account of potential passenger receipts, but also for freight traffic in agricultural produce and building materials such as cement, lime and bricks.[117] Although most traffic from the Sittingbourne and Faversham brickyards continued to be by barge, some manufacturers took advantage of the railway to reach other destinations. Both Henry Millichamp at Teynham and the Abbey Brick Fields at Faversham informed potential customers that they could supply bricks by barge, but also by rail via the LCDR. The former's works were adjacent to the Teynham station, while the latter had its own siding.[118] The Sittingbourne brickmaker A.E. Stacey offered to send bricks to any station on the LCDR or the London Brighton & South Coast Railway.[119]

---

111 Hanson, *Canal boatmen*, p. 94.

112 TNA RAIL 830/78 GJCC Collector's Account Book 16 September 1863; 2 July 1853.

113 J. Simmons, *Railways in town and country, 1830–1914* (Newton Abbot, 1986), p. 130.

114 *Post Office London Directory*, 1882.

115 Simmons, *Railways in town and country*, p. 115; Cox, 'Bricks to build a capital', p. 14.

116 Simmons, *Railways in town and country*, p. 173.

117 Gray, *London, Chatham and Dover Railway*, p. 96.

118 *South London Press*, 1 November 1884.

119 The fact that his advert appeared in a Surrey local paper suggests that one of the target markets was the south-east suburbs of London. *Croydon Chronicle and East Surrey Advertiser*, 1 March 1879.

From brickfield to building site

On the other side of the Thames the Eastern Counties Railway (later the Great Eastern Railway) opened up routes into East Anglia in the 1840s. Freight services to Colchester started in 1843, with intervening stations on the line including Ilford, Romford, Brentwood, Mark's Tey and Chelmsford. Brick and tile making were among businesses that followed the railway and by the 1870s there were three brickfields at Colchester near the railway, one of which had its own siding.[120]

The London, Tilbury & Southend Railway (LTSR) opened in 1856 and provided an alternative distribution route for the south Essex brickfields as well as areas closer to London. The brickmaker James Brown, long established at Braintree and Chelmsford, acquired a brickfield in Upminster in 1885, almost certainly because of the opening of the LTSR extension to the town. He quickly added a horse-drawn tramway to carry bricks over the mile-long journey to Upminster station.[121]

The North London Railway, serving the northern inner suburbs such as Islington, Camden Town and Hampstead, opened to freight traffic in 1852.[122] The Lea Valley had always been served by its network of rivers, and the north-eastern suburbs were highly industrialised. The area was opened up to rail transport starting with the formation of the Northern & Eastern Company in 1836, with authorisation to build a line from Islington to Cambridge.[123] Tottenham, Edmonton, Enfield and Walthamstow were now provided with an alternative connection to inner London. Edmonton remained an important brickmaking area, with four firms there in 1914. In Enfield the North London Estates Company established a brickfield as part of its development of Bush Hill Park and had a railway siding from the Great Eastern Railway, which had opened a station there in 1880.[124] A brickfield at Chapel End, Walthamstow was marketed as being in 'one of the fastest developing districts around London' and was within easy reach of Hoe Street (now Walthamstow Central) and Wood Street stations.[125]

West of London the route of the Great Western Railway' (GWR) to Bristol passed through the same part of Middlesex as the Grand Junction Canal and at West Drayton the two were less than a hundred yards apart.[126] Because of its proximity to the canal the railway inevitably cut through some existing brickfields or land containing workable brickearth. The landowner Hubert de Burgh claimed £15,000 compensation from the GWR for land, part in use as a brickfield, that would now be separated from the canal by the railway, allegedly rendering it of little or no value.[127] The GWR also acquired some of the land of the Southall Brick Company as part of the widening of the main line in the 1870s.[128]

---

120 D.I. Gordon, *A regional history of the railways of Great Britain, vol. 5: eastern counties* (Newton Abbot, 1968), pp. 41, 47, 50; Paar and Gray, *Great Eastern Railway*, p. 8.

121 'Upminster's lost brickworks' <www.upminsterhistory.net>, accessed 20 September 2021.

122 H.P. White, *A regional history of the Railways of Great Britain, vol. 3: Greater London* (Newton Abbot, 1971), pp. 75–6.

123 *Ibid.*, pp. 171–2.

124 D. Pam, *A history of Enfield, vol. 2, 1837 to 1914: a Victorian suburb* (Enfield, 1992), p. 20.

125 *London Evening Standard*, 21 February 1903.

126 E.T. MacDermot, *History of the Great Western Railway vol. 1: 1833–63* (London, 1927), pp. 51–2.

127 LMA Acc. 742/107. It is not recorded if he received this sum from the GWR.

128 TNA MR1/1977/1 (plan extracted from RAIL 258/522).

Bricks of Victorian London

The termini of the canal and railway were side by side at Paddington. There are some early indications that the GWR was interested in brick traffic. In 1837 it offered to carry bricks from the West Drayton area at the same rate brickmakers currently paid to the canal company, but was reluctant to authorise sidings because of the potential disruption to its express trains. Nevertheless, in the 1860s at least two brickfields had sidings connected to the GWR main line, one at Botwell, the other at Southall. In the case of the latter the railway was closer than the canal to the brickfield; this may have been the brickfield of contractors Brassey, Ogilvie & Harrison while they were building part of Bazalgette's sewerage scheme. When it was sold it was said that:

> The Railway Company [the GWR] will convey bricks either to the Thames at Brentford, or to the North London Railway, at a very moderate rate, and a tramway can be formed to connect the brickfield with the Grand Junction Canal which is within a quarter of a mile.[129]

In 1873 the New Heston brickfield offered to supply bricks by water or to any station on the London & South Western Railway or the GWR.[130]

Up until 1879 the brickmakers in the Iver–Langley–Slough area were dependent on the GWR for their distribution, as the railway had opened up the brickmaking potential of the district. They felt this put them at a disadvantage compared with their Cowley neighbours, complaining that capacity issues on the railway forced them to limit production and that there were delays to deliveries and uncertainty over when empty trucks would be returned. Canal boats, on the other hand, were easy to come by and could carry more than a ten-ton railway wagon. They therefore enthusiastically supported the proposed Slough arm of the canal.[131]

Since the railway opened up new markets, even major barge-owning firms sent some deliveries by that route. Smeed, Dean had a siding to the LCDR. However, water transport remained the dominant means of the bulk distribution of bricks to the London market during the nineteenth century and into the twentieth. Sailing barges were carrying bricks from the Swale brickfields in the 1930s, and barges carrying the Red Triangle logo and the legend 'Cement, bricks, dependability' remained a familiar site on the tideway.[132]

There was a differential between the price charged at the brickfield gate and that on delivery at a London wharf or depot, but in many cases the price a brickmaker charged included the freight cost. So Smeed, Dean held the same price for deliveries to any wharf on the Thames below Battersea Bridge or up the canals, except that the purchaser paid any tolls.[133] In 1879 one Slough brickmaker charged purchasers 5s per thousand carriage to send bricks by rail to Paddington, or 4s if he used his own

---

129 Ordnance Survey 6-inch map, 1866; *London Evening Standard*, 18 January 1865.

130 *The Builder*, 12 July 1873.

131 *Buckinghamshire Advertiser, Uxbridge and Watford Journal*, 12 July 1879, reporting the parliamentary committee scrutinising the bill for the Slough canal extension.

132 For the latter years of the Smeed, Dean barge fleet see Perks, *George Bargebrick*, pp. 56–7.

133 *The Builder*, 25 June 1870.

From brickfield to building site

trucks. In 1860 a brick merchant from the same area advertised best yellow stocks, all carriage costs paid and sent in GWR trucks to Paddington, for 34s per thousand.[134]

It is difficult to calculate what percentage of the sale price of bricks was attributable to transport costs, since only rarely do brickmakers' account books survive. However, one does for bricks sold by Beart's company at their King's Cross depot. In 1860 transport accounted for 20 per cent of the sale price and, while the company was able to hold down the manufacturing cost over the next fifteen years, the cost of carriage fluctuated considerably. In 1865 carriage costs were 15.8 per cent, in 1870 21.2 per cent and in 1875 back down to 18.3 per cent.[135]

If transport costs were an important consideration for all brickmakers, the biggest element of expenditure, especially for those brickmakers relying on hand-moulding, was the wages paid to the moulding gangs. As we have seen, these accounted for a quarter of the manufacturing costs. The experience of the men, women and children who worked on the brickfields is the subject of the next part of the book.

---

134 *Buckinghamshire Advertiser, Uxbridge and Watford Journal,* 12 July 1879; *The Builder,* 23 June 1860.
135 Bedfordshire Archives Z41/A4/1/1. Beart's Patent Brick Company. Ledger, 1852–74; A. Cox, *Survey of Bedfordshire: brickmaking, a history and gazetteer* (Bedford, 1979), pp. 44–5.

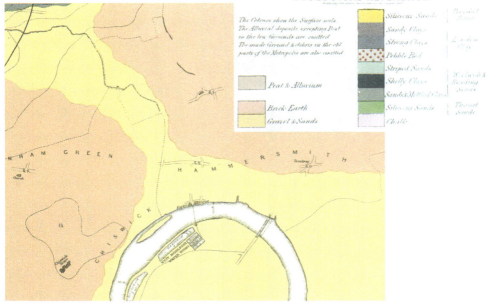

Plate 1. A section of R.W. Mylne's map of the *Geology and contours of London and its environs* (1856), showing brickearth in Chiswick and Hammersmith. (London Topographical Society/Bishopsgate Institute)

Plate 2. Westminster from Chelsea Fields. Drawn by C. Marshall, engraved by J.C. Varrall. From *The history of London, illustrated with views of London and Westminster* (1837–8). (Author's copy)

Plate 3. Hammond Road brickfield, Southall by E.A.L. Ham (1896). (London Borough of Ealing Local History Centre)

Plate 4. 'London going out of town, or the March of Bricks and Mortar'. Designed, etched and published by George Cruikshank (1829).

Plate 5. Brickwork in the Houses of Parliament, the cone over the central lobby. (UK Parliament/A. Watrobski)

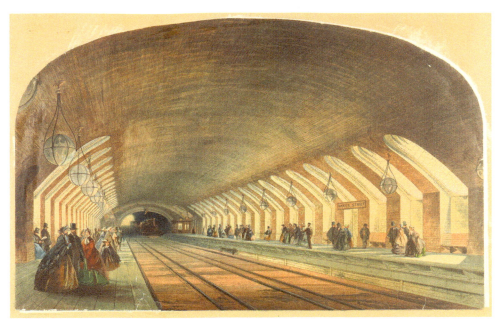

Plate 6. Metropolitan Railway, Baker Street station (c.1865). (London Picture Library/London Metropolitan Archives)

Plate 7. English country brickworks, probably in Edmonton (c.1840). Oil painting attributed to Nicholas Condy, but probably by G. Forster. (Science Museum, Science & Society Picture Library)

Plate 8. Brickmaking on the Stonefields estate, Islington. The parish workhouse in Barnsbury Street in the distance. Watercolour. (London Borough of Islington Local History Centre)

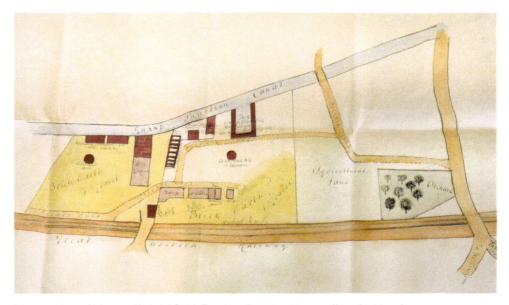

Plate 9. Map of Maynard's brickfield, Dawley. (London Metropolitan Archives)

Plate 10. Kingsland Road, brickfields near Ball's Pond Road. (London Picture Library/London Metropolitan Archives)

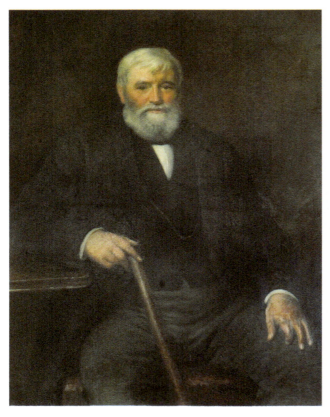

Plate 11. George Smeed (1878) by E.U. Eddis. (Art UK/ Swale Borough Council)

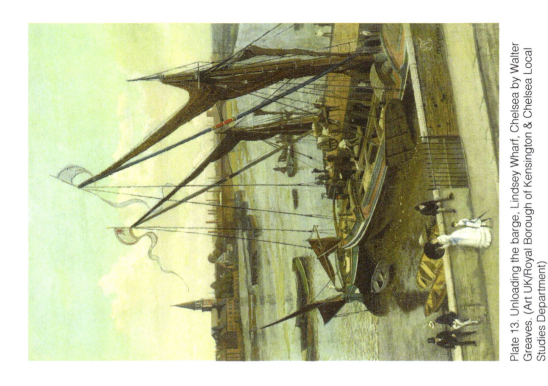

Plate 13. Unloading the barge, Lindsey Wharf, Chelsea by Walter Greaves. (Art UK/Royal Borough of Kensington & Chelsea Local Studies Department)

Plate 12. Garfield House, Sittingbourne, the home of Daniel Wills. (Author's photograph)

Plate 14. A family moulding gang. 'Brickmakers', from W.H. Pyne, *The world in miniature: England, Scotland and Wales* (Ackermann, 1827). (Author's copy)

Plate 15. Young woman pulling a crowding barrow. 'The Brickmaker', from W.H. Pyne, *Costume of Great Britain* (1808). (Author's copy)

Part III: Brickies

Chapter 10

'Hard and inappropriate labour': the brickies at work

In a chapter in *Capital* devoted to the application of machinery in industry and its effects on workers, Karl Marx wrote:

> A classical example of over-work, of hard and inappropriate labour, and of its brutalising effects on the workman from his childhood upwards, is afforded not only by coal-mining and miners generally, but also by tile and brick making, in which industry the recently invented machinery is, in England, used only here and there. Between May and September the work lasts from five in the morning till eight in the evening, and where the drying is done in the open air, it often lasts from four in the morning to nine in the evening.[1]

Marx wrote this in the 1860s, when he was living in London. He did not have direct experience of the workers whose plight he described, but he deployed a wealth of information obtained from his extensive research in the British Museum Reading Room, chiefly from government reports. In this section he quotes from the 5th Report of the Children's Employment Commission, published in 1866.

By contrast, one of the best descriptions of nineteenth-century brickmakers comes not from the pen of Marx or a socially engaged novelist like Charles Dickens, but, surprisingly, from Anthony Trollope. The brickmakers of his fictional Hogglestock could stand for any of the more rural brickfields in the vicinity of London:

> And on the brink of this canal there had sprung up a colony of brickmakers, the nature of the earth in those parts combining with the canal to make brickmaking a suitable trade. The workmen there assembled were not, for the most part, native-born Hogglestockians, or folk descended from Hogglestockian parents. They had come thither from unknown regions, as labourers of that class do come when they are needed. Some young men from that and neighbouring parishes had joined themselves to the colony, allured by wages, and disregarding the menaces of the neighbouring farmers; but they were all in appearance and manners nearer akin to the race of navvies than to ordinary rural labourers. They had a bad name in the country; but it may be that their name was worse than their deserts. The farmers hated them, and consequently they hated the farmers. They had a beershop, and a grocer's shop, and a huxter's shop for their own accommodation, and were consequently vilified by the small old-established tradesmen around them. They got drunk occasionally, but I doubt whether they

---

1   K. Marx, *Capital: a critique of political economy* [1867] (1996), vol. 1, p. 302.

Bricks of Victorian London

drank more than did the farmers themselves on market day. They fought among themselves sometimes, but they forgave each other freely, and seemed to have no objection to black eyes. I fear that they were not always good to their wives; nor were their wives always good to them; but it should be remembered that among the poor, especially when they live in clusters, such misfortunes cannot be hidden as they may be amidst the decent belongings of more wealthy people. That they worked very hard was certain; and it was certain also that very few of their number ever came upon the poor rates. What became of the old brickmakers no one knew.[2]

In his description he touches on many of the issues that we shall encounter in the following pages regarding the manners and behaviour of brickmakers.

There are four aspects of the lives of the brickies that are worth examining. The first is the length of the working day during the moulding season, to which Marx drew attention, and the work discipline that developed from it. The second is the use of subcontracted labour and the skill differences within the moulding gang and the way this was reflected in the wage structure. The third is the seasonality of employment and the fourth the physical demands of the work and the health of the workers.

As we have seen, brickmaking was a seasonal activity, concentrated in a period from April to September when the weather was warm enough and the hours of daylight long enough to allow for work outdoors with minimal protection from the elements. Brickfields contained few, if any, permanent buildings; contemporary descriptions and illustrations suggest that a thatched awning was usually provided to cover the moulding bench, more effective at shielding the sun than excluding the rain. Brickmaking of this kind was inevitably dependent on the vagaries of the English weather. On wet days moulding came to a halt as the newly made bricks in the hacks were vulnerable to damage from heavy rain; one owner estimated that over the course of the season it was possible on average to make bricks on only four days per week.[3] As well as the danger of rain, at the beginning and end of the season, when the days were shorter and the nights colder, there was the threat of frost, which would also affect the drying bricks. One of Mr Rhodes' workers at his Britannia Fields brickfield described going out at 11.30pm on an early April evening to check the bricks and protect them from frost with straw.[4] Although the season usually ended in September, it could be extended a week or two if the weather stayed fine, allowing time lost earlier in the summer to be made up. All in all, the prevailing weather affected both the quantity and quality of that year's make, the fine summer of 1892,

---

2   Brickmakers have only a background role in the Barsetshire novels, standing symbolically for marginalised groups in society. A. Trollope, *The last chronicle of Barset* [1867] (Oxford, 1980), p. 117.

3   Notes of a visit to the Hayes brickfield by the Factory and Workshops Acts Commission, PP 1876, vol. 30, p. 190; Messrs Stroud calculated on the basis of the number of bricks made in a season that it was 'rather less than 4 days a week'. Reports of the Inspectors of Factories, PP 1873, pp. 39–40.

4   *Evening Mail*, 3 April 1844.

'Hard and inappropriate labour'

for example, proving 'exceptionally favourable' compared with the disastrous one of 1879, discussed earlier at p. 70.[5]

The moulding gangs worked during the hours of daylight, the usual hours in the 1860s being from 5am to 8pm. Even these long hours might be exceeded, around mid-summer, when the gangs could work from 4am to 9pm, as Marx had found in the sources he used. The 5th Report of the Children's Employment Commission, mentioned above, described attempts by owners to restrict the hours of work. This was achieved by not allowing the horses turning the pug mills to work before 6am or after 6pm, or by shutting down the steam engines after a similar period. It was also suggested that shorter working hours could lead to an improvement in productivity. Mr Reed, the foreman at a Dawley brickworks, thought that the moulding teams should only need to work a twelve-hour day to achieve an acceptable level of production. In those fields where bricks were made by machinery the hours of work were always less than where they were made by hand.[6] These excessively long working days, when they were worked by children alongside the adults, became the target of attempts to regulate working conditions through legislation. This is a subject to which we will return.

There were breaks in the day for refreshment, but in most cases food and drink were brought to the brickfield, rather than the men going home for them. Some of the stoppages in the day were occasioned by the need to rest the horses that turned the pug mills. The horse was taken off for half an hour at breakfast time and an hour at lunch time; the gang, however, might take a shorter break, making use of clay that had already been 'pugged out' beforehand.[7]

It was understandable, however, that, being paid piece rates, the gang would work longer hours to compensate for time lost to inclement weather, the illness of a key member of the team or impromptu holidays and other forms of ill-discipline.[8] In this respect brickmaking on the gang, or family, system in a largely unmechanised workplace bore many of the characteristics of pre-industrial work discipline, in which working hours were determined not by the owner but by the men themselves. At its most extreme this produced a pattern of 'alternate bouts of intense labour and idleness, and ... heavy weekend drinking'.[9] Working excessive hours one week reduced the men's capacity in the following one; a foreman commented that 'on the Sunday and Monday they are fit for nothing'.[10] This recalls the custom of 'St Mondays' – taking Mondays off – that had been common in domestic industries such as handloom weaving.[11] Irregular holidays were all too frequent in brickmaking too. It was alleged

---

5   *British Clayworker*, January 1893, p. 218; *Daily News*, 5 September 1879.

6   Children's Employment Commission, 5th Report, PP 1866, p. 137.

7   *Ibid.*, pp. 135–6.

8   *Ibid.*, pp. 131.

9   E.P. Thompson, 'Time, work discipline and industrial capitalism', in *Customs in common* (London, 1991), pp. 370–8.

10   Mr Ives to the Children's Employment Commission, 5th Report, PP 1866, p. 136.

11   S. Pollard, *The genesis of modern management: a study of the industrial revolution in Great Britain* (London, 1965), p. 182.

Bricks of Victorian London

that 'Fairs, races, or fetes of any kind within six miles or more of the brickfields are tolerably sure to empty half the stools for the day at least.'[12]

In factories owners or managers used a number of techniques to condition workers to a new kind of work discipline, among which were payment by results and subcontracting.[13] Both these methods were in use within the brick industry, but in circumstances that were unlike the more regulated atmosphere of a factory building. Piece rates did not in themselves impose a discipline on brickmakers, as we have seen, but the widespread use of subcontracting was a key element of workforce management in brickfields.

Within the moulding gang there was a hierarchy, with the moulder being regarded as the most skilled worker as well as the leader of the gang, and the temperer his assistant. Several roles within the gang could be undertaken by boys, girls or women, and this was reflected in the wages that were paid to them – far less than that paid to the adult males. One owner suggested that from a piece rate of 4s 4d per 1000 bricks, the moulder paid the temperer and the off-bearer 1s each, the walk-flatter 4d and the same to the pusher-out (in this case half-paid by the temperer), the pug boy 3d and the barrow loader 2d, leaving himself 1s 5d. On this basis it was thought that the moulder could earn about £3 a week in summer, but during the winter he would be paid only 30s a week for digging out the clay for the following season, as well as any back pence received at the end of the moulding season.[14]

The early decennial censuses tend to place most people involved in the industry into one of two categories: 'brickmakers' and 'brickfield labourers'. There are more of the latter than the former, which suggests that 'brickmaker' equates to 'moulder' and a 'labourer' was any of the other gang members. Later censuses introduce greater differentiation of job titles, with the terms 'moulder' and 'setter' beginning to appear, and occasionally 'brick burner', although the all-purpose term 'brickmaker' still predominates. The other terms, such as barrow loader, temperer and off-bearer, seem to occur more rarely, and their appearance may be the result of the way the census enumerator chose, or was told, to categorise what the men said to him. The Southall census of 1881 was one in which the enumerator reflected the individual roles that people had in the moulding gang: Philip Iron was recorded as a brick moulder, his younger brother Henry as an off-bearer, Thomas Hamborough as a brick loader, George Wasts as a temperer and James Peel as a brick setter. As a sign of the increased use of machinery in brickfields, there were as many as six engine drivers in Southall that year, some of them with the qualification 'stationary'.[15]

Without any kind of formal apprenticeship in the brick industry skills were learnt on the job, and the task that required the most skill and was best paid was undertaken by the moulder. He subcontracted with the employer and was responsible for recruiting and managing his team. In order to maximise the earnings of his gang he needed to ensure the efficiency of his fellow workers. Not everyone who came into the trade

---

12   Children's Employment Commission, 5th Report, PP 1866, p. 131.

13   Daunton, *Progress and poverty*, p. 182; Pollard, *Genesis of modern management*, pp. 189–91.

14   R. Smythe in Children's Employment Commission, 5th Report, PP 1866, p. 138.

15   Census Enumerator's Book, Southall 1881.

'Hard and inappropriate labour'

as a child, perhaps as a pug boy or a barrow loader, could aspire to becoming a moulder, but it would be a mark of independence for a young man to manage his own team, marry and settle down, in the knowledge that moulders had greater job security. Because of the imprecision about job titles in the census books it is difficult to be sure about such progression, but two examples from Northolt seem persuasive. Aged 23, Thomas Evans was boarding with two other labourers at the home of brickmaker Thomas Prince in 1851, but a decade later was a married man, still in Northolt and described as a brickmaker. Thomas Leonard was a 47-year-old labourer in 1851, but a brick setter ten years on. However, from the same censuses, there are examples where the process seems to have gone into reverse: both John Reynolds and John Prince seem to have taken on labouring roles after having been previously described as brickmakers.[16]

The seasonality of brickmaking had many implications. There was only limited job security because of both the annual cycle of production and the fluctuations in demand for bricks from one year to the next. Employers adjusted their production levels through the number of gangs they recruited each spring.[17] This did not, however, result in the kind of casualisation of labour that happened in the London docks, where men were hired by the day. Brickmakers signed on for the season and they were expected to remain until moulding stopped; if individual workers deserted they could find themselves pursued through the courts, since both the moulding gang and the owner lost out if a gang ceased working. A Hammersmith moulder who left early in the 1853 season was apprehended even though he was now working some miles away in Holloway.[18] A firm in Grays, Essex went as far as to offer a five-guinea reward for information about eight of their workers who had absconded, and a newspaper advertisement included a brief physical description of each of them.[19]

Many brickfield labourers were not permanent residents in the brickmaking areas, coming just for the season and lodging with the resident brickmakers. Seasonal workers were, of course, not unusual in rural areas, as there was a significant influx of workers at harvest times, many of them from Ireland. There were even examples of itinerant labourers from continental Europe, such as the Italian labourers in Greenford in 1881.[20] The seasonal workforce in brickmaking, however, was drawn largely from the indigenous population. It is not clear how the summer workers were recruited. There do not seem to have been newspaper advertisements for labourers, and many might not have been able to get sight of newspapers, or read them if they could. It is likely, then, that they returned to areas where they had worked in previous years or went on the tramp through the known brickmaking districts in the hope of finding vacancies. Presumably news of the availability of work was also spread by word of mouth. There was, of course, no guarantee of success, especially in seasons when the

---

16   Census Enumerator's Books, Northolt 1851, 1861.

17   S. Webb and A. Freeman, *Seasonal trades, by various writers* (London, 1912), p. 6.

18   *Standard,* 2 April 1853.

19   *Morning Advertiser,* 2 June 1809.

20   P. Horn, *Life and labour in rural England, 1760–1850* (London, 1987), p. 74; Census Enumerator's Book, Greenford 1881.

Bricks of Victorian London

demand for bricks was low and the manufacturers chose to scale back production. In Dickens' *Bleak House*, Inspector Bucket encounters two couples in a London lodging house. These brickies and their wives have come up from St Albans in search of work, but to no avail, as one of the women explains: 'We walked up yesterday. There's no work down with us at present, but we have done no good by coming here, and shall do none, I expect.'[21]

At the end of the season much of the workforce was dispersed and it was mainly the senior men whose labour was wanted in the winter. There was some tidying up of equipment used that summer; moulds were checked for wear and washed, benches and barrows repaired and put away, machinery such as pug mills cleaned and oiled. Where hacks were covered with wooden louvres these needed to be taken down and stored and the grass on the hack ground kept short by grazing horses on it.[22] Fewer than a third of the employees working in the summer months were required in the winter, when the main task was the digging out and preparation of clay for the following season. On one brickfield in the 1860s only the moulders and a few setters worked between October and Christmas; from Christmas to March the temperers and off-bearers were also employed.[23]

If there was no work at the beginning of the season in one locality, men either moved on to try their luck elsewhere, accepted other kinds of work or became a charge on the poor rate.[24] Any large-scale reduction in activity in a particular area had a marked impact; the complete cessation of brickmaking in Heston in the early 1890s, which may have arisen from the failure of a local business, had, it was said, 'an adverse effect on the parish'.[25]

In rural areas there was little other local winter employment, since agriculture and horticulture had similar seasonal requirements as brickmaking. Once the harvest had been got in, which mobilised the whole population, including women and children, there was much less work until the start of spring sowing. In the winter months there was often much economic distress and a marked increase in the numbers entering the workhouse. This was a cause of some resentment, as one temperer explained:

> I am obliged to walk to and fro the mile in the burning sun, or not, all day long: am often fit to drop and faint; so lear and sickish like, I can't eat a bit of victuals; but if I give out, the whole gang is throwed. I work like a slave all the time, but as soon as the day comes that I takes home my horse for the last time, 'cos work is struck, there's ne'er another job for me. I may beg, starve, or go to the Union for all as my employer cares.[26]

---

21   C. Dickens, *Bleak House* (London, 1853), chapter xxii.

22   'Winter in summer season yards', *British Clayworker*, October 1896, p. 165.

23   Evidence of Mr Smythe. Children's Employment Commission, 5th Report, PP 1866, p. 138.

24   Inwood, *A history of London*, pp. 473–5.

25   *British Clayworker*, September 1896, p. 152.

26   Unnamed workman, reported by Rev J. Dennett, Children's Employment Commission, 5th Report, PP 1866, pp. 148–9.

'Hard and inappropriate labour'

There were a few ways to provide some protection against winter distress. Owners hoped that brickmakers saved enough money from their good summer wages to allow them to get by during the winter, supplementing this with the back pence deducted from their wages each week and paid at the end of the season. Some had gardens or kept pigs to supplement their income: at West Drayton a pig was known as the 'brickies' bank'.[27] A Southall brickmaster suggested that in the gardens attached to his cottages the men could grow ten to twenty sacks of potatoes, and Mr Smeed said his men were able to grow potatoes and other vegetables on spare land he provided.[28]

Even those who had employment on the brickfields in the winter months could find themselves stopped from working by adverse weather, especially when the ground was frozen solid, leaving them without means to support themselves. In the winter of 1879, for example, a large number of brickmakers applied to the Uxbridge Board of Guardians for poor relief. They asked for outdoor relief – in effect, cash payments – but the authorities only offered admission to the workhouse, where the men would be employed breaking stones at 1s 6d a day. It was said that a number of their children were suffering from measles.[29]

Those who could not get winter employment in the brickfields had to seek work elsewhere. Henry Mayhew interviewed a destitute brickworker in a hostel in January 1850 who had been working at a seasonal yard at Northfleet in Kent until November and had then gone on the tramp following leads about where there might be work, taking him to Peterborough, Grimsby, Grantham, the Isle of Dogs, Portsmouth and the London Docks. By the time Mayhew encountered him he was penniless, and admitted that 'Not many of the brickmakers save. They work from 17 to 18 hours every day when its fine, and that requires a good bit to eat and drink. The brickmakers most of them drink hard.'[30]

It has long been known that a major source of employment for brickmakers in the off-season was in gasworks.[31] Gasworks were one of the few enterprises that had a substantial demand for largely unskilled labour in the winter months, when the demand for gas lighting increased significantly, creating a load three times that experienced in the summer.[32] For much of the nineteenth century the retorts in gasworks were stoked by hand, and brickfield labourers, used to heavy repetitive work and long shifts, were well placed to supply this labour demand, as this report confirms.

> Hand brickmaking requires the same characteristics of good physique and capacity for sustained strenuous effort as does gas stoking. In the old days when brickmaking and gas stoking were largely manual trades, there appears to have

---

27 G.F.L. Packwood and A.H. Cox, *West Drayton during the nineteenth century* (West Drayton, 1967), p. 67.

28 Children's Employment Commission, 5th Report, PP 1866, pp. 138, 143.

29 *Illustrated Police News*, 20 December 1879.

30 Letter XXVI (Tuesday 15 January 1850) in H. Mayhew, *The* Morning Chronicle *survey of labour and the poor: the metropolitan districts*, vol. 2 (Firle, 1981), pp. 316–18.

31 Webb and Freeman, *Seasonal trades*, p. 160.

32 E.J. Hobsbawm, *Labouring men: studies in the history of labour* (London, 1964), p. 161.

Bricks of Victorian London

been a regular interchange of men between the gasworks and the brickfields, the dovetailing being almost perfect in point of seasons.[33]

Kent brickmakers could go to the gasworks on the east side of London. Harry Matthews' father, who worked at a Faversham brickworks at the end of the nineteenth century, told him that he

used to go up to Woolwich gas-house, Greenwich gas-house and get a job in there for the winter. But you'd got to be in the know and in line to get them jobs. Sheerness too, they always wanted men over there. You could get a job in them in the winter when the gas was wanted more. Most times night work it was.[34]

Other jobs for Kent brickmakers in the off season included potato digging, hopping, wurzel pulling, corn threshing or casual labour unloading barges at the creeks. If all else failed they were forced to go to the workhouse and asked for tickets that could be exchanged for food.[35]

There would also be opportunities for brickmakers in many places on the outskirts of London, as gasworks were generally sited close to larger residential centres to meet domestic demand. There were around twenty within a five-mile radius of the centre of the capital, which could accommodate a large number of brick labourers. Even in a largely rural area like west Middlesex there were gasworks at the two main urban centres, Southall and Uxbridge, which were opened in 1869 and the 1830s respectively. The latter's proprietor in 1838 was James Stacy, described as an engineer and wharfinger in 1845, and almost certainly the owner of a brickfield in Hillingdon as well.[36]

It is, therefore, debatable whether brickmaking should be thought of as a summer alternative for gas workers, or the other way about, or whether these workers were 'men of two trades'.[37] Eventually some brickmakers made the transition to full-time employment in gasworks; a study of one Southall family shows a move over time from Waring's brickfield to the local gasworks, prompted perhaps by the decline of local brickmaking. Of six members of the family working in brick manufacture in the census of 1881, five were employed at the gasworks in 1901.[38] The close connection between brickmaking and the gas industry became institutionalised during the 1890s through the formation of trade unions, particularly the Birmingham-based Amalgamated Society of Gasworkers, Brickmakers and General Labourers in 1889 and the Gasworkers and General Labourers Union formed in London the same year, which recruited heavily in

---

33 F. Popplewell, 'Seasonal fluctuations in employment in the gas industry', *Journal of the Royal Statistical Society*, 74/7 (June 1911), p. 706.

34 M. Winstanley, *Life in Kent at the turn of the century* (London, 1978), p. 182.

35 *Ibid.*, pp. 182–3.

36 *Victoria County History. Middlesex, vol. 4*, pp. 47, 86.

37 Popplewell, 'Seasonal fluctuations', p. 706.

38 Ex inf. Andrew Snelling.

'Hard and inappropriate labour'

the brickfields.[39] Different types of winter work were available in other districts. In the Medway area, for example, cement manufacture was also a major industry and, unlike brickmaking, was a year-round activity.[40]

Quantifying the seasonal movement of labourers presents problems. The decennial census, which is so useful for analysing occupation in the nineteenth century, has major disadvantages for investigating seasonal employment, as it records a snapshot taken on a particular day in the year. The census was usually taken in April, and thus at the divide between winter and summer jobs, but an exception was that of 1841, which was taken on 7 June in the middle of the hay harvest and the brickmaking season.[41] In that year the Northolt enumerator noted that 'haymakers and mowers, with brickmakers, will make an increase of at least twenty-five persons' over the resident population of about 600.[42] In 1851, when the census was taken in April, the enumerator for Yiewsley observed that the recorded population of brickmakers was 200, 'but during the brickmaking season the temporary residents would be nearly three hundred in a busy time'.[43] There is occasionally some direct evidence. In Rutters' yard at Crayford in Kent in 1865, 382 men, women and children were employed in the moulding season, but only thirty-three in the winter: twenty-five men and eight boys.[44]

While some families remained in the same parish for much of their lives and stayed with the same employer, others were more mobile, following the best opportunities for work. Tracking brickmaking families through the census reveals that many families moved from one brickfield area to another, sometimes in adjacent parishes, or across the London brickmaking area and even further afield. They might also encounter the same owners for, as we have seen, some of the owners had brickfields in more than one district.

Despite the uncertain nature of their work and their sometimes itinerant lives, many brickmakers were married with families. A few examples may illustrate this. Henry Dodd owned a large number of cottages on his brickfield in Yeading, between Hayes and Northolt, and the inhabitants of these cottages in 1861 were almost certainly his employees. Among them was William Wellman. He had been born in Pentonville and his children had been born in Islington, St Pancras and Heston; only the youngest two were born in Hayes. A neighbour was Edward Sherwood, born in Kingsland (Hackney), with children born in Chelsea, Kensington and Hammersmith. Joseph Newman also hailed from Hackney, and his children had been born in Battle Bridge (King's Cross), Kentish Town, Botwell (Hayes) and Hammersmith, with only the youngest (aged three months) born in Yeading. William Sage originally came from Kent, and he appears to

---

39 For trade unionism in the brick industry see chapter 15; H.A. Clegg, A. Fox and A.F. Thompson, *A history of British trade unions since 1889: vol. 1 1889–1910* (London, 1964), p. 65.

40 R. Samuel (ed.), *Miners, quarrymen and saltworkers* (London, 1977), p. 5.

41 M. Drake, 'The census 1801–1891', in E.A. Wrigley (ed.), *Nineteenth-century society: essays in the use of quantitative methods for the study of social data* (Cambridge, 1972), p. 29.

42 Census Enumerator's Book, Northolt 1841.

43 Samuel, *Miners, quarrymen, and saltworkers*, p. 5.

44 Statistics from H.W. Lord from his visit to Rutters' brickfield. Children's Employment Commission, 5th Report, PP 1866, p. 146.

Bricks of Victorian London

have started his brickmaking career there; through the birthplace of his children we can trace his movements to Sittingbourne, Gravesend, Milton (near Sittingbourne), Hoxton, Norwood Green and Hayes.[45] On Smythe's brickfield in 1871 occupants included the Brown family. Charles the father had been born in Marylebone and married a woman from Heston, where his eldest child had been born. The remaining seven children had been born in Hillingdon, Plaistow (Essex), Hayes, Egham (Surrey), Sunbury (Middlesex), Isleworth and Hayes.[46]

The most travelled of the Hayes inhabitants in that year was the Reed family. George Wood Reed came from West Drayton, but emigrated in 1849 to Australia, where he initially made bricks but later took a share in an alluvial gold drift. Returning to England in 1861 with his family, he became the foreman of a brickfield in Yiewsley, before moving to a similar position at Botwell, to the same brickfield and same house he had occupied before he emigrated. His eldest son had been born in Hayes before the emigration, two other sons had been born in Australia, and by 1871 there were two further children who had been born in Hayes. His eldest son, by now 22 years old, was also a brickfield foreman, a role held by three generations of the family.[47]

These examples should not obscure the fact that some brick workers were recruited from local villages or from neighbouring areas. Another of Henry Dodd's employees, James Fields, had been born in Hayes and had married a local girl, and his children had been born there with the exception of the youngest, who had been born in the neighbouring parish of Harlington.[48] In Burham in Kent in 1861 the majority of brickmakers were local or from other places in Kent relatively close by, such as Maidstone and Aylesford. In Murston, near Sittingbourne, the workforce in 1871 came from a range of towns in Kent as far away as Dover, Deal and Canterbury, but there were no brickmakers born in Essex or Middlesex. In Crayford in Kent in 1881 most of the workers were local or from other towns in Kent, predominantly along the south side of the Thames Estuary, such as Dartford, Erith and Northfleet. However, here there was a handful of men who had been born in Middlesex or London itself. Great Wakering, in Essex, the site of one of Rutters' brickfields in 1891, drew a sizeable number of its workers from Middlesex, where the Rutters also had brickfields, suggesting that the firm may have encouraged the transfer. Altogether twelve different places in Middlesex are recorded, but there were also men from Kent, Buckinghamshire and even Cornwall.[49]

Most of the brickmakers working in the London area seem to have come from the south of England. There seems to have been little immigrant labour in brickfields. Irish emigrants seem to not to have been drawn to brickmaking, despite the fact that an estimated 46,000 Irish arrived in London in the 1840s as a result of the Famine,

---

45   Census Enumerator's Book, Hayes 1861.

46   Census Enumerator's Book, Hayes 1871.

47   *Ibid.*; Reed, 'Reminiscences of a Middlesex brickmaker', pp. 13–15. See also excerpts from A.H. Reed, *An autobiography* (Wellington, 1967), in *Journal of the Hayes and Harlington Local History Society*, 13 (Spring 1976), pp. 5–8.

48   Census Enumerator's Book, Hayes 1861.

49   Census Enumerators' Books, Burham 1861; Murston 1871; Crayford 1881; Great Wakering 1891.

'Hard and inappropriate labour'

and smaller numbers came in later decades.[50] Occasionally workers from the near continent came to work in brickfields, and in the 1891 Census there were one Dutchman, one Belgian, three Frenchmen, five Germans and a Spaniard.[51] In 1883 the family business of L. Normand and Co., originally from Hesdin, near Calais, leased a brickfield in Heston.[52]

Although the moulding gangs operated with a degree of autonomy, there was a need for supervision of the whole brickfield, including the setters, horsekeepers and enginemen. This might be undertaken by the owner, but often a foreman managed the day-to-day operations. 'Foreman in brickfields' is an occupation that appears in Census returns. We have already encountered George Reed. In Southall in 1881, Welsh-born Benjamin Chandler probably worked for John Minter, a 'brick manufacturer employing 100 men and boys' who was living a few doors along the same street. A clerk might be recruited to handle the paperwork, tabulating the number of bricks made, processing orders and issuing invoices. Peter Blaker was described as a 'commercial clerk (bricks)' in Crayford in 1881 and the 20-year-old son of Francis Newell, a Southall brickmaker and landlord of the Hamborough Tavern, was described as 'assistant in brickfield', suggesting that he may have played a similar role for his father.[53]

Once a man was established as a foreman in a brickfield it was possible for his children to follow him into that role. William Reed (b.1796 at Heston) was only a labourer at the time of his wedding in 1822, but by 1851 he was the foreman of a brickfield in Hillingdon.[54] His family of ten children gave rise to a dynasty of brickfield foremen and managers. Eldest son Henry W. (b.1823) evidently spent time working in Crayford between 1848 and 1850, but by 1861 he was manager of Smythe's brickfield at Heston, and ten years later he was manager of a different brickfield in Hayes.[55] Henry's youngest brother John (b.1844) spent some time around 1870 as manager at the Rutters' brickfield in Great Wakering, Essex, but later he was back in the Cowley district at Heston.[56] In the next generation, Henry's eldest son, William (b.1846), worked for a period in Hendon in the late 1860s, where two of his children were born. By 1878 he was back in the Cowley district as the licensee of the Hamborough Arms in Hayes, and in 1891 he was described as an innkeeper and manager of a brickfield. By 1901 he seems to have acquired his own brick business, and now lived a few miles away in the desirable suburb of Ealing.[57] His brother George (b.1849) became manager of a brickfield in South Benfleet in Essex, but he had returned to west Middlesex by 1891.[58] In the fourth generation two sons of William H. were at times

---

50 Inwood, *A history of London*, p. 412; Census Enumerator's Book, Burham 1861.

51 *British Clayworker*, November 1893, p. 150.

52 LMA Acc. 405/7.

53 Census Enumerators' Books, Crayford 1881, Southall 1881.

54 Census Enumerators' Books, Hillingdon 1841, 1851; Baptism Register, Heston 27 May 1825.

55 Census Enumerators' Books, Heston 1851, Hayes 1861.

56 Census Enumerators' Books, Great Wakering 1871, Heston 1881.

57 Census Enumerators' Books, Hayes 1881, 1891, Ealing 1901.

58 Census Enumerators' Books, South Benfleet 1881, Hillingdon 1891.

Bricks of Victorian London

clerks in brickfields, Frederick Charles (b.1872) in 1891 and Albert (b.1878) in 1901, either working for their father or at another local brickfield.[59]

Larger concerns had a manager, whose name appeared as the business contact in commercial directory entries. John Andrews fulfilled this role for Smeed, Dean for many years. He had started out as a pug boy, graduating to be a foreman for a contractor on the LCDR and then for George Smeed. He worked for the firm for forty-three years, and for much of that time was a director of the company.[60] Henry Juniper managed Rutters' brickfield at Great Wakering in the 1880s, and still held that position in 1901, when he was 70 years old. Born at Stock in Kent, he also started as a brickfield labourer, being employed in Heston in 1861. His son John was born there, and probably worked with his father at Great Wakering as a clerk.[61]

Brickmaking made physical demands on all its workers and especially on children.[62] Brickmakers undertook physical, repetitive tasks for long hours during the moulding season, and needed to be fairly strong, or at least develop stamina.[63] We might imagine the impact that weeks of intensive labour had on the brickies, but doctors, who were beginning to take an interest in what we would now call occupational health, held that brickmaking was a largely benign activity. The main reasons behind this conclusion were that the brickmakers were not working with toxic or dust-producing materials, and that their work took place in the open air. In one of the earliest inquiries of this kind, Charles Thackrah stated:

> Brickmakers, with the advantage of full muscular exercise in the open air, are subject to the annoyance of cold and wet. These, however, appear little, or not at all injurious. Brickmakers, half-naked, and with their bare feet in the puddle all day, are not more liable to catarrh, pneumonia and rheumatism, than men whose work is under cover and dry. Of twenty-two brickmakers of whom we have made personal inquiry, only one had been affected with rheumatism, or could state himself subject to any disease. All declare that neither rheumatism, nor any inflammatory complaint is frequent among them. Individuals of great age are found at the employ [sic].[64]

To our modern view this judgement seems over-optimistic, and Trollope's description of the fictional brickmaker Hoggett seems more persuasive; despite suffering from rheumatism he nevertheless went to work, like many others did, otherwise he and his family would be in want.

---

59 Census Enumerators' Books, Hayes 1891, Ealing 1901.

60 Perks, *George Bargebrick*, p. 37.

61 Census Enumerators' Books, Heston 1861; Great Wakering 1881, 1901, 1911.

62 The effect on children's health and wellbeing is discussed in Chapter 14.

63 Ten blind and thirty deaf and dumb workers were employed in brickfields across England and Wales in 1891. *British Clayworker*, November 1893, p. 150.

64 C.T. Thackrah, *Effects of the principal arts, trades and professions ... on health and longevity* (London & Leeds, 1832), pp. 14–15.

'Hard and inappropriate labour'

> The best treatment for rheumatism might be to stay away from the brick-field on a rainy day; but if so, there would be no money to keep the pot boiling, and Hoggett would certainly go to the brick-field, rheumatism and all, as long as his limbs would carry him there.[65]

A pioneer of public health and of the use of medical statistics, Dr William Guy produced a comparative study of the health of dustmen, bricklayers and brickmakers in the 1840s. He examined twenty-eight brickmakers employed by Henry Dodd, either at Hackney or Yeading. The eldest was 68 years old and only two were under 20; mainly, they were men in their twenties or thirties. Guy concluded that scavengers (comprising nightmen, street sweepers and dustmen) were the healthiest of the three groups he studied and least likely to be absent from work because of sickness, but he didn't speculate why this might be so, and conceded that more research was necessary to understand his observations. However, despite listing a range of specific conditions from which individual brickmakers suffered, he classified 82 per cent of those he met as being in 'robust' or 'good' health, although he identified that six of them suffered from rheumatism, a higher percentage than he found in the other two groups.[66]

The same spirit of investigation prompted the Medical Officer of Health for Islington to undertake in 1864 a comparative study of the health of those involved in sixteen kinds of largely male occupations and five kinds of largely female ones. He placed brickmakers third highest in his list of male occupations in relation to death rates, at 176 per annum per 10,000 population, and with a life expectancy of thirty-eight years, while commenting that 'they appear to come close upon the average for England generally'. His comments echo a familiar tale of high wages undermined by a lifestyle in which alcohol featured heavily.

> Brickmakers obtain good wages, but are very improvident; more than half the deaths in my table took place in the workhouse. They suffer from their customary habitations, much as labourers do; and acute chest infections carried off a large proportion. On the other hand, their working in places open to air, and with materials moist, and so not giving off dust, give them a remarkable immunity from phthisis [tuberculosis]. Were these people habitually temperate and provident, their trade would prove, I am convinced, one of the most salubrious of those followed in their rank of life.[67]

---

65 Trollope, *The last chronicle of Barset*, p. 675.

66 His findings are open to objection on two grounds: first that his sample size of brickmakers was smaller than for the other two groups, and secondly that his study had been undertaken to counter suggestions that working with filth, as the nightmen, scavengers and dustmen did, was necessarily injurious to health. His views, like Thackrah's, reinforced the prevailing view that working outdoors was inherently healthier than working in badly ventilated buildings. W.A. Guy, 'On the health of nightmen, scavengers and dustmen', *Journal of the Statistical Society of London*, 11/1 (March 1848), pp. 72–81.

67 Islington Vestry, Medical Officer of Health, *Report of the sanitary condition of the parish of St Mary, Islington during the year 1864* (London, 1865), p. 14 and table XIV.

Bricks of Victorian London

There were dangers from repeated physical actions – what would later be termed repetitive strain injuries – by all the members of a moulding gang, but there were more immediate threats from accidents, especially involving machinery.[68] Trailing cables linking stationary engines to pug mills and chalk mills were a particular hazard. In 1879 James Gillham, a chalk washer on Henry Kyezor's brickfield in Hounslow, was caught up by the mechanism turning the chalk mill and thrown into it, sustaining injuries that kept him away from work for eight weeks. He claimed compensation from the owner and Kyezor agreed to pay him £10, a sum less than the loss of wages he had sustained.[69] In the same year, at an inquest into the death of a girl who had been playing on a brickfield where her father worked, and where her two playfellows were badly injured when they became caught up in the shafting that drove the mills, the jury recommended that the whole of the shafting should be covered in.[70] In 1885, in one of the worst incidents of its kind, a boiler exploded on a brickfield in Beckenham in Kent, causing the death of five men.[71]

Brickfields could have hidden health hazards. In 1866, during the last cholera outbreak to affect Britain, a brickmaker and his son living in a newly built house in Kentish Town, succumbed to the disease, despite there being no other cases in the near neighbourhood. The local Medical Officer was at a loss to explain how they had contracted the disease, although he did comment that the house was badly built and damp, but he did offer another explanation arising from the fact that both worked at the same brickfield: 'Another supposition occurred to my mind, that this man and boy working in the fields where there are open sewers, may have introduced into their stomachs, either from their hands at their meals, or by drinking water, some sewage matter.'[72]

In fact, this raises the wider question of what if any sanitary provisions were made on brickfields. Inspections of brickfields by factory or nuisance inspectors do not seem to comment on facilities for the workers, and there were no stipulations about what provision should be made in the factory acts themselves. In all probability it is likely that very little in fact was done to provide the men with washing and toilet facilities. A supply of water was always needed as part of the brickmaking process but how it was provided is not usually described and there must be doubts about its potability. Some brickfields would have had natural streams crossing them, or ponds, and the digging out of clay created depressions in the ground that would have filled up with water. Wells could be sunk if necessary. Many brickfields in the Cowley district were close to the canal, and water may have been drawn from it for use around the brickfield. We have already noted the dangers posed by ponds on brickfields.

Engravings and early photographs of brickmakers at work suggest that the clothes they wore were typical of the clothing of working people of the period, and no special protective clothing was thought necessary for most activities on a brickfield

---

68   A legal right to compensation for injuries received at work was established in 1880.

69   *Middlesex Chronicle*, 2 August 1879.

70   The brickfield was the Beckenham and Penge brickworks. *Kentish Mercury*, 16 August 1879.

71   *Standard*, 14 February 1885.

72   St Pancras Vestry, *Eleventh annual report of the Medical Officer of Health for the year 1866* (London, 1867), p. 5.

'Hard and inappropriate labour'

Figure 10.1. The Crockett family at Starveall, West Drayton (*c*.1897). (A. Beasley/P. Sherwood)

(Figures 10.1 and 10.2). The one area where the workers might have needed to protect themselves was when unloading hot bricks from a kiln, when gloves, or 'cotts' would be worn. Cotts were fashioned from offcuts of leather or similar materials.[73]

Despite the hard and repetitive nature of their work, brickmakers worked on into their fifties and sixties. In this respect they were no different from other members of the labouring classes in the period before the introduction of old age pensions; you continued working until you were physically unable to do so, unless your children were

---

73 *Morning Post*, 23 September 1875; in the twentieth century they might also be made from the inner tubes of lorry tyres. Haynes, *Brick*, p. 269.

Bricks of Victorian London

Figure 10.2. Setters at a Crayford brickfield. (London Borough of Bexley, Local Studies and Archive Centre)

able to support you. It was said that in 1869 some 80 per cent of men applying to the Uxbridge Union for relief were brickmakers.[74] The census rarely records anyone who seems to have retired from the industry, so a census entry of 'formerly brickfield labourer' is unusual.[75] Inevitably, some brickmakers ended up in the workhouse, usually as result of old age and infirmity. In the Hillingdon Union workhouse in 1871 there were eighteen sometime brick workers aged 50 or over, of which seven were in their seventies and the oldest 80. However, there were younger men as well, and some teenagers. One 17-year old was with his widowed father and his siblings, and a 14-year old was with his mother and siblings. Emma Odell, a 22-year old, whose occupation was recorded as 'brickfield work', seems to have been in and out of the workhouse, and was now looking after her illegitimate baby, which had been born there. There were fewer ex-brick workers in the same workhouse in 1861, only seven, suggesting 1871 had been a tough year in the trade. Surprisingly, then, there were very few brickmakers in the Faversham Union workhouse in 1871 and 1881, only two in each year.[76]

Many brickmakers lived in accommodation rented to them by their employees, so the next chapter considers their home life and the conditions in their cottages.

---

74 G. Smith, *The cry of the children from the brickyards of England: a statement and appeal, with remedy*, 4th edn (London, 1871), p. 11.
75 He was 69 years old. Census Enumerator's Book, Southall 1881.
76 Census Enumerators' Books, Hillingdon 1861, 1871, Faversham 1871, 1881.

Chapter 11

'The perfection of untidiness, dirt and disease': the brickies at home

The most familiar description of a nineteenth-century brickmaker's home occurs in Dickens' *Bleak House* when his protagonist Esther visits a group of workers' cottages near St Albans. Dickens satirises the kind of middle-class meddling in the lives of the poor, represented by Esther's companion Mrs Pardiggle, and the recipients' reaction to it. To her, their living conditions were a reflection of their moral and social degradation, out of which she wished to lift them, but they are resistant to her entreaties.

> I was glad when we came to the brickmaker's house; though it was one of a cluster of wretched hovels in a brick-field, with pigsties close to the broken windows and miserable little gardens before the doors growing nothing but stagnant pools. Here and there, an old tub was put to catch the droppings of rain-water from a roof, or they were banked up with mud into a little pond like a large dirt-pie. At the doors and windows some men and women lounged or prowled about, and took little notice of us except to laugh to one another or to say something as we passed, about gentlefolks minding their own business and not troubling their heads and muddying their shoes with coming to look after other people's ... Mrs Pardiggle conducted us into a cottage at the farthest corner, the ground floor room of which we nearly filled.[1]

The scene is nicely caught by Dickens' illustrator, 'Phiz' (Hablot Knight Browne) (Figure 11.1), but we do not know if this description is based on direct experience or owes more to Dickens' imagination. The home described is chaotic and the husband an irreligious drunk, but we should not assume that all brickmakers lived like this. Nevertheless, it is likely that many brickmakers' homes were poorly built and overcrowded. The small space of the interior had to be put to a multiplicity of uses, an experience shared by many working-class households.

The housing needs of brickmakers differed, depending on where the brickfield was situated. In towns, they could no doubt find a home, temporary just for the season, or longer term if they were employed all year round, in lodgings in the neighbouring streets. In more rural communities it was common for the owner of the brickfield to provide cottages for his employees. These might be designed for short-term use, when a brickworks was opened to serve only one piece of construction work, and be built of timber, creating shanty towns like those provided for navvies building the railways. But generally brickfield cottages were of more permanent construction, expected to last for several decades, and sometimes passing from one employer to another. In the

---

1   Dickens, *Bleak House,* chapter VIII.

Bricks of Victorian London

Figure 11.1. Brickmaker's house from the illustrations to Dickens' *Bleak House* by 'Phiz' (Hablot Knight Browne) (1852–3).

1860s Mr Smythe refers to his older properties as three roomed 'huts', whereas his newer ones were 'comfortable cottages', a distinction reflected in a higher rent.[2]

Groups of cottages are identifiable in many brickmaking districts. Sales, leases and rate books often refer to them and they appear as addresses in the census and can be seen adjacent to brickfields on Ordnance Survey Maps. Heron & Rutter paid insurance premiums on four cottages at North Hyde, Heston, probably in the 1840s (Figure 11.2).[3] There were many workers' houses in Southall; the Southall Brickmaking Company, which may have employed as many as 150 people in the 1860s, owned thirty-two alone.[4] In the same period Smythe built twelve cottages for his moulders and their families and proposed, he claimed, building a similar number to accommodate temperers and off-bearers.[5] Waring Brothers had more than twenty dwellings and brickmakers occupied the sixteen Hamborough cottages, also in Southall, in 1871.[6]

---

2   Rents were 2s 6d a week for the huts and 3s 6d for the cottages, at a time when his moulders could earn £3 in summer and 30s in winter. Children's Employment Commission, 5th Report, PP 1866, p. 138.

3   LMA Acc. 328/31 undated policy document.

4   Children's Employment Commission, 5th Report, PP 1866, p. 137; Southall Rate Book 1863.

5   Children's Employment Commission, 5th Report, PP 1866, p. 137.

6   Census Enumerator's Book, Southall 1871.

'The perfection of untidiness, dirt and disease'

Figure 11.2. Brickfield cottages at North Hyde, Heston. (London Borough of Ealing Local History Centre)

The picture was similar in other parts of the Cowley district. Henry Dodd's cottages at Yeading later passed into the ownership of Thomas Clayton and sixteen of these one-storey dwellings survived until 1897, when they were pulled down.[7] In Northolt the New Patent Brick Company built the twelve 'Invicta cottages' in the 1890s, some of which are still standing.[8] Many sets of cottages bore the name of the brickmaker who owned or leased them: Stroud's Row and Stroud's Cottages in Southall; Stacy's Cottages in Stavehall Road, Hillingdon; Rigby's Row in Dawley.[9] Samuel Tildesley owned a number of cottages bearing his name, including a group with the address of Tildesley's Bottom.[10] Odell Ltd owned thirty cottages at Yeading, six at Northolt and nineteen at Dawley.[11] There is visual evidence in the plans that accompany leases. Maynard's brickfield at Harlington includes eight dwellings on the field and six cottages are shown on the map of Samuel Pocock's West Drayton works in 1882.[12]

---

7   *Middlesex Chronicle*, 23 January 1897.
8   TNA IR58/29130.
9   Census Enumerator's Book, Southall 1871; TNA IR58/39628/444–457; IR58/39732/919–920.
10 LMA Acc. 328/59; Census Enumerator's Book, Southall 1881.
11 TNA BT31/5649/39405.
12 LMA Acc. 969/69; LMA DL/D/L/028/Ms12335.

Bricks of Victorian London

The owner of the brickfield did not necessarily own the freehold of his cottages. Quite often he only leased them and then rented them to his workers. Rigby's Row was owned by the de Salis family but leased by Thomas Clayton in 1899, whose company was responsible for their upkeep and repairs.[13] In Hayes Edward Shackle owned the thirteen units of Austin's Row, named after Henry Austin who leased the adjacent brickfield, and a further ten in Pantile Row in the 1860s. Austin's Row still stood in 1897.[14]

By contrast with the Cowley district, at Crayford in Kent the workers at the brickfields seem to have lived alongside workers in other local industries and tradesmen, and there were only two 'Rutters' Cottages' in 1881, one of them occupied by the works foreman.[15]

The location of brickfield cottages close to the brickfield often meant that they were outside the historic village centres and might remain isolated or be absorbed in their subsequent expansion. This may have contributed to a sense of distance between the brickies and the other residents of the district, and reinforced the prejudice against them. This sense of alienation, however, can be overstated. As well as being concentrated in these rows of tied cottages, brickfield employees can be found living or boarding in houses in the adjacent villages. It is also the case that not all the brickmakers were incomers to the areas where the brickfields were located: some had been born in the areas in which they worked and would have kinship and friendship links with other people who lived there.

In a few cases a group of brickfield cottages could be the basis of a new settlement. The village of Eccles, near Aylesford in Kent, was largely built to house the workers of Thomas Cubitt's brickfield at Burham. Identifying a need for housing for the workers, some of whom had relocated from Cubitt's now closed brickfield in the Caledonian Road, Thomas Abbot erected twenty-two terraced cottages in the 1850s; further cottages were later added, together with a school in 1865.[16]

Sittingbourne brickmaker Smeed, Dean built houses at Murston, together with a shop and post office, in the 1920s owning 303 cottages that housed many of its 1000 workers.[17] An undated photograph of the company's cottages shows terraces of two-storey brick-built dwellings, as you might expect a brickmaker could readily provide (Figure 11.3). However, some of Smeed's earlier dwellings in Murston Row were said to have been built without indoor facilities for cooking, which had to be carried out on open fireplaces in the back yard. The accidental death of a child in one of these fireplaces in 1861 prompted a local newspaper to campaign about the squalor in which Smeed's labourers lived. Thirteen years later the Sittingbourne Inspector of Nuisances complained about the insanitary conditions of these homes, since the water supply for 174 dwellings came from just four wells.[18] These cottages, whatever

---

13   TNA IR58/39628/444–457.

14   London Borough of Hillingdon, Museum and Archives Service Hayes Valuation, 1865, 1897.

15   Census Enumerator's Book, Crayford 1881.

16   Hann, *The Medway valley*, p. 111.

17   Perks, *George Bargebrick*, p. 33.

18   *East Kent Gazette*, 22 and 29 June 1861.

'The perfection of untidiness, dirt and disease'

Figure 11.3. Smeed, Dean's houses at Murston. (Sittingbourne Museum)

their shortcomings, may have been preceded by even more basic accommodation. In 1851 it was estimated that over 5000 people existed in the 'shanty' towns of Milton, Sittingbourne and Abbey Fields at Faversham.[19]

The proximity of their houses to the brickfield was no doubt highly desirable for workers whose summer hours were extremely long, but it also gave the employer a degree of control over his labour force, something clearly in the mind of George Smeed:

> All who work in my fields live in cottages which I have built for them; the men bind themselves under agreement for the year; they are fined 5s if they leave their work without a good excuse; the fines go to a general sick fund; I also give each of them a plot of spare land, on which they grow potatoes and other vegetables. By these and other similar means I think I manage to attract steady men and to keep them; I have, of course, from time to time under pressure from want of hands had to take whomever I could get without very close inquiries, but then I can weed out the bad ones by degrees.[20]

---

19 Perks, *George Bargebrick*, p. 25.
20 Children's Employment Commission, 5th Report, PP 1866, p. 143.

Bricks of Victorian London

For tenants of tied accommodation, the loss of one's job, whether as a result of real or alleged misbehaviour or through downsizing by the employer when demand was low, also created homelessness. This was an issue faced by brickmakers involved in strike action in the 1890s, when there was a real threat, sometimes carried out, of evicting men for non-payment of rent. By offering tied accommodation the employer ensured that a proportion of the wages he paid out returned to him in the form of rent and, to make sure the rent was paid, in some cases the owners deducted it from the men's wages at the end of the week.[21]

Some seasonal workers found lodgings in local public houses. Not all the boarders were young single men. Living at the Wool Pack public house in Hayes in 1861 were the landlady's son and two boarders aged 49 and 61, all three of them brickfield labourers.[22] In 1851 an unmarried man originally from Leamington in Warwickshire was boarding at the Prince of Wales at Norwood Green, Southall, while James Macdonald and his wife lodged at the Bridge House in Botwell and James Pizzey, born locally and aged 52, was lodging at the Red Cow public house.[23]

More commonly, however, seasonal labourers boarded with a brickmaking family, and there was an assumption that a moulder would provide accommodation for members of his gang. For example, in their cottage on Dodd's brickfield in 1861 the Payne family boarded four brickfield labourers aged from 13 to 58. In the same year in Northolt the Doman family, whose three teenage boys were all brickmakers, also lodged a man and two teenagers, who appear to have been a father and his sons, as well as a widower of 68.[24] Boarders, for all the inconvenience of their presence in a crowded cottage and their noisy bachelor ways, paid for their keep, but they were often resented by the wives who had to cater for them. A moulder's wife complained that boarders she encountered were 'a filthy, drunken, lousy lot, and that's the truth, the most of them; at all events those that don't live in the neighbourhood, but just come down for the summer work and then go off, and are never seen again'.[25]

Like other working-class housing of this period, when families with five or more children were not uncommon, brickfield cottages with only two or three rooms and sometimes only a single storey would often have been overcrowded. This raised sanitary concerns, but also moral ones, with shared bedrooms and a lack of privacy resulting in undesirable intimacies, a situation exacerbated when boarders were unattached young men. So, despite their ambivalent feelings about employing their own children in the brickfields, moulders and their wives recognised both the financial incentives, in terms of retaining more of the gang's income, and the moral advantages, in putting them to work 'as soon as they can lift a brick almost' and thus avoiding the boarding of strangers in their homes.[26]

21　See chapter 12.

22　Census Enumerator's Book, Hayes 1861.

23　Census Enumerator's Book, Hayes 1851.

24　Census Enumerator's Book, Northolt 1851.

25　Evidence of Mrs Serjeant. Children's Employment Commission, 5th Report, PP 1866, p. 135.

26　Evidence of R.M. Smythe. Children's Employment Commission, 5th Report, PP 1866, p. 137.

'The perfection of untidiness, dirt and disease'

Although we might dismiss Dickens' description of the scene that presented itself to Esther Summerson and Mrs Pardiggle as exaggerated for dramatic reasons, other investigators were also taken aback by the squalor they encountered: 'The bodies of all are greatly exhausted with the profuse perspiration of the day so that neither health, cleanliness nor decency can be much, if at all regarded, and some of the huts are the perfection of untidiness, dirt and dust.'[27] Mr Metters, a missionary active in brickmaking districts for many years, reflected on the improvement he had seen in living conditions over time, but recalled that 'On entering his work among them [in Heston and Southall], he never remembered witnessing so much wretchedness before in all his life. Cottage windows were generally stuffed with old rags, in some instances there were no tables and chairs, but a general ruin.'[28]

Many of these cottages survived for decades, even after the brickfields to which they were attached had been closed, until swept away to make way for new houses or condemned as insanitary. For example, some cottages were demolished in Hackney to make way for a mission church in 1889, removing what was said to be 'so great an eyesore'.[29] In 1894 the Medical Officer at Harefield gave his opinion that the Brickfield Cottages ought never to have been built on a site so close to a river, and that they were unfit for human habitation. He had previously condemned them after an outbreak of diphtheria had caused five deaths.[30] On the other hand, in the same year his counterpart at Bromley had inspected brickfield cottages in his parish and was far more positive: 'The WCs of all the houses are at the ends of the gardens and each house has a constant supply of water. With the exception of the afore-mentioned defects, these cottages are in very fair order. They appear to be dry. The occupants are respectable and cleanly in their habits.'[31]

Those brick firms that continued in production in the early decades of the twentieth century were still renting cottages, and new ones continued to be built. Eleven dwellings at Horton Bridge, owned by Thomas Clayton Ltd, were newly built of brick and slate in about 1910.[32] Not surprisingly, some cottages remained in occupation long past the end of their useful life. Wooden Row, also known as 'Rabbit Hutch Row', was a series of single-storey cottages sandwiched between the railway and the canal near West Drayton (Figure 11.4). Leased by Broad & Co., they remained in use until the 1930s, when brickmaking in the area was on its last legs. The cottages, by then fifty years old, were finally condemned as unfit for human habitation and demolished, as a letter explains:

> There are a number of brickmakers cottages belonging to the lessees on the land … and these have recently been condemned by the Local authority … owing to the lack of drainage facilities and water supply and are about to be removed.

---

27 Evidence of Rev. J. Dennett. Children's Employment Commission, 5th Report, PP 1866, pp. 148–9.

28 *Middlesex County Times*, 1 December 1866.

29 *Hackney and Kingsland Gazette*, 26 August 1889.

30 *Middlesex and Buckinghamshire Advertiser*, 24 February 1894.

31 *Bromley and District Times*, 23 February 1894.

32 TNA IR58/39732/951–65; IR58/39731/875–885.

Figure 11.4. The Wooden Row, West Drayton. (London Borough of Hillingdon/Reach plc)

> Drainage facilities will no doubt be provided in due course, but the advantage thereof to the land included in Messrs Broad & Co's lease will be qualified by the fact that the larger part has been excavated down to a level below that of the drainage system of the district.[33]

The provision of cottages was an important part of recruiting and retaining a brickfield workforce. Conditions in them will often have been cramped and that is one reason why an evening at a public house or a beershop would have been attractive after a long day's work. It is to the brickies' consumption of alcohol that we turn next.

---

33   TNA IR58/39732/951–65; Church of England Record Centre ECE/7/1/7583/4 Letter from Cluttons to Ecclesiastical Commissioners 23 July 1935.

Chapter 12

'Habits of intemperance':
the brickies and the beershop

Nineteenth-century brickmakers have had a bad press. They were widely described as uncouth, uneducated, irreligious, spendthrifts, drunken and given to fighting: a rough lot altogether. For many brickmakers 'the only change from work is eating, drinking and sleeping', and the public house was the main place where they did their drinking.[1] Some of that received prejudice against brickmakers is present in the scene in Dickens' *Bleak House* to which we have already referred. In reply to Mrs Pardiggle's questioning, the brickmaker retorts:

> How have I been conducting of myself? Why, I've been drunk for three days; and I'd a been drunk four if I'd a had the money. Don't I never mean for to go to church? No, I don't never mean for to go to church. I shouldn't be expected there, if I did; the beadle's too gen-teel for me. And how did my wife get that black eye? Why, I give it her; and if she says I didn't, she's a Lie![2]

Whenever brickmakers were discussed the problem of drink was raised, since it was thought to result in a laxity of morals and a want of religion. The brickmakers' reputation for excessive drinking not surprisingly drew the attention of temperance reformers. Drink, they thought, underpinned the brickmakers' other ills; it led to rowdy and violent behaviour on the part of the men, and some women as well, and the money drunk away on summer nights left families short of food and heating in the winter. Beer was at the heart of the brickmakers' social stigma.

Brickmakers were by no means at the bottom of the employment ladder; a brick moulder, with an experienced gang to support him, could earn good money during the season, allowing him to put money aside for the winter. This did not always happen, as the temptation to spend the money in his pocket often proved too much. Mary Bayly, who undertook missionary work in the Potteries slum of Notting Hill in the 1850s, observed the problem at first hand.

> One man informed me that he and his family had earned £2–18s nearly every week through the season; and yet this man's wife and three children were shivering at my door, one bitterly cold morning in December, and begging for food and clothing. The effects of hard work and hard drinking had been to bring on a terrible illness, and not a sixpence was left of all the money which they had earned 'when the sun was shining'. After enduring privation and suffering too

---

1   M. Bayly, *Ragged homes and how to mend them* (London, 1860), p. 43.

2   Dickens, *Bleak House*, chapter VIII.

Bricks of Victorian London

terrible to contemplate the man and one of the children died, and the poor widow with the remaining children went to the workhouse.[3]

In her view, if the families were more prudent in the way they used the high summer wages, then there should be adequate resources to see them through the other six months of the year. What they needed was a means by which to save their money, such as a savings bank.

> Now the earnings of the family ... averaged for five months in the summer £2–10s per week. They could, of course, have lived very well upon 25s. If we reckon 10s for paying off old scores, buying new clothes, furniture and sundries, there would still be 15s left, which might have been put into the savings bank to meet the demands of the ensuing winter.[4]

She set one up for them, but it did not prove to be a great success.[5]

Of course, brickmakers were not alone in their drinking habits. Drunkenness was an issue that affected many occupations and concerns about its impact prompted the formation of temperance societies. The British and Foreign Temperance Society in London, formed in 1831, had over 85,000 members across the country by 1834. As a result of pressure from it and other parts of the temperance movement parliament was induced to appoint an inquiry into drunkenness, focusing, at this point, on the dangers of drinking strong spirits rather than beer.[6] It took evidence from a range of witnesses, including Thomas Hartley, who claimed to know of a brickfield where

> the workmen earn very high wages during the summer; but each man is obliged to contribute 6s or 7s per week, to be spent in drink. In consequence of these habits of intemperance, their families are reduced to the greatest distress in the winter; but even then, their wives have said there was more peace and less ill-treatment than during the summer, while their husbands were receiving their high wages.[7]

We should not assume that rough behaviour was universal. The owners of brickfields thought that the itinerant workers were rougher in their manners than those who had put down roots and worked in the same brickfield for many years. The Strouds

---

3   Bayly, *Ragged homes*, pp. 39–40.

4   *Ibid.*, p. 42. £2 10s per week over five months would provide an income of about £50. Average wages in 1863 were just under £40, which equates to £27,976 in 2019. For the calculation of wages see <https://measuringworth.com/datasets/ukearncpi/result2.php>, accessed 23 September 2021.

5   Bayly, *Ragged homes*, p. 50.

6   B.H. Harrison, *Drink and the Victorians: the temperance question in England, 1815–1872* (London, 1971), pp. 107–10.

7   Evidence of Thomas Hartley. Report of the Select Committee on Inquiry into drunkenness among the Labouring Classes of the United Kingdom, with minutes of evidence and appendix, PP 1834, vol. 8, p. 162.

'Habits of intemperance'

noticed a difference between the workers in their brickfield in Stoke Newington and those in their field in the Cowley district, to the latter's disadvantage.

> The men in this field are very steady, but there are some in the other field who are not at all so. We had a strike, and were obliged to take whom we could get. I think the brick makers in this district are, as a rule, tolerably steady; at all events, those who have lived in the neighbourhood some time; they are certainly better than they are about Uxbridge and Drayton.[8]

Support for this view comes from the Kent brickfields, where it was alleged that the navvies who built the London to Dover railway and later joined the brickfield labour force in Faversham and Sittingbourne were rough, hard-drinking and fighting men.[9]

Brickies regularly ended up in magistrates' courts for offences such as leaving their employ in the middle of the season, theft, drunkenness, fighting and assaults on women. On many occasions drink was an obvious factor. In October 1876 George Olliffe, a brickmaker from Botwell, was arrested in Finchley Road for being drunk and disorderly and using obscene language in the company of Emma Riddlesworth, a prostitute. Both were convicted. Olliffe's friends paid his fine (15s), while the less fortunate Emma went to prison.[10] A Sittingbourne brickmaker, Edward Harman, and a local bargeman were arrested for being drunk and fighting in the High Street in September 1871. In one week in 1894 George Hudson, a brickfield labourer, and Alfred Thomas, a walk-flatter, were both charged with being drunk and disorderly in Milton and Sittingbourne respectively.[11] Under the newspaper heading 'Brutal assault by brickmakers', three brickmakers of Aylesford named John Coulter, Alfred Mercer and James Baldwin were charged with assaulting Thomas Clegg on Good Friday 1866. They had been drinking in Maidstone and were returning home 'in a state of intoxication'. Near the Gibraltar Inn they encountered Clegg and, for whatever reason, set upon him and beat him so badly that he was still receiving medical treatment when the case reached court. They received short custodial sentences with hard labour.[12]

Drink, as well as leading to fighting and other sorts of anti-social behaviour, could endanger the brickies' lives. Walking back from a canalside beer shop was fraught with danger, as one brickmaker found.

> _Effects of intemperance._ On Monday, Mr Wakley held an inquest at Norwood Green on the body of John Sandford, aged 39, whose body was found in the Grand Junction Canal. The deceased, a brick moulder in the employ of Mr Tanner of Norwood, left the brickfield with his fellow workmen at dusk and accompanied them to a public house, where they remained until half past nine, having each

---

8   Children's Employment Commission, 5th Report, PP 1866, p. 139.

9   Perks, _George Bargebrick_, p. 30.

10   _Hampstead and Highgate Express_, 14 October 1876.

11   _East Kent Gazette_, 2 September 1871, 21 June 1894.

12   _Dover Telegraph and Cinque Ports General Observer_, 14 April 1866.

Bricks of Victorian London

drunk no less than two gallons of beer. Deceased then left and was not seen again alive. Next morning his body was found in the canal.[13]

The drinking of beer was an integral part of the brickmakers' working day as well as their leisure time. 'The quantity of beer consumed by brickies is almost incredible' was the view of one factory inspector. He went on to describe the sort of scenes he witnessed as he made his visits to the brickfields of Kent.

> Carts laden with beer regularly make the rounds of some fields. Many of the master brickmakers were, and still are, publicans. Some even have public houses in their own fields. I remember myself on a brilliant day of last summer driving into a field where I expected all would be busily at work. Nobody was at work at all; but at the door of the public house, in semi-drunken conversation with the portly gentleman, who was brickmaster and publican in one, lounged three or four stalwart brickies.[14]

However, the consumption of beer has to be seen in the context of heavy work in the open air on brickfields that almost certainly had poor access to clean drinking water and no facilities for heating it. Although refreshment breaks were built into the working day there was no real opportunity to leave the brickfield, and drinks were either brought from the nearest beershop or from the homes of the workers, which were often close by. To this end, the licensee of the Royal Oak beershop, Yiewsley, operated a delivery service to the nearby brickfields, and his son took out a donkey and cart, with the beer in stone bottles. The contents of the cart, on the particular day he was stopped by the police around five o'clock in the morning, came to over eight gallons.[15]

Beer was consumed by the moulding gangs throughout the working day and, according to some reports, in prodigious quantities, although we can't be certain how strong the beer was. One factory inspector reported that the men were supplied with five pints a day, and another that a brickfield master allowed ten pints a day to each setter. Mary Bayly was told that the men consumed seven pints a day, but in his memoirs James Reed suggested that the daily allowance was eight. He even described how this consumption was fitted into the working day, which started at 5am, as follows: at 6am a pint of beer and a mouthful of food, standing; breakfast, lasting half an hour, at 8am; three half pints and more food at 10am, sitting down for fifteen minutes; a pint at 11am; dinner, lasting one hour, at 12 noon; a pint at 2pm; three half pints and food during a fifteen-minute break at 3pm; a pint at 4.30pm; and a pint with food during another fifteen-minute break at 6pm.[16]

---

13 *Bell's Weekly Messenger*, 22 December 1845.

14 *The Times*, 14 August 1873, p. 9, reporting comments made by Factory Inspector Whymper.

15 He was stopped on the presumption that the licensing laws had been broken by selling beer during prohibited hours. *Uxbridge & West Drayton Gazette*, 24 August 1878.

16 Factory and Workshops Acts Commission, Report, Appendix E, PP 1876, vol. xxix, p. 190; *The Times*, 14 August 1873 p. 9; Bayly, *Ragged homes*, p. 42; Reed, 'Reminiscences of a Middlesex brickmaker', pp. 13–15.

'Habits of intemperance'

To provide for a regular supply of beer, there was usually a public house or a beershop close to a brickfield and the brickies probably made up the bulk of the clientele. However, when brickfields were located near canals or rivers, public houses would also have provided refreshment for boat crews as well as brickmakers.

Beershops were a new category of licensed premises, established, as the name implies, to supply only beer, and were one attempt to combat the excessive consumption of spirits, such as gin, that had been a problem in the eighteenth century and early decades of the nineteenth. Unlike the more onerous licensing requirements for public houses, with the passing of the Beer Act in 1830 any rate-payer could apply for a licence costing only two guineas, which permitted the recipient to brew and sell beer.[17] It is not surprising that, with a low entry qualification, a large number of beershops were opened. By 1833 there were some 35,000 licensed beershops nationally, and by the early 1840s there were five beershops in Botwell alone.[18] The foreman of a Kent brickfield estimated that 'there are now nearly 30 public-houses-and-beer-shops in that parish [Sittingbourne], besides several in the outlying districts, like this of Murston'.[19]

There was often a close link between the brickfield and the beershop. Beershops and public houses could be operated by the owner of the brickfield or by a foreman, or even by a member of a moulding gang. In 1851 William Tilbury was described as a foreman of brickfields and beershop keeper in Yeading, Hayes, and Charles Mole was a brickfield labourer who operated the Anchor beershop in Botwell.[20] Francis Newell was the owner of both the Hambrough Tavern in Southall and the local brickfield.[21] Some public houses and beer shops that served the brickfields bore names that related to the trade. The Brickmaker's Arms in Yiewsley still exists, and there may have been a Brickmaker's Arms in North Hyde, Heston. In Murston, George Smeed built the Brickmaker's Arms for his workers in 1859, although, as he pointed out when applying for a licence for the premises, it would also be patronised by the crews of barges docked at Murston Wharf (Figure 12.1). It was one of five public houses in the district. There was also a Brickmaker's Arms beershop in Faversham in 1867, and there is a Brickmaker's Arms in Maidstone, but this may have once been known by the more common name the Bricklayer's Arms.[22]

The Dawley Arms in West Drayton is well documented. The building was erected during the long tenancy of the brickfield by Samuel Pocock, and was taken over by his successors, Broad & Harris, in 1884. They let the house to John Shepherd of the Hayes Brewery at an annual rent of £70 and a barrelage of 2s 6d on all malt liquors, another way in which the brickfield owner benefited by the spending of his employees. In addition, Shepherd was asked to pay an entry fee of £100. The original seven-year

---

17 Harrison, *Drink and the Victorians*, chapter 3.

18 *Ibid.*, pp. 69, 81–2; London Borough of Hillingdon, Museum and Archives Service. Hayes Rate Book 1842–4.

19 Evidence of Mr Dean, foreman at Scott's Field, Murston. Children's Employment Commission, 5th Report, PP 1866, p. 143.

20 Census Enumerators' Book, Hayes 1851.

21 Census Enumerators' Book, Southall 1881.

22 For Kent public houses see <www.dover-kent.com>, accessed 10 January 2022.

Figure 12.1. Brickmakers' Arms, Murston. (Sittingbourne Museum)

lease was extended for a further term, but then assigned to Isleworth Brewery in 1891 and renewed for fifteen years in 1898.[23] Such a relationship between the owner of the brickfield and a beershop was probably not unusual, but there were some ground landlords who discouraged the opening of licensed premises on their land. The de Burgh family specifically forbade D. & C. Rutter from opening a public house on the brickfield and, despite their long tenancy of the site, there is no evidence that one was ever built. This stipulation may have been designed to protect de Burgh's interests in the licensed premises he already owned, or may have come from a desire to encourage abstinence among the workers.[24] By contrast, another local landowner, de Salis, allowed Messrs Rigby to open a public house on the land they leased for an additional rent of £6 per annum, but stipulated that it was not to interfere with the digging of brickearth. One assumes that this was intended to ensure that the main focus of the business remained brickmaking rather than beer retailing.[25]

Brickmaster R.M. Smythe argued that intemperate habits among the men could best be restrained by the master owning and managing the beershop and keeping beer off the brickfield itself.

> I have endeavoured to restrain the habit of drinking by prohibiting beer from being brought on the ground, but allowing men to get it for themselves at a beershop, built by me close to the field, and kept by the foreman, in whom I have

---

23 LMA Acc. 1214/1340–1343.
24 LMA Acc. 1386/105.
25 LMA Acc. 969/4.

'Habits of intemperance'

every confidence; he is instructed to turn the tap off and not allow a drop more to be supplied, if any symptom of drunkenness appear.[26]

The beershop in question was presumably the Brickmaker's Arms at North Hyde.[27]

The involvement of brickfield owners in the running of public houses inevitably encouraged abuses. If the owner supplied the men with beer during the working day, he could stop its cost from their wages. This is presumably what concerned the factory inspectors in 1876: 'Nearly all the fields have a beershop in connection, and some are the property of the beerhouse keepers. The men have about five pints a day in wages. It may be worthy of consideration whether the occupier of a brickfield should have a licence.'[28]

With the lack of proper offices on many brickfields, it was the custom to pay the men their wages on a Saturday evening in a public house, especially if it was under the control of the employer. Once the men arrived to collect their wages the foreman could delay payment on some excuse, so that the men started drinking to pass the time before they were paid and were encouraged to make a night of it once they had been. The writer of a letter to the *East Kent Gazette* in 1865, complaining of this deplorable practice, proposed an alternative.

> I would suggest that if all the foremen of brickfields make every effort to induce their masters to pay the men in their offices in the fields not later than 3 o'clock on Saturday afternoon, this would confer a lasting benefit to the masters, workpeople and tradesmen. What a blessing if the half-holiday system could be adopted. More respect would be shown to the masters, and the poor brickie could attend to his little plot of ground; the wife would be able to go to market earlier; the dear children would be cared for; and different places of worship would be better attended; and our missions receive greater support.[29]

Another Kent philanthropist, in promoting the idea of a working men's hall in Sittingbourne, complained that at present the public house was the only place where the men could meet to socialise. As they couldn't stay in a public house without having a drink, 'thus they drank a glass, a pint or a quart, not so much for the love of drink as to make a sort of payment for the accommodation offered'.[30]

An even greater abuse was the habit of unscrupulous owners of paying the men not in coin of the realm but with a chitty or token that was redeemable only in a pub or shop managed by the company. Shops of this kind were known as 'tommy shops' and the practice of paying in anything other than legal currency was known as 'truck'. It is not possible to know how widespread this practice was, but complaints emerged from

---

26   Evidence of R.M. Smythe. Children's Employment Commission, 5th Report, PP 1866, p. 138.

27   LMA Acc. 328/105.

28   Notes of a visit to the brickfields of Hayes in Factory and Workshops Acts Commission, Report, Appendix E, PP 1876, vol. xxix, p. 190.

29   *East Kent Gazette*, 23 December 1865.

30   *Ibid.*, 26 January 1878.

Bricks of Victorian London

time to time and, where brickmakers lived in more isolated places, a company-owned beershop or general store might have been the only place to purchase articles of food after a long day on the brickfield.

This description of the payment system, and the way it could be manipulated by some owners, comes from the foreman of a brickfield at Murston in Kent in the 1860s:

> One of the best things that could be done for brickfields would be to make the Saturday half-holiday general, and to allow no wages to be paid at public houses. As it is they don't leave off in most fields till 3 or 4p.m. on Saturday, and the money is not all paid till 7 or 8 p.m.; all have to go to the public house (where the habit is to pay there), even the little girls and boys, who are thus, as you may say, taught drunkenness in their childhood. The moulder is paid by the foreman of the field, and has to distribute among his gang; sometimes he is paid by a cheque; at all events, he generally requires change; that he can get only at the public-house, but the publican of course does not care to give change, unless, some of his beer goes with it. But the worst of all is the practice, which, though unknown to employers, I know as a fact, to exist in some cases, that the publican actually allows the foreman a per-centage upon all the money which he pays in wages at the public-house.[31]

At the same time a clergyman in the Cowley district is explicit in identifying a local publican and owner of a brickfield who was exploiting his employees.

> He works on the truck system, selling beer, grocery &c., and deducts on Saturday from the wages payable ... . One was asked how much he spent per week in beer. 'One pound, sometimes more, at least the feller docks it; when he gets me 'toxicated he puts down two or three scores for one; he takes good care to have my money on pay night.'[32]

Suspicion about possible truck payments came to light in a Southall courtroom because the description of the way that the men were paid was important to the case. The son of the manager of the Southall Brickmaking Company's field operated The Three Tuns and also sold provisions such as bread, cheese, saveloys and black pudding. The manager was at great pains to suggest that the men were paid their wages before any payments were taken for the rent of their cottages or any provisions that they were had on credit, but counsel for the defendant suggested that the manager might have been infringing the Truck Act.[33]

Truck was a long-standing problem. The first Truck Act had been passed in 1725 and there was a further act in 1831, but attempts to challenge truck payments in the courts could be difficult because of the way the legislation had been drawn up. In 1857 Thomas Ingram agreed with Richard Barnes, a railway contractor, to make bricks

---

31 Children's Employment Commission, 5th Report, PP 1866, p. 143.

32 *Ibid.*, p. 149. Evidence of Rev J. Dennett, Cranford.

33 *Uxbridge & West Drayton Gazette*, 10 July 1866.

'Habits of intemperance'

for the West End & Crystal Palace Railway. He was to be paid at a rate of 10s 6d per thousand, and he hired a team, in the usual way, to assist him. He was responsible for paying the other members of the team. Ingram received his payment partly in cash and partly in tickets for goods that were redeemable only in Barnes' own shop. While this seemed a clear breach of the act he lost the case in the Queen's Bench on the technicality that because he did not make the bricks on his own, but recruited a team to help him, he was not an 'artificer' as specified in the Act.[34]

The payment of wages in public houses was stopped by the Truck Amendment Act of 1887, which extended the provisions of the earlier act to all manual labourers except domestic servants and the employees of public houses themselves. The framers of the legislation expected this to benefit particularly dock workers and the employees of brickfields. It also placed responsibility for enforcing the legislation with the Factory Inspectorate.[35] Charles Bradlaugh MP, who had introduced the legislation, became an active campaigner to see that the law was enforced. In 1888 he became aware that Henry Haynes, a brickmaker and owner of a public house, The Alperton, in Alperton, Middlesex, seemed to be paying his men in cheques rather than in money. The cheques had a nominal value of 1s and could be redeemed at some local shops, but they only had the purchasing power of 11d. The shopkeepers presented these cheques to Haynes, who redeemed them, but again at a discount. The factory inspectors took statements and tried to build a case, but the witnesses were reluctant to appear in court lest they should lose their employment and their homes. Bradlaugh tackled the home secretary about the failure to deal with these 'great and flagrant' offences and the factory inspectors were asked to 'keep a careful watch' on Haynes' activities. Although he was not prosecuted, Haynes became sufficiently worried about the attention he was getting that in January 1889 he abandoned his illegal practices.[36] However, this was not the end of the story. In June 1889 Haynes was summoned before the magistrates on the allegation of factory inspector Gould for supplying one of his employees, John Watts, and two others with drink as an advance on their wages and then deducting it when they were paid. This looked like a breach of the act, but real money had changed hands and so the act had not been broken. The magistrates initially dismissed the charges, but a higher court decided that there was a violation of the Act and ordered the magistrates to hear the case again. Finally, in January 1890 Haynes was convicted and fined £5 12s plus costs. Half of the fine was given to Watts, who was no longer in Haynes' employ.[37]

Apart from its economic effects, excessive drinking was thought to have an impact on the health and productivity of brickmakers. Mary Bayly's view was that continued heavy drinking resulted in mental and physical degeneration: 'his life thus literally resembles that of the brute ... and when this has gone on for several years, all

---

34 *The Jurist*, new series, III/1 (1857), pp. 156–8.

35 50 & 51 Victoria c. 46; G. Hilton, *The truck system, including a history of the British Truck Acts, 1465–1960* (Cambridge, 1960), pp. 139, 144.

36 C. Frank, *Workers, unions, and payment in kind* (London, 2020), chapter 3.

37 *Barnet Press*, 1 June 1889; Frank, *Workers, unions*, chapter 3.

Bricks of Victorian London

intellectual power seems extinct'.[38] There were a number of assertions made, largely in the temperance literature, as you might expect, about how this affected the output of brickmaking gangs. A temperance textbook published in 1914, aimed at children in elementary schools, included this passage:

> Some men were making bricks. Some drank a glass or two of beer with their food, some were water drinkers. By calculating it was found that on the average each water drinker made 795,400 bricks a year, each beer drinker made 760,269 bricks a year. ... Also, the best workman among the teetotal men made 10,000 more in the year than the best beer drinker. Can you suggest any reason why beer should thus make one set of men think and move – for it is chiefly movements that are concerned in brick-making – so much slower than another set who had no beer but drank water instead?[39]

There is no source given for these figures, but we can identify them from a much earlier temperance work. A 'gentleman residing at Uxbridge' and presumably familiar with the workmen in the Cowley district had made that calculation as far back as 1840, following a conversation with 'our largest maker'; he provided exactly these figures based on a survey of gangs producing a total output of 23 million bricks.[40] The same figures appear again in a temperance dictionary of 1861 that had a separate section on 'Brickmakers'.[41] A different set of figures appeared in an 1886 volume, reprinting some statistics from a decade before. In 1875 the owner of a brickfield in the Slough area reported that he had eleven abstainers working for him, and that he had compared the output of four gangs led by abstainers with four where the moulders were drinkers. In the work done from the beginning of the season until 5 June the first four had made a total of 1,469,000 bricks to the second four's 1,284,500, a 24 per cent variation. However, disaggregating the figures reveals that one of the 'drinker' gangs had made more bricks than two of the 'abstainer' gangs, and there were considerable variations on both sides between the teams, indicating that factors other than drink determined output.[42]

Temperance supporters were always looking for instances that demonstrated the efficacy of abstinence. So, it was reported that a gang working for Stephen Watkins in West Drayton had made 52,500 bricks in a week, working eighteen-hour days, 'without a single individual among them tasting a drop of intoxicating liquor', but sadly without indicating whether this impressive total was sustained across the season.[43]

---

38 Bayly, *Ragged homes*, p. 43.

39 H. Coomber, *Lessons and experiments on scientific hygiene and temperance for elementary schoolchildren* (London, 1914), pp. 50–1.

40 W.B. Carpenter, *Temperance and teetotalism: an inquiry into the effects of alcoholic drinks on the human system in health and disease* (Glasgow, 1849), p. 20.

41 D. Burns, *Temperance dictionary* (London, 1861), p. 409.

42 Temperance Congress, *Temperance progress: facts and figures for temperance workers* (Croydon, 1886), pp. 171–2.

43 R.B. Grindrod, *Bacchus: an essay on the nature, causes, effects and cure of intemperance* (London, 1851), p. 342.

'Habits of intemperance'

Other brickfield proprietors also claimed that abstainers were more productive. George Smeed's experience was that 'the teetotallers [were] the steadiest and most useful of all the men; they never lose time; once I had a field full of them, and I wish I could always have'.[44]

Not surprisingly, brickmaking areas were fertile ground for the temperance societies and Christian missionaries. This description in a temperance journal gives a flavour of the kind of outreach work undertaken:

> *Norwood Green and North Hyde.* A few weeks since we held a meeting at Norwood Green, under a tent belonging to the Christian Instruction Society; we had about 200, many of the roughest brickmakers; the subject was evidently new to many of them; they were very orderly, and expressed themselves pleased with the meeting; several signed [the pledge?]. Our speakers were three reformed drunkards, working men. Two weeks since we got up a meeting at North Hyde, a very small place, surrounded by brickfields, only about 200 inhabitants, with five drunkeries [sic]; two poor drunkards have been suffocated by lying upon the kiln when intoxicated; the brickmakers there were described by a lady as being scarcely like human beings, indeed the ignorance is almost past conception; they, however, behaved well, and we had a good meeting; the same speakers, one of whom is a brickmaker, and a good speaker. I think there were about 150 present. I imagine thou never yet saw such a set of rough looking beings; my sister and I were told we should be thrown into the canal, the meeting being held close to it, but we were not afraid; we distributed a great many tracts. I am sorry to say our stock is exhausted, but I am ashamed to beg again; nevertheless, there is no place where they will be more gratefully received, or where they will be more needed. We intend holding a meeting in the chapel at this place next week; the cause is certainly progressing round here; we are but a few, yet we are in earnest.[45]

The temperance movement seems to have made considerable inroads among the brickmakers of West Drayton. In 1840 J. Metters, described as Missionary to the District, contrasted the indifference, and even obstruction, he had encountered early on with the present state of things. He now had 170 people signed up. Two years later this sanguine view was confirmed in a report of the West Drayton Rechabite Anniversary and Public Teetotal Fête.

> The teetotal brickmakers of this place have deservedly attracted much public attention and interest; yes, when it is considered what a miserable degraded set of men they generally used to be, it may well excite the wonder of many in beholding what has been done among them by means of teetotalism; and truly a worthier set of fellows does not now exist. Nor are they content to eat their morsel alone, but are anxious that those benefits should be extended to others,

---

44 Children's Employment Commission, 5th Report, PP 1866, p. 143.
45 *Temperance Recorder for Domestic and Foreign Intelligence*, 1 (August 1842), p. 363.

Bricks of Victorian London

which they, from the adoption of total abstinence principles, have experienced themselves. And, in order to do this, they earnestly invite their fellow countrymen to a participation of some of those pleasures of which they shortly anticipate the enjoyment, when they hope to have their hearts cheered by the coming together of a goodly number of their brother teetotallers and rechabites from all quarters.[46]

As well as the work of missionaries converting individual brickmakers and their families to sobriety, there were some brickfield owners who took the lead in limiting or excluding alcohol from the workplace. At Smeed, Dean, John Andrews, the works foreman and later a director of the company, found the workers to be a particularly rough lot when he joined the company in 1865 and 'attempted to instil in the workforce the maxims of temperance and religion'.[47] The neighbouring firm of Wills & Packham prohibited the sale of drink on its brickfield, and celebrated the end of the 1874 season with 'the cup that cheers but not inebriates'. The men were said to have 'confessed that with continuous good health and strength they had done their work better without the beer than others had with it, and this is proved by the amount of work performed by them and other men in the neighbouring brickfields'.[48]

As well as preaching the message of abstinence, the temperance reformers were keen to improve the circumstances of brickmakers. Many were illiterate.

As soon as they became sober men, they felt what a bad thing ignorance is; and in the winter evenings, the persons who used to be once found drinking, and smoking, and quarrelling in the ale-house, were to be found in the house of the good missionary – *learning to read and write.*[49]

There were only limited opportunities for educational activities in the summer months because of the long working days, but for those living in the area during the winter months there was more scope. To keep the men out of the beer shops it was necessary to provide alternative places for them to meet, where they could socialise and where they had access to reading material. There was said to be a brickmakers' reading room in West Drayton about 1845.[50] While educational work was largely confined to the winter months, to maintain contact with the reformed brickmakers in the summer it was important to provide social activities: fêtes, cricket matches and tea parties seem to have been popular, and 270 people joined a tea festival in Uxbridge in 1842.[51]

---

46 *London Teetotal Magazine and Literary Miscellany* (1840), pp. 115–16; *Temperance Recorder,* 1 (August 1842), p. 26. Rechabites were a religious order or clan of ancient Israel that had strict rules about abstinence from wine. The name was adopted in nineteenth-century England by some total abstainers within the temperance movement.

47 Perks, *George Bargebrick*, p. 30.

48 *The Temperance Record*, 14 November 1874 – 'Teetotalism in a brickfield'.

49 C.L. Balfour, *Morning dew drops or the juvenile abstainer*, 4th edn (London, 1859), pp. 246–7.

50 Copies of the Temperance Herald were dispatched to this reading room. *Christian Witness and Church Members Magazine* (1845), p. 200.

51 *Temperance Recorder*, 1 (1842), p. 131.

'Habits of intemperance'

One of the ways to wean working men away from public houses was by establishing alcohol-free alternatives, such as the coffee tavern. These started to appear in the working-class areas of London in the 1860s, and one opened in Southall, near the railway bridge, in 1879. As well as providing food and drink, there were dining, smoking and reading rooms, and a space that could be hired for events. Lodgings for single men were also provided at a charge of 6d or 7d per night. The activities of this coffee house were particularly directed at the brickmakers of the district and shareholders in the company running it included brickmaster Mr Minter. The company

> proposes to do all that is possible by means of coffee barrows, which in summer months will be taken into the brickfields to provide for the wants of the thirsty workers during the day. They may in this materially assist the cause of temperance, while the brickmakers themselves will be both morally and physically benefited.[52]

Sadly, there is no evidence to indicate whether this happened and, if it did, what success attended it. In the same year there was a proposal to set up a similar establishment in Faversham for the brickmakers and bargemen who made up a large part of the local working population. Another tavern opened in Milton near Sittingbourne two years later, which was designed to be 'conducted as a public house [where] all-comers will be made welcome'.[53]

Conditions in brickfields improved as the century went on, especially as, with mechanisation and the increasing size of businesses, manufacturing sites began to take on the character of a works or a factory, where it was easier to provide toilet and mess facilities. There was also a reduction in seasonal employment, as some manufacturers installed drying sheds and kilns that made all-year production a possibility. This greater security of employment may have encouraged the men to become steadier in their habits. But perhaps changes in the behaviour of brickmakers are a reflection of larger changes in British society, as a broader range of leisure activities became available to the working classes. The 1869 and 1872 Licensing Acts imposed reduced hours on public houses.[54] The peak year for beer consumption was 1876, at 34.4 gallons per head of population, and the same was true for spirits.[55]

The work of temperance reformers across society and specifically among the brickmakers had also made an impact. Weaning men and women off drink was also a prerequisite to improving their education and saving their souls.

---

52 Harrison, *Drink and the Victorians*, pp. 303–4; Mrs Westbrook, the widow of the Heston brickmaker, and W.W. Deloitte, the founder of the eponymous accountancy firm and a Southall resident, were both present at the opening of the Tavern. *Uxbridge & West Drayton Gazette*, 19 November 1879.

53 *Whitstable Times and Herne Bay Herald*, 10 May 1879; *East Kent Gazette*, 29 January 1881.

54 Harrison, *Drink and the Victorians*, pp. 271–5.

55 Figure from G.B. Wilson, *Alcohol and the nation: a contribution to the study of the liquor problem in the United Kingdom from 1800–1935* (London, 1940).

Chapter 13

'Profane workmen':
the brickies at prayer

As well as having a reputation for drunkenness, brickmakers were generally regarded as uneducated and irreligious. One Hayes resident concluded that 'brickmaking ... seems one of these employments more especially carried on by profane workmen'.[1] So, as well as attracting the attention of temperance reformers, brickmakers were fertile ground for Christian missionaries. When Trollope's Mr Crawley goes about his pastoral work among the brickmakers he sees himself as a missionary, as he indicates by his reference to St Paul.

> Mr Crawley, ever since first coming into Hogglestock, had been very busy among these brickmakers, and by no means without success. Indeed, the farmers had quarrelled with him because the brickmakers had so crowded the parish church, as to leave but scant room for decent people ... . But Mr Crawley had done his best to make the brickmakers welcome at the church, scandalising the farmers by causing them to sit or stand in any portion of the church which was hitherto unappropriated. He had been constant in his personal visits to them, and had felt himself to be more a St Paul with them than with any other of his neighbours around him.[2]

As well as its avowedly religious aim, this kind of missionary work was designed to promote sober habits and opportunities for self-improvement. Encouraging temperance among brickmakers was a necessary prerequisite to reforming their lives, as missionary J. Metters had discovered in West Drayton. When attempting to distribute religious tracts he 'found my way almost entirely thwarted', but once the habit of sobriety took hold he felt that 'they have begun to open their eyes to the delusion they have been under', becoming more amenable to his other attempts to improve their lot.[3]

Impelled by Christian charitable and paternalistic instincts, missionaries and the local clergymen undertook a whole range of practical activities on behalf of brickmakers and their families. These included the operation of soup kitchens in the winter months[4] and treats in the summer, but most important was the establishment of meeting places that would provide an alternative to the public house or the beershop.

---

1   E. Hunt, *Hayes, past and present* (Hayes, 1861), p. 4.

2   Trollope, *The last chronicle of Barset*, chapter XII, pp. 117–18.

3   *London Teetotal Magazine and Literary Miscellany* (1840), p. 115.

4   E.g. in 1891 at Yiewsley, *Uxbridge & West Drayton Gazette*, 31 January 1891, and Sittingbourne, *East Kent Gazette*, 24 January 1891.

'Profane workmen'

Mission halls provided a place for Christian worship, but, just as importantly, offered social and educational facilities.

The London City Mission was founded in 1835 with a mandate 'to extend the knowledge of the Gospel among the inhabitants of London and its vicinity (especially the poor)'. It recruited and paid full-time workers who were assigned to particular districts and were expected to make regular visits, going door-to-door, with a goal of persuading families to attend local churches. In the early days the districts that were targeted were closer to the centre of London, but then coverage spread out into the more rural parts of Middlesex. Brickmakers were not specifically targeted, but in some areas, such as West Drayton, they made up a significant proportion of the working-class population.

In the 1840s missionary work was undertaken in a corner of Islington where the inhabitants were principally mechanics, labourers and brickmakers.[5] In 1861 S.R. Brown was allocated to a district just to the north of the Potteries, in Notting Hill. Here he started house visits, and worked with Mrs Bayly, whom we have already encountered, who organised a regular mothers' meeting in a laundry drying room in Latimer Road. There was no church, chapel or school in the area, so services initially took place in the open air, until a Mission Hall was opened in 1863.[6]

Harrow School also established a mission in the Latimer Road area in the 1880s, paid for by Old Harrovians and organised by William Law. In his view

> nothing could have been more forlorn, neglected or desolate than the condition of the district at starting ... the livelihood of the men – brickmakers, costermongers, casual labourers – was always precarious, while the women, the real breadwinners of the families were mainly employed in steam laundries away from their homes and children.

Eventually a church, Holy Trinity, Latimer Road, was opened in 1889.[7]

The London City Mission was non-denominational, but the Anglican Church and the Methodists, among others, had their own home missionary societies. One clergyman, Ernest Bull, who worked in Heston and Southall for the London Diocesan Home Mission, was a champion of the brickies and felt impelled to take issue with the regular reporting of incidents of drunkenness and violence by local brickmakers. Responding to a piece in the local newspaper with the headline 'The brickies again', he wrote

> From my connection with the brickmakers as chaplain to several fields in the neighbourhood of Southall, extending, in fact from Hayes Bridge to Heston, I feel a peculiar interest in their welfare, and I am specially grieved when anything takes place amongst them tending to add, in any degree, to the opprobrium which for so long a time has been attached to their name.

---

5   *London City Mission Magazine*, January 1840, p. 12.

6   Bayly, *Ragged homes*, p. 109; *Latymer Road Mission centenary, 1863–1963* (London, 1963).

7   C. Griffin, *Nomads under the West Way: Irish travellers, gypsies and other trades in West London* (Hatfield, 2008), pp. 70–1; *The Times*, 14 June 1883, 20 May 1887; B. Cherry and N. Pevsner, *The buildings of England: London 3, north west* (London, 2002), p. 226.

Bricks of Victorian London

However, despite his sympathy with the brickies, he agreed that their reputation was often deserved, but

> considering the vast numbers of brickmakers who are working in these fields in the summer season, the occasional or even frequent appearance of some of their number in the police courts is not at all to be wondered at, nor does it place them in unfavourable contrast with other large bodies of workmen.[8]

He devoted much of the rest of his letter to describing the work he and his fellow clergy had undertaken to improve the behaviour of the workmen. They felt it was important to provide educational opportunities such as evening classes in the winter months, and to find a building that would act as a reading room, where newspapers and 'such books as shall lead to their interest and profit' would be available. However, he was adamant that such reading rooms should be under the control of the men themselves, not managed by others, however well-intentioned.

> To make such an institution successful, I believe it to be of primary importance that it be made as far as possible self-supporting. They must be able to feel that it is THEIR reading room, in the support and management of which THEY have an active part. Nor have we any reason to fear that they will be behind hand in this. They came forward very nobly with their subscriptions to the late Cholera Fund, which was for the relief of those who were quite strangers to them; and I doubt not but that they can and will do the same for their own moral benefit.[9]

A couple of months later it was reported that a mutual improvement society had been established, whose aims were 'the promotion of the social, intellectual, and moral welfare of its members by means of a reading room, library, classes for instruction, occasional lectures, and such other things as shall tend to the furtherance of this object'. The society was self-governing, at least in part, the committee being elected from the honorary members (presumably the middle-class supporters, who paid 12s per annum) and the general members (who paid 6d per month, or 6s per annum). A building with gas lighting was made available by Samuel Tildesley, the local brickmaster, part of which had been fitted out as a reading room. Two hundred tickets were sold, at 6d a time, for the inauguration of the new enterprise on 19 November 1866, and many more were turned away. Not surprisingly, the room was overcrowded. It is not clear, however, how long the society remained in existence and what the continuing level of support was.[10]

---

8   *Middlesex County Times*, 29 September 1866. Letter to the editor by Alfred Ernest Bull, Southall Green. Bull was a graduate of Emmanuel College, Cambridge. Between 1865 and 1867 he worked for the London Diocesan Home Mission, and then became curate of Heston 1867–72, before taking up a post at St Paul, Hounslow Heath.

9   *Ibid.*

10   'Southall – the brickmakers', *Middlesex County Times*, 1 December 1866.

'Profane workmen'

Reflecting on his first year as a missionary to the brickies, Bull counted himself satisfied that some progress had been made, but more needed to be done. He wrote:

> Your recent efforts to improve your social, intellectual and moral welfare, the establishment of Mutual Improvement Societies amongst yourselves, and the good success which have attended the two such societies already started, have cheered me much. Above all the earnest Christian characters which some of you have exhibited, have given me unmixed delight, and proved to me that true religion can and does exist in a brickfield. It is possible to be a hardworking brickmaker, and a God-fearing, Christ-loving man at the same time.[11]

A decade later, a Primitive Methodist Chapel was opened in Southall. With a site secured at a nominal rent, Tildesley and Minter provided the clay and local brickies made the bricks in their own time. The men had previously met in a barn that Tildesley had offered them without charge. As well as a place for worship that could hold 300 people there was space for a schoolroom in the new chapel.[12]

Despite the activities of missionaries such as Bull, there was still much to do to improve the religious observance of the brickmakers. A correspondent, referring to an editorial in a local paper, was pessimistic about progress in the Yiewsley area.

> I know our indefatigable minister (Mr Stedman) has done all in his power to reform them, but I am afraid, with very little success, as I very seldom see many of them at church. I have known brickfields visited by well-meaning Christians, and tracts distributed among them many times, but all to no effect.[13]

Missionaries, of course, were not to be put off by the difficulty of the challenge. The London City Mission remained active and there were 450 missionaries in the London area in the early 1880s, who made upwards of three million visits in the course of a year. Some visited Harefield, Middlesex in 1882, and one of them addressed a tea organised by a local parishioner for the brickmakers, and also toured the public houses. There was, in the view of the local parish priest, cause for hope, for one public house was now entirely shut on a Sunday, while the licensee of another went to church in the morning and his wife went in the evening.[14]

The London Female Bible & Domestic Mission had been founded by Ellen Ranyard in 1857.[15] In 1880 its workers were active among the brickmakers and their families in West Drayton, holding mothers' meetings, Bible classes and evening classes in the winter months, which drew attendances of about fifty people. The cottages of the

---

11 'Southall – the moral and social reformation of brickmakers', *Buckinghamshire Advertiser and Uxbridge Journal*, 9 February 1867.

12 *Acton Gazette*, 5 August 1876.

13 'The brickfield mission', *Uxbridge & West Drayton Gazette*, 26 May 1866, 2 June 1866.

14 *Uxbridge & West Drayton Gazette*, 6 August 1882.

15 <https://infed.org/ellen-ranyard-lnr-bible-women-and-informal-education>, accessed 16 October 2021.

Bricks of Victorian London

brickmakers were visited and the 'Bible woman', Mrs Paytor, conducted a service on Sunday evenings in one of them.[16]

Other missionary societies targeted particular groups of working men. As brickmakers in the Sittingbourne area lived side by side with bargemen, many of whom worked for brick companies, it is not surprising that a representative of the Wesleyan Seamen's mission, T.C. Garland, could be found preaching in the Primitive Methodist chapel in Milton and the Wesleyan Chapel in Sittingbourne in 1881. He also held a large camp meeting at Murston, which was addressed by a number of bargemen and brickmakers.[17] In 1887 it was a missionary from the Thames Church Mission, which covered the river from Putney Bridge to the Nore, who lectured in the Town Hall at Sittingbourne and drew applause from his audience when he said 'he was sure that, taking them as a whole, the Sittingbourne bargemen and brickmakers were an exceptionally sober, decent and hardworking community'.[18]

Some brickfield owners, like Mr Tildesley, evidently took a paternalistic attitude towards their employees' welfare and provided chapels or mission halls near to their rows of tied cottages. In Crayford in Kent Messrs Lucas built a room for worship at the prompting of local missionary Mr Baker in 1865. This mission room seated around fifty and would be full on Sunday evenings. There were fifty-five children on the books of the Sunday school, and a night school met on two evenings a week. There were plans to start a temperance society.[19]

A mission hall was established close to the Starveall (West Drayton) brickfields of Samuel Pocock as a daughter church in the parish of St Matthew, Yiewsley. In this isolated area the congregation was drawn chiefly from the local brickmakers and their families. A service was held on Sunday evenings, and there was a weekday mothers' meeting, as well as social activities. Around Christmas time in 1885 some seventy people sat down to a meat tea and an entertainment presided over by Mr Broad, of the brickmaking firm of Broad Harris and Company.[20]

Although not exclusively designed for the benefit of brickmakers, the Heston Institution for Working Men, also known as the Westbrook Memorial, was founded by Mrs Westbrook in 1868 in memory of her husband Edward, one of the district's best-known brickmasters (Figure 13.1). In the high-minded tone of the period the Institution was to be 'a place of innocent recreation as for mental improvement' with a library and reading room and was designed to promote 'the welfare of the inhabitants of Heston, by contributing to the comforts, and aiding in the great work of the improvement of the moral and social condition of the poorer classes of such inhabitants'. It was strictly temperance. The subscription in the 1890s was 2d a week.[21]

---

16   *Uxbridge & West Drayton Gazette*, 4 December 1880.

17   *East Kent Gazette*, 22 October 1881.

18   *East Kent Gazette*, 12 November 1887.

19   Children's Employment Commission, 5th Report, PP 1866, p. 146.

20   The Mission Hall is shown on OS maps; *Uxbridge & West Drayton Gazette*, 2 January 1886.

21   London Borough of Hounslow Archives, Cuttings book SC2, p. 183 [n.d.]; article in *Heston Ratepayers' Association Magazine*, January 1938; *West London Observer*, 14 March 1868. The building was demolished in 1966.

'Profane workmen'

Figure 13.1. Westbrook Memorial Hall, Heston. (London Borough of Hounslow, Local Studies Service)

John Andrews, the foreman at Smeed, Dean's works, was keen to look after the spiritual needs of his men. To that end he established cottage prayer meetings at Lower Murston.

> A cottager would offer the use of his front room on one or two evenings a week for this purpose, perhaps one shilling would be paid for each evening's use; this was not always done, but as the meetings were held in the winter when a fire was needed, the extra cost for warmth and light was met in this way ... .
> As many as twenty would crowd into a small room, but usually about twelve, the scripture would be read and expounded, hymns sung, interspersed with extempore prayers.[22]

Andrews accumulated and distributed stocks of hymn books and Bibles and the inexpensive publications of the British & Foreign Bible Society. He insisted on his own sons joining the Band of Hope, and their signed pledges were framed and hung on the

---

22   G. Andrews, *Memories of Murston* (Sittingbourne, 1930), p. 64.

Bricks of Victorian London

walls of their bedroom as a constant reminder of their promises.[23] His fellow director of Smeed, Dean, George Hambrook Dean, was a leading light in the Baptist chapel.[24]

Churches in the nineteenth century were at the heart of the social life of their communities and so it is not surprising to find entertainments for brickies taking place there, but the events that were reported in local newspapers, of course, do not allow generalisations to be made about how common they were or what their impact was on those who participated. Nevertheless, they give a sense of the kind of activities that the brickies were drawn into and the paternalistic attitudes of their employers. In 1867 Thomas Norton laid on an 'abundant' meat tea for his workers and their wives at Hillingdon in the Chiltern View Road Primitive Methodist Chapel on a Friday night in November. Typically for such events, there was preaching: first, to stress the importance of the owners of brickfields taking an interest in the welfare of their employees and, secondly, to draw a contrast between Norton's employees and the brickmakers of nearby Starveall, who did not benefit from the same paternalistic attention, and were coarse in behaviour.[25]

Despite the fact that it was in the midst of the moulding season, the brickmakers in West Drayton had a day off on the August Bank holiday of 1874 (which at this period occurred at the beginning, rather than the end of the month) and a cricket match was organised for teams representing Stacey's and Rutters' firms at the West Drayton race course. Stacey's team won. The match was followed by a dinner in a tent in the grounds of the De Burgh Arms. Contrary to the usual description of brickmakers' drunken behaviour, the event was accompanied by 'sobriety and moderation supposed to be unpossessed by the brickmaking tribe'.[26]

Missionaries and temperance reformers alike were interested in the welfare of the brickmakers, and of their families. A particular concern was for the children, many of whom were themselves employed by their parents in the brickfield. It is to the work of children in brickfields and the attempts to regulate it that we now turn.

---

23 *Ibid.*, p. 61.

24 *East Kent Gazette*, 4 April 1869, 2 March 1889.

25 *Uxbridge & West Drayton Gazette*, 9 November 1867.

26 *Ibid.*, 8 August 1874.

Chapter 14

Pug boys and barrow loaders: the children of the brickfields

In the eighteenth and early nineteenth centuries the idea of childhood as a particular phase in life had not yet been formed, and there was little understanding of the different stages through which children went as they developed physically and psychologically.[1] Child labour was common, and working-class children often started work at an early age. Consequently, they attended school for only short periods of time, if at all. As we have already seen, children were widely employed in the brickmaking gangs that made the stock bricks of London. To contemporaries it seemed inevitable that children would follow in their parents' footsteps into the business; 'a moulder's child is born, as the saying is, with a brick in his mouth' (Plate 14).[2]

Since for much of the nineteenth century, until the passing of the 1870 Education Act, education was not compulsory, there was no school leaving age. Young people, whom we would call teenagers today, would enter the labour market before they had finished growing physically, but even more troubling was the employment of primary school age children. In the mid-1860s factory inspector W.H. Lord estimated that under-18s made up between 43 and 57 per cent of the complement of the moulding gangs in the Cowley district and, of those, half were children under the age of thirteen, say between 350 and 500.[3] They were employed at a number of different tasks around the brickfield, often as pug boys or barrow loaders. They might be given other jobs, too, such as looking after the horses, sifting ashes or raking sand to dry it ready for the moulding table. James Reed recalled that his first job on the brickfield was screening breeze, and in the process finding coins, jewellery and bits of metal that had been missed by the rubbish sorters in London.[4] Since brickmaking families often lived close to their work, a child's first venture onto the brickfield might be to bring refreshments for family members or to run errands. Children would then progress to become part of a moulding gang, often alongside their parents and older siblings.

Their employment in such work was open to objections from several points of view: first, the physical effect of heavy labour on young and still growing bodies; secondly, the exposure to coarse language and manners that came with working alongside adults, who were notorious for their uncouth behaviour; and, thirdly, the lack of opportunity for education and the self-fulfilling effect of that on their prospects. Such objections were not, of course, restricted to children working in brickmaking,

---

1   E. Hopkins, *Childhood transformed: working class children in the nineteenth century* (Manchester, 1994), p. 2.

2   Children's Employment Commission, 5th Report, PP 1866, p. 136.

3   *Ibid.*, p. 128.

4   Reed, 'Reminiscences of a Middlesex brickmaker', pp. 13–15.

Bricks of Victorian London

and attempts to remedy the situation of brickies' children formed part of a bigger campaign to regulate working conditions during the nineteenth century. For a number of reasons brickfields were one of the last places of employment to be taken into the legal framework of the Factory Acts.

These issues were all investigated by the Children's Employment Commission when it undertook its research in the early 1860s. Let us consider each of these concerns in turn, starting with the physical effects of heavy work and long hours. While brickmaking did not involve the dust and fumes of many factory tasks, and the workers were said to be generally healthy, the weights that were lifted or pushed by the younger employees could be physically damaging.

> In spite of this [the long hours] the children grow up strong and healthy; they are at times put to work that is too much for them, but not generally; ... sometimes after a heavy rain has saturated the ground you may see a girl of only 12 years old staggering up the hacks with a barrow which she can scarcely move along.[5]

When the government started to investigate the role of children in the brickfields, calculations were made of the weight of clay that a child might lift in the course of the working day, working either as a pug boy or as a barrow loader. The foreman of a Faversham brickfield gave this answer.

> I never calculated how many miles a day a pug boy will go but you may get at it in this way: from the bottom of the pug mill to the stool is about 14 feet; a moulder will make from 7000 to 8000 bricks in the day from 5 a.m. to 7 p.m. allowing an hour for meals; a pug boy of 12 or 13 will carry each time on an average enough to make four bricks. I dare say he runs up and down from 120 to 150 times in an hour. Our bricks weigh 12 lbs. each when green.[6]

Such exertion could produce physical deformities. One girl, it was said, 'has a crooked ankle and her knee is grown out on one side' and another lad had 'his leg put quite out'.[7] The foreman of a brickfield in Shepherd's Bush claimed that he knew of boys who had ruptured themselves by trying to lift too heavy a load.[8] Even if such dangers could be avoided the children were often exhausted at the end of a long summer day.[9] A clergyman commented on a girl who doggedly attended Sunday school, only to fall asleep as soon as she sat down in class; she attempted to cope with the difficulty by remaining standing.[10] Inevitably, children grew up to be tough; a police officer in the Cowley district commented on the resilience of the brickfield children:

---

5   Children's Employment Commission, 5th Report, PP 1866, p. 136.

6   *Ibid.*, p. 145.

7   *Ibid.*, p. 135.

8   *Ibid.*, p. 139.

9   *Ibid.*, p. 138.

10   *Ibid.*, p. 149.

Pug boys and barrow loaders

> I often wonder that the children can stand the work as they do, but nothing seems to hurt them; they are as hardy as ground toads, as the saying is; yet I have seen them so tired at the end of the day's work that the men have had to take them up in their arms to carry them home.[11]

The second concern was about the kinds of behaviour and language to which children were exposed. Boys in the brickfield learned bad habits from their fathers and the other men they worked alongside, including drinking and smoking. A school teacher in Crayford complained that 'boys of the age of 9 to 12 have actually been seen drunk with beer'.[12] One boy in a Southall brickfield was overheard to have said '"Well, I've been teetotalling for 9 months, I must go and get beery now". He had learned it of course from his father or some of the men in the field; but he said it quite seriously, and no doubt meant it too.'[13] Across in Kent, a foreman was worried about smoking:

> There is a great too much smoking and drinking in brickfields generally. It is to the boys that the harm comes of smoking; you may see little things not as high as the table with pipes in their mouths; that must injure them, but when I speak to their fathers about it they never try to prevent it.[14]

Social reformers were particularly concerned about the effect that the drunkenness, bad language and rough manners of the men had on the morals of the women and children who worked alongside them. This fear of moral corruption was a strand in many of the reform movements of the mid-Victorian period, informing, for example, campaigns against domestic overcrowding and the types of working conditions that might encourage intimacy. The Rev. Dennett of Cranford summed up the prevailing attitude when he wrote about the boys and girls he encountered in his missionary work:

> The language that they constantly hear, the oaths and blasphemy that are frequently poured forth, the utter want of religion and of any religious feeling of any kind, and the impious ridicule often cast upon the mere observance of the Sunday or any religious ordinance, without mentioning the filthy, indecent and shameless habits of many among them, is quite sufficient to satisfy the most sceptical of the baneful effects on an ignorant and juvenile mind. It need surprise none that many in after years should rank among the lawless, the depraved and the dissolute.[15]

George Smeed took a paternalistic view of the women in his brickfields, and revealed the conventional attitudes of the period about a women's place being in a domestic environment.

---

11 *Ibid.,* p. 138.
12 *Ibid.,* p. 151.
13 *Ibid.,* pp. 136–7.
14 *Ibid.,* p. 145.
15 *Ibid.,* p. 149.

Bricks of Victorian London

> I am quite convinced that the employment of girls in brickfields has a very bad and demoralising effect upon them; in the first place they begin young and work hard all their lives there, and never know how to cook, or wash, or mend clothes, and can never make good housewives. At the same time as they grow up into young women, they are thrown into constant contact with young men, working, so to speak, side-by-side, for the walk flatter is often a young woman, and the off-bearer a young man of 17 or 18 upwards. Granting that they work perhaps under their parent's eye in the field – the moulder's gang usually consists more or less of members of his family – still when there happens to be a fair or race or any other amusement in the neighbourhood they go off there together, or meet there, and too often the girl's virtue is gone before her holiday is over.[16]

Having said that, young women from working-class backgrounds needed to work and had few employment opportunities in the areas where brickfields were sited (Plate 15). Many could only expect to go into service if they did not work in the brickfields, but, unfortunately, working in brickfields as children was not a good preparation for domestic service in their teenage years: 'they grow up wholly ignorant of all domestic duties, and are quite unfit to be servants in other families; or, when the time comes, wives and mothers in their own.'[17]

The brickmakers themselves, or at least some of them, recognised that their children were exposed to bad influences from the adults, especially from the male labourers without families who arrived just for the season. Close proximity to foul-mouthed and drunken men rubbed off on the children, who became equally coarse in their speech and manners. A teacher in Crayford summed up the behaviour of young brickies in his school: 'Some of such boys use filthy expressions and blasphemous language; exhibit sullen demeanour and show habits of untidiness; also show dispositions of cruelty.'[18]

The circumstances in which the children found themselves resulted mainly from the attitudes of their parents, many of whom had themselves enjoyed little or no education. Parental indifference to their children was, in the view of one brickfield foreman, 'the great evil'. Parents, he suggested, 'take no interest in their improvement; they drag them up instead of bringing them up, and don't care what becomes of them afterwards'.[19] Working in brickfields from as young as six, seven or eight years old inevitably prevented children from receiving much in the way of education and was likely to determine that they followed their parents into similar work. Their parents, either as a result of their financial circumstances, through a lack of responsibility or because they believed that what was good enough for them was good enough for their child, were unlikely to take a lead in ensuring that their children went to school.

Education was not compulsory for most of the nineteenth century. Middle- and upper-class children attended public schools or were privately tutored, and children

---

16   *Ibid.,* p. 142.

17   *Ibid.,* p. 136.

18   *Ibid.,* p. 151.

19   *Ibid.,* p. 140.

Pug boys and barrow loaders

Figure 14.1. Heston National School. (London Borough of Hounslow, Local Studies Service)

in towns could attend one of the historic grammar schools, but working-class children were reliant on 'dame schools', which required a modest payment and in which the standard of education was unregulated and variable. In response to this lack of provision and the poverty of many local families, wealthy people with a philanthropic disposition endowed schools for the poor. In west Middlesex, for example, schools like this were established by Elisha Biscoe on Norwood Green in 1767 and by the Rev. Edward Betham in Greenford in 1780. These schools were designed to teach literacy and numeracy and to give girls needlework skills, but there was always a strong religious element, as children were also to be taught 'the principles of the Christian religion'.[20]

Churches developed an important role in providing education for poor children, especially in the form of Sunday schools. These were established across the country following the initiative of Robert Raikes, a Gloucester newspaper editor, in 1781. The movement had supporters such as Sarah Trimmer, who opened a Sunday school in Ealing in 1786. Mrs Trimmer had first-hand experience of brickfields, as she was married to James Trimmer, the second generation of a major brickmaking dynasty, and lived close to their brickfields in Brentford. By 1801 there were 2290 such

---

20   J. Oates, *Southall and Hanwell: history and guide* (Stroud, 2003), pp. 37–8; F.A. Hounsell, *Greenford, Northolt and Perivale Past* (London, 1999), pp. 28–9. Children from Northolt brickmaking families attended the Greenford school.

Bricks of Victorian London

schools and 23,135 in 1851, when the number of children on the books had risen to more than 2 million.[21]

Day schools for poor families were established by the National Society for Promoting the Education of the Poor in the Principles of the Established Church (usually referred to as the National Society), founded in 1811. Its rival was the British & Foreign School Society (the British Society), founded three years later, which provided education that included non-denominational religious teaching.[22] Eventually the National Society took over responsibility for many existing charity schools. By the 1860s there were national schools in major brickmaking centres such as Heston, Southall, Crayford and Sittingbourne (Figure 14.1).[23]

It was a typical response of local people with a philanthropic disposition to want to provide schools for the more disadvantaged children in their district, but one that was not always shared by other local ratepayers. Novelist Margaret Oliphant captures this equivocal attitude in this exchange:

> 'By the by, Mr Green, I think of asking Philip for a bit of ground behind the hill yonder for our district school; a good situation, sir; capital for the poor brickmakers, who begin to squat about there in these wretched huts of theirs. We must do something for these poor fellows, Mr Green.'

> 'Rogues and reprobates,' said Mr Green laconically, shaking his head.

> 'The more reason we should do something for them – the more reason,' said Mr Wyburgh.[24]

We have already encountered brickmasters who took a paternalistic interest in the welfare of their employees, but in ways that allowed them to exercise a degree of social control over them, including building cottages for their workers. These were often close to the brickfield, but outside established villages and towns, so there might not be a convenient school for the children to attend. There was an incentive for the owner or a local clergymen to try and establish one to meet the need, in a similar way to providing mission halls. This is what happened in the Yeading district of Hayes parish, the location of a large brickfield operated by Henry Dodd and at least two others. In the 1860s these brickfields together operated forty stools and employed a workforce of at least 250 people.[25] In 1858 an advert appeared in *The Times*:

---

21 Hopkins, *Childhood transformed*, p. 130; Hounsell, *Greenford, Northolt and Perivale past*, p. 91; for information about the Trimmer family see <www.bhsproject.co.uk/families_trimmer.shtml>, accessed 7 February 2019.

22 Hounsell, *Greenford, Northolt and Perivale past*, p. 92.

23 Returns on average attendance made by schoolmasters. Children's Employment Commission, 5th Report, PP 1866, pp. 150–1.

24 M. Oliphant, *Zaidee: a romance*, 3 vols (Edinburgh, 1856), vol. 1, p. 139.

25 London Borough of Hillingdon, Museum and Archives Service. Hayes valuation, 1865.

Pug boys and barrow loaders

> Subscriptions are earnestly requested to enable the undersigned to erect in a remote part of his parish, and in the heart of the brickfields, a plain and commodious schoolhouse and master's residence. A free site has been generously granted for the proposed buildings, and subscriptions amounting to £85–10s, besides the gratuitous services of an eminent architect, have already been obtained. The entire cost will be under £400, and it is earnestly hoped that this attempt at bettering the religious and moral condition of the families of the labouring brickmakers will meet with a speedy response from a christian (sic) and charitable public. ... subscriptions most thankfully received by the Rev J.T. Willis, the Vicarage, Hayes, Middx.[26]

Dodd was one of the subscribers, giving £50, but it is not clear how successful this appeal was overall. A school house is visible on the 1894 Ordnance Survey map close to the brickfields but it was said that the school closed in 1861, when the master and the mistress transferred to Biscoe's school in Southall. The building was later used as a Mission Hall. No new school was opened until 1903.[27]

In Murston, on the outskirts of Sittingbourne, a school was needed after George Smeed built houses for his workers in Church Road. One house had its ground floor made into a single long room, which was used for the school, and it was only in 1868 that a national school was opened to serve the district.[28] Incidentally, both partners in the firm of Smeed, Dean were nonconformists and allowed the grounds of their houses to be used by the children of the Congregational and Baptist Sunday schools for their annual treats.[29]

Not all such initiatives were successful. Mr Smythe complained that he had endeavoured to establish a school at North Hyde, Heston, but it proved a failure 'as the people could not be got to send their children'.[30] The presence of a school did not necessarily mean that the brickmakers' children would attend it, especially once they had begun to work in the brickfield, and many lacked basic literacy and numeracy. On one visit to a brickfield in Dawley, Middlesex, in the 1860s an inspector found 'six children (out of 15) who could not read or write; one of these was 17 and another 15 years of age; the two youngest in the field were 10 years old, but one had worked in the previous summer; he could not read, though he said he had been to school in the winter'.[31] The last comment is important. Because children were generally employed in the period April to September each year, it was possible for them to attend school in the winter months. As a result, schools in brickmaking districts experienced a drop in attendance in the summer of around 15 to 20 per cent, and in the case of Sittingbourne

---

26 *The Times*, 27 November 1858, p. 5.

27 B. Holloway, *Rural Yeading in the industrial parish of Hayes 1900–1940* (Hayes, 1974), p. 24; *Victoria County History. Middlesex, vol. 4*, pp. 38–9; Ordnance Survey, Middlesex sheet 15.06.1894; *Kelly's Directory of Middlesex*, 1899.

28 B. Clarke, *A history of Murston* (Stroud, 2011), chapter 6.

29 *East Kent Gazette*, 21 July 1866, 13 July 1867.

30 Children's Employment Commission, 5th Report, PP 1866, p. 138.

31 *Ibid.*, p. 137.

Bricks of Victorian London

and Southall of as much as 40 per cent. The children were said not even to attend Sunday school, because on that day they would prepare the sand for the following week's work. Beneficial though winter attendance could be, in providing some sort of education, it came with disadvantages. Such a discontinuous style of learning was not conducive to children making progress with skills such as reading and, moreover, the arrival of the brickmakers' children in schools in winter was regarded as detrimental to good discipline. The teachers at Heston National School expressed this problem in forthright terms:

> When the children return to school from the brickfields they are generally rough in manner, dirty in habits, and have contracted the habit of swearing. Almost all that they have learned is forgotten, and usually with the quickest [it] takes two months to revive and learn again … . The regular attendants slacken in their discipline, and get more rough in manners. Their habitual swearing is the cause of the tradesmen's children not attending school.[32]

The master of a school in Sittingbourne made similar observations:

> They have forgotten much that they had learnt; have generally neglected their church and Sunday school; they have become ill-mannered, unruly, addicted to swearing and men's vices generally; indifferent about personal cleanliness and the notice of the clergy; the effect is so far felt that in much of the moral and religious education in many it is necessary to begin *de novo*, to awaken in them afresh the love of instruction and to exhort them not to regard the advice and ill example to which they have been exposed.[33]

A Government Committee investigating education in the 1860s came to the same conclusion:

> It frequently happens that the scholars make the requisite number of 200 attendances at the beginning of the school year, and are absent all the rest of the time till close upon the inspection. To give an actual instance: a scholar J.B. was presented to me in October; he had just come back to school after being at work since March in the brickfields helping his father; he was now 12 years old, but had been accustomed to work all the summer since he was 6; he then earned about 3s per week, but now 6s. It need scarcely be added, that he did not pass in any subject after his mind had lain fallow 6 months, but he would most likely have reached the standard if he had been examined just before he returned to his summer work.[34]

---

32 *Ibid.*, pp. 150–1.

33 *Ibid.*, p. 151.

34 Report of the Committee of Council on Education (England and Wales), PP 1865–6, vol. 27, Appendix, pp. 173–4.

Pug boys and barrow loaders

Campaigns to restrict child labour and improve access to education had started early in the nineteenth century, but at that point the focus of reformers was on children in factories or mines, although they accounted for only a small proportion of the total child workforce.[35] The first Factory Act was passed in 1833, and it restricted the hours of work for children aged nine to twelve in factories to eight per day, and required them to receive two hours' education daily. It took a further forty years to extend similar provisions to all the other types of manufacture in which children were engaged.[36] As the Victorians tended to regard working in the open air as inherently healthier than working in buildings in occupations that created dust, regulating brickfields was not an early priority.

In the House of Lords in 1861 the earl of Shaftesbury moved that a fresh enquiry should be undertaken into those trades and manufactures that were still not regulated by law, and as a result the Children's Employment Commission was established. During the 1860s it investigated a number of areas where women and children were employed, in agriculture, workshops and other occupations, of which the most notorious was chimney sweeping, with its 'climbing boys'.[37] The focus had now shifted away from the large factories to smaller units of production, where it was felt even worse evils might exist. In its fifth report, published in 1866, the Commission turned its attention, among other trades, to brickmaking, and took evidence from businesses in the Cowley district, in parts of inner London, at Crayford and in the brickmaking districts of Sittingbourne and Faversham in Kent. Inspectors spoke to a range of people, including owners and their foremen, individual workers, local policemen, clergymen and schoolteachers.

Following this report, in 1867 two Acts were passed which should finally have included the remaining unregulated trades, including brickmaking: the Factory Acts Extension Act, covering manufacturing premises employing more than fifty people; and the Workshop Regulation Act, applied to units with fewer employees.[38] These acts stipulated that no child under the age of eight should be employed in any handicraft; that children between the ages of eight and thirteen should be employed only half-time and should attend school the other half; and that young persons between the ages of fourteen and eighteen and women should be employed for no more than twelve hours per day, minus one and a half hours for meal breaks. It also prohibited children, young people and women from working on Sundays or after 2pm on Saturdays.[39] Specially appointed doctors, known as certifying surgeons, were

---

35 In 1830, before the first Factory Act, some 26,000 children were employed in textile factories. E. Hopkins, 'The Victorians and child labour', *The Historian*, 48 (Winter 1995), p. 10.

36 Hopkins, *Childhood transformed*, pp. 76–7.

37 Climbing boys were investigated by the Children's Employment Commission in its First Report, published in 1861.

38 30 & 31 Victoria, c. 103 (1867) *An act for the extension of the Factory Acts* (Factory Acts (Extension) Act); c. 146 (1867) *An act for regulating the hours of labour children, young persons and women employed in workshops* (Workshops Regulation Act).

39 B.L. Hutchins and A. Harrison, *A history of factory legislation*, 3rd edn (London, 1966), pp. 168–72; J. Roach, *Social reform in England, 1780–1880* (London, 1978), pp. 191–2.

required to provide certificates for children who were employed, confirming their age and their fitness for work.

At first the two acts were enforced by different bodies. Larger businesses were regulated by the Factory Inspectorate, while the enforcement of the regulations for smaller businesses was put in the hands of local sanitary authorities. This approach proved ineffective, especially as brickfields of different sizes often existed side by side and the factory inspectors could see that the regulations were being flouted in brickfields over which they had no jurisdiction. There were many attempts in the early years to evade the new requirements, and a failure actively to apply the new acts prompted a celebrated press campaign by George Smith, a man who had first-hand experience of brickfields in the Midlands.[40] In the particular style of manufacture practised there, children and teenagers carried weights of raw clay and finished bricks that were detrimental to their health, causing muscular and skeletal injuries. Even if each individual load was not beyond their strength, the cumulative effect of the constant repetition of the task for as long as twelve hours per day meant that a young worker could have carried a total weight of some 43lbs the equivalent of six and a quarter miles a day.[41] The investigations of the Children's Employment Commission in general supported these claims, as did the more lurid observations of an American, Elihu Burritt, in the Black Country.[42]

Smith's campaign was very effective, and the illustrations that accompanied his newspaper articles and his book *The cry of the children from the brickyards of England* were designed to touch the heart and fire the anger of his middle-class readers (Figure 14.2).[43] His attempts to influence government to toughen the law finally bore fruit in 1871 when an act was introduced in parliament by A.J. Mundella and the veteran campaigner the earl of Shaftesbury, who specifically cited George Smith as the 'zealous and long-tried friend of these sufferers': 'Now the state of things existing in the brickfields has risen to such a height of cruelty and abomination that a cry has gone forth through the whole country, and I most earnestly appeal to your Lordships to step in and arrest it.'[44]

By the 1871 Factory and Workshops Regulation Act smaller brickfields were placed under the control of the factory inspectors, alongside the larger ones.[45] This and many earlier acts were repealed by a further act in 1878, which consolidated the requirements on working hours and educational attendance as well as covering areas such as workplace safety.[46]

40　George K. Behlmer, 'George Smith (1831–1892)', *Oxford Dictionary of National Biography* (Oxford, 2004) <https://doi.org/10.1093/ref:odnb/25807>, accessed 10 January 2021.

41　Smith, *The cry of the children*, p. 11.

42　Smith quotes extensively from E. Burritt, *Walks in the Black Country and its green borderland* (London, 1868).

43　His campaign was reported in local and national newspapers such as *The Graphic*, 27 May 1871.

44　*Hansard House of Lords debates*, 11 July 1871.

45　Hopkins, *Childhood transformed*, p. 220; 34 & 35 Victoria, c. 104 (1871). An act to amend the acts relating to factories and workshops.

46　41 Victoria, c. 16 (1878) *An act to consolidate and amend the law relating to factories and workshops* (Factory & Workshops Act).

Figure 14.2. Children at work in a brickyard. Illustration to an article by George Smith, in *The Graphic* (1871).

Once children were expected to attend school half-time there were problems with the operation of the traditional moulding gang, which depended on all its members being present during working hours. Similar difficulties had already occurred in other industries.[47] In the aftermath of the passing of the 1867 Acts there was discussion about how the half-time system could best be accommodated; the alternatives were sending children to school for half of each day, or letting them attend on alternate days, an option sanctioned by the legislation. The problem was exacerbated by the distance many of them had to walk from their isolated villages to reach school. But, in either case, in order to allow production to continue unchecked, it was necessary to employ two sets of children to work with the adults in each gang. This clearly added to costs, and, it was argued, became additionally difficult because of a scarcity of children. In some districts in the London area the moulders were given an additional 4d per thousand bricks in recognition of the increased costs involved in using older boys to do the work previously done by younger children.[48]

---

47 U. Henriques, *Before the welfare state: social administration in early industrial Britain* (London, 1979), p. 96.
48 *Islington Gazette*, 8 August 1878.

Bricks of Victorian London

In the first few years after the passing of the 1867 acts there were some discrepancies, especially in relation to school attendance, as the regulations were written differently for factories and workshops, with a more flexible approach being available to the latter while strict half-time or alternate day attendance was required of the former. The close proximity of large and small brickfields in some districts led to some discontent and, as a Rainham schoolmaster put it, 'Parents may with some justice complain of a concession granted to small brickmasters withheld from larger ones.'[49] Prior to the passing of the acts there had been no compulsion for children to attend school at all, although, as we have seen, some parents chose to send them in the winter months. Now children who were employed were required by law to attend school for part of the day or part of the week, but in the winter months, when they weren't working, there was no such requirement. But there is some evidence that school attendance in the summer created a disposition for attending school throughout the year. One Kent schoolmaster told a factory inspector

> that he had children now [i.e., after the end of brickmaking season] coming to school, who had only first come to school last summer under the compulsion of the Act, and who [he was convinced] would never have come at all but for that compulsion. The Act was therefore not only bearing fruit during the season of work, but also originating a habit of school attendance during the winter, when schooling was no longer compulsory.[50]

The position would be changed with the passage of the 1870 Elementary Education Act, which created the groundwork for a national education system in which schooling could be provided for all children aged 5–13, but which still required parents to pay fees. The Elementary Education Act six years later placed a duty on parents to see that their children went to school. Furthermore, the 1876 Act required children entering work from age 10 to provide proof that they had previously been attending school.[51] This helped curb child labour in industries such as brickmaking, since factory inspectors did not need to prove that children had been working, only that they had not been attending school.[52]

The new regulations did not bring the employment of children in the brickfields to an end, but placed their employment under a new level of scrutiny. Generally, in the view of factory inspector Frederick Whymper, the new regulations were well observed, at least in the brickfields of Kent:

> The result of my inquiries was that the Act had been most strictly observed, and had already done a very great amount of good, in making work more regular, and

---

49 Rev J.S. Hoare quoted in Reports of the Inspectors of Factories to her Majesty's Principal Secretary of State for the Home Department for the half year ending 31st October 1869 (c.77), PP 1870, vol. 15, p. 63.

50 *Ibid.*, p. 51.

51 33 & 34 Victoria, c. 75 (1870) *An act to provide public elementary education in England & Wales*; 39 & 40 Victoria, c. 79 (1876) *An act to make further provision for elementary education*.

52 C. Nardinelli, 'Child labour and the Factory Acts', *Journal of Economic History*, 40 (1989), p. 754.

Pug boys and barrow loaders

in causing the very young children either to be dismissed or attend school. I was surprised greatly by the unanimity with which these statements were made.[53]

His view was corroborated by George Smeed, who praised Whymper's 'tact, energy and perseverance'. He claimed that the provisions of the Act had been 'strictly and universally' carried out in the Kent brickfields, and had proved to be 'productive of much good to the workpeople, and to have caused no unreasonable inconvenience to the employer'.[54] In the spirit of mutual admiration, Smeed was specifically praised by the inspectors:

> The principal masters, however, among whom Mr. G. Smeed has been conspicuous, have done their best to insist on the observance of the law, and their foremen have seconded them industriously. Mr. Ray, too, the certifying surgeon for Sittingbourne, has lost no opportunity in giving me his valuable advice.[55]

Notwithstanding these comments, there were a number of prosecutions of owners and parents of children in Sittingbourne and Faversham in 1869.[56] Despite the Inspector's high opinion of him, Smeed himself was among those taken to court for allowing a 12-year-old girl to be employed on his fields. His partner George Dean's argument that the girl was not employed by the company but by the moulding gang did not impress the magistrates, who fined the company 2s 6d with costs, noting that 'we cannot deal with Mr Smeed differently from other people'.[57] Owners often tried to hide their own responsibility in this matter behind the cover that the children were not directly employed by them, but by the moulding gangs. This claim rarely saved them when cases came to court.

On the other side of London factory inspector James Henderson came to the same conclusion as his Kent colleague in respect to the brickfields of west Middlesex:

> When I first went among the 'brickies' of West Middlesex and Buckinghamshire, I was gravely assured that I had an impossible task before me, and some even hinted that my interference would be resisted by physical violence, so lawless were these people assumed to be. Experience has disproved all these prognostications of evil. The Act has been accepted by both employers and their workpeople, the employment of young girls in the fields has been abolished, and the law is generally well-observed.[58]

---

53 Reports of the Inspectors of Factories, PP 1870, p. 51.
54 Letter to *The Times*, 5 August 1871, p. 11.
55 Reports of the Inspectors of Factories, PP 1873, p. 17.
56 Nine owners and nine parents were convicted in Sittingbourne; the cases against one owner and six parents were withdrawn on payment of costs. Report of the Inspectors of Factories, PP 1870, p. 61.
57 *East Kent Gazette*, 24 July 1869.
58 Report of Inspector of Factories, PP 1877, p. 30.

Bricks of Victorian London

However, not all owners seemed to have a proper understanding of their responsibilities. When questioned by the Factory and Workshops Commission in 1876 the representative of the Association of Master Brickmakers, Robert Maclean Smythe, showed a poor grasp of the legislative requirements and appeared not to realise that the act allowed the alternate day arrangement. Ideally, as far as the masters were concerned, the half-time system should operate as it had informally beforehand, with the children working during the summer months and attending school in the winter. Such a compromise flew in the face of the aims of the legislation and was one that the Inspectorate was unwilling to accept.[59] The commissioners also disputed the owners' contention that the statutory age limits – 13 before young people could work a twelve-hour day and 10 before a child could be employed at all – were set too high, and that the work undertaken in the Middlesex brickfields was much less arduous than that which was done elsewhere. The masters wanted compulsory school attendance to end at age 11.[60]

The legislation did not solve all issues of school attendance. The tendency for children to be absent in summer months, either regularly or occasionally, when they were substituting for an absent brother or sister, persisted into the 1890s, as school log books show.

> Betham School, Greenford, 21 October 1879 'We have recently received six boys from this quarter [Northolt] who were employed in the brickfields.'
>
> Northolt School. 15th May 1882 'Henry Saunders and Henry Rose still absent from school to work in the brickfields.'
>
> 20th April 1894 'Brickmaking recommenced and some children are absent barrow loading.'[61]

Both employers and parents could be fined for employing a child who should have been at school. In 1873, for example, George Wethered was fined £1 for employing a child under the age of 13 without a school certificate, and the child's father, Edward Leaver, a Hayes brick moulder, 5s for neglecting to send his child to school.[62] Brickmaker J.E. Butcher was called before Sittingbourne Police Court for failing to produce attendance certificates for two boys.[63] Even major businesses fell foul of the law. In 1880 Messrs Rutter were convicted of eight offences of employing boys who had not been certified and fined 20s in each case, and Samuel Pocock was convicted on four summonses in relation to the employment of two boys in 1878.

---

59 Report of the Commissioners appointed to inquire into the working of the Factory and Workshops Act., Vol. II Minutes of evidence (c.1443) (1876) vol. XXX, pp. 173–5.

60 *Ibid.*

61 Betham School, Greenford. Transcript of Log Book for 1879–1890; Northolt School. Transcript of Log Book 23 July 1866–23 December 1891. Both transcribed by C.H. Keene.

62 *Report of the Inspector of Factories for the half-year ending 31st October 1873.* PP 1874, xiii, p. 25.

63 *Aldershot Military Gazette,* 14 September 1878.

Pug boys and barrow loaders

These prosecutions were brought by the factory inspectors. In the case relating to Pocock, Inspector Gould argued for a conviction and fine in one case but only costs in respect to the others, but the magistrates took a tougher line:

> The chairman remarking that the Act [of 1876] had been so greatly infringed in the district during the season that he was sorry proceedings of this nature had not been taken before. The school attendance officer had repeatedly reported cases in which children were illegally employed in brickfields. Mr Gould said he could only take proceedings when he saw a child at work, and it was not always easy to do so ... the boy who had been called as a witness said that when it was known that the inspector was coming the children were 'popped' under some straw.[64]

The legislation necessitated a certain amount of bureaucracy, as every employed child had to be seen by a certifying surgeon and records maintained at the workplace. Not surprisingly, these regulations were sometimes contravened, either accidentally or deliberately. In 1896 the firm of Coles, Shadbolt & Co. was convicted at Uxbridge Magistrates' Court of employing boys without obtaining the proper certificates of fitness from the doctor and failing to keep a register in the required form.[65]

It is difficult to gauge the prevalence of women and girls in the brickfields of the London area. It is rare to find in the Census returns the wives of brickmakers recorded as having any occupation, but this may be a convention that masks some degree of employment in brickmaking. Even if they were not part of the moulding gang, they were kept busy caring for those children too young to work and providing meals for their husbands and sons, as well as for the casual labourers who boarded with them in the summer months. Likewise, only occasionally are girls recorded as working in the brickyards and this may be an accurate reflection of the practice in this part of the country, but one that differed from, say, the brickyards of the Black Country. In the mid-1860s Tildesley admitted to employing about twenty females of all ages and the Southall Brickmaking Company two per stool, a total of between thirty-five and forty. The Rev. Dennett thought the average for the Cowley district was about two per stool.[66] In 1869 there were 288 women and girls employed in the Kent brickfields, about 18 per cent of the total workforce, of whom half were over 18 and the rest between the ages of 8 and 18.[67] In 1876, nearly a decade after the 1867 Acts had imposed restrictions on the working hours of young people under the age of 18 and women, Middlesex brickmaster R.M. Smythe stated unequivocally that girls were not employed at all, and the following year Sub-Inspector Henderson declared that 'the employment of young girls in the fields has been abolished, and the law is generally well-observed'.[68] Yet the Inspectorate had prosecuted several employers in the previous few years for employing girls under the age of 16. In 1873 Francis Newell of Southall was fined £2

---

64 *Manchester Times*, 23 October 1880; *Bucks Herald*, 2 November 1878.
65 *British Clayworker*, September 1896.
66 Children's Employment Commission, 5th Report, PP 1866, pp. 135–49.
67 *Reports of the Inspectors of Factories... for the half-year ending 31 October 1869*, p. 59
68 Report of the Factory and Workshops Commission, pp. 173–6 (Smythe); p. 165 (Henderson)

Bricks of Victorian London

with 7s costs and Waring Brothers £1 13s with similar costs for this offence. Individual moulders would also be prosecuted for allowing an under-age girl to be employed, as happened to William Pigott of Dawley.[69] Owners might not always know that under-age children were working in their brickfield. In 1876 Mr Savage, the manager of the Southall Brick Company, made this claim in respect of Mary Hill, a barrow loader, but this did not prevent the company being fined. In another case a 14-year-old girl was found on the site, but it was alleged that she was not working but merely bringing her father a pot of beer. This explanation was accepted when, upon examination, her hands proved to be soft and white. Her father, however, was cautioned for impeding the factory inspector.[70]

In 1873 Inspector Redgrave was alerted to a number of offences at Messrs Rutter's Crayford brickfields, and found upwards of fifty cases of infringement. A sample case of a 10-year old girl was taken to court. The defendants made the familiar defence that the young people were not employed by the company but by the moulders, an argument that was inevitably rejected. The company was fined 20s.[71] The following year Smeed, Dean was prosecuted for employing girls under the age of 16 and failing to produce certificates of school attendance in respect of three boys. Eleven parents were also summoned in respect of these offences. The company offered an explanation that there was a misunderstanding about whether an open-air works was defined as a factory.[72] The law continued to be contravened later in the decade; a Highgate brickmaker was fined in 1878 for employing a girl under 16 in 1878, and an Edmonton brickmaker in 1879, both at the prompting of the same factory inspector.

The extension of the factory acts and the introduction of machinery progressively reduced the number of children working in the brickfields, and it is possible that the regulations hastened the introduction of machinery. This had been a hope expressed as far back as the 1850s by a parliamentary committee examining schools:

> I trust that employment in the brickfields will shortly be superseded by brickmaking machinery. The neighbourhood of a brickfield is always a serious injury to a pauper school. It furnishes a large demand for children for about 6 months in the year during which they earn high wages in a simple manual labour. At the end of that period they are turned off, thoroughly demoralised by the work. This high-priced casual employment seems equally demoralising of the men, and it forms one of the numerous instances in which it seems obvious that the introduction of machinery would be of great and immediate benefit to the labouring classes.[73]

---

69 Reports of the Inspectors of Factories, PP 1873, p. 25; Reports of the Inspectors of Factories, PP 1877, p. 34.

70 *Marvel and Middlesex Register*, 27 July 1876, p. 3.

71 *The Times*, 16 September 1873.

72 *East Kent Gazette*, 24 July 1874.

73 Committee of Council on Education (Schools of Parochial Unions and Reformatory schools in England and Wales). Minutes. With reports by Her Majesty's Inspector of Schools, House of Lords (1856–7), p. 35.

Pug boys and barrow loaders

Figure 14.3. Moulding gang at Edmonton. (London Borough of Enfield Local History Centre)

It has been argued that child labour in non-textile industries was already declining before it became subject to factory control, although the legislation helped to accelerate the process.[74] Although steam-powered pug mills and moulding machines had been introduced in the late 1850s, the increased labour costs imposed by the provisions of the Workshops Act may have encouraged their more widespread adoption. It was claimed that the exclusion of the youngest children after 1867 had added 6d per thousand bricks to the cost of moulding and raised the wages of boys from 5s to 7s a week. There was now a clear incentive to design machinery that would substitute for part of the child labour, by, for example, setting up pug mills so that they fed clay directly on to the moulding bench, thus obviating the need for a pug boy. Sub-Inspector Henderson reported that

> The pug-mill is now generally placed so as to deliver the clay direct on to the moulder's table: and one hand in the gang, the 'pug-boy', whose work was most laborious, having to stoop and lift from twenty to twenty-five tons of wet clay, has been dispensed with.[75]

---

74 Nardinelli, 'Child labour', pp. 739–55.
75 Factory and Workshops Acts Commission, Report, Appendix E, PP 1876, vol. 30, p. 190.

Bricks of Victorian London

By the end of the century many of the abuses that reformers had campaigned against had been removed by successive factory acts, and the provision of compulsory elementary education kept younger children out of the workforce. These changes, together with the introduction of machinery, undermined the structure of family-based moulding gangs. Now the workers in the brickfields were mainly adult males and teenage boys (Figure 14.3). Yet, despite these improvements, it was felt that the relationship between workers and employers in the brick industry remained an unequal one, and the brickies turned to industrial action to effect changes.

Chapter 15

'The great struggle': industrial disputes and trade unions in the brick industry

In parallel with the changes that the government had imposed on the industry by means of the Factory Acts, the brickmakers themselves took collective action over wage rates and employment practices. In challenging the terms of their contracts they sought to shift the balance in the relationship between themselves and their employers, and in so doing they became part of the bigger struggle between capital and labour in the 1890s.

At the beginning of the nineteenth century trade unions were outlawed, but with the passing of a new Combination Act in 1824 it became possible for workers to join together to campaign for increased wages or improved conditions.[1] There was, however, no explicit right to strike, and violence, intimidation and picketing could result in imprisonment. Although there was trade union activity in some parts of the country and in some trades, there appears to have been little involving brickmakers in southern England until the 1860s, although a Brickmakers' New United Friendly Benefit Society was registered as a Friendly Society in June 1845 and met at the King's Head Inn in West Drayton.[2]

Early unions were generally localised, small-scale and confined to more skilled workers. Usually they were more assertive in times of economic upturn, when employees were in a stronger bargaining position, but quieter during depressions in trade, when the demand for their members' skills was lower. For this reason London trade unions were relatively unsuccessful during 1837–42, but revived in the late 1840s. The formation of the Amalgamated Society of Engineers in 1851, which brought together a number of smaller bodies, marked the beginning of the so-called New Model Unionism. The relative prosperity of the 1850s dampened down political campaigning, which had peaked with the Chartist demonstration in Kennington in 1848, but encouraged union activity.[3]

Unionism developed in the brickmaking industry in the 1860s but there was no single union for the whole country and the causes the unionists fought varied from place to place. In the London area brickmakers may have been encouraged by a strike of the building trades in 1859 over calls for a nine-hour day. Other unions joined the strike committee, from which developed the London Trades Council, raising £23,000 for the strike fund.[4] A leading figure on the council was William Burn, secretary of the

---

1   The new legislation repealed the Acts of 1799 and 1821.

2   Little else is known about it. TNA FS2 2422; J.B. Smethurst and P. Carter, *Historical directory of trade unions*, vol. 6 (Farnham, 2009), pp. 5–6.

3   A. Briggs, *The age of improvement, 1783–1867* (London, 1959), pp. 405, 408.

4   Inwood, *A history of London*, pp. 623–4.

Bricks of Victorian London

London brickmakers. Although he was a shoemaker, he 'gave up his trade to devote himself to organising the brutally exploited brickmakers'.[5]

In the 1860s a series of violent strikes took place in the north of England, including among the brickmakers of Manchester, causing injuries and death. So dangerous did these 'outrages' appear that there was widespread demand for a public inquiry. A Royal Commission was appointed in 1867, which delivered several reports in the following years.[6] The focus of the men's grievances was the introduction of machinery and their union sought to protect its members from deskilling and from workforce reductions. The changes created a different work organisation, where the workers were paid by the hour rather than on piece rates, thus undermining the traditional gang system. Local bricklayers supported the action by refusing to use machine-made bricks. It was said that similar practices were 'rather common about Lancashire', but did not extend to London and there seemed to be no obvious co-operation between the southern brickmakers and their northern brethren.[7] There were, however, attempts to form amalgamations of local trade unions, such as the Operative Brick-Makers' General Amalgamation, which met in Birmingham in 1867 and attracted 35 delegates.[8]

Disputes in the London area were more likely to be about wage rates and employment contracts. Adopting the title 'operative brickmakers' to distinguish themselves as workers rather than owners, the Friendly United Society of Operative Brickmakers of London and Vicinity was formed in 1859, later changing its name to the United Operative Brickmakers' Benevolent and Protective Society of the South of England. It claimed to have nearly 1000 members in 1866, organised in twenty-six 'lodges'.[9] In his annual report for 1866 its secretary William Burn noted that 'We have been put to severe test this last year by the many attempts to reduce the prices [paid to moulders], but I am happy to say we have prevented them, and at the same time we have been enabled to advance the wages of some lodges, thanks to the firmness of the men.'[10] The union was successful in a number of the battles it fought to resist pay cuts and to protect its members' rights. It took on employers in the courts over contracts of employment and the payment of back pence, the money held back by the owner and paid at the end of the season. Back pence could be withheld if, for example, the men failed to cover the hacks in inclement weather and bricks were spoilt. A brickie explained what this meant in practice.

---

5 G. Tate (ed.), *London Trades Council 1860–1950: a history* (London, 1950), pp. 5, 8.

6 Price, 'The other side of respectability', pp. 110–32. An earlier Manchester strike, in 1843, by members of an early Operative Brickmakers' Society resulted in bloody confrontations with blacklegs and the military. F. Engels, *The condition of the working class in England* (London, 1987), pp. 234–5.

7 Evidence of Mr A Mault to the Royal Commission appointed to inquire into the organisation and rules of trade unions and other associations, 11th report, PP 1868–9, vol. 31, p. 30.

8 P.S. Brown and D.N. Brown, 'Industrial disputes in Victorian brickyards, 1: the 1860s', *BBS Information*, 99 (February 2006), p. 7.

9 *Ibid.*

10 *The Beehive*, 15 December 1866.

'The great struggle'

> Our work is of a most laborious kind; we toil 14 hours per day. Even then our work is not done. Should it rain on Sundays, or in the night, we have to get up out of our warm beds and hasten off to our different fields, facing the pitiless storm, getting drenched with wet, for the purpose of protecting the employers' property by covering the fresh made bricks with straw, occupying a considerable time in the pouring rain, for which extra and dangerous labour (for it is dangerous, we know, to our cost, bringing on cramp, rheumatism, and other disorders – in fact, making old men of us when we ought to be in the prime of our lives), we do not get paid one farthing, but it all goes in as part of our work.[11]

In the winter of 1864 there was a strike, lasting several weeks, by more than 250 men in Highbury and Stoke Newington against a proposed reduction of moulding rates for the following year from 5s 6d to 5s per thousand, for which no reason was given. The men's union argued that the 'prosperous state of our trade, and the great demand there is for bricks, and the prices obtained, would enable the employers to give an advance rather than reduce our wages'.[12] A second source of dispute arose because employers had started trying to tie down the moulding rate for the following season by issuing contracts in December, rather than in the spring (Figure 15.1). The response of the masters to the strike action was to lock the men out. Strike pay was paid by the union, and through subscriptions from other trades. Journalists praised the demeanour of the men; at one of the union meetings they 'found a quiet attentive assemblage of hard-handed men, and heard the labour question handled in an able manner by successive speakers'.[13] The men, who went back to work at the end of March at a rate of 5s 5d per thousand, felt satisfied with the result, especially as the union had recruited many new members during the dispute.[14]

The same issues occupied the union throughout the 1860s. In May 1866 a crowded courthouse at Brentford heard a case brought against forty striking moulders from the Heston area for alleged breach of contract under the Masters and Servants Act of 1823. In November 1865 Thomas Avery, an employee of James Burchett, had signed an agreement to make bricks at 4s 4d per thousand but had left work on 24 April 1866 and did not return. Burchett instigated legal action, but admitted in court that he had promised that if any of his neighbours agreed a wage rise he would also give it, notwithstanding the terms of the agreement. He claimed that none had, but witnesses confirmed that indeed some had, including Keyzor and Rutter. The defendant's solicitor Mr Merriman, retained by the Union, argued that a moulder was not a servant under the terms of the act as he employed the men in his gang, suggesting, rather fancifully, that a brick moulder 'was as much a contractor as Sir Morton Peto [one of the leading railway builders]'. The magistrates, while agreeing that it was bad practice for masters to make these half promises, still sentenced Avery

---

11   *Ibid.*, 31 December 1864, 7 January 1865. One of the brickfields involved in the dispute was that of James and Alfred Stroud at Clapton.

12   *Ibid.*, 4 February 1865.

13   *Morning Advertiser*, 2 February 1865; *The Beehive*, 4 February 1865.

14   *The Beehive*, 1 April 1865.

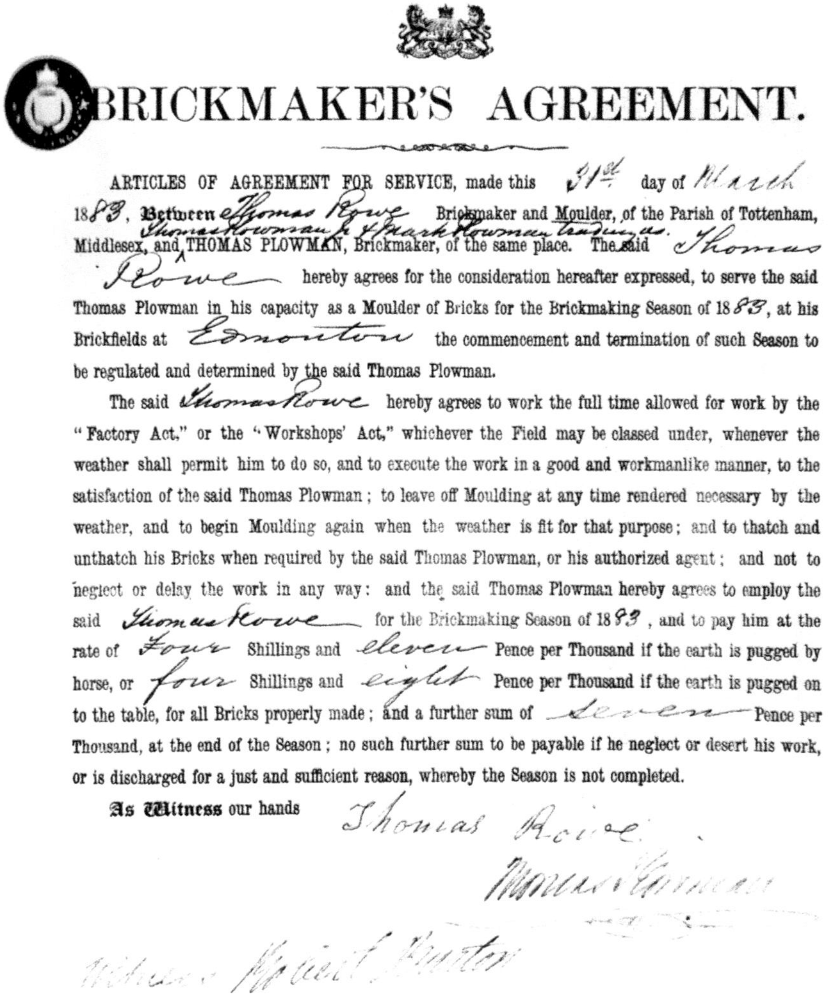

BRICKMAKER'S AGREEMENT.

ARTICLES OF AGREEMENT FOR SERVICE, made this 31st day of March 1883, Between Thomas Rowe Brickmaker and Moulder, of the Parish of Tottenham, Middlesex, and THOMAS PLOWMAN, Brickmaker, of the same place. The said Thomas Rowe hereby agrees for the consideration hereafter expressed, to serve the said Thomas Plowman in his capacity as a Moulder of Bricks for the Brickmaking Season of 1883, at his Brickfields at Edmonton the commencement and termination of such Season to be regulated and determined by the said Thomas Plowman.

The said Thomas Rowe hereby agrees to work the full time allowed for work by the "Factory Act," or the "Workshops' Act," whichever the Field may be classed under, whenever the weather shall permit him to do so, and to execute the work in a good and workmanlike manner, to the satisfaction of the said Thomas Plowman; to leave off Moulding at any time rendered necessary by the weather, and to begin Moulding again when the weather is fit for that purpose; and to thatch and unthatch his Bricks when required by the said Thomas Plowman, or his authorized agent; and not to neglect or delay the work in any way: and the said Thomas Plowman hereby agrees to employ the said Thomas Rowe for the Brickmaking Season of 1883, and to pay him at the rate of Four Shillings and eleven Pence per Thousand if the earth is pugged by horse, or four Shillings and eight Pence per Thousand if the earth is pugged on to the table, for all Bricks properly made; and a further sum of seven Pence per Thousand, at the end of the Season; no such further sum to be payable if he neglect or desert his work, or is discharged for a just and sufficient reason, whereby the Season is not completed.

As Witness our hands Thomas Rowe

Thomas Plowman

Witness Robert Baxter

Figure 15.1. Brickmaking agreement between Thomas Plowman, brickmaker, and Thomas Rowe, moulder, for the 1883 season. (London Brick Company archive/Forterra Building Products Ltd)

to two months' imprisonment, but suspended the sentence for a week in the hope that other brickmakers would return to work.[15]

Later in the year a case about the same issues came before Uxbridge Magistrates Court, this time involving the Southall Brickmaking Company. Mr Merriman again appeared on behalf of the employees and the Brickmasters'

15 *Reynold's Newspaper,* 13 May 1866.

'The great struggle'

Association was also represented. Like the Heston case, the moulders had signed agreements in December 1865 fixing the rates for the 1866 moulding season at 4s 10d per thousand, but when the season commenced they were told that rates might be lowered by 6d, but not when. When their gang members were told of the likelihood of a wage cut, some of them walked off to find work elsewhere. Without them the moulders were unable to work, and went off themselves to see if they could find replacements in neighbouring districts. Five out of sixteen gangs stopped work. Tebbutt, the manager, did not cut an impressive figure in court, and his description of the way he and his son also ran a public house and a shop prompted Merriman to suggest he might be contravening the Truck Act. The magistrate convicted the men, but sentenced them to only fourteen days' imprisonment. Merriman referred the case to the Court of Common Pleas, which was already considering a similar case, and one outcome of these challenges was that the Masters and Servants Act was amended the following year to limit the prosecution of strikers for breach of contract. Unions, however, remained dissatisfied, as criminal action was still possible in what were described as 'aggravated cases'.[16]

As if to prove the point about subcontracting, in May 1865 Daniel Dixey, a moulder, summoned two members of his gang before the Uxbridge magistrates for having deserted their work without just cause. They had been hired for the summer season, one as his pug boy, the other as his off-bearer. In court neither produced any satisfactory reasons as to why they had walked off the job, but Dixey offered to take the men back on. The defendants agreed to this, faced by the magistrates' warning that otherwise they faced time in jail.[17]

In January 1867 brickmakers in Essex, working for a Mr Hill, who had brickfields in Ilford, Wanstead Flats and Chobham, were locked out for refusing to accept a 6d cut in rates. As the strike dragged on into April the union's strike fund became exhausted and it had to reach out to fellow unionists for contributions, including an impassioned plea directed at northern brickmakers. The brickmasters were able to take advantage of the union's precarious financial position. A large employer in Stoke Newington also locked out his men for refusing to accept a cut in wages, and other incidents occurred in Sydenham and Deptford where the masters evicted families from the cottages they rented.[18]

Issues about the payment of back pence also came before the courts. One brickmaker took his employer to court because of his failure to pay out at the end of the season the 6d per thousand back pence he had been deducting, although there had been no complaint of neglect against the moulder. The claimant had difficulty proving his case, as the employer had retained his tally book, and the case was

---

16 C. Cook and J. Stevenson (eds), *Longman handbook of modern British history 1714–2001*, 4th edn (London, 2001), pp. 210–11.

17 *Broadwater's Buckinghamshire Advertiser & Uxbridge Journal*, 27 May 1865.

18 Brown and Brown, 'Industrial disputes, 1', p. 8, quoting *The Beehive*, 12 January, 2 February, 13 April 1867. *The Beehive*, edited by George Potter, who had led the building trade strike in 1859, was a newspaper that devoted itself to trade union activities and radical politics. At its peak in 1865 it sold 8000 copies a week. Briggs, *Age of improvement*, p. 408fn.

Bricks of Victorian London

referred from Sittingbourne to the Court of Common Pleas, where the judgement went in favour of the claimant.[19]

The union had several successes, but was left with legal fees for the court cases it had defended. Secretary Burn subsequently found himself in a debtor's prison in 1868 owing £96 to the solicitors Merriman and Buckland, whose costs for the work they had undertaken came to over £200.[20]

In the next decade there were other cases involving alleged verbal agreements. In a dispute at Pocock's Hillingdon brickfield in 1876 (discussed earlier on p. 123) a group of moulders left their work when they did not receive an anticipated increase that they claimed was part of a verbal agreement. Pocock argued that the men had breached their contract of employment as they had signed an agreement including the paragraph:

> the said moulders shall each forfeit and pay 5s for every day if the work of the berth or stool shall be hindered or obstructed, or not proceeded with through their default, or the default of any of their assistants, such forfeit to be deducted from the current week's wages at the discretion of the said Samuel Pocock.

Pocock demanded compensation. Whether the men were able to read or not, the agreement had only been read to them, and they hadn't been given a copy. Here again there was a verbal agreement that wages would be increased if other fields in the area started paying more. The outcome of the dispute was not recorded in the local press.[21]

However, despite this evidence of trade union activity, it was estimated that only about 6 per cent of the 42,623 workers in the industry nationally were members of a union.[22]

There appear to have been far fewer trade disputes in the second half of the 1870s, but one occurred in Sittingbourne early in the next decade, involving employees of Smeed, Dean, Wills & Packham and Charles Burley, again about signing an agreement in the winter binding them to the rates to be paid the following season. The men based their claim for an increase in wages on an unexpected rise in the price of bricks, having been persuaded the previous autumn to agree to rates that were lower than those paid in 1880. The men's case was weak in legal terms as they had indeed signed the new contracts and lacked the support of a trade union. They also encountered a hostile public reaction and were accused of being 'malcontents' and using intimidation to persuade workers in other fields to down tools. Later in the season a large meeting at the Town Hall, Sittingbourne, was addressed by Alfred Simmons, leader of the Kent & Sussex Labourers' Union, who noted that these autumn contracts were not enforced in other brickfields in Kent. He asserted that if the men had been part of the union, the strike could have been averted and the

---

19 Knox v. Inkly. *Reynold's Newspaper*, 3 May 1868.
20 *Ibid.*
21 *Marvel and Middlesex Register*, 18 May 1876; *Buckinghamshire Advertiser*, 20 May 1876.
22 Brown and Brown, 'Industrial disputes, 1', p. 8.

'The great struggle'

dispute settled by arbitration. Based on what had occurred elsewhere, this sounds like wishful thinking.[23]

Within a few years the economy had sunk into depression and there was a marked fall in the demand for bricks. As a result, masters scaled back production and reduced the price paid to the moulding gangs. The men tried to combat these reductions, including by an unsuccessful strike at Stroud's in Southall and some other brickfields in 1883, but were not in a good bargaining position.[24] As conditions began to improve at the end of the 1880s there was a resurgence of disputes about pay or working hours as the men attempted to return wages to the level from which they had been reduced earlier in the decade.[25] The major strikes that occurred after 1887 arose out of the unwillingness of the owners to respond to improving market conditions and pay the men more. Brickmakers in the London area at this point did not seem to belong to a union, the earlier union having disappeared.

Between the 1860s and 1890s changes had taken place affecting the relationship between employer and workman, with legislation giving employees greater protections and placing new obligations on the owners. As well as adhering to the requirements of the Factory Acts, firms now had to take account of the Employers' Liability Act of 1880 requiring them to pay compensation for injuries sustained at work.[26] The *British Clayworker* started to carry a regular column listing accidents in the workplace, some horrific, especially when they involved limbs caught in machinery. However, a wide if not exhaustive reading of these reports suggests that the London area was remarkably free from incidents of this kind.[27] Nevertheless, even if the risk seemed low, employers had to be prepared to meet claims. In the aftermath of the passing of the Workmen's Compensation Act of 1897 they formed the Brickmasters' Employers' Liability Association Ltd, capitalised at £100,000, whose first directors were G.H. Dean, of Smeed, Dean, A. Rutter of D. & C. Rutter and G.E. Wragge, the managing director of Eastwoods.[28]

For several years, from 1887 onward, there were disputes in one brickmaking district or another. One occurred in the Cowley district in April that year, starting in

---

23 *East Kent Gazette*, 2 April, 9 April, 23 April, 4 June, 11 June 1881.

24 *Uxbridge Gazette & Middlesex and Bucks Observer*, 28 April, 5 May 1883.

25 P.S. and D.N. Brown, 'Industrial disputes in Victorian brickyards, 2: the 1890s', *BBS Information*, 101 (July 2006), pp. 14–19.

26 The Employers' Liability Act of 1880 established a right to compensation for injury or death when the injury was caused by a defect in equipment or machinery, negligence of any person placed in a position of authority by the employer or any act or omission made by following the orders of the employer or their representative. The burden of proof was on the employee. Compensation was limited to the equivalent of three years' pay of someone in the same type of job in the same location. A. Ruegg, *A treatise upon the Employers' Liability Act, 1880* (London, 1880); it was replaced by the Workmen's Compensation Act of 1897, under whose terms the employees only had to show that they had been injured on the job. D.M. Walker, *The Oxford companion to the law* (Oxford, 1980), pp. 1307–8.

27 *British Clayworker*, passim.

28 *Ibid.*, August 1898, p. xxvii.

Bricks of Victorian London

Southall, and quickly spread to the surrounding areas. The men argued that following the revival in trade the masters were in a position to pay more. The men in Heston brickfields joined the strike, and the masters responded by closing their brickfields for a fortnight. Many more men were thrown out of work, although some of them, it was said, were able to find work elsewhere in the neighbourhood. The total loss in wages in the district was estimated at £1000 a week, and inevitably had a wider impact.[29] The men demanded an immediate increase of 6d per thousand or, if it was not conceded within a week, an increase of 8d, the amount said to have been lost since 1885. An unsympathetic local press supported the masters, but conceded that the striking men's families would 'experience the severest pinch' and the local economy would suffer from the 'injurious action of the men'.[30] The Cowley Brickmasters' Association put their side of the argument in letters to *The Times* and other newspapers, claiming that 'for the past three years brickmaking has been carried on at an almost ruinous loss to the manufacturer, and in the present depressed state of the building trade there appears to be no probability of a sustained advance to fairly remunerative prices'.[31] They agreed that moulding rates had been reduced by 15 per cent, but argued that the selling price of bricks had fallen by 40 per cent.[32]

It was asserted, by a correspondent who labelled himself 'A working man', that the masters were attempting to undermine the men's resolve by asking local shopkeepers 'to stop the poor brickies' credit'.[33] The strike continued with angry words but without violent behaviour, although 'had it not been for the fact of bodies of police being placed in the neighbourhood of the fields, some noisy outbreaks might have occurred'. However, by the end of May the men could no longer sustain the strike and, without support from a union, returned to work. As the local paper uncharitably suggested, some of the strikers got into financial difficulties and were 'at length driven to taste humble pie from sheer necessity'.[34]

Industrial action returned to the brickfields of the London area at the start of the 1889 moulding season. A large meeting at St Matthew's Church, Yiewsley, chaired by the vicar, the Rev. H.G. Bird, heard the men argue the same case: that market conditions had improved and the masters were in a position to restore moulding rates to the old level. 'You took the price off when bricks were low, and now we want you to put 6d per 1000 on.' One of the moulders who spoke at the meeting complained that the owners had used underhand tactics to get the men to return to work:

> In the unfortunate strike ... two years ago, certain cases had since come to light when men had been offered £5 to decoy them to go to work, as a means of inducing other men to do so, and this plan, he understood, had succeeded very well. He heard that the same bait had been held out in the present case, but he

---

29 *Southall News and Norwood Advertiser*, 27 April 1887; *County of Middlesex Independent*, 27 April 1887.

30 *Middlesex Independent*, 17 April 1887; *Uxbridge and West Drayton Gazette*, , 7 May 1887.

31 *The Times*, 11 May 1887

32 *Acton Gazette*, 14 May 1887; *Uxbridge & West Drayton Gazette*, 14 May 1887.

33 *Middlesex Independent*, 18 May 1887.

34 *Middlesex and Surrey Express*, 21 May 1887; *Uxbridge & West Drayton Gazette*, 28 May 1887.

'The great struggle'

hoped that the men would not be thus induced to sell their mates, but would act like true heroes.[35]

It was proposed that Bird should meet with Mr Broad, of Broad, Harris, to try and resolve the dispute. They agreed a compromise whereby the masters offered the men an increase of 4d, which they accepted. However, Eastwoods broke ranks with their fellow masters by offering a rise of 7d but refusing to re-employ two men who had spoken at the public meetings. At a later meeting a letter from Mr Broad was read out in which he applauded the mediation of Revd Bird in the dispute, warned the men about the competitiveness of the Cowley district and condemned Eastwoods' stance.

> The motives of Messrs Eastwood & Co in giving their men sevenpence, are only known to themselves, but, as you remark, it is obvious that it can have been done out of no sympathy with the men. All the other masters in the district have unanimously agreed to abide by the arrangements made by Mr Bird, as representing the men, to pay fourpence advance on last year's prices ... their action is based on purely personal motives, and totally opposed to the general interests of the Cowley brickmaking industry. It cannot be too clearly pointed out that the cost of brickmaking in the Cowley district is greatly in excess of that in Kent, where by far the larger quantity of bricks for supplying the London market is made, any attempt therefore to increase the cost of production must operate against the Cowley trade ... at the prices agreed upon [i.e. the additional 4d] we are paying 7d per 1000 more for moulding than is paid in Kent, the work being precisely similar.[36]

It will be remembered that Eastwoods had substantial brickfields in Kent as well as in Middlesex.

Similar demands were raised by the men working in brickfields across north and east London, in Edmonton, Ponders End, Temple Mills, Stratford, Ilford, Woodford, Wanstead Flats, Walthamstow, Mayors Hill, West Green, Green Lanes and Tottenham. Here, too, the men lacked union backing and, therefore, strike pay, and had to collect money from other workmen to support themselves and their families.[37] In order to help sustain industrial action, it was suggested that a union be formed once the men were back in employ and able to afford subscriptions.[38]

The situation changed after 1889, with the advent of the 'New Unionism'. In this phase of the trade union movement larger unions were established that reached beyond skilled tradesmen to the semi-skilled and unskilled labour force, whose conditions of employment were often more precarious. These new unions included the Dock, Wharf, Riverside and General Labourers' Union, founded by Ben Tillett,

---

35 _Uxbridge & West Drayton Gazette,_ 4 May 1889.

36 _Ibid.,_ 18 May 1889.

37 _The People,_ 12 May 1889.

38 _Uxbridge & West Drayton Gazette,_ 18 May 1889.

Bricks of Victorian London

Figure 15.2. Will Thorne, leader of the Gas Workers and General Labourers Union. (GMB website, www.gmb.org.uk.)

and the Gas Workers and General Labourers Union (GWGLU), led by Will Thorne.[39] Interestingly, both these men had been brickmakers in their youth, and Thorne, who had grown up in Birmingham, had started work at about the age of seven as an offbearer. For a time he had combined summer work in the brickfields with winter work in a gasworks, before moving to the Beckton gasworks in London (Figure 15.2).

Gas workers, in common with others thought of as unskilled, were believed to be unable to organise effectively until the events of 1889 proved otherwise.[40] The GWGLU, formed in March that year, grew quickly and had up to sixty branches in London and the provinces by mid-summer.[41] A strike at Beckton and other London

---

39 Hobsbawm, *Labouring men*, pp. 179–85; Clegg *et al.*, *British trade unions*, pp. 65–88. The relationship between brickmaking and work in gasworks has already been noted in chapter 10.
40 Hobsbawm, *Labouring men*, pp. 158, 164–5.
41 W. Thorne, *My life's battles* (London, n.d. [1925]), p. 80.

'The great struggle'

gasworks resulted in the employers conceding an eight-hour day.[42] Buoyed by this success, Thorne looked to the brickfields as a new challenge.

> There were new fields to conquer. The brickfields of Kent, Surrey and Essex claimed my attention, and I soon had them well organised within the union ... . A demand was made for an increase in wages. The brickmasters refused to make any concessions. They sneered at the fact that the brickmakers had joined the union, which they likened to a mushroom that had sprung up overnight, and would die as quickly.[43]

Branches of the GWGLU were set up in a number of brickmaking districts. In August 1889 Thorne spoke at a meeting in Southall that was attended by contingents from Hounslow, Notting Hill, Yiewsley, Hillingdon and West Drayton.[44] He was back there in October, in the aftermath of the London Dock strike, which he claimed had been inspired by the earlier success of the London gas workers. As Southall had a gasworks as well as brickfields, his audience was probably drawn from men working in both industries. The local branch was, he claimed, one of the strongest of the 'country' branches, but he urged the importance of solidarity and stressed the value of teetotalism. He focused on the need to campaign to get Sunday accepted as a rest day and, if Sunday work was necessary, for it to be rewarded with extra pay. Leisure time, he argued, was essential for the long-term health of the working class, contrasting the average life expectancy of a labourer in Lambeth (25 years) with that of a middle-class man in Westminster (70 years).[45]

A West Drayton branch had also been formed by 18 August 1889, when a meeting was held at which 1200 attended. A month later a local committee was formed, with John Brown elected branch secretary. In November Thorne returned to address a well attended meeting. By January 1890 the branch had 500 members and at its first anniversary it had 600. By then there were 500 members of the Southall branch. There was also a branch in Slough.[46]

Despite having become established in the Cowley district during 1889, the GWGLU was not immediately involved in any disputes there. However, there was a strike in the autumn at Eastwoods' brickfield at Shoeburyness. Given the time of year, the dispute was not about moulding rates but arose because a group of fifteen men digging clay for the following season asked for wages to return to the old levels. Although the increase probably meant an additional cost to the owners of only £70 spread over the winter months, they responded by locking out a further sixty to seventy men. The men had the support of the GWGLU and the sympathy of many people in the area. A public meeting was held, preceded by a torchlight procession at

---

42   *Ibid.*, p. 72.

43   *Ibid.*, p. 121.

44   *Middlesex County Times*, 10 August 1889.

45   *Uxbridge & West Drayton Gazette*, 12 October 1889.

46   *Ibid.*, 17 August 1889, 24 August 1889, 21 September 1889, 16 November 1890, 18 January 1890, 16 August 1890.

Bricks of Victorian London

which a collection was taken up to add to the strike fund. The strike lasted ten weeks, but the men finally returned to work on the owner's terms.[47]

The GWGLU made an attempt to impose closed shops in those brickfields in which it had strong representation. In July 1890 the men at Eastwoods in West Drayton struck over the employment of a man whose union membership had lapsed, and only agreed to return to work if he was dismissed. Despite Mr Brown's best efforts at persuasion, the man refused to pay his subs and the moulder who employed him discharged him. The following month three non-union men at Rutter's were forced to join the GWGLU to avoid a similar fate.[48]

The major industrial action of that year was in the Medway area and badly affected the brickmakers, although it was not their dispute. At the end of 1889 the Bargemen's and Watermen's Protection Society challenged the barge owners' refusal to raise the rates paid for carrying bricks in line with the rising sale price of bricks, mirroring the demands that the brickmakers themselves had made. It issued its own scale of rates, which the masters at Faversham and Sittingbourne declined to accept. The ensuing dispute affected only vessels involved in the brick trade, as the employers of barges carrying other commodities had settled with the bargemen.[49] When the bargemen struck at the beginning of March, the Sittingbourne brickmasters, many of whom were barge owners themselves and therefore directly involved in the dispute, retaliated by closing their brickfields and locking out their employees. This was a devastating response, as a local paper commented:

> The majority of people ... speak of the action of the brickmasters in throwing the brickmakers out of work as being harsh in the extreme. The suffering which these poor fellows and their families will undergo is ever present to the hearts and minds of those who can sympathise with working men in their struggles with adversity.[50]

The dispute quickly escalated, as barge crews arriving back at their home ports tied up their craft and walked away, leaving some 300 barges idle. The Faversham brickmasters followed their Sittingbourne colleagues and closed their brickfields.[51] As many as 5000 men were now out of work, with a huge impact felt by their families and the local economy.[52] Appeals were made in national newspapers for funds to support the unemployed brickies and save them from starvation and the workhouse.[53]

---

47 *Barking, East Ham & Ilford Advertiser*, 2 November 1889, 9 November 1889; *Uxbridge & West Drayton Gazette*, 21 December 1889.

48 *West Drayton & District Historian*, 94 (1990), p. 6; 82 (1982), p. 7; *Uxbridge & West Drayton Gazette*, 26 July 1890.

49 Report on the strikes and lockouts of 1890, by the labour correspondent of the Board of Trade (c.6476) (1891), pp. 214–15.

50 *East Kent Gazette*, 8 March 1890.

51 *Thanet Advertiser*, 8 March 1890.

52 *Maidstone Journal & Kentish Advertiser*, 11 March 1890.

53 *Pall Mall Gazette*, 8 March 1890.

'The great struggle'

Essex brickfields were also affected. At a mass meeting at Southend Mr Watkinson, the local union branch secretary, argued that unions needed to federate so they could support each other in strikes like these. They were not engaged in isolated dispute, he said: 'this was a class war!' He raised the concern that some brickmasters were using other routes to get their bricks into London, and he singled out Eastwoods, which was sending bricks by rail from its Shoeburyness brickfield.[54]

Most of the locked out brickmakers were members of the GWGLU, but the disputes also affected non-union members, some of whom may have been encouraged to join a union as a result of the lockout. To maintain their morale the men held public meetings, and they were supported by the local clergy and parts of the local press, which condemned the uncompromising position of the owners. Mr Wragge, the chairman of the Kent and Essex Brickmasters' Association, was accused of having 'shut the door of conciliation, and his attempt to place the responsibility for the whole state of affairs upon the bargemen was, to say the least, ungenerous'.[55] After an abortive attempt at conciliation, the owners claimed that the hard line they had taken was necessary in the face of increasing competition from machine-made bricks and that the Kent and Essex trade was in a critical condition and any more burdens placed upon it would 'probably result in its destruction'. They placed the blame on the bargemen, who by their actions had closed the market for bricks, making it impossible to keep producing them if they could not be sold.[56]

Although they might have been resentful of the bargemen's action, which had resulted in their present plight, the brickies showed solidarity with their fellow unionists in processions and public meetings under the slogan 'Stick like bricks. No Surrender.'[57] One meeting was addressed by the Liberal MP Robert Cunninghame Graham, who took a distinctly socialist tone, saying that he

> wanted to strike at the root of the system which made their interests and those of their employers absolutely opposed ... did it not seem a very extraordinary fact that their class, which produced all that value, was precisely the class which had the smallest enjoyment of it when it was produced (hear, hear and applause).[58]

Nevertheless, despite the GWGLU supporting its members with 10s a week in strike pay, the continuation of the lockout brought hardship. The general sympathy of the local community led to many offers of help; some local tradesmen agreed to provide temporary credit, and local school managers allowed children to attend without paying the usual fees.[59] One trader offered to distribute bags of coal. Soup kitchens were opened in Murston, Sittingbourne, Milton, Grovehurst and Faversham. Faversham's Benevolent Committee provided free dinners to brickmakers' children and the Board

---

54   *Barking, East Ham & Ilford Advertiser,* 15 March 1890.
55   *East Kent Gazette,* 15 March 1890.
56   *East Kent Gazette,* 15 March 1890; *Maidstone Journal,* 18 March 1890.
57   *Daily Telegraph,* 17 March 1890.
58   *East Kent Gazette,* 22 March 1890.
59   *Maidstone Journal,* 18 March 1890.

Bricks of Victorian London

of Guardians accepted applications for financial support, including the payment of school fees. It also asked the Local Government Board to sanction the payment of outdoor relief to able-bodied men who had been thrown out of work.[60]

Meetings took place between the bargemen and the brickmasters in an attempt to come to a settlement. The solidarity of the Brickmasters' Association was demonstrated when one of its members, Mr Horsford at Oare, near Faversham, reopened his field thinking that an agreement had been reached, only to receive a delegation informing him that this was not the case, whereupon he laid the men off again.[61]

The leaders of the Gas Workers came to Kent to rally the men. A meeting in Faversham was addressed by Will Thorne and Edward Aveling, who was married to Eleanor Marx, Karl Marx's daughter. As a socialist, Aveling spoke in terms of class war and asserted that the men 'were simply claiming their mere human rights'. Thorne pledged the support of the gas workers in making collections and doing all they could to help the brickmakers.[62]

As the lockout entered its third month hardship was seriously biting, such that the Local Government Board conferred with the Rochford Board of Guardians as to how best to relieve distress.[63] However, at this point the bargemen conceded, it was said, out of consideration for the brickmakers, who had been 'involuntary sufferers in the contest', and withdrew the list of rates they had drawn up the previous autumn. The masters still refused to negotiate and issued their own list of rates that had to be adopted without any possibility of arbitration.[64] The bargemen accepted the masters' new rates, and on 28 April the brickfields were reopened.[65]

On the other side of London support for the West Drayton branch of the Gas Workers remained strong. In September 1890 a meeting was held to dedicate a new banner, which was then paraded from West Drayton to Yiewsley and back. Then the crowd was addressed by John Brown, Will Thorne and Eleanor Aveling. Thorne said that

> they as brickmakers, had been divided for many years and in consequence the masters had taken advantage of them, but now that they had joined the Union they could work more freely than they otherwise could have done. They had set an example to all brickmakers which he hoped would soon be followed. (Hear, hear.) Before they joined the union they fought and competed like a lot of slaves, but now they went about their work in a quiet way.[66]

Eleanor Aveling said that she had been told that she was the first woman to address a meeting on Drayton Green, and she hoped she would not be the last. She congratulated the branch on having a beautiful banner:

---

60 *East Kent Gazette*, 22 March 1890.
61 *East Kent Gazette*, 29 March 1890.
62 *Ibid.*
63 *Barking, East Ham & Ilford Advertiser*, 5 April 1890.
64 *Acton Gazette*, 19 April 1890.
65 *St James Gazette*, 28 April 1890.
66 *Uxbridge & West Drayton Gazette*, 4 October 1890.

'The great struggle'

> Under that banner they recognised no difference of sex, and that men and women were both fighting the same fight … . The women knew best as to the miserable way in which they were starving – they could hardly call it living – at the present day. … She was called an agitator, and she could assure them that she should keep on agitating so long as working men or women, who had lived honest, sober and hard-working lives, had nothing before them, when they could work no longer, but the workhouse (applause); so long as a woman worked 10 hours a day, and only got 5s or 6s a week, and so long as every working man and woman did not belong to the Union. So long as these things continued, she would continue to agitate.[67]

Her speech ended with a rallying call:

> The great struggle had commenced between capital and labour. Capital had been victorious hitherto, simply because labour was not united, but when the second half of the labour army fell into the ranks, then would come the re-action, and where labour had failed, it would come off victorious. (Applause.) … They must not rest until every working man and woman in the kingdom belonged to the Union.[68]

Although wage rates remained the main issue for the GWGLU, the problem of back pence reappeared from time to time. A case was brought by a brickmaker, Rogers, against his employer Henry Odell claiming that he was owed £5 18s 2d back pence. The case had more general implications, and Rogers was legally represented. In court it was said that the contractual arrangements had been altered some nine years previously by mutual consent and that, under the new terms, the master could stop work at any moment and the moulder might leave at any time, but, notwithstanding that, 4d per thousand was left in the hands of the master for a certain period as back pence. The moulders agreed that the master might keep back the pence so long as the moulder had a batch of bricks under his care but as soon as a 'set' was handed over to the setter to build the clamp, the back pence should be paid out. Odell had not followed this practice. Rogers had been moulding all summer and had made, by his own estimate, over 400,000 bricks, but in the middle of July his walk flatter had stopped working and he had been forced to disband his gang. He asked for the back pence, which he felt he was due, but Odell argued that he had contracted for the season and was not entitled to his back pence. The judge found in favour of Odell but gave Rogers leave to appeal.[69] The result of the appeal, if lodged, is not known.

At the beginning of the 1891 moulding season 750 men in the Cowley district demanded a wage rise of 6d per 1000 for moulding and related increases for setting, loading and skintling in order to restore rates to the level that had prevailed before the reductions of the early 1880s. Although an increase of 4d had been paid in 1888, the

---

67 *Ibid.*

68 *Ibid.*

69 *Uxbridge & West Drayton Gazette,* 18 October 1890.

Bricks of Victorian London

men contended that the price of bricks was now higher than it had been for eight or nine years, and that a further increase could therefore be justified, pointing out that men in Tottenham were getting 5s 8d as against the 4s 4d that they received.[70] They made two other demands. The first was that the difference between what the pug boy was actually paid and the allowance made for him in the wage structure of the gang be made up by the employer. The moulders argued that they were allowed only 3d per 1000 for the pug boy when they were obliged to pay an additional penny as they were now employing older boys as a consequence of the Factory Acts. The second grievance related to back pence.[71]

The Cowley Brickmakers' Association rejected the men's demands on the basis that, although brick prices had indeed risen, they were still lower than they had been and the Middlesex men were paid better than the employees in Kent and Essex. They also opposed any change to the 'back pence' custom, since it provided, in their view, the necessary security that the men would remain at work throughout the season. All in all, they felt that to accede to the men's demands would cripple the industry.[72]

As many as 2000 people joined the strike, which lasted until 15 August, when, despite the masters' early intransigence, the dispute was settled and the rise of 6d granted. Of course, by then, much of the season had been lost and the Labour Correspondent of the Board of Trade held 'that the strike was of such long duration as to greatly discount the advantage gained'.[73] The GWGLU, however, regarded it as a triumph of the men's resistance to

> the desperate attempt of the brickmasters to starve out the brickmakers. Never has wealth more cynically tried its strength against hunger. And wealth failed, and failed after a fight of seventeen weeks, and a fight that came on the top of a winter of unprecedented severity.[74]

Support for the GWGLU had remained firm and there had been no recorded instances of blacklegging. The strike had been well organised and the Union had paid out a total of £4890 in strike pay, supported by donations from as far afield as Australia, Germany and France, demonstrating the strength of international working-class solidarity.[75]

However, these protracted disputes had an impact beyond just the brickmakers and their families, as there was less money circulating in the local economy. When the Uxbridge draper Carrick & Coles announced its stocktaking sale at New Year 1892 it cited two reasons for the poor trading of the previous year; one was the weather, the other 'the brickmakers' strike which has proved most disastrous to a very large

---

70 *Brick, Tile & Potteries Journal*, 9 June 1891, p. 360.

71 *Ibid.*, p. 360; evidence of Will Thorne to Royal Commission on Labour, Minutes of Evidence, Group C. Vol. 3 (c.6894), PP 1893–4, vol. 34, p. 131.

72 *Brick, Tile & Potteries Journal*, 9 June 1891, p. 360.

73 Report on the strikes and lockouts of 1891 by the Labour Correspondent to the Board of Trade (c.6890) (1893–4), p. 10.

74 *Ibid.*, quoting a union official.

75 *Ibid.*

'The great struggle'

number of working people who have had little money to spend'.[76] In 1894 a Southall shopkeeper attributed his bankruptcy in part to a strike of local brickmakers.[77]

In 1892 brickmasters in Kent and Essex continued to behave cautiously, restricting output by starting the moulding season later than usual and reducing the number of gangs they employed. They claimed that market conditions made this step necessary, but the men, unsurprisingly, thought it was a scheme to force up the price of bricks.[78] That year strike action shifted to the Acton and Shepherd's Bush area, where the moulders, perhaps emboldened by the success of the Cowley workers the previous year, made a claim for an extra 9d per thousand to bring their rates up to 5s 9d, arguing that they were being paid a shilling less than they had been ten years before. Initially affecting two brickfields, within a week all of them had been closed and 250 men locked out, of whom 100 were members of the Starch Green branch of the GWGLU. The Union represented the men in negotiations and paid strike pay each day. The masters refused to concede, suggesting the current rate was generous compared to the 3s 8d being paid in Kent and Essex yards and relying on the fact that at the start of the season they still had stock in hand.[79] The GWGLU claimed that comparisons between local rates of pay and those in Kent and Essex were misleading, because, as the branch secretary explained:

> the superior quality of the Kentish earth enabled the men there to make 1,200 or 1,400 bricks in the same time it took the Acton men to make 700 or 800. ... the owners of the brickfields were receiving the same prices for their bricks now as they were 15 years ago, when they paid 6s per thousand to the brickmakers as against the present rate of 5s.[80]

Once the last of the men engaged for the winter had completed their work, they too were laid off, and eight brickfields were at a standstill. However, the dispute affected only the stock brickmakers, while those making red bricks, with a different wage structure, remained open.[81]

That year, the west London brickmakers found themselves part of a wider pattern of industrial action involving a number of trades across the capital, including clerks and domestic servants, together with a widespread agitation in favour of an eight-hour day.[82] The masters met at the offices of Mr Willett, owner of the Clifton Brickworks, and decided to remain firm in their rejection of the men's demands. Local clergymen, such as the Rev. A.G.H. Dicker from the Mission Church in Acton Vale and the vicar of St Alban, Acton Green, attempted to act as mediators, but their efforts proved ineffective.

---

76   *Uxbridge & West Drayton Gazette*, 2 January 1892.

77   *Ibid.*, 10 February 1894.

78   *Ibid.*, 12 March 1892.

79   Harper Smith, *Brickfields of Acton*, p. 31; *Acton Gazette*, 16 April 1892.

80   *Acton Gazette*, 23 April 1892.

81   *Ibid.*; the eight fields were Wright's, Daw's, Willett's, Stroud's, Bird's, Richardson's, Williams, Son and Wallington's.

82   *London Evening Standard*, 25 April 1892.

Bricks of Victorian London

They came back with the offer of a sliding scale of pay based on the cost of bricks, but this was rejected by the men.[83]

Not all the Acton brickfields remained shut. The men employed by Hewlett John Cooper at his Bedford Brickworks, coming to the end of their winter's employment, accepted an increase of 6d per thousand and carried on working.[84] The GWGLU pushed for arbitration, but a meeting at the Conciliation Board of the London Chamber of Commerce at which four owners – Wright, Willett, Williams and Bird – met six of the men produced no solution.[85]

Some of the striking men were able to obtain work elsewhere, not as lucrative as brickmaking, enabling them 'to keep the wolf from the door'. The GWGLU appealed to other brickmaking centres for donations to the strike fund, which would be shared between their own men and the non-union men. The Union also said that if the strike continued it would petition the County Council to close the fields for the season, on the grounds that 'the bricks must be made somewhere, and if the trade is diverted to other districts we can follow it', prompting the local paper to comment that they were cutting off their nose to spite their face.[86] The masters, meanwhile, arranged for bricks to be supplied to them at cost from other districts sufficient to meet their customers' needs until June of the following year.[87]

As the strike dragged on the brickmakers faced a further threat, that of losing their homes as well as their livelihood. Many of the employees of the East Acton Brickworks lived in tied cottages and 'put forward the startling proposition that they are not required by law to pay rent while a strike is in progress!' The owners offered to write off seven weeks of rent if the men returned to work, an offer that was declined. In court the men lost the argument and evictions were ordered in most cases. It was reported that the men peacefully gave up their cottages.[88]

However, the brickmasters' position was undermined once a second firm settled with the men. Stroud's was being run by executors following the owner's death, and they feared that they might be found personally liable for any losses incurred. When they proposed a 5d increase if the men immediately returned to work, the offer was accepted. Stroud's was a small operation compared with some of the other firms, which kept their fields closed for the remainder of the 1892 season.[89]

The dispute was only finally settled the following April by conciliation, with an advance of 6d given. One firm that had settled earlier explained the motivation behind it:

> Our neighbour and ourselves were the only firms who gave way to the demands of the workmen, the rest of the manufacturers in this district stopping their works

---

83   Harper Smith, *Brickfields of Acton*, p. 31.
84   *Acton Gazette*, 7 May 1892.
85   *Ibid.*, 14 May 1892.
86   *Ibid.*, 4 June 1892.
87   *Ibid.*, 4 June 1892, 18 June 1892.
88   *Ibid.*, 25 June 1892.
89   *Ibid.*, 2 July 1892, 30 July 1892.

'The great struggle'

the whole of the season. Our neighbour gave in at once, as he holds his brickfield under a lease, and is obliged to pay a royalty on a minimum quantity, whether made or not. We did not consider that the price realised for bricks justified the men in asking for an advance, but we felt compelled to give in, in order to protect ourselves against our neighbour, who would not only be making an extra price by the stoppage of our works, but would be taking our customers.[90]

A less widely reported dispute that occurred in north and north-east London districts resulted in the men getting an increase of 5d per thousand. The success of this dispute was put down to the strength of the GWGLU, as it regularly reminded its members, pointing to the firmness of the Kent men in the face of the lockout in 1890 and the defiant attitude of the Acton men as they entered the winter months of 1892.[91]

So, it was not surprising that the brickmakers of the Cowley district, including those at Iver, Langley and Slough, launched a further attempt to increase moulding rates at the beginning of the 1893 season. This strike, however, was poorly supported; the Heston men remained at work and not all the Southall men came out, and it lasted a mere eight days before the men returned to work.[92] An ugly side to the dispute was the attempt by some of the strikers to intimidate their fellow workers into joining them. Thomas Harris, from Yiewsley, and his wife were convicted and fined 10s for having assaulted an Eastwood's employee while attempting to prevent him going to work.[93]

As the strike came to an end Strouds closed their Southall works for good and sold off their stock of bricks, machinery and plant. Whether this decision was prompted by the recent dispute is difficult to say, but the firm had also been hit by the Acton strike the previous year.[94]

There were no reported strikes in the Medway or Cowley brickfields in 1894, but, as a sympathetic newspaper, the *Labour Leader*, reported, every spring at the start of the moulding season the GWGLU was inclined to flex its muscles. This year there was industrial action in two areas, in both cases to prevent the masters from reducing wage rates again; in Grays in Essex the men fought a reduction of 9d, while in Edmonton they challenged an attempt to remove the 5d increase granted the previous year.[95]

Concerns over the level of industrial action were such that a new clause was inserted in some brickmaking leases to address the loss of production that strikes caused. This provided for an exemption from minimum royalty requirements if the manufacturing season was disrupted by stoppages. In 1895 Rutter's new lease of their West Drayton field provided for a lowering of the minimum royalty payment from

---

90 Report on the strikes and lockouts of 1892 by the Labour Correspondent to the Board of Trade (c.7403) (1893), pp. 41, 157.

91 *Ibid.*, p. 397.

92 *London Evening Standard*, 6 May 1893; *Middlesex Independent*, 6 May 1893; Report on the strikes and lockouts of 1893 by the Labour Correspondent of Board of Trade (c.7566) (1894), p. 27.

93 *Uxbridge & West Drayton Gazette*, 20 May 1893.

94 *Ibid.*, 13 May 1893.

95 *Labour Leader*, 28 April 1894.

Bricks of Victorian London

£350 to £150 when there was 'a general strike or lockout in the district ... for any period exceeding two calendar months'.[96]

There continued to be strikes in the last few years of the old century and in the early years of the new, and the GWGLU had several successes. One strike at the beginning of the 1897 season affected twelve works in the London district employing 350 people. It was over within a fortnight when the owners conceded the demand for an 9d increase in moulding rates. This was followed by a strike in the Acton area in June that involved 600 men from four works seeking a 6d increase, which was secured after less than two weeks.[97] In 1898 there was again a strike of north London brickmakers, bringing 400 men from eleven works out. The demand for a 6d increase in rates at the beginning of the season was conceded after four weeks.[98]

There seem to have been fewer strikes in the following years, or at least ones that attracted the attention of the press, but the same issues persisted. In 1905 the centre of attention was the south-eastern corner of London, where the men rejected an attempt to stem a trend in rising wages that had increased from 4s 9d per 1000 to 6s 6d in the course of seven years. The masters claimed that they could now only afford to pay 5s 9d. A number of firms in Croydon, Norwood, Deptford, Crofton Park and Lewisham, among other districts, closed their works and locked the men out. However, the London County Council, which owned a brickworks on its Norbury housing estate, continued to pay the higher rate. Strikes also affected other brickmaking districts, with mixed results. In Crayford a strike was successful and the men went back to work at the previous year's rates, but at Edmonton and Langley, owing to, as Will Thorne put it, 'the disorganised state of the men', the action collapsed and the men accepted a reduced rate.[99]

It is perhaps strange, therefore, that in a report published the following year H.G. Montgomery, representing the Institute of Clayworkers, had confidently claimed to a government enquiry that

> The brick trade does not suffer so much from strikes as do other trades, possibly owing to the fact that the trade is split up into small portions all over the country, and that brickmakers have no trade organisation of their own. In some of the larger brickmaking centres, such as Sittingbourne, Peterborough and West Bromwich, a number of men belong to the Gas Workers' Union, but they do not subscribe to it regularly ... At Sittingbourne no strike has occurred of any importance since 1890.[100]

---

96 LMA Acc. 1386/382.

97 Report on the strikes and lockouts of 1897 by the Labour Correspondent of Board of Trade (c.9012) (1898), pp. 92, 94.

98 Report on the strikes and lockouts of 1898 by the Labour Correspondent to the Board of Trade (c.9437) (1899), p. 80.

99 *London Daily News*, 9 June, 21 June 1905.

100 Royal Commission on Trade Disputes and Trade Combinations, Minutes of evidence before the RC (Cd. 2826) (1906), p. 291.

'The great struggle'

He was correct in so far that, compared with other industries, the strikes in the brick industry were localised affairs and there was never a general stoppage of brickmaking across the country. Similarly, in his evidence to the same commission, Mr Wragge, Eastwoods' chairman, asserted, surprisingly, that 'he has no trouble with his men, and that, so far, any disputes in regard to wages have been amicably settled between the masters and their employees'.[101] This hardly reflected the experience of the industry in the 1890s. As the economy came out of the recession of the 1880s and brick prices rose, so the workers in brickfields attempted to improve their rates of pay, and in this they were supported by an active trade union in a series of disputes.

In the first decade of the twentieth century the incidence of industrial action was much reduced; a much greater threat came from falling demand and the increasing hold of the much cheaper Fletton bricks on the London market. However, stock brickmakers might have taken some comfort from the fact that strikes also affected their Fletton competitors. There were unsuccessful strikes in 1898, and again in 1901, but more seriously two in 1902 in which the GWGLU was involved. J.C. Hill, the founder of the London Brick Company, claimed that the Union was dominated by men from the Kent & Essex brickfields whose aim was to cause trouble in the Fletton yards as a way of disrupting production.[102] It is to the history of the Fletton brick that our attention now turns.

---

101 *Ibid.*

102 Hillier, *Clay that burns*, pp. 58–9, quoting *Peterborough Standard*, 19 July 1902.

Part IV: An industry in decline

Chapter 16

'The chief market is London':
the challenge of the Fletton brick

Until the 1880s the stock brick industry did not face any significant competition except from some specialist bricks that carried a premium price, but the discovery of an extensive seam of clay – the Lower Oxford Clay – near the village of Fletton, near Peterborough, led to the development of a new style of brickmaking. This type of clay was not suitable for hand moulding, and heavy machinery was required to make effective use of it. Bricks made from it were noted for two things: their compressive strength and their low production costs. Although manufactured at some distance from the capital, they could be sold at prices significantly below those of stocks in London.

The story of the Fletton brick started when the 400-acre Fletton Lodge estate, just south of Peterborough, was put up for auction in 1877. Brickmaking using the superficial clays was already practised in the area, and so it was not surprising that the sale catalogue referred to the presence of 'good brick earth'.[1] One lot was purchased by a local draper, James McCallum Craig, who started a small brickworks on part of his newly acquired land. Around 1880 a Grantham firm, Hempsted Brothers, took over the running of Craig's brickfield and soon a number of other brickmakers were working at Fletton. One of them attempted to use not just the superficial clays but the Lower Oxford Clay, which lay beneath it. This stratum exists as a belt across England from Yorkshire to Dorset, but was mainly worked for brick production in the area around Peterborough and in Bedfordshire. Apart from the thickness of the seam and the uniformity of its quality, this clay did not require the addition of water to make it malleable and contained a much higher level of carboniferous material than other clays. As a result, bricks made from it required less time to dry before firing and less fuel for the firing process.

As this clay was too hard to be moulded by hand, a different production method was required; this became known as the semi-dry process. The shaley clay was ground to a powder and then heavy machinery compressed it into a brick. Breaking a Fletton brick in half makes the granular structure of the brick readily apparent. By 1890 several firms had produced machines that worked with the semi-dry process, but eventually those manufactured by Whittaker & Co. of Accrington dominated the market. Whittaker's machinery was promoted as being suitable for making bricks from a variety of hard substances, such as slate debris, fireclay and ground shale, and found an ideal material in the Lower Oxford Clay.[2] Between 1890 and 1900 sixteen firms of Fletton brickmakers between them bought fifty units from Whittaker's.[3]

---

1   Hillier, *Clay that burns*, p. 7.
2   The pressure required was about thirty tons. Watt, 'Nineteenth-century brickmaking inventions', pp. 219–20.
3   Hillier, *Clay that burns*, p. 24.

Bricks of Victorian London

Unfired bricks made in this way were sufficiently resilient not to require the careful handling of a soft moulded brick, and could be stacked straight away in a kiln without the intermediate period of drying. It is likely that in the early days of experimentation with the new clay brickmakers tried clamps, as a flexible, cheap and familiar method of burning bricks. Unfortunately, when fired at lower temperatures the high carboniferous content of the clay produced offensive oily fumes.[4] In order to overcome this problem, Hempsted's installed the first of many Hoffman multi-chamber kilns. When the bricks were fired to a temperature of about 400°C the clay gave off combustible gases which then burned the bricks to a temperature of 1050°C, and only a small amount of coal dust was required to help maintain the temperature.[5]

The thick seams of clay resulted in deep clay pits. In the early decades the clay was won by hand from a steep cliff by men on ladders; later, mechanical excavators were employed.[6] The new industry found it hard to get established, as the 1880s proved to be a very difficult decade for all brickmakers because of low levels of demand. While stock brickmakers reduced production and expected their workers to accept lower rates of pay, the Fletton brickmakers were in a different position, as their kind of operation was more capital intensive, needing investment in machinery and kilns.

As we have seen, during the period 1887–92 brickmakers in the London area were pre-occupied with a series of labour disputes affecting one district after another as their employees sought to return to the levels of pay that they had enjoyed in earlier years. The employers, on the other hand, were reluctant to concede too much, partly because they were operating in a market environment that now included the cheaper Fletton brick.

Positioned near the Great Northern Railway's main line into King's Cross, the early Fletton yards had a direct route into the capital for their bricks. By 1882 Hempsted's brickworks had been provided with a siding, by which coal was brought to the site and the manufactured bricks distributed. In the words of a contemporary report, 'The Great Northern has built a siding into the yards, and an engine from Peterborough runs into them every day and takes away a train of trucks loaded with bricks consigned to various destinations. The chief market, however, is London.'[7] Hempsted's also had interests in housing development in the capital through the North London Freehold Land and House Co. Ltd, which built houses in Finchley, Hornsey and Islington, and acquired their Fletton brickmaking sites.[8]

The low price of the Fletton brick clearly appealed to speculative builders. Builders' price books, though, seem to have been reluctant to quote prices for Flettons up to the end of the century, despite the fact that they were already established in the market. However, in 1898 the ex-works price of a Fletton was 22s per thousand,

---

4   *Ibid.*, pp. 15–16.

5   *Ibid.*, p. 17.

6   *Ibid.*, pp. 25–6.

7   *Peterborough Advertiser*, 8 April 1882, quoted in Hillier, *Clay that burns*, p. 19.

8   The company seems to have over-extended itself and went into liquidation after eleven months. Hillier, *Clay that burns*, p. 19.

'The chief market is London'

as against a stock brick at 50s and a place brick at 34s.[9] After only a decade of production it was thought that Peterborough bricks had already captured an eighth of the London market, a matter naturally of concern to their competitors.[10] 'Sittingbourne brickmakers', it was said, 'are perturbed at the preference being shown by many builders for Peterborough bricks.'[11]

The Fletton was not expected to be used as a facing brick; it was valued for its strength, not its appearance. Tests carried out by Kirkaldy & Son to establish the breaking weight of four well-known kinds of brick showed that a Peterborough pressed brick could withstand up to 178 tons and a Beart's Arlesey brick 157.8 tons, while stock bricks cracked at much lower pressures: an Essex stock at 129.9 tons and a Kent one at 125.9 tons.[12] The Fletton manufacturers therefore pitched their product against the place brick, rather than the best stocks: 'The Fletton bricks are very largely used in London for inside work, but up to the present time there has been a good deal of prejudice against their use for outside work.'[13] Over time that reluctance would fade and Fletton bricks would begin to be used for the side and rear elevation of houses, leaving just the fronts with yellow stocks or red bricks. The Fletton makers would also mitigate the blandness of their products by giving them textured finishes, starting with the herringbone patterned 'Rustic' in 1922.[14] As Brunskill and Clifton-Taylor note,

> half a century ago Fletton was a byword for an anaemic kind of machine-pressed brick whose only virtue was its cheapness; but these were 'commons', in which appearance was of no consequence. Fletton facing bricks, which are either faced with sand or machine textured, are visually more acceptable.[15]

A major moment in the acceptance of Fletton bricks came with the use of ten million of them in the construction of Westminster Cathedral in 1898. These, however, were not pressed Fletton bricks; rather, the architect, John Francis Bentley, specified wire-cut bricks, but ones sourced from a yard at Fletton. Nor were they used as facing bricks; they do, however, form the core of the building and account for around 80 per cent of the total number of bricks used overall. The same Kirkaldy & Son advised on the compressive strengths of the different types of brick chosen for the building.[16]

The upswing in the housebuilding market in the 1890s was a relief to stock brickmakers but also an opportunity for the Fletton producers. The Edmonton

---

9   Fletton prices from Woodforde, *Bricks*, p. 149; the prices for stocks and place bricks from *Laxton's Builders' Price Book*, 1898, p. 73.

10   *British Clayworker*, November 1892, p. 161.

11   *Ibid.*, September 1893, p. 102.

12   *Ibid.*

13   *Builders' Merchant*, March 1898, p. 53.

14   Woodforde, *Bricks*, pp. 192–3.

15   Brunskill and Clifton-Taylor, *English brickwork*, p. 57. Commons were ordinary cheap bricks not usually exposed, and place bricks were used in a similar way.

16   T.P. Smith, 'Westminster Cathedral: its bricks and brickwork', *BBS Information*, 110 (July 2009), pp. 8–26.

Bricks of Victorian London

stock brickmaker T. & M. Plowman, sensing an opportunity, bought a 23-acre site at Fletton in 1891. As well as being used in housebuilding, Flettons gained a share in infrastructure projects, and the London Brick Company secured a contract for 25 million bricks in 1895 for the Great Central Railway, opening a new brickfield at Calvert in Buckinghamshire on the strength of that order.[17] The title of the London Brick Company is itself instructive. Its founder, J.C. Hill, was a speculative builder in north London who attended an auction of bricks and tiles at Fletton in 1888, where he bought most of the stock. He then looked at ways to secure a continuing supply for his business and was able to buy up a struggling yard in 1889. He was also the owner of two other yards, one near Colchester in Essex and another in Enfield.[18]

The late 1890s were optimistic times for brickmakers supplying the London area:

> A brick famine threatens London. The Grand [sic] Central Railway, and the new City and Waterloo Railway, and the electric railway from the City to the West End have used up nearly all the available stock. Prices have risen 2s or 3s a thousand, much to the consternation of the speculative builder.[19]

Good market conditions led to the formation of new companies wanting to benefit from what seemed a profitable way of manufacturing bricks. Output from Fletton yards, which had been about fifty million in 1890, had grown ten times by the end of the century (Figure 16.1). In 1891 the Great Eastern Railway loaded 7130 tons of Fletton bricks at Whittlesea, a station close to many of the brickfields, but the traffic grew rapidly to 108,000 tons by 1898.[20] By 1900 it was not unreasonable to claim that 'Fletton is a force to be reckoned with. Its amazing strides are one of the commercial wonders of the century.'[21] The sector was able to supply 25 million bricks for the construction of the War Office building in Whitehall (1903–4) at a price of 27s a thousand delivered to site, a price one contemporary observer thought was unsustainable.[22]

There were a number of ways in which the stock brickmakers could respond to the Fletton challenge. The first approach was to make different types of brick. At the end of the nineteenth century some London brickmakers, while maintaining their production of yellow stocks, diversified into other types of brick, such as red facings. In the Acton area, the Clifton Brickworks stopped making stocks and focused on red bricks after 1879, while its neighbour, the East Acton Brickworks, made both yellow stocks and moulded red bricks burnt in Scotch kilns. The Springfield Park brickworks, the last of the Acton brickfields to close in 1915, also made red bricks, and several small kilns are visible on an Ordnance Survey map from 1913. The Willesden & Acton brickworks were, unusually, making red wire-cuts.[23] Over in Sittingbourne the Smeed,

---

17   Hillier, *Clay that burns*, p. 38.

18   *Ibid.*, pp. 44–6.

19   *British Clayworker*, May 1897, p. lxxxi.

20   Hillier, *Clay that burns*, p. 36.

21   Woodforde, *Bricks*, p. 150.

22   The Fletton bricks are not visible. A. Service, *Edwardian architecture* (London, 1977), p. 148.

23   Harper Smith, *Brickfields of Acton*, pp. 44, 46, 50, 62.

'The chief market is London'

Figure 16.1. London Brick Company yard at Fletton. (London Brick Company Archive, Forterra Building Products Ltd)

Dean company directors decided to try their hand at manufacturing red facings and installed a 'Monarch' moulding machine, together with drying equipment and a continuous kiln in 1906. The machine was capable of producing 100,000 bricks a week.[24] In Faversham, Cremer & Whiting's works also turned to making red bricks.[25]

The second approach adopted by some London brickmakers was, in the spirit of 'if you can't beat 'em join 'em', to try their hand at Fletton making. As we have seen, north London brickmaker Plowman's bought a brickfield in Fletton and Eastwood also acquired interests in brickfields at Fletton in the 1890s and maintained a presence there for some decades.[26]

A third possibility was to try and adapt the Fletton style of brickmaking to utilise other clays, and this is what the New Patent Brick Company of London seems to have done by using the clay beds that lay below the superficial clays at its site in Northolt.

---

24 Perks, *George Bargebrick*, p. 45, and illustration of the Monarch machine p. 54.
25 A. Perceval, 'Faversham bricks', *BBS Information*, 109 (March 2009), p. 13. The brickworks still operates at Faversham as part of W.T. Lamb and Sons Ltd. See <www.lambsbricks.com>, accessed 31 May 2020.
26 Eastwoods were a member company of the Pressed Brick Makers Association formed in 1910, as were T. and M. Plowman Ltd. Hillier, *Clay that burns*, pp. 53, 98–9.

Bricks of Victorian London

Here it was not the Lower Oxford clay that it encountered, but the heavy London clay, which had always been thought too difficult to work by traditional methods. As a press correspondent remarked on a visit to the works, 'if it can make bricks out of London clay, we shall be the first to give it welcome, for it will undoubtedly help the London maker out of a considerable difficulty'.[27] The thick seams of London clay presented a seemingly inexhaustible resource, with depths of up to 100 metres recorded at some places in the London region. The New Patent company invested in 'Invicta' machines from Australia, which were said to operate in a similar way to Whittaker's. Long after the initial owners had gone bust, brickmaking on this site continued into the 1930s, by which time clay was being fetched from forty feet down by means of a bucket ladder excavator. The company claimed at that point to have clay reserves for 120 years' production.[28]

The last approach was the one most often employed: reducing costs in order to compete with Flettons on price. There was a large gap to make up, as Fletton bricks were being sold in the London market below the manufacturing cost of the local products. Employers attempted to achieve this by reducing the rate they paid to the moulders, a strategy they had adopted before. In 1897 the Kent & Essex Brickmasters had agreed to a 10 per cent increase in wages, costing about £40,000 in all, but in spring 1900 they proposed a reduction in wage rates back to those prevailing in 1896.[29]

The high level of demand for bricks in the London area began to tail off after 1902, and this downturn in the market affected both London brickmakers and Fletton producers. The period from 1895 to 1900 had been one of spectacular growth for the Fletton industry, with the formation of nine new companies in the area around Peterborough and increasing capacity from established businesses. The high level of housebuilding that had sustained this boom peaked in 1898 and then levelled off for five years. By 1903, however, demand was falling away at a dramatic level, as had been predicted two years earlier:

> Common brickmaking has been always looked upon as an easy trade needing no technical knowledge, and the immediate effect of any rise in prices had been to induce the novice to rush in, lured by the prospect of large and easy profits. The consequent over-production has in each case immediately had the effect of lowering prices and causing ruin to the inefficient. Such a period occurred in the early eighties … now, again … a similar result seems threatened.[30]

The Fletton producers sought to protect themselves by establishing a trade association, as the Cowley makers and the Kent & Essex brickmasters had done before them. The first, the Fletton Brickmasters Association, was formed in 1890, followed in 1900 by the Peterborough & District Brick Manufacturers Association.[31] In 1901 the *British Clayworker* suggested that it was in the interests of both parties

---

27 *British Clayworker*, September 1895, pp. 145–6.
28 *Ibid.*, September 1936, p. 178.
29 *Ibid.*, April 1897, p. 24, October 1900, p. 251.
30 *Ibid.*, January 1901, quoted by Hillier, *Clay that burns*, p. 40.
31 Hillier, *Clay that burns*, pp. 50–3.

'The chief market is London'

that the Fletton masters' association should come to agreement with the Kent & Essex Brickmasters Association to regulate prices and avoid the kind of cutthroat competition that could ruin them all. This could probably have been achieved only on the basis of the allocation of market shares and nothing came of it.[32]

Conditions continued to worsen for both the stock brickmakers and their Fletton competitors. By 1908 the price of Flettons had fallen catastrophically from 28s to a price of only 8s, causing several companies near Peterborough to shut their works. At the same time the Cowley district was despondent, mainly due to the lack of demand, but also because of a sense that during the industrial disputes of the early 1890s a large portion of the trade had been gifted to the Fletton makers. The north Kent makers 'from Belvedere to Sittingbourne', though perhaps not as badly placed as the Cowley district, were also sharing the common misery.[33]

It is at this point, where the Fletton makers found themselves selling their own bricks below cost price, that they formed their new association, the Pressed Brick Makers Association, setting minimum prices and quotas for their members.[34] Yet this was not enough to meet the challenge of difficult market conditions and one or two yards had already shut before wholesale closure became necessary when war broke out in 1914. With construction work at a standstill except for buildings connected with the war effort, the demand for bricks was very low and from 1916 conscription into the armed forces removed much of the labour force. Some of the Fletton companies mothballed their smaller plants, and their empty kilns were offered to the Ministry of Munitions as storage sites for high explosives.[35]

After the war the Fletton industry consolidated with a series of amalgamations. The London Brick Company & Forders Ltd, formed in 1923, began to dominate the sector. There followed a period of increased stability for the producers, and the price of Fletton bricks barely altered in the London market between 1923 and 1931, only falling slightly during the mid-1930s, when the bricks were widely used in the extensive speculative suburban housing boom of that period.[36] Fletton bricks achieved rapid popularity and, with more decorative products becoming available following the success of the 'Rustic' brick, they began to be used as a substitute for the traditional facing brick. It was not uncommon for Fletton bricks to be used on all the exterior walls except for the street front, or to be used throughout a building hidden under a coating of render or pebbledash, much like the habit of using stucco over a century earlier.[37]

The London Brick Company dominated national brick manufacture and was making as many as 1750 million bricks a year in the interwar period from its many plants, including what was then the largest brickworks in the world at Stewartby in

---

32 *Ibid.*, p. 52.

33 *British Architect*, 21 August 1908.

34 Hillier, *Clay that burns*, p. 53.

35 *Ibid.*, p. 60.

36 *Ibid.*, pp. 64–8.

37 A.A. Jackson, *Semi-detached London: suburban development, life and transport, 1900–39*, 2nd edn (Didcot, 1991), p. 108.

Bricks of Victorian London

Bedfordshire.[38] Between 1968 and 1971 London Brick bought out its three remaining Fletton brick competitors, thus achieving a monopoly of the sector. In 1973 its brick sales totalled 2.88 billion units, some 43 per cent of the total UK output.[39]

Since then Flettons' market share has shrunk and there has been an overall reduction in the use of bricks, as commons have been largely replaced with concrete blocks. Fletton bricks now account for less than 10 per cent of the market. Hanson Brick (now part of Forterra), which took over London Brick in 1984, still has a division known as London Brick. Production at Stewartby closed in 2008, bringing an end to large-scale brick production in Bedfordshire. The company still operates from Kings Dyke brickworks at Whittlesey near Peterborough.

The rise of the Fletton brick industry had its counterpart in the decline of stock brickmaking in the London area. When the London Brick Company exerted dominant control in the supply of bricks to London after the Second World War stock brickmaking had all but disappeared.[40]

---

38 Hillier, *Clay that burns*, p. 77.

39 Monopolies & Mergers Commission, *Building bricks: a report on the supply of building bricks* (London, 1976), p. 10.

40 British Geological Survey, *Brick clay*, Mineral planning factsheet (London, 2007), p. 8; *Construction Enquirer*, 2 June 2011.

Chapter 17

Into the new century: stock brickmaking after 1900

The decennial census of 1891 identified 43,688 brickmakers in England and Wales, an increase of 11 per cent in a decade. In the County of London (corresponding to the modern inner London) there were just 447 brickmakers. Kent was now the dominant south-east county, with 3335 workers, followed by Essex with 1205 and Middlesex with 974. Reflecting the changes that had occurred because of the Factory Acts, only 6 per cent of the national workforce was female and in these three counties just over thirty women gave their occupations as brickmakers, the majority in Essex. Stock brickmaking had become an occupation largely carried out by adult men and teenage boys.[1]

This census was taken at the time when London brickmaking was just coming out of the depression of the 1880s with an upturn in activity in the construction sector that peaked at the end of the century. Growth in demand, however, would not last forever and at the end of the 1900 season there were 100 million unsold bricks in Kent and Essex yards.[2] The 1902 season was weather-affected, with rain in the early part of the season causing a reduction in output, and while the second half of the season was better, the net result was a shortfall of about 100 million bricks.

At this point the building boom that had sustained the industry for several years showed signs of slowing, because there was now a surplus of houses on the market. 'The speculative builder, not finding purchasers, is disposed to curtail his operations, and as two-thirds of the London trade is speculative, it will have a certain effect on the brick market.'[3] In fact, this was the beginning of a long slump causing considerable difficulties for the London brickmakers. Weather again played a part. In 1903 heavy rain flooded brickfields at Southall and Ilford in the same week.[4] In 1904 the weather was kinder, 'all that could be desired', but this proved little consolation as demand was falling and prices with it, leaving the trade 'unremunerative'.[5] By the summer of 1905 conditions were dire, as the economy had entered the most acute depression for twenty-five years and 'every branch of clay working is slack, all trades are depressed which depend on internal commerce', while at the same time there was robust export growth.[6] The slump in demand continued, resulting in a 'sensational fall' in the price

---

1   *British Clayworker*, November 1893. As the census was taken that year on 6 April, some workers who arrived in brickmaking areas for the summer moulding season may not have been counted.

2   *Ibid.*, October 1900, p. 251.

3   *Ibid.*, January 1903, p. 331.

4   *Middlesex County Times*, 20 June 1903; *Barking, East Ham & Ilford Advertiser*, 20 June 1903.

5   *British Clayworker*, January 1905, p. 315.

6   *British Clayworker*, June 1905, p. 74; Lloyd-Jones and Lewis, *British industrial capitalism*, p. 103.

Bricks of Victorian London

of bricks of all types, and affecting Flettons particularly. The Cowley district was said to be in a 'slough of despond', as trade had almost dried up, and the brickmakers of north Kent were also affected.[7] The number of brickies in Kent fell during this decade, and this was reflected in the age structure of the workforce: men over the age of 45 comprised 23 per cent of the workforce in 1901 but 30 per cent in 1911.[8]

There were mixed fortunes for brickmakers in the London area in the first decade of the twentieth century. In the summer of 1903 the West End Brick and Joinery Company, the successor to the New Patent Brick Company in Northolt, sold off its brickmaking plant.[9] By contrast, a few miles away, the Willesden & Acton Brick Company's works were in the process of expansion. They were located at West Acton and connected by a siding to the new railway line to High Wycombe being built by the Great Western Railway, with whom it had a contract for 20 million bricks. This 13.5 acre site, with an output of 60,000 pressed bricks a day, drying sheds of the Wolff type and two 16-chamber Hoffman kilns, was thought interesting enough to attract a visit from a group of French brickmakers who were in England on a fact-finding tour.[10]

The severe downward trend in demand for bricks is evident in economic indices. They show a peak in demand, nationally and in London, at the turn of the century, and then a steep decline after 1904. The peak years nationally were 1898, 1899 and 1901, and in London 1898, 1899 and 1903, but by 1913 demand had fallen by two-thirds from those high points.[11] In 1918 a statistician looking at the building cycles since 1870 suggested 'that a period of increasing building activity would, in normal conditions, have been due in or about 1914'.[12] As it was, the outbreak of war suppressed demand even further. The number of houses built nationally fell to only 7000 in 1916, and no figures are available for the rest of the war. The lack of house building immediately before and during the Great War resulted in a housing emergency when war ended. In John Burnett's phrase, the '1919 shortage was, therefore, the 1914 shortage accentuated'.[13]

The Great War had a huge impact on the building trades and the suppliers of building materials. By the middle of the war the government was exerting considerable control over the economy, and although some brick production was required for government contracts this was insufficient to compensate for the dearth of commercial projects. Production costs rose steeply in the face of increased taxation and rising wages, and, with conscription in force after 1916, there were labour shortages as well.[14] All brickmakers suffered. The Fletton producers reacted to these challenging

---

7 *British Architect*, 21 August 1908.

8 Winstanley, *Life in Kent*, pp. 174–5.

9 *Ealing Gazette & West Middlesex Observer*, 4 July 1903.

10 Despite the obvious optimism of the owners in 1903, the company was not very long-lived, closing in 1910, by which time the clay pit was around twenty feet deep. *British Clayworker*, July 1903, p. 153; Harper Smith, *Brickfields of Acton*, pp. 44–5.

11 Lewis, *Building cycles*, pp. 316–17; Mitchell, *British historical statistics*, p. 390; Saul, 'House building in England', p. 125.

12 Spensley, 'Urban housing problems', p. 170.

13 J. Burnett, *A social history of housing 1815–1970* (Newton Abbot, 1978), p. 217.

14 Musson, *British industry*, pp. 260–1.

Into the new century

conditions by closing down or mothballing many of their yards and by taking in other kinds of war work, utilising the mechanical skills of their workshops. Those that stayed in operation stockpiled bricks against the anticipated post-war demand.[15] Stock brickmakers reduced their production.

The labour force became depleted by the number of men who volunteered for the armed forces in the early months of the year, but increasingly by the call-up of men once conscription was introduced in 1916. In the face of the military's inexorable demand for more and more soldiers, the government had to balance the needs of the army with those of the economy as a whole. It established a large number of reserved occupations and a system of appeals to local military tribunals.[16] Brickmaking had some protection, and the more skilled workers were most likely to be granted exemption.

A number of cases involving brickmakers came before these military tribunals. In the first year of the scheme some of the bigger firms applied for large numbers of exemptions. In November 1916 Wills & Packham appealed on behalf of nine younger men who were needed to prepare the brickearth for the following season. If they were taken for military service, Mr Wills claimed, 'it practically meant that they would have to close the brickfield. They had certain contracts running, and practically the whole of them were with the government.' Temporary exemptions were given to seven of them, but the youngest two were refused. At the same time Smeed, Dean sought exemption for sixty-five of its men, of whom about half were granted temporary exemptions. Its workforce had already been reduced to 702 employees from a pre-war total of 1130.[17] In all some 400 Smeed, Dean employees served in the military, among them the grandson of the chairman, Donald Dean, who was awarded the Victoria Cross.[18] There are thirty-five names on the Murston war memorial.

Appeals continued throughout the war. In November 1917 eight employees of another Kent firm applied for renewal of their exemptions, and the employer successfully made the case that, although his firm was only making one fifth of the bricks it made in peacetime, the workforce had been reduced by the same ratio. Nearly all the current output was destined for government contracts.[19] In June 1918 the East Kent Appeal Tribunal considered the cases of thirty-four brickmakers and cement workers, the employees of the two largest brickmakers in Sittingbourne – unnamed, but presumably Wills & Packham and Smeed, Dean. Five moulders and brick sorters belonging to one firm who had been granted temporary exemption the previous year found their exemptions were now opposed on the grounds that their occupation did not appear in the official list of reserved occupations. However, as the men's employer pointed out, exemptions applied to men employed making bricks by machinery, whereas in this case the bricks were made by hand. The twenty-nine

---

15   Hillier, *Clay that burns*, p. 60.

16   G.J. DeGroot, *Blighty: British society in the era of the Great War* (London, 1996), p. 96.

17   *East Kent Gazette*, 4 November 1916.

18   He was a director of Smeed, Dean and after the war started his own brickmaking business, Newington Brick. He died in 1985. See <www.hrgs.co.uk>, accessed 17 October 2021.

19   *East Kent Gazette*, 24 November 1917.

Bricks of Victorian London

employees of the other firm were all married men and carried munitions protection certificates. All the exemptions were upheld.[20]

Not all those seeking exemption were working brickmakers. Reginald Montague Rowse, aged 34, a director and manager of the East Acton Brickworks & Estates Ltd, argued that his presence was essential to the operation of the business. Another man, described as a clerk and salesman at a Heston brickfield, who had six sons serving in the military, was granted an exemption on the grounds that he was the only member of the workforce left and was needed to protect the stock of bricks that was sitting on the field and to send out batches to customers.[21]

We can observe the impact of the war on brickyards in the London area by looking at the experience of the Cowley district. In 1910 there were eleven brickfields, but by 1917 there were only seven and by 1926 just three. Of the bigger concerns, Rutters and Eastwoods had stopped working on the west side of London and the remaining three were Broad & Co (West Drayton) and the East Acton Brickworks and Estates Ltd (Hayes), along with a newcomer, the West End Brickworks Ltd, which now operated from the Northolt site of the New Patent Brick Company.[22]

The Uxbridge Road Brick Co Ltd in Southall was one firm that did not survive the war. This small outfit had been formed in 1906, taking over an existing brickfield with twenty-nine acres of land. In 1909 the firm worked just two stools; it made a loss in the following year on account of the poor weather (of £265), and a smaller one in 1911 (£136). Sadly, the improving trend was reversed in 1913, as the season was exceptionally wet and the bricks were of poor quality. In the early months of 1914 there was some optimism, but once war commenced demand fell and prices with it. Halving their output to 1,224,000 bricks, the company made a loss of £291. By 1916 it had lost its labour force and, unable to recruit enough men to carry on, put itself into voluntary liquidation. The company was formally wound up in 1918 and in February that year a clearance sale of the remaining stock, plant and equipment was held.[23]

There does not seem to have been any significant replacement of men in brickfields by women during the war. Unlike other industries, where capacity needed to be maintained, brickmaking was operating at a very low level and there would always have been a part of the workforce that was too old to be called up for military service; additionally, as we have seen, it was possible to get exemptions for some younger men.

Coming after a long pre-war slump in demand, the smaller firms were at greater risk of going out of business during the war, and there was a fear that whole brickmaking districts could face extinction. Even while the war continued the government was

---

20   *Ibid.*, 22 June 1918.

21   TNA MH/47 Southall-Norwood Tribunal 19 January 1917 Case No: M2676; *Middlesex Chronicle*, 26 August, 25 November 1916.

22   *Kelly's Directory* of Essex, Hertfordshire and Middlesex, 1910; *Kelly's Directory* of Middlesex, 1917. The story of the New Patent Brick Company and its successors on the site is a complex one. Hounsell, 'Cowley stocks', pp. 282–5.

23   TNA BT31/17793/89188 Uxbridge Road Brick Company Ltd; Sale Particulars, *Middlesex Chronicle*, 2 February 1918.

Into the new century

planning for the construction work that would be required once hostilities ceased, especially to make good the deficit in housing stock, prompting the Homes for Heroes initiative. Responding to a Local Government Board circular in the autumn of 1916, the Faversham Board of Guardians discussed the issue. Charles Cremer, an established local brickmaker, gave his opinion that there would be no more brickmaking in the district after the war. Discussion revolved around the weakness of the traditional method of brickmaking that resulted in the production of too large a proportion of inferior bricks. There remained a market for good stocks, but place bricks could not compete with Flettons. This had already resulted in accumulations of millions of place bricks at brickyards, some of them, it was said, in stock for twenty years. The position of Sittingbourne was thought to be better, but even here some of the fields were thought likely to close.[24]

Clement B. Broad (of Broad & Co.) was appointed to the Building Industry Committee set up by the Ministry of Reconstruction in 1917 to represent the brick industry. Anticipating that the demand for bricks to meet the post-war reconstruction, including the building of 300,000 homes, would be about six billion a year, compared with the pre-war average of 2.8 billion, the committee came up with several recommendations. These included the handing back of brickyards that were currently being used for other purposes, such as the storage of munitions, and the early release, before general demobilisation, of 'pivotal' workers. At demobilisation priority should be given to other workers involved in the supply of building materials and the 'immediate provision of labour to get and prepare earth during the ensuing winter [that of 1918/19] for the making of stock bricks so as not to miss manufacture in 1919'.[25]

As a result, in the summer of 1918, with the war not yet won, some brickfields started to recruit workers again. Both the Milton Hall Brick Company Ltd in Southend and Cullis's brickfield in Heston advertised in local newspapers for experienced brick moulders, presumably attempting to attract older men who had not been called up.[26]

Although war time restrictions had created severe challenges for all brickmakers, the stock brick industry, contrary to Mr Cremer's prediction about Faversham, did not disappear. Many plants went back into production, Cremer's included, and continued throughout the interwar period. However, it was some time before national production returned to the level experienced before the pre-war slump.

In 1924 the national Census of Production listed 1600 firms engaged in the brick and fireclay industries nationally, with an average of 43.8 employees each. Between 1924 and 1937 the output of United Kingdom brickworks doubled from 3.7 billion to 7.7 billion, of which Flettons then accounted for one third.[27]

There was no wholesale reduction in the number of brickfields in the post-war period in the London area, but a steady erosion. Five manufacturers were still operating in Faversham in 1918, one fewer than in 1914, and only one Sittingbourne

---

24 *East Kent Gazette*, 23 September 1916.

25 Ministry of Reconstruction, Report of the committee appointed by the minister of reconstruction to consider the building industry after the war (Cd. 9197), PP 1918, vol. 7, pp. 4, 6.

26 *Middlesex Chronicle*, 15 June 1918.

27 M. Bowley, *Innovations in building materials: an economic study* (London, 1960), pp. 60, 163.

Figure 17.1. Brickfields at Murston in the early twentieth century. (Sittingbourne Museum)

manufacturer had disappeared. However, overall numbers across the three counties were down. In Kent as a whole there were 30 per cent fewer brickmaking businesses in 1918 than there had been in 1913; in Essex 25 per cent fewer by 1922. In Middlesex there had been twenty brickworks at the outbreak of war, but this number had halved by 1926, with one in Willesden and three in the Edmonton/Enfield area, as well as the three in the Cowley district.[28]

Smeed, Dean faced the postwar era with some confidence, with a visit from the duke of York (the future King George VI) in 1921. The firm had returned to volume production and was now making 52 million bricks a year, still predominantly yellow stocks, but also an increasing number of machine-made red facings, and was experimenting with a cheap pressed brick to be known as 'S.D. Flettons'. Like many other companies, they recognised that mechanisation was important in order to improve productivity. In a brochure produced for the royal visit, the company could also point to the flexibility it enjoyed in terms of distribution of its product, by rail, road and river, its long history, the quality of its products and the many London landmarks that had been constructed with them, claiming that the 'S.D' mark, pressed into the frogs of its bricks, stood for 'Strength and Durability' (Figure 17.1).[29]

The output of brick plants nationally increased dramatically between the wars. It has been estimated that about 38 billion bricks were produced in the 1920s and 70

---

28 *Kelly's Directories* of Kent, 1913, 1918; of Essex 1914, 1922; of Middlesex 1914, 1926.
29 Perks, *George Bargebrick*, p. 49.

Into the new century

billion in the following decade.[30] The high level of demand came from a large volume of house building across the country and particularly in the London area – what Alan Jackson termed 'speculators' suburbia'. Nationally, the peak years for housebuilding of all kinds were between 1934 and 1938, when more than 300,000 houses were completed each year, of which over 200,000 were built by speculative builders. In greater London the peak year for speculative building was 1934, when 72,750 houses were completed, 21 per cent of the total number of houses built in Britain that year.[31]

The large increase in output during the 1920s and 1930s was not achieved by a significant growth in the number of brickmaking firms or by a large increase in the number of employees in brickworks. Rather it was the result of increased mechanisation and higher productivity. Productivity gains between 1907 and 1935 were spectacular, amounting to 31 per cent output per employee, or 47 per cent per man hour, taking account of shorter working hours. Less efficient firms disappeared and well-established and better-managed concerns increased capacity. Overall, brickworks became larger. The average yearly output for a brickworks in 1930 was between 4.8 and 5.4 million; by 1935 it was 7.2 million.[32]

Although Flettons were the cheapest brick in the London market, and were used where they would not be seen – in interior work, in side elevations or behind render or pebbledash – good-quality facing bricks were still required for street fronts. While Fletton bricks captured a large part of the London market, brickmakers in the London region could still have a share in the booming local market for bricks, and there were still 365 works in the south of England in 1937, contributing 12.5 per cent of the national brick output.[33] Although the factory price of Flettons remained low, the stock brickmakers of Kent had the advantage of lower distribution charges, as river transport continued to be cheaper than rail.[34]

A bigger threat to the brickmakers of the south-east of England came from the import of bricks from continental Europe. In the early 1920s these were being sold in Britain at prices below the manufacturing cost of the local product. For example, in 1923 a Belgian firm offered Folkestone Corporation bricks at 50s a thousand, while locally produced ones were twice the price.[35] Significant quantities of bricks were imported during the following years. In 1924 there were 83 million imports and in 1925 185 million, of which 38 per cent came from Belgium, 44 per cent from France and 16 per cent from the Netherlands; but, to put this in context, this accounted for less than 5 per cent of British production.[36] By 1927 imports had grown further, to over 278 million, prompting questions in parliament, as at the time there were said to be 6 billion

---

30 D.H. Kennett, 'Britain 1919–39: brick and economic regeneration', *BBS Information*, 88 (July 2002), p. 9.

31 Mitchell, *British historical statistics*, p. 390; Jackson, *Semi-detached London*, p. 61.

32 Bowley, *Innovations*, pp. 159–62; H.W. Richardson and D.H. Aldcroft, *Building in the British economy between the wars* (London, 1968), p. 412.

33 Bowley, *Innovations*, p. 172.

34 *East Kent Gazette*, 14 July 1923.

35 *Ibid.*

36 *Mid-Sussex Times*, 14 September 1926.

251

Bricks of Victorian London

bricks in stock at brickfields across the country.[37] The government finally responded to demands to protect a range of products from foreign competition by the Import Duties Act of 1932, which introduced a general tariff of 10 per cent on manufactured goods and a greater one for some sectors.[38]

Some of the firms identified in this book survived the 1930s and the Second World War and continued to operate into the second half of the twentieth century. In 1953 it was Eastwoods' Conyer brickworks that supplied the bricks that were used to rebuild the House of Commons after it was damaged in the Blitz.[39] However, there was an increasing trend towards consolidation within the industry, with fewer firms and larger units of production. In 1950 Kent brickmakers produced about 162 million bricks, but in the same year the London Brick Company had produced 1.4 billion, giving it 24 per cent of the national market.[40] In 1959 the Stock Brickmasters' Association celebrated its 50th anniversary with a dinner at the Connaught Rooms, Holborn, with Mr John E. Wills, of the Sittingbourne firm, in the chair.[41]

The East Acton Brickworks & Estates Ltd, the last remaining firm in the Cowley district, ceased trading in the 1950s. Broad & Co. stopped brickmaking in the 1930s and reverted to being a building materials supplier, later acquired by Travis Perkins in 1975. Eastwoods became part of the Redland Group in 1963. The last firm to operate in Edmonton, W.D. Cornish, closed in 1936.[42]

In 1900 there had been about 3500 brickyards in Britain, but this had fallen to about 350 in the mid-1970s; at that point seven companies, each delivering between 100 million and 349 million bricks, contributed about 20 per cent of the total UK output. By then rather more bricks were being produced than in 1938 but the number of brickworks had fallen by two-thirds.[43] In 1980 there were still 300 brick firms, but in 2022 just twelve companies are members of the Brick Development Association, and between them account for most of the bricks produced in Britain.[44] The four largest are Ibstock, Forterra, Wienerberger and Micklemersh. These companies are the results of multiple amalgamations and acquisitions, and each operates from several sites. In 1984 the London Brick Company was acquired by Hanson Brick and is now owned by Forterra. Wienerberger is a 200-year-old Austrian business which is the largest brickmaker in the world; it entered the UK market in 2001 and still makes a Smeed, Dean stock brick at a factory in Sittingbourne. At the other end of the scale, small companies such as W.H. Collier and H.G. Matthews still make hand-made bricks by

---

37   *Hansard*, 18 December 1928, 19 April 1926.

38   22 & 23 George V, c. 8 (1932) *Import Duties Act*.

39   *East Kent Gazette*, 30 January 1953.

40   *Ibid.*, 23 February 1951; Monopolies and Mergers Commission, *Building bricks*, p. 10.

41   *East Kent Gazette*, 9 January 1959.

42   *Victoria County History. Middlesex, vol. 5: Hendon, Kingsbury, Great Stanmore, Little Stanmore, Edmonton, Enfield, Monken Hadley, South Mimms, Tottenham*, ed. T.F.T. Baker and R.B. Pugh (London, 1978), pp. 161–72.

43   Woodforde, *Bricks*, p. 155; Monopolies and Mergers Commission, *Building bricks*, p. 11.

44   D. Gann, *Building innovation: complex constructs in a changing world* (London, 2000), p. 29; Brick Development Association <brick.org.uk/about/our-members>, accessed 8 April 2022.

Into the new century

traditional methods which are sought after for the restoration of historic buildings and new builds.

There is a thriving trade in reclaimed London stock bricks and new bricks giving a similar appearance are being produced by a few manufacturers. However, the industry, which throughout the nineteenth century supplied the needs of the London market from the local brickearth, has now disappeared, and it is only if you look carefully that you can still see signs of where the hundreds of brickfields that supplied those millions of bricks once were, perhaps in a piece of land whose surface is lower than its neighbours'. Many old brickfields are now under buildings, but some are still open land, in the form of public parks and recreation fields. The Television Centre in Wood Lane, Shepherd's Bush, and the neighbouring housing estate are on the site of former brickfields and similar stories will be found across London.

Finally, in some parts of Greater London streets perpetuate the names of brickmakers who once worked there. Rutters Close and Eastwood Road are close to each other in West Drayton, not far from Pocock Avenue and Brickfields Way, while Westbrook Road is in Heston and Rigby Lane is in Hayes. Cornish Court is close to the site of the company's brickfield in Edmonton. There will be many more.

The London stock brick was the mainstay of building in the capital and its suburbs for most of the nineteenth century, taking advantage of the particular qualities of the local brickearth, which was found widely across the region and was ideally suited to hand moulding. Thousands of men, women and children made thousands of millions of such bricks, but the industry eventually fell victim to its own success. The expansion of the capital and the exhaustion of clay reserves caused brickfields to close, and finally machine-made bricks from outside the area made the local product expensive in a highly competitive market.

Its legacy remains in the many thousands of buildings in London built of yellow bricks. These have stood the test of time. As you go into King's Cross station, or while waiting for a train at Baker Street, remember to look up and enjoy the stock bricks our ancestors made.

Glossary

Sources
1. J. Whittow, *The Penguin dictionary of physical geography* (Harmondsworth, 1984)
2. R.W. Brunskill, *Brick building in Britain* (London, 1990)
3. M.J. Crute, 'Brickmaking terms: a collected list, mainly from South-East England', *BBS Information*, 72 (October 1997), pp. 3–11
4. Peter Hounsell

Barrow loader: the person in a **moulding gang** (q.v.) responsible for taking the freshly moulded brick and placing it on the **hack barrow** (q.v.). (4)

Breeze: cinders or coarse ashes remaining when the finer ash has been sieved out of domestic refuse collected by scavengers. As breeze resulted from incomplete combustion in domestic fires it was sufficiently combustible to act as fuel for burning bricks in clamps or kilns. (2)

Brickearth: a general term for any loamy clay that can be used for brickmaking, but used more specifically to describe the wind-blown, fine-textured soils that were re-sorted and redeposited by water, frequently in old river terraces. Many of the brickearths of southern England and northern Europe were initially blown southwards by glacial winds that picked up many deposits formed by the melting Pleistocene ice sheets. Brickearths give fertile, easily worked soils and are generally classified as of high agricultural value. (1)

Brickfield: a field containing brickearth, and where bricks are made. (4)

Brickie: informal name for a brickmaker, a person who makes bricks. (4)

Brickmaker: name applied both to a person who makes bricks, but also to the owner of a brickmaking business. (4)

Brickmaster: the owner of a brickmaking business. (4)

Brickworks: similar to a brickfield, but likely to have more buildings and machinery. (4)

Callow: the topsoil that must be removed from a clay ground before the clay can be extracted for brickmaking. Hence **uncallowing** (q.v.). (4)

Clamp: a method of firing bricks without a permanent kiln. A carefully constructed stack of unburnt bricks with gaps for fuel and to allow hot gases to circulate, which was the traditional method of firing bricks in the London area. The different temperatures achieved at the centre and edges of a clamp produced varying degrees of over-burnt and under-burnt bricks that were sorted into a number of different grades. Clamps normally contained 30,000 to 45,000 bricks, but could contain as many as 150,000. Clamps took two to three weeks to burn through, but large clamps took much longer. (2, 3, 4)

Clay: a natural argillaceous substance of soft rock which develops plastic qualities with the addition of a small amount of water. It then becomes malleable into different shapes that will retain their form when either air- or oven-dried. Clays have different physical properties because of their differing chemical and mineralogical compositions, but in general they are based on a hydrous aluminium silicate. (1)

Bricks of Victorian London

Crowder: another name for a **setter** (q.v.).

Crowding barrow: barrows used by crowders (or setters) to wheel dried bricks to clamp or kiln, and for moving fired bricks to loading areas for carts or barges. They differed from **hack barrows** (q.v.) in being shorter and more upright. The bricks on crowding barrows were firm enough to be stacked rather than laid out in a single layer, as on the hack barrow. (4)

Flattie: a **walk flatter** (q.v.).

Fletton: common bricks made from the Lower Oxford Clays in Bedfordshire, Buckinghamshire and the Peterborough area. These bricks, notable for their granular consistency when broken open, are produced by the semi-dry process, in which the clay is ground and dampened, then subject to high-pressure moulding. After the 1880s they were widely used in the London area, and became the most common brick produced in the United Kingdom. They take their name from the village of Fletton near Peterborough. (4)

Frog: an indentation in the surface of a brick which reduces its weight, makes it easier to handle and minimises the clay used in its manufacture. When laid 'frog-up' the indentation is filled with mortar by the bricklayer. (2)

Gault brick: brick made from the gault clays associated with the chalk belt of eastern England. They are normally yellowish in colour but may emerge as pink or red according to their position in the kiln. (2)

Grizzle: an underburnt brick, usually of a grey colour, intended to be hidden or used in an unobtrusive location. (2,3)

Hack: an area of ground on which freshly moulded bricks were laid out to dry. Also known as the hack ground. Bricks were often protected from the weather, especially against the effects of rain, by wooden covers. (4)

Hack barrow: a long flat barrow with a single front wheel, used for carrying bricks from the moulder's bench to the drying hack. Each barrow could hold 28–30 bricks, laid out in two rows. (3, 4)

Hoffman kiln: a type of kiln, circular in plan and designed for the continuous production of bricks. The kiln was divided into many chambers, usually about a dozen, and each chamber in turn was loaded with 'green' bricks that were dried, burnt, cooled and removed chamber by chamber, so that a batch of bricks was produced every day. By means of a series of ducts and flues the heat from the continuously burning furnace was directed to pre-heating and firing, while the waste heat from a chamber that was cooling was used to help in drying the green bricks that had just been loaded into another chamber. (2)

Loess: an unstratified, homogeneous, fine-grained yellow brickearth. Majority opinion favours a wind-blown genesis, whereby widespread dust clouds were carried outwards from the newly deposited glacial and glacio-fluvial deposits of northern Eur-Asia by strong anticyclonic winds blowing from the Pleistocene ice-sheets. (1)

Malm: brick made out of a naturally occurring or artificial mixture of fine yellow alluvial clay and about one-sixteenth proportion of chalk. Such a clay is found in the London area. (2)

Malming: the process of artificially adding chalk to brickearth to create a clay that approximates to a natural malm. (4)

Mould: a wooden box without top or bottom and with inner sides usually lined with brass or thin sheet iron. In brickmaking the mould is placed over a wooden **stock**

Glossary

(q.v.) to form the complete mould into which the clay is thrown. The dimensions of the mould allow for the shrinkage of the bricks in drying and firing. (2)

Moulder: the member of a brickmaking gang who actually forms the brick in the mould. The moulder was the most skilled member of the gang and usually its leader, subcontracting with the owner of the brickfield and responsible for finding the remainder of his gang. (4)

Moulding gang: a group of usually six persons, led by the moulder, working together to make hand-made bricks. The gang comprised the **moulder**, the **temperer**, the **pug boy**, the **walk flatter**, the **barrow loader** and the **pusher out** (all q.v.) (4)

Off-bearer: person, often a woman or child in traditional brickmaking, who takes the newly moulded bricks from the moulder's bench to the **hack** (q.v.) using an off-bearing or hack barrow. Also known as a pusher-out or bearer-off. (3)

Operative brickmaker: a person who physically makes bricks, in distinction to a brickmaker who is the owner of a brickfield. (4)

Pallet board: thin board on which newly moulded bricks are placed before they are taken to the hacks. (4)

Place brick: slightly under-burnt brick from the clamp, used for inside work. (3)

Pug boy: the person in the moulding gang responsible from bringing prepared clay from a pug mill to the moulding bench. (4)

Pug mill: a device for mixing and refining clay for brickmaking. The pug mill consists of a tub of iron placed vertically, and usually tapering downwards, in which there is a shaft from which project a set of knives arranged in a spiral fashion. The shaft was usually turned by a horse treading a circular path around the mill. Clay was inserted at the top, mixed by the knives and forced out through an orifice at the bottom to be taken away to be moulded into bricks. (2)

Pusher out: The person who takes the newly moulded bricks from the moulder's bench to the **hack** (q.v.) using an offbearing or **hack barrow** (q.v.). Also known as a pusher-out, or off-bearer. (3)

Setter: man who took the dried bricks from the hacks and loaded them into a kiln or built them into clamps. They did not form part of the moulding gangs and were employed by the owner of the brickfield. Also known as crowders, hence **crowding barrows** (q.v.). (4)

Shales: hard laminated rocks that may be crushed or broken down through weathering and mixed with water so as to form a plastic mass from which bricks can be moulded and fired. Suitable shales are found in the coalfields, expecially those of Durham, Yorkshire, Lancashire and Yorkshire. (2)

Skintling (or scintling): the herringbone placing of bricks for drying, arranged when the bricks are half dry. The spacing allows air to pass freely between the bricks. (3)

Soil: finely sieved ashes mixed with the clay, so helping to provide an integral fuel for burning the green bricks. Hence **soiling**, the process of adding the ashes to the clay. Also known as **Spanish**. (2)

Stiff plastic process: a brickmaking process in which ground, screened and dampened shale is pressed to make a roughly rectangular clot, and then pressed again to make a smooth sided brick ready for firing. (2)

Stock board, or stock: an iron-faced block of wood fixed to the surface of the moulder's bench. The mould fits over the stock. (2)

Stock brick: the term has three main meanings. (1) The name given to any bricks

Bricks of Victorian London

made with the aid of a **stock board** (q.v.); (2) the ordinary brick of any particular locality; (3) the yellowish common brick of the London area. (2)

Stool: also known as a **berth**. The bench on which the moulder shapes the brick. Consequently the unit of measurement of traditional brickfields, indicating the number of moulding teams employed and the likely output. (4)

Temperer: the member of a gang responsible for preparing the clay ready for the moulder. He worked the clay by hand, or using a pug mill, adding ashes and chalk to the mix. Temperers, like moulders, were usually adult males in the London area and were also employed during the winter months, ensuring enough clay was dug and weathered ready for the next season. (4)

Tempering: the action of bringing brick clay into a state ready for use by the brickmaker. Weathered clay is turned over, mixed with the right amount of water, chopped and then wheeled either directly to the moulder's bench or, later, the pug mill. (2)

Uncallowing: the removal of vegetation and topsoil preparatory to digging brickearth or gravel from the ground. (4)

Walk flatter: the member of the brickmaking gang who broke off a piece of clay sufficient to make a single brick and passed it to the moulder. The name was often shortened to **flattie**. The position was sometimes known as a **clot moulder**. (4)

Washback: a slurry of clay and chalk contained in a pond and allowed to settle before being made into London stock bricks. (2)

Wire-cut bricks: brick clay extruded through an aperture, cut (like cheese) into brick shapes by wires and then burnt in the kiln. Wire-cut bricks are less dense than pressed bricks; they may be perforated, but do not have a **frog** (q.v.), and they often show in the surface the parallel scratch lines resulting from the extrusion process. (2)

Bibliography

Primary sources

Bedfordshire Archives
Z41/A2/1/1 Minutes of Beart's Patent Brick Company, 1853–57
Z41/A4/1/1 Beart's Patent Brick Company. Ledger, 1852–74

Canal & River Trust, Waterways Archive
BW99. GJCC Brentford Toll Books 1897, 1901
BW99/6/5 Grand Junction Canal, gauging registers
BW99/10/3/1 Shackle's Dock 1825
Correspondence file. Dutton's Dock, West Drayton
Diary of W.H. King for the year 1895

Church of England Record Centre
ECE/7/1/7583 Records of the bishopric of Worcester's estates in West Drayton & Hillingdon

City of Westminster Archives
D Misc. 69B/1 Contract between St Marylebone Vestry and Thomas Wheatley, 1808
Paddington Vestry, minute books
Paddington Vestry, Works Committee minute books

Kent Archives and Local History Centre
Miscellaneous deeds and sales catalogues

London Borough of Camden Archives
Hampstead Vestry MOH Report for the Year 1885–6

London Borough of Ealing, Local History Centre
Partnership agreements 1894, 1898
Sale particulars New Patent Brick Company of London Ltd, 1901
Sale particulars Osterley Estate, 1919
Southall Rate Book, 1863

London Borough of Enfield Archives
Enfield Local Board of Health Minute Book 1 (1850–5)

London Borough of Hackney Archives
D/F/RHO Rhodes family estates, Hackney
M569, M570, M717, M721, M724, M725, M760 Miscellaneous deeds

Bricks of Victorian London

London Borough of Hillingdon, Museum and Archives Service
Hayes valuations 1827, 1865, 1893, 1897
Holloway, B., *Rural Yeading in the industrial parish of Hayes 1900–1940* (1974), typescript
Minet estate papers

London Borough of Hounslow Archives
Cuttings book SC2: Westbrook Memorial
Heston Highway rate books 1868, 1872
Heston Poor Rate book 1868

London Metropolitan Archives
Acc. 180 Hayes manorial records
Acc. 289 Northolt manorial records
Acc. 328 Passingham estate papers
Acc. 397/11 Passingham estate act
Acc. 405 Jersey estate papers
Acc. 506 Jersey estate papers
Acc. 538 Papers of Woodbridge & Son, Uxbridge, solicitors
Acc. 742 De Burgh estates in Hillingdon and West Drayton
Acc. 969 De Salis estates in Harlington
Acc. 1103 Papers of Theodore Bell, Cotton and Curtis, solicitors
Acc. 1214 Records of Isleworth Brewery
Acc. 1261 Shadwell estates in Greenford and Northolt
Acc. 1386 De Burgh estates in Hillingdon and West Drayton
DL/D/L/028/Ms12335 Ecclesiastical Commissioners. Colham Garden Manor estates
DL/D/L/136/Ms12292 Ecclesiastical Commissioners. Fulham Manor estates
SC/PZ/HK/01/019 Kingsland Road, brickfields near Ball's Pond Road. Watercolour
WCS Westminster Commission of Sewers

The National Archives, Kew
B3 Cases of the Bankruptcy Commission
BT31 Board of Trade. Files of dissolved companies registered from 1856 onwards
BT34 Board of Trade. Dissolved companies, liquidators' reports
BT41 Board of Trade. Files of joint stock companies registered under the 1844 Act and dissolved by 1856
Census Enumerators' Books 1841–1911 (accessed via Ancestry.co.uk)
FS2 Friendly Societies, indexes to rules and amendments, series 1
IR29 Tithe Apportionment Awards, 1836–60 (accessed via thegenealogist.co.uk)
IR58 Board of Inland Revenue, Valuation Office, field books
MH47 Records of the Middlesex Appeal Tribunal 1916–19
RAIL 830 Records of the Grand Junction Canal Company

Westminster Abbey Muniments
Class N Shadwell estate papers relating to Northolt

Bibliography

Printed works

Anon. [Benjamin Ellis-Martin], 'Through London by canal', *Harper's New Monthly Magazine* (1885), reprinted by British Waterways Board (1977).

Bacon's new large-scale Ordnance Atlas of London and Suburbs (London, 1888).

Balfour, C.L., *Morning dew drops or the juvenile abstainer*, 4th edn (London, 1859).

Bayly, M., *Ragged homes and how to mend them* (London, 1860).

Bazalgette, J.W., 'On the main drainage of London ...', paper read to the Institution of Civil Engineers (14 March 1865).

Bourry, E., *A treatise on ceramic industries: a complete manual for pottery, tile and brick manufacturers*; translated by A.B. Searle (London, 1911).

'Bricks and brickmakers', *Chambers Journal of Popular Literature, Science and Arts*, issue 682 (3 July 1880), pp. 428–30.

Burns, D., *Temperance dictionary* (London, 1861).

Burritt, E., *Walks in the Black Country and its green borderland* (London, 1868).

Campbell, R., *The London tradesman, being a compendious view of all the trades, professions, arts ... now practised in the cities of London and Westminster* [1747] (Newton Abbot, 1969).

Carpenter, W.B., *Temperance and teetotalism: an inquiry into the effects of alcoholic drinks on the human system in health and disease* (Glasgow, 1849).

Chamberlain, H., 'The manufacture of bricks by machinery', *Journal of the Society of Arts*, 185/4 (6 June 1856), pp. 491–524.

Cheshire, E., 'Results of the Census of Great Britain in 1851 ...', *Journal of the Statistical Society of London*, 17/1 (March 1854), pp. 45–72.

Clutterbuck, J.C., 'The farming of Middlesex', *Journal of the Royal Agricultural Society of England*, 2nd series, 5 (1869), pp. 2–27.

Collins, W., *Hide and seek* [1854] (Oxford, 1993).

Coomber, H., *Lessons and experiments on scientific hygiene and temperance for elementary schoolchildren* (London, 1914).

Crees, F.W., *The life story of F.W. Crees*, ed. C.H. Keene (Ealing, 1979).

Defoe, D., *A tour through the whole island of Great Britain*, abridged and edited by P.N. Furbank and W.R. Owens (London, 1991).

Dickens, C., *Bleak House* (London, 1853).

Dickens, C., *Dombey & Son* (London, 1847).

Dobson, E., *A rudimentary treatise on the manufacture of bricks and tiles*, 1st edn (London, 1850) and 10th edn (London, 1899).

Elmes, J., *General and bibliographical dictionary of the fine arts* (London, 1826).

Engels, F., *The condition of the working class in England* [1892], ed. V.G. Kiernan (London, 1987).

Galsworthy, J., *To let* (London, 1921).

Gissing, G., *The Netherworld* [1889] (Oxford, 1999).

Greenwood, J., 'Mr Dodd's dust yard', in *Journeys through London; or, byways of modern Babylon* (London, 1873), pp. 64–71.

Grindrod, R.B., *Bacchus: an essay on the nature, causes, effects and cure of intemperance* (London, 1851).

Guy, W.A., 'On the health of nightmen, scavengers and dustmen', *Journal of the Statistical Society of London*, 11/1 (March 1848), pp. 72–81.

Hammersmith Vestry, Annual Report of the Medical Officer of Health of the parish of Hammersmith for the year ending 29th December 1894 (London, 1895).

Hughson, D., *London, being an accurate history and description of the British metropolis and its neighbourhood*, 6 vols (London, 1805–9).

Bricks of Victorian London

Hunt, E., *Hayes, past and present* (Hayes, 1861).

Hunt, R., *Mineral statistics of the UK of Great Britain and Ireland, being part two for 1858*, Memoir of the Geological Society of Great Britain (London, 1860).

Hunt, R., *Mining records: mineral statistics of the United Kingdom of Great Britain and Ireland for the year 1855*, Memoir of the Geological Society of Great Britain and the Museum of Practical Geology (London, 1856).

Hunter, H., *A history of London and its environs*, 2 vols (London, 1811).

Islington Vestry, Medical Officer of Health, *Report of the sanitary condition of the parish of St. Mary, Islington during the year 1864* (London, 1865).

Law Journal Reports for the year 1847, XVI (1847).

Lockwood, J., 'Bricks & brickmaking', *The Builder* (19 April 1845), pp. 182–3.

London: what to see and how to see it (London, 1853).

Lysons, D., *The environs of London, vol. 2: county of Middlesex* (London, 1795); 2nd edn (London, 1811).

Marx, K., *Capital: a critique of political economy*, vol. 1 [1867] (1996).

Mayhew, H., *The* Morning Chronicle *survey of labour and the poor: the metropolitan districts, vol. 2* (Firle, 1981).

Measom, C., *The illustrated guide to the Great Western Railway* [1852] (1985).

Middleton, J., *View of the agriculture of Middlesex*, 2nd edn (London, 1807).

Milne, T., *Land use map of London and environs in 1800*, ed. G.B.G. Bull, London Topographical Society, nos 118 and 119 (London, 1975–6).

Montgomery, H.G., 'Bricks and brickmaking', *Journal of the Society of Architects, vol.3, no.6* (April 1896), pp. 97–104.

Mylne, R.W., *Map of the geology and contours of London and its environs 1856*, with an introduction by Eric Robinson, London Topographical Society no. 146 (London, 1993).

Oliphant, M., *The rector and the doctor's family* [1863] (London, 1986).

Oliphant, M., *Zaidee: a romance*, 3 vols (Edinburgh, 1856).

Owen, R., *A history of British fossil mammals and birds* (London, 1846).

Parnell, H., *On financial reform*, 3rd edn (London, 1831).

Popplewell, F., 'Seasonal fluctuations in employment in the gas industry', *Journal of the Royal Statistical Society*, 74/7 (June 1911), pp. 693–734.

Pyne, W.H., *Artistic and picturesque groups for the embellishment of landscape, in a series of above 1,000 subjects* (London, 1817).

Pyne, W.H., *Microcosm; or, a picturesque delineation of the arts, agriculture, and manufactures of Great Britain*, 2 vols (London, 1808).

Redford, G. and Riches, T.C., *The history of the ancient town of Uxbridge: being a reprint of the original edition published in 1818* (London, 1885).

Reed, A.H., *An autobiography* (New Zealand, 1967).

Reed, J., 'Reminiscences of a Middlesex brickmaker by James Reed (1925)', *Hayes & Harlington Local History Society Journal*, 79 (Spring 2009), pp. 13–16.

The repertory of patent inventions and other discoveries and improvements in arts, manufactures and agriculture, vol. I (London, 1825), vol. XVI (London, 1833).

Ruegg, A., *A treatise upon the Employers' Liability Act, 1880* (London, 1880).

St Pancras Vestry, *Eleventh annual report of the Medical Officer of Health for the year 1866* (London, 1867).

Sewell, A., *Black Beauty* (London, 1877).

Shoreditch Vestry, *Report of the Medical Officer of Health of the Parish of St Leonard, Shoreditch* (London, 1878).

Bibliography

Smith, G., *The cry of the children from the brickyards of England: a statement and appeal with remedy*, 4th edn (London, 1871).

Spensley, J.C., 'Urban housing problems', *Journal of the Royal Statistical Society*, lxxxi (1918), pp. 161–210.

Stow, J., *A survey of London reprinted from the text of 1603*, ed. C.L. Kingsford (Oxford, 1908).

Temperance Congress, *Temperance progress: facts and figures for temperance workers* (Croydon, 1886).

Thackrah, C.T., *Effects of the principal arts, trades and professions ... on health and longevity* (London & Leeds, 1832).

Thorne, J., *Handbook to the environs of London* (London, 1876).

Thorne, W., *My life's battles* [1925] (London, n.d.).

Tremenheere, H., 'Agricultural and educational statistics of several parishes in the county of Middlesex', *Journal of the Statistical Society of London*, VI (May 1843), pp. 120–30.

Trollope, A., *The last chronicle of Barset* [1867] (Oxford, 1980).

Ward, H., 'Brickmaking', *Institution of Civil Engineers, Minutes of Proceedings* (Session 1885–86, part iv), pp. 1–26.

Ware, I., *A complete body of architecture* (London, 1756).

Webb, S. and Freeman, A. (eds), *Seasonal trades, by various writers* (London, 1912).

White, W., *History, gazetteer and directory of the county of Essex* (Sheffield, 1848).

Yeoman, J., *Diary of the visits of John Yeoman to London in the years 1774 and 1777*, ed. M. Yearsley (London, 1934).

Newspapers and journals (most cited)

The Beehive
Brick & Tile Gazette
Brick, Tile & Builders' Gazette
Brick, Tile & Potteries Journal
British Clayworker
The Builder
Builders' Merchant
East Kent Gazette
London Teetotal Magazine and Literary Miscellany
Marvel & Middlesex Register
Middlesex Chronicle
Middlesex County Times
Southall-Norwood Gazette
The Times
Uxbridge & West Drayton Gazette
Uxbridge Gazette & Middlesex & Bucks Observer

Trade directories

Kelly's Directories of Essex, 1862, 1894, 1914, 1922
Kelly's Directory of Essex, Hertfordshire and Middlesex, 1910
Kelly's Directories of Kent, 1862, 1891, 1913, 1918
Kelly's Directories of Middlesex, 1862, 1882, 1886, 1890, 1894, 1899, 1914, 1917, 1926
Kelly's Directories of Surrey, 1855, 1891
Kelly's London Suburban Directory, 1876

Bricks of Victorian London

Marchant and Co's Builders and Building Trades' Directory, 1857
Pigot & Co.'s London and provincial new commercial directories for 1822–3, 1826–7, 1828–9, 1838
Post Office Directory of the Building Trades, 1870
Post Office Directory of Essex, Hertfordshire, Kent and Middlesex, 1855
Post Office Directory of the Six Home Counties, 1845, 1870
Post Office London Directories, 1863, 1882, 1883
Post Office London Trades and Professional Directory, 1870

Price books

Laxton's Builders' Price Book, 1856, 1860, 1862, 1884, 1890–9
Spon's Architects, builders and contractors pocket book ... 1880
Taylor's Builders' Price Book, 1825, 1830

Acts of parliament

James I (1607) *Proclamation touching new buildings and inmates, 12 October 1607*
Charles I (1622) *A proclamation for the due making and sizing of bricks*
18 & 19 Charles II, c. 2 (1667) *An act for the rebuilding of the city of London*
12 George I, c. 35 (1726) *An act to prevent abuses in making of bricks and tiles, and to ascertain the dimensions thereof, to prevent all unlawful combinations amongst any brickmakers or tile makers within 15 miles of the City of London in order to advance or enhance the price of bricks or tiles*
10 George III, c. 49 (1769–70) *An Act for continuing and amending several acts for preventing abuses in making bricks*
24 George III, c. 24 (1785) *An Act for granting to his Majesty certain rates and duties upon bricks and tiles made in Great Britain and for laying additional duties upon tiles imported into the same*
7 & 8 Victoria, Pr.c. 22 (1844) *An act for enabling the Trustees under the will of the late Mr Jonathan Passingham to grant leases of the devised estates, with licences to dig brick earth*
9 & 10 Victoria, c. 96 (1846) *An act for the more speedy removal of certain nuisances* (Nuisances Removal Act)
10 & 11 Victoria, Pr. c. 35 (1847) *An act to authorise the construction of a canal on the estates devised by the Will of the late Mr Jonathan Passingham*
11 & 12 Victoria, c. 63 (1848) *An act for promoting the public health* (The Public Health Act 1848)
16 & 17 Victoria, c. 128 (1853) *An act to abate the nuisance arising from the smoke of furnaces in the metropolis and from steam vessels above London Bridge* (Smoke Nuisance Abatement (Metropolis) Act)
18 & 19 Victoria, c. 133 (1855) *An act for limiting the liability of members of certain joint stock companies* (The Limited Liability Act)
30 & 31 Victoria, c. 103 (1867) *An act for the extension of the Factory Acts* (Factory Acts (Extension) Act)
30 & 31 Victoria, c. 146 (1867) *An act for regulating the hours of labour children, young persons and women employed in workshops* (Workshops Regulation Act)
33 & 34 Victoria, c. 75 (1870) *An act to provide public elementary education in England & Wales*
34 & 35 Victoria, c.104 (1871) *An act to amend the acts relating to factories and workshops* (The Factory and Workshops Act, 1871)
39 & 40 Victoria, c. 79 (1876) *An act to make further provision for elementary education*
41 Victoria, c. 16 (1878) *An act to consolidate and amend the law relating to factories and workshops* (Factory & Workshops Act)

Bibliography

50 & 51 Victoria, c. 46 (1887) *An Act to amend and extend the Law relating to Truck* (The Truck Amendment Act)

22 & 23 George V, c. 8 (1932) *An Act to provide for the imposition of a general ad valorem duty ....* (Import Duties Act)

Government reports

Census of Production, Final Report on the 1st Census of Production of the United Kingdom, 1907 (Cd. 6320), PP 1912–13, vol. 109 (1912–13)

Children's Employment Commission (1862), 5th report of the Commissioners, with appendix, PP 1866, vol. 24, Report on brickfields by H.W. Lord and evidence

Eighteenth report of the Commissioners of Inquiry into the Excise establishment, Bricks, PP 1836, vol. 26

Committee of Council on Education (Schools of Parochial Unions and Reformatory schools in England and Wales). Minutes. With reports by Her Majesty's Inspector of Schools. House of Lords (1856–7)

Factory and Workshops Acts Commission, Report of the commissioners appointed to inquire into the working of the Factory and Workshops Act, Vol. II – Minutes of evidence (c.1443), PP 1876, vol. 30

Hansard: official reports of debates in Parliament (accessed online <hansard.millbanksystems.com>)

Ministry of Reconstruction, Report of the committee appointed by the minister of reconstruction to consider the building industry after the war (Cd. 9197), PP 1918, vol. 7

Monopolies and Mergers Commission, Building bricks. A report on the supply of building bricks, PP 1975–6, vol. 22

Report from the Select Committee on Metropolitan Communications, PP 1854–55, vol. 10

Report of the Committee of Council on Education (England and Wales), PP 1865–6, vol. 27. Appendix

Report of the Select Committee on Inquiry into drunkenness among the Labouring Classes of the United Kingdom, with minutes of evidence and appendix, PP 1834, vol. 8

Report on the strikes and lockouts of 1890, by the Labour Correspondent of the Board of Trade (c.6476) (1891)

Report on the strikes and lockouts of 1891 by the Labour Correspondent to the Board of Trade (c.6890) (1893–4)

Report on the strikes and lockouts of 1892 by the Labour Correspondent to the Board of Trade (c.7403) (1893)

Report on the strikes and lockouts of 1893 by the Labour Correspondent of Board of Trade (c.7566) (1894)

Report on the strikes and lockouts of 1897 by the Labour Correspondent of Board of Trade (c.9012) (1898)

Report on the strikes and lockouts of 1898 by the Labour Correspondent to the Board of Trade (c.9437) (1899)

Reports of the Inspectors of Factories to her Majesty's Principal Secretary of State for the Home Department for the half year ending 31st October 1869 (c.77), PP 1870, vol. 15

Reports of the Inspectors of Factories to her Majesty's Principal Secretary of State for the Home Department for the half year ending 31st October 1872, PP 1873, vol. 66

Reports of the Inspectors of Factories to her Majesty's Principal Secretary of State for the Home Department for the half year ending 31st October 1876, PP 1877, vol. 69

Reports of the Inspectors of Factories to her Majesty's Principal Secretary of State for the Home Department for the half year to 30 April 1877 (*c*.1794), PP 1877, vol. 56

Bricks of Victorian London

Royal Commission appointed to inquire into the organisation and rules of trade unions and other associations, 11th report, PP 1868–9, vol. 31

Royal Commission on Labour, Minutes of Evidence, Group C. Vol. 3 (c.6894), PP 1893–4, vol. 34

Royal Commission on Trade Disputes and Trade Combinations, Minutes of evidence before the RC (Cd. 2826) (1906)

Secondary sources

Airs, M., *The Tudor and Jacobean country house: a building history* (Far Thrupp, 1975).

Andrews, G., *Memories of Murston* (Sittingbourne, 1930).

Armstrong, J. and Jones, S., *Business documents: their origins, sources and uses in historical research* (London, 1987).

Atkins, P. (ed.), *Animal cities: beastly urban histories* (London, 2016).

Bale, J., *The location of manufacturing industry*, 2nd edn (Harlow, 1981).

Barker, T.C. and Gerhold, D., *The rise and rise of road transport, 1700–1990* (Cambridge, 1993).

Bastian, F., *Defoe's early life* (London, 1981).

Baxter, B., *Stone blocks and iron rails* (London, 1966).

Beckett, J., 'The Chandlers Ford brickworks 1860–1915', *BBS Information*, 145 (May 2020), pp. 8–29.

Behlmer, G.K., 'George Smith (1831–1892)', *Oxford Dictionary of National Biography* (Oxford, 2004).

Bell, W.G., *A short history of the Worshipful Company of Tylers and Bricklayers of the City of London* (London, 1938).

Benham, H., *Down tops'l: the story of the east coast sailing barges*, 2nd edn (London, 1971).

Bennett, L.G., *The horticultural industry of Middlesex*, University of Reading, Department of Agricultural Economics Miscellaneous studies, 7 (Reading, 1952).

Blunden, J., *The mineral resources of Britain* (London, 1975).

Bowley, M., *Innovations in building materials: an economic study* (London, 1960).

Briggs, A., *The age of improvement 1783–1867* (London, 1959).

British Geological Survey, *Brick clay*, Mineral planning factsheet (London, 2007).

British Regional Geology, *London and the Thames Valley*, 4th edn, compiled by M.G. Sumbler (London, 1996).

Brodribb, G., *Roman brick and tile* (Far Thrupp, 1987).

Brown, P.S. and Brown, D.N., 'Industrial disputes in Victorian brickyards, 1: the 1860s', *BBS Information*, 99 (February 2006), pp. 6–9.

Brown, P.S. and Brown, D.N., 'Industrial disputes in Victorian brickyards, 2: the 1890s', *BBS Information*, 101 (July 2006), pp. 14–19.

Brunskill, R.W., *Brick building in Britain* (London, 1990).

Brunskill, R.W. and Clifton-Taylor, A., *English brickwork* (London, 1977).

Bull, G.B.G., 'T. Milne's land utilisation map of the London area in 1810', *Geographical Journal*, 122 (1956), pp. 25–30.

Burnett, J., *A social history of housing 1815–1970* (Newton Abbot, 1978).

Cairncross, A.K. and Weber, B., 'Fluctuations in building in Great Britain, 1785–1849', *Economic History Review*, 2nd ser., 9 (1956) reprinted in E.M. Carus-Wilson (ed.), *Essays in Economic History*, vol. 3 (London, 1962), pp. 318–33.

Campbell, J.W.P., *Brick: a world history* (London, 2003).

Campbell, J.W.P., *Building St Paul's* (London, 2008).

Chambers, J.D. and Mingay, G.E., *The agricultural revolution, 1750–1880* (London, 1966).

Bibliography

Chapman, M., 'Brick for a day: H.G. Matthews Brickworks, Bellingdon, near Chesham, Buckinghamshire', *BBS Information*, 142 (August 2019), pp. 39–46.

Cherry, B. and Pevsner, N., *The buildings of England: London 3, north west* (London, 2002).

Churchill, D., *Crime control and everyday life in the Victorian city: the police and the public* (Oxford, 2018).

Clarke, B., *A history of Murston* (Stroud, 2011).

Clarke, L., *Building capitalism: historical change and the labour process in the production of the built environment* (London, 1992).

Clegg, H.A., Fox, A. and Thompson, A.F., *A history of British trade unions since 1889: vol.1 1889–1910* (Oxford, 1964).

Clements, D. (ed.), *The geology of London*, Geologists' Association Guide No. 68 (London, 2010).

Clements, P., *Marc Isambard Brunel* (London, 1970, reissued 2006).

Collins, M., *Banks and industrial finance in Britain, 1800–1939* (London, 1991).

Cook, C. and Stevenson, J. (eds), *Longman handbook of modern British history 1714–2001*, 4th edn (London, 2001).

Cooney, E.W., 'Capital exports and investment in building in Britain and the USA 1856–1914', *Economica*, new series, xvi/64 (1949), pp. 347–54.

Coppock, J.T. and Prince, H.C., (eds) *Greater London* (London, 1964).

Cottrell, P., *Industrial finance 1830–1914: the finance and organisation of English manufacturing industry* (London, 1980).

Cox, A., 'Bricks to build a capital', in H. Hobhouse and A. Saunders (eds), *Good and proper materials: the fabric of London since the Great Fire* (London, 1989), pp. 3–17.

Cox, A., *Survey of Bedfordshire: brickmaking, a history and gazetteer* (Bedford, 1979).

Cox, A., 'A vital component: stock bricks in Georgian London', *Construction History*, 13 (1997), pp. 57–66.

Crompton, G.W., 'Canals and the industrial revolution', *Journal of Transport History*, 14/2 (1993), pp. 93–110.

Darby, M., *Early railway prints, from the collection of Mr and Mrs M.G. Powell* (London, 1974).

Daunton, M.J., *Progress and poverty: an economic and social history of Britain, 1700–1850* (Oxford, 1995).

DeGroot, G.J., *Blighty: British society in the era of the Great War* (London, 1996).

Dennis, R., *Cities in modernity: representations and productions of metropolitan space, 1840–1930* (Cambridge, 2008).

Dixon, R. and Muthesius, S., *Victorian Architecture*, 2nd edn (London, 1985).

Drake, M., 'The census 1801–1891', in E.A. Wrigley (ed.), *Nineteenth-century society: essays in the use of quantitative methods for the study of social data* (Cambridge, 1972), pp. 7–46.

Drummond, A.J., 'Cold winters at Kew Observatory, 1783–1942', *Quarterly Journal of the Royal Meteorological Society*, 69 (1943), pp. 17–32.

Duckham, B.F., 'Canals and river navigation', in D. Aldcroft and M. Freeman (eds), *Transport in the Industrial Revolution* (Manchester, 1983), pp. 100–41.

Dyos, H.J., 'Speculative builders and developers of Victorian London', *Victorian Studies*, XI (1968), pp. 641–90.

Faulkner, A.H., *The Grand Junction Canal*, 2nd edn (Rickmansworth, 1993).

Feinstein, C.H., 'Capital formation in Great Britain', in P. Mathias and M.M. Postan (eds), *The Cambridge economic history of Europe, vol. VII: the industrial economies: capital, labour and enterprise* (Cambridge, 1978), pp. 28–94.

Frank, C., *Workers, unions, and payment in kind* (London, 2020).

Fraser, W.H., *The coming of the mass market 1850–1914* (London, 1981).

Bricks of Victorian London

Fredericksen, A., 'Parliament's genus loci: the politics of place after the 1834 fire', in C. and J. Riding (eds), *The houses of parliament: history, art, architecture* (London, 2000), pp. 99–112.

Freer, W., *Women and children of the Cut* (Nottingham, 1995).

Gallois, R.W., *A guide to the Pinner chalk mine*, 3rd edn (Hillingdon, 1998).

Gann, D., *Building innovation: complex constructs in a changing world* (London, 2000).

George, D., *London life in the eighteenth century* (Harmondsworth, 1966).

Gordon, D.I., *A regional history of the railways of Great Britain, vol. 5: eastern counties* (Newton Abbot, 1968).

Gray, A., *The London, Chatham and Dover Railway* (Rainham, 1984).

Griffin, C., *Nomads under the West Way: Irish travellers, gypsies and other trades in West London* (Hatfield, 2008).

Hadfield, C., *The canals of the East Midlands* (Newton Abbot, 1966).

Hall, J. and Merrifield, R., *Roman London* (London, 1986).

Halliday, S., *The Great Stink of London: Sir Joseph Bazalgette and the cleansing of the Victorian metropolis* (Stroud, 1999).

Hammond, M., *Bricks and brickmaking* (Aylesbury, 1981).

Hann, A. *et al.*, *The Medway valley: a Kent landscape transformed* (Bognor Regis, 2009).

Hanson, H., *The canal boatmen 1760–1914* (Manchester, 1975; Gloucester, 1984).

Harper Smith, A. and T., *The brickfields of Acton*, 2nd edn (Acton, 1991).

Harrison, B.H., *Drink and the Victorians: the temperance question in England, 1815–1872* (London, 1971).

Haynes, C., *Brick: a social history* (Cheltenham, 2019).

Henriques, U., *Before the welfare state: social administration in early industrial Britain* (London, 1979).

Hillier, R., *Clay that burns: a history of the Fletton brick industry* (London, 1981).

Hilton, G., *The truck system, including a history of the British Truck Acts, 1465–1960* (Cambridge, 1960).

Hobhouse, H. (ed.), *Survey of London, vol. 42. Southern Kensington: Kensington Square to Earls Court* (London, 1986).

Hobhouse, H., *Thomas Cubitt: master builder* (London, 1978).

Hobsbawm, E.J., *Labouring men: studies in the history of labour* (London, 1964).

Holderness, B.A., 'Agriculture 1770–1860', in C.H. Feinstein and S. Pollard (eds), *Studies in capital formation in the United Kingdom, 1750–1920* (Oxford, 1988), pp. 9–34.

Hopkins, E., *Childhood transformed: working class children in the nineteenth century* (Manchester, 1994).

Hopkins, E., 'The Victorians and child labour', *The Historian*, 48 (Winter 1995), pp. 10–14.

Horn, P., *Life and labour in rural England, 1760–1850* (London, 1987).

Hounsell, F.A., *Greenford, Northolt and Perivale Past* (London, 1999).

Hounsell, P., 'Cowley stocks: brickmaking in West Middlesex from 1800', PhD thesis (Thames Valley University, 2000).

Hounsell, P., *Ealing and Hanwell past* (London, 1991).

Hounsell, P., 'Henry Dodd', in *Oxford dictionary of national biography* (Oxford, 2004), vol. 16, pp. 393–4.

Hounsell, P., *London's rubbish: two centuries of dirt, dust and disease in the metropolis* (Stroud, 2013).

Hounsell, P., 'Robert Beart', in *Oxford dictionary of national biography* (Oxford, 2004), vol. 4, pp. 546–7.

Hounsell, P., 'Spanish practices: dustbin rubbish and the London stock brick', *BBS Information*, 146 (October 2020), pp. 25–37.

Hutchins, B.L. and Harrison, A., *A history of factory legislation*, 3rd edn (London, 1926).

Inwood, S., *A history of London* (London, 1998).

Jackson, A.A., *Semi-detached London: suburban development, life and transport, 1900–1939*, 2nd edn (Didcot, 1991).

Bibliography

Jackson, G., 'Ports', in D. Aldcroft and M. Freeman (eds), *Transport in the Industrial Revolution* (Manchester, 1983), pp. 177–209.

Jeremy, D.J., *A business history of Britain, 1900–1990s* (Oxford, 1998).

Juby, C., 'London before London: reconstructing the Palaeolithic landscape', PhD thesis (Royal Holloway College, 2011).

Keeling, P.S., *The geology and minerology of brick clays* (London, 1963).

Kennett, D.H., 'Britain 1919–1939: brick and economic regeneration', *BBS Information*, 88 (July 2002), pp. 3–21.

Kirby, M.W. and Rose, M.B. (eds), *Business and enterprise in modern Britain: from the eighteenth to the twentieth centuries* (London, 1994).

Latymer Road Mission centenary, 1863–1963 (London, 1963).

Lee, C.E., *The District Line* (London, 1973).

Lewis, J.P., *Building cycles and Britain's growth* (London, 1965).

Lewis, W.A., *Growth and fluctuations, 1870–1913* (London, 1978).

Lipson, E., *The economic history of England*, vol. 3 (London, 1934).

Lloyd-Jones, R. and Lewis, M.J., *British industrial capitalism since the Industrial Revolution* (London, 1998).

MacDermot, E.T., *History of the Great Western Railway vol.1: 1833–63* (London, 1927).

McDonnell, K., *Medieval London suburbs* (London, 1978).

McKellar, E., *The birth of modern London: the development and design of the city, 1660–1720* (Manchester, 1999).

Maddox, B., *Reading the rocks: how Victorian geologists discovered the secret of life* (London, 2017).

Malcolmson, P.E., 'Getting a living in the slums of Victorian Kensington', *London Journal*, 1 (1975), pp. 28–55.

March, E.J., *Spritsail barges of the Thames & Medway* [1948] (London, 1970).

May, T., *Gondolas to growlers: the history of the London horse cab* (Stroud, 1995).

Mills, A.D., *Oxford dictionary of London place names* (Oxford, 2001).

Mitchell, B.R., *British historical statistics* (Cambridge, 1988).

Moore, N.J., 'Brick', in J. Blair and N. Ramsay (eds), *English medieval industries: craftsmen, techniques, products* (London, 1991), pp. 211–36.

Mordaunt Crook, J. and Port, M.H. (eds), *The history of the king's works, vol.VI: 1782–1851* (London, 1973).

Morris, L.E., 'The genius of Perkin: story of his discovery and the courageous venture by which he founded the coal-tar dyestuffs industry', *The Dyer & Textile Printer*, CXV (1956), pp. 747–64.

Musson, A.E., *The growth of British industry* (London, 1978).

Muthesius, S., *The English terraced house* (London, 1982).

Nail, N., 'Brick and tiles taxes revisited', *BBS Information*, 67 (March 1996), pp. 5–14.

Nardinelli, C., 'Child labor and the factory acts', *Journal of Economic History*, 40/4 (1989), pp. 739–55.

Nevett, T.R., *Advertising in Britain: a history* (London, 1982).

Nightingale, P., *A medieval mercantile community: the Grocers Company and the politics and trade of London, 1000–1485* (London, 1995).

Oates, J., *Southall and Hanwell: history and guide* (Stroud, 2003).

Oxley, J., *Barking vestry minutes and other parish documents* (Colchester, 1955).

Paar, H. and Gray, A., *The life and times of the Great Eastern Railway, 1839–1922* (Welwyn Garden City, 1991).

Packwood, G.F.L. and Cox, A.H., *West Drayton during the nineteenth century* (West Drayton, 1967).

Pam, D., *A history of Enfield, vol. 2, 1837–1914: a Victorian suburb* (Enfield, 1992).

Bricks of Victorian London

Payne, P.L., *British entrepreneurship in the nineteenth century* (London, 1974).

Pearce, A. and Long, D., *Chalk mining and associated industries of Frindsbury*, Kent Underground Research Group, Research report 3 (1987).

Perceval, A., 'Faversham Bricks', *BBS Information*, 109 (March 2009), pp. 12–16.

Perks, R.-H., *George Bargebrick Esquire: the story of George Smeed, the brick and cement king* (Rainham, 1981).

Perry, P.J., *British farming in the Great Depression, 1870–1914: an historical geography* (London, 1974).

Pollard, S., *The genesis of modern management: a study of the Industrial Revolution in Great Britain* (London, 1965).

Port, M.H. (ed.), *The commission for building fifty new churches: the minute books 1711–27, a calendar*, London Record Society (London, 1986).

Porter, M.E., *The competitive advantage of nations* (London, 1990).

Porter, R., *London: a social history* (London, 1994).

Porter, S., *The Great Fire of London* (Stroud, 1996).

Porter, S. (ed.), *Survey of London, vol. 43. Poplar, Blackwall and the Isle of Dogs* (London, 1994).

Powell, C., *The British building industry since 1800: an economic study*, 2nd edn (London, 1996).

Prentice, J.E., *The geology of construction materials* (London, 1990).

Preston, J.M., *Industrial Medway: an historical survey* (Maidstone, 1977).

Price, R., 'The other side of respectability: violence in the Manchester brickmaking trade 1859–1870', *Past & Present*, 66 (1975), pp. 110–32.

Price, R., *Masters, unions and men: work control in building and the rise of labour, 1830–1914* (London, 1980).

Prince, H.C., 'North-west London 1814–1863', in J.T. Coppock and H.C. Prince, *Greater London* (London, 1964), pp. 80–119.

Reddaway, T.F., *The rebuilding of London after the Great Fire* (London, 1940).

Richardson, H.W. and Aldcroft, D.H., *Building in the British economy between the wars* (London, 1968).

Roach, J., *Social reform in England, 1780–1880* (London, 1978).

Robbins, M., *A new survey of England: Middlesex* (London, 1953).

Robinson, E., 'Geology and building materials', in B. Cherry and N. Pevsner, *The buildings of England: London 3, north west* (London, 2002), pp. 91–3.

Rodger, R., *Housing in urban Britain, 1780–1914* (Cambridge, 1989).

Ryan, P., *Brick in Essex from the Roman conquest to the Reformation* (Chelmsford, 1996).

Ryan, P., *Brick in Essex: the clayworking craftsmen and gazetteer of sites* (Chelmsford, 1999).

Samuel, R. (ed.), *Miners, quarrymen and saltworkers* (London, 1977).

Saul, S.B., 'Housebuilding in England, 1890–1914', *Economic History Review*, 2nd series, xv/1 (1962), pp. 119–37.

Saul, S.B., *The myth of the Great Depression, 1873–1896* (London, 1969).

Schofield, J., *The building of London from the Conquest to the Great Fire* (London, 1984).

Service, A., *Edwardian architecture* (London, 1977).

Shannon, H.A., 'Bricks – a trade index, 1785–1849', *Economica*, 1/3 (1934); reprinted in E.M. Carus-Wilson (ed.), *Essays in Economic History*, vol. 3 (London, 1962), pp. 188–201.

Shannon, H.A., 'The limited companies of 1866–1883', *Economic History Review*, 4/3 (1932), pp. 290–316.

Shenton, C., *Mr Barry's war: rebuilding the Houses of Parliament after the Great Fire of 1834* (Oxford, 2016).

Bibliography

Sheppard, F.H.W. (ed.), *Survey of London, vol. 27. Spitalfields and Mile End* (London, 1957).

Sheppard, F.H.W. (ed.), *Survey of London, vol. 37. North Kensington* (London, 1973).

Sheppard, F.H.W. (ed.), *Survey of London, vol. 38. South Kensington museums area* (London, 1975).

Sheppard, F.H.W. (ed.), *Survey of London, vol. 39. The Grosvenor Estate in Mayfair, Part 1: General history* (London, 1977).

Simmons, J., *Railways in town and country, 1830–1914* (Newton Abbot, 1986).

Simmons, J., *St Pancras Station*, 2nd edn, with additional chapters by R. Thorne (London, 2012).

Simmons, J. and Biddle, G. (eds), *The Oxford companion to British railway history* (Oxford, 1997).

Smalley, I., 'London stock bricks: from Great Fire to Great Exhibition', *BBS Information*, 147 (March 2021), pp. 26–34.

Smalley, I., 'The nature of brickearth and the location of early brick building in Britain', *BBS Information*, 41 (February 1986), pp. 4–11.

Smalley, I., Assadi-Langroudi, A. and Lill, G., 'Choice or chance: the virtues of London stock bricks for the construction of the Bazalgette sewer network in London c.1860–1880', *BBS Information*, 148 (September 2021), pp. 10–19.

Smethurst, J.B. and Carter, P., *Historical directory of trade unions*, vol. 6 (Farnham, 2009).

Smith, T.P., 'The brick tax and its effects', *BBS Information*, 57 (November 1992); 58 (February 1993); 63 (October 1994), pp. 4–13.

Smith, T.P., *The medieval brickmaking industry in England, 1400–1450*, British Archaeological Reports British Series 138 (Oxford, 1985).

Smith, T.P., '"Upon an adventure with others": John Evelyn and brickmaking after the Great Fire of London', *BBS Information*, 103 (April 2007), pp. 10–15.

Smith, T.P., 'Westminster Cathedral: its bricks and brickwork', *BBS Information*, 110 (July 2009), pp. 8–26.

Spencer-Silver, P., *Pugin's builder: the life and work of George Myers* (Hull, 1993).

Stedman Jones, G., *Outcast London: a study of the relationship between classes in Victorian society* (Harmondsworth, 1984).

Stratton, M., *The terracotta revival: building innovation and the image of the industrial city in Britain and North America* (London, 1993).

Summerson, J., *Georgian London*, rev. edn (Harmondsworth, 1978).

Tate, G. (ed.), *London Trades Council 1860–1950: a history*, with a foreword by Julius Jacob (London, 1950).

Tawney, R.H. and Power, E. (eds), *Tudor economic documents* (London, 1924).

Taylor, S. (ed.), *The moving metropolis: a history of London's transport since 1800* (London, 2001).

Temple, P. (ed.), *Survey of London, vol 47. Northern Clerkenwell & Pentonville* (London, 2008).

Thomas, B., *Migration and urban development* (London, 1972).

Thompson, E.P., 'Time, work discipline and industrial capitalism', in *Customs in common* (London, 1991), pp. 352–403.

Thompson, F.M.L., *English landed society in the nineteenth century* (London, 1963).

Tilling, J., *Kings of the highway* (London, 1957).

Turnbull, G., 'Canals, coal and regional growth during the Industrial Revolution', *Economic History Review*, 2nd series, xl/4 (1987), pp. 537–60.

Turner, M.E., Beckett, J.V. and Afton, B., *Agricultural rent in England, 1690–1914* (Cambridge, 1997).

Twist, S.J., *Stock bricks of Swale* (Sittingbourne, 1984).

Velten, H., *Beastly London: a history of animals in the city* (London, 2013).

Victoria County History. Essex, vol. 6: Becontree hundred now within the London Boroughs of Newham, Waltham Forest and Redbridge, ed. W.R. Powell (London, 1973).

Bricks of Victorian London

Victoria Country History. Essex, vol. 8: Chafford and Harlow hundreds, including Brentwood, Harlow and Thurrock, ed. W.R. Powell (London, 1983).

Victoria County History. Middlesex, vol. 4: Harmondsworth, Hayes, Norwood with Southall, Hillingdon with Uxbridge, Ickenham, Northolt, Perivale, Ruislip, Edgware, Harrow with Pinner, ed. T.F.T. Baker (London, 1971).

Victoria County History. Middlesex, vol. 5: Hendon, Kingsbury, Great Stanmore, Little Stanmore, Edmonton, Enfield, Monken Hadley, South Mimms, Tottenham, ed. T.F.T. Baker and R.B. Pugh (London, 1978).

Victoria County History. Middlesex, vol. 9: Hampstead and Paddington parishes, ed. C.R. Elrington (London, 1989).

Victoria County History. Middlesex, vol. 10: Hackney, ed. T.F.T. Baker (London, 1995).

Walford, N.W., 'Bringing historical British population census records into the 21st century: a method for geocoding households and individuals at their early twentieth century addresses', *Population, Space, and Time* (2019) <https://doi.org/10.1002/psp.2227>, accessed 1 May 2022.

Walker, D.M., *The Oxford companion to the law* (Oxford, 1980).

Watt, K.A., 'Nineteenth-century brickmaking inventions in Britain: building and technological change', PhD thesis (University of York, 1990).

Weaver, C.P. and C.R., *Steam on canals* (Newton Abbot, 1983).

White, H.P., *A regional history of the railways of Great Britain, vol. 3: Greater London* (Newton Abbot, 1971).

Whiting, P.D., *A history of Hammersmith, based upon that of Thomas Faulkner in 1839* (Hammersmith, 1965).

Wight, J., *Brick building in England from the Middle Ages to 1550* (London, 1972).

Willmott, F.G., *Bricks and brickies* (Rainham, 1972).

Wilson, G.B., *Alcohol and the nation: a contribution to the study of the liquor problem in the United Kingdom from 1800–1935* (London, 1940).

Winstanley, M., *Life in Kent at the turn of the century* (London, 1978).

Wolmar, C., *Fire & steam: how the railways transformed Britain* (London, 2008).

Woodforde, J., *Bricks to build a house* (London, 1976).

Index

Abbey Brick Fields, Faversham 119
Acton (Middx) 3, 39, 41, 42, 76, 87, 97, 99, 105, 130, 246
    industrial action in 229–32
Agriculture 17, 37–8, 41, 75, 87, 93, 102, 156, 203
    and brickfields 49–51, 74, 83–4
    and land drainage 43, 49, 50, 93
    and rates 112
    and rents 43–4
Andrews, John 99, 162, 186, 193
Arlesey (Beds) 121, 125, 127
Arlesey Brick Company 126
Artificers, Statute of (1563) 11, 183
Ashenden, Edward 119
Ashes and breeze 12, 22–3, 27, 70, 87–8, 111, 133, 143, 195
Austin, Henry de Bruno 93, 141, 170
Aveling, Edward 226
Aveling, Eleanor (née Marx) 226–7
Aylesford (Kent) 33–4, 44, 74, 94, 132, 140fn, 160, 170, 177

Baker, Isaac 133
Baker Street station 253, Plate 6
Bakewell, Samuel Roscoe 32–3
Bargemen 132–3, 187, 191
    strike action 224–6
Bargemen's and Watermen's Protection Society 224
Barges, Thames spritsail 127, 132–6, 146
Barlee, Herbert 99, 113
Barrow loader 26, 154–5, 195–6, 210
Bastin, E.P. & Co. 106
Battersea 113, 139, 146
Bawden's brickmaking machines 33, *107*, 109
Bayly, Mary 175–6, 178, 183–4, 189
Bazalgette, Joseph 60
Beart, Robert 34, 93, 121, 125, 127–8, 144, 147, 239

Bedfordshire 64, 121, 125, 237, 244
Beer 179–82, 184
    consumption of 175–82, 184, 186, 187, 197
    delivery to brickfields 178, 210
Beershops 179–81, 186
Bell Brick Field, Orpington 119
Belvedere wharf, Lambeth 100, 125–6
Bentley, John Francis 239
Betham School, Greenford 199, 208
Bird, Revd. H.G. 220–1
Bird, Stephen 65–6, 93
Biscoe's School, Norwood 199, 201
Booth, William 102–3
Bradlaugh, Charles MP 183
Bradley & Craven Ltd 33–4, 108
Brassey, Thomas 74, 146
Brentford (Middx) 19, 64, 215
    and Grand Junction Canal 57, 133, 136–7, 141–3, 146
    brickmaking at 15–16, 62, 77, 87, 199
Brick Excise Duty 32, 46, 62–7, 98, 109, 111
Brickfield cottages 93, 112, 159–60, 167–74
    sanitary condition of 170–4
Brickfields
    assessment for rates 111–12, 118
    and crime 84–6
    and fossilised remains 87
    and hazards in 86–7
    and leases of 37–48, 50, 83, 92, 93, 94, 95, 100, 104, 105, 113, 114, 115, 118–19, 136, 139–40, 169–70, 231–2
    sales of 104–5
    sanitary provision on 164
    water supplies to 42
Brick Lane, Spitalfields 13, 15
Brickmaking
    labour costs of 109–11
    legislation 19
    machinery 30–1, *30*, 34–6, 91, 106–9, *107*, 151, 164, 210–11, 214, 219, 237–8

Bricks of Victorian London

piece rates 11, 153–4, 214
seasonality 18–19
sub-contracting in 24–6
Brickmaking tools and equipment 26–36, 97,
     104, 106–11, 156, 219fn, 241
  costs of 106–10, Table 7.1
  crowding barrows 28, 72, 106, 108
  hack covers 26, 108
  moulding stools 13, 106, 109
  moulds 10, 13, 26, 106, 108, Table 7.1
  navvy barrows 72, 106
  off-bearing barrows 106, Table 7.1
  sales of 30–1
  suppliers of 106–8
  pumps 31, 106–7, 108, 109fn
  tramroads 29, 108
Brickmakers (employees)
  contracts of employment 11, 24, 26, 69, 123,
     213–15, **216**, 217–18, 227
  foremen 72, 92, 99, 104, Table 8.1, 153,
     160–2, 170, 179, 180–2, 186, 193, 196, 197
  health of 162–4, 173, 183–4, 186, 196, 203–4
  hours of work of 153, 157, 196, 203, 209, 215,
     219, 227, 251
  winter employment 154, 156–9
Brick manufacturers
  background of 92–4
  limited companies 97–102
  partnerships 92, 94, 96–7, 99, 100–1
  wealth of 95
Brickmasters 3, 91, 122, 187, 190, 192, 200,
     206, 209, 242–6, 252
  and industrial disputes 217, 219, 220, 224–6,
     228–30
Brickmasters' Employers' Liability Association
     Ltd 219
Bricks
  auction sales of 61, 118–19
  branding 120–1
  compressive strength of 117, 121, 237, 239
  imports of 61–2, 251–2
  shortages of 66, 69
Bricks, types of
  Accrington Reds (NORI) 117
  Beart's Patent Perforated 34, 121, 127–8, 239
  Flettons 238–44, 246, 249
  gault 16, 34, 52fn, 74, 121

place 28, 61, 75fn, 111, 118–19, 123, 249
  pressed 32–3
  Reading Greys 117
  red facings 14, 70–1, 95, 121, 229, 240–1
  Staffordshire Blue 117, 128
  Suffolk Whites 16, 117, 121
  wire-cuts 33–4, 239, 240
Brickworks *see* Brickfields
British & Foreign Bible Society 193
British and Foreign Temperance Society 176
British Clayworker 68–9, 102, 105, 242–3
Broad, Clement Burgess 101, 192, 221
  and Building Industry Committee (1917) 249
Broad, Harris & Co, 48, 84, 101, 104, 122, 179,
     192, 221
Broad & Co Ltd, 21fn, 68, 71, 100–1, 104, 107,
     126, 173–4, 248–9, 252
Bromley (Kent) 79, 123, 173
Brown, James 145
Brown, John 223–4, 226
Brown & Mecklenburg 94, 97
Browne, Hablot Knight ('Phiz') 167, **168**
Brunel, Isambard K & Marc 60
Builder, The, 54, 61, 104, **107**, 118, **120**, **129**
Bull, Rev Ernest 189–91
Bull's Bridge, Grand Junction Canal 136, 144
Burchett family, brickmakers 42, 100, 119, 122,
     215–16
Burham (Kent) 29, 33–4, 41, 68, 74, 108, 119,
     132, 160, 170
Burham Brick and Cement Works 68, 119
Burley, Charles 218
Burn, William 213–14, 218
Butcher, J.E. 100, 119, 208
Butterfield, William 32fn, 53, 128

Calvert (Beds) 240
Canal boats 49, 139, 141–4, **142**, 146
Canals, construction of 57 *see also* Grand
     Junction Canal
Cawte, William 121
Chalk
  availability of 21, 23, 37, 117
  and brickmaking 12, 20–2, 24, 31, 40
  cost of 23, **120**
Chalk mills 20–1, **20**, 72–3, **73**, 106, table 7.1,
     164

Index

Cherry Garden Stairs, Bermondsey 139
Child workers in brickfields 72, 159–60, **165**,
   172, 175, 195, 211
   education of **198**, 198–202, 225
   Factory Acts and 203–4, 206–7, 209, 210
   health of 157, 196–7
   moral concerns about 197–8
   school attendance of 192, 201–2, 205–6, 208
   working conditions of 153, 195, 203, 204, **205**
Children's Employment Commission 203
   5th Report of (1866) 18fn, 33, 67–8, 78, 151,
   153–4, 156–7, 171–3, 177, 179, 180–2,
   185, 192, 195, 196, 200–1, 209
Chobham (Surrey) 217
Cholera 164, 190
Churches, chapels and mission halls 75, 88,
   173, 185, 188, 189, 191–2, 200, 201,
   202, 229
Clamps, Brick 15–16, 22–3, 34, 66, 73–4, 119,
   121, 238
   construction of 26–8, **27**, Plate 3, 73, Plate 7
   dangers of 84–5
   nuisances caused by 79–80, 83
Clay mills 17, plate 2, 21, 72, **73**, 107, 109–10
Clayton, Thomas (Paddington) Ltd 88, 101,
   169–70, 173
Clayworkers, Institute of 105, 232
Clerkenwell (Middx) 32, fn52, 77
Cliff, Joseph 125, 144
Clot Moulder *see* Walk Flatter
Coade stone 16
Coal Duties 23
Coggeshall Abbey 8
Collier, S. & E. 117
Collins, Wilkie *Hide and seek* 52
Convict Prisons, H.M. 74
Conyer (Kent) 132, 252
Cooper, Hewlett John 230
Cowley (Middx) 80–1, 83, 93, 100, 130, 136,
   141
Cowley Brick Company Ltd 99, 113, 139
Cowley Brickmasters' Association 122, 123,
   220, 228
Cowley district 2, 3, 18fn, 42, 54, 105, 114, 137,
   182, 184, 242, 243, 246
   brickfield cottages in 169–70
   brickmakers in 161–2, 164, 177

brickmaking companies in 98–102, 126, 248,
   250, 252
child workers in 195, 197, 203
costs of brickmaking in 117, Table 8.1
gravel digging 88
growth of 80–1, 83
industrial action in 219, 221, 223, 227, 229,
   231
output of 64, 68, 69, Table 4.3
transport 133, 139, 143, 146
women workers in 209
Cowley stock bricks 54, 66, 80–1, 119, 121–2,
   120, 125
Craig, James McCallum 237
Crayford (Kent) 19, **30**, 36, 39, 68, 83, 112, 132,
   134, 135, 159, 160, 161
Cremer, Charles 241, 249
Crowder *see* Setter
Croydon (Surrey) 79, 86–7, 232
Cubitt, Thomas 60, 72, 75–6, Table 5.1, 85, 92,
   124, 127
   and Burham brickworks 29, 34–5, 41, 108,
   170
Cullis Bros. 105
Cullis, Philips & Co. Ltd. 115, 249
Cunninghame Graham, Robert MP 225
Curnock, John 130
Curry, W.T. 105

Dartford (Kent) 29, 160
Dawley (Middx) 41, 44–5, 46, 48, 83, 97, 100,
   140, 142, 153, 169, 201, 210, col.pl. 9
De Beauvoir wharf, Regent's Canal 137
De Burgh, Hubert 38, 41, 46, 48, 145, 180, 194
De Salis family 38, 41, 44fn, 46, 140, 170, 180
Dean, Donald 247
Dean, George Hambrook 97, 99, 193–4, 207,
   219
Defoe, Daniel 13, 15
Dennett, Rev. J. 156, 173, 182, 197, 209
Dennis, William 125
Deptford (Kent) 8–9, 79, 217, 232
Dickens, Charles
   Bleak House 156, 167, **168**, 175
   Dombey & Son 59
   Our Mutual Friend 23
Dicker, Rev A.G.H. 229–30

Bricks of Victorian London

Dobson, Ernest 18–21, **20**, **25**, 26, 28, 77–8, 109–10, Table 5.1, Table 7.1, Table 7.2

Docks *see* London docks

Dodd, Henry 49, 66, Table 5.1, 95, 123, 128, 163, 200–1
- brickfield at Yeading 95, 200
- brickfield cottages 159–60, 169, 172
- canal boats 141
- refuse business 23–4, **24**, 95
- Thames barges 135–6

Dodd, Ralph 141

Dove, Robert 118

Ealing (Middx) 93, 94, 100, 119, 124–5, 130, 161, 199

East Acton Brickworks and Estates Ltd. 70, 98, 142, 230, 240, 248, 252

East Kent Railway 144

Eastern Counties Railway 145

Eastwood and Co Ltd 29, 68, 78, 98, 100, 119, 125, 128–9, **129**, 131, 248, 252
- barges 132–5, 135
- canal boats 141–2
- Fletton bricks 241
- industrial relations 219, 221, 223–5, 231, 233

Eccles (Kent) 170

Edmonton (Middx) **27**, 79, 145, 210, **211**, 239–40, 250, 252, 253
- strikes at 221, 231, 232

Education
- adult education 186, 187, 188–91
- Education Acts 195, 206
- Factory Acts and 203–4
- *see also* Schools

Employers' Liability Act (1880) 219

Enfield (Middx) 79–80, 145, 240, 250

Erith (Kent) 29, 160

Everest, Henry 47, 66fn, 112, 135

Factory Acts 196, 203
- and brickfields 203–5, 210, 228, 245
- certifying surgeons 203, 207, 209
- Factory inspectors 181, 183, 204, 206, 209

Faversham (Kent) 34, 83, 94, 144, 158, 166, 171, 177, 179, 187, 196, 203, 207, 241, 249
- strikes at 224–6

Fellows, Morton, & Clayton Ltd 143

Fifty New Churches Act (1711) 15

Finchley (Middx) Table 5.1

Finchley Road, Camden (Middx) 101, 123–4, 177

Finsbury (Middx) 10, 13

First World War 246–9

Flemish bricks 8

Fletton (Cambs) 237

Fletton Brickmasters' Association 242

Fletton bricks 117, 126, 237–44, **241**, 252
- competition with stock bricks 128, 240–2
- cost of 242, 245–6
- dominance of English market 249, 251
- 'Rustic' facing bricks 239

Forder, B.J. & Son Ltd 126

Fossils 87

Foster, W. & Co Ltd 108

Frindsbury (Kent) 39, 100, 112, 132

Frindsbury Manor Farm brickfield 46–7, Table 3.1

Furness, George 95–6

Gale, George 144

Galsworthy, John *To Let* 81

Gasworkers' and General Labourers' Union 158, 222–33

Gasworks 157–8, 222–3

Gauged brickwork 16

Gibbs, James 14

Gibbs and Canning 101, 121

Gissing, George *The Netherworld* 52

Gladdish, W & T.N. 126

Goldsmiths of Grays 135

Grand Junction Canal 42, 101, 145, 177
- boats on 141–3, **142**
- brickfields near **63**, 69, 81, 98, 128, 146
- construction of 57
- docks on **138**, 139–41
- tolls on 142–3
- traffic on 133, 136–7

Gravel digging 3, 37, 40, 48–9, 50, 75–6, 87–8, 99, 126, 137, 139fn, 141, 143

Grays (Essex) 39, 83, 132, 135, 155, 231

Great Eastern Railway Table 4.3, 145, 240

Great Exhibition (1851) 53, 62, 97–8

Great Northern Railway 59, 74, Table 4.3, 127–8, 238

Index

Great Wakering (Essex) 160–2
Great Western Railway 43, 58, 81, 128, 130,
    145, 246
Greenwich (Kent) 15, 58, *59*, 132, *135*, 158
Gregory, Joseph 101
Gripper, Edward 127, 144
Grissell, Thomas 130
Guy, William 163

Hackney (Middx) 22, 33, 38, 39, 41, 45, 46, 64,
    68–9, 77, Table 5.1, 85, 87, 93, 124, 136,
    140, 159, 163, 173
Hacks 26, 32, 33, 72–3, 75, 85, 106, 110, 111,
    152, 196, 214
  hack covers 26, 156
  skintling bricks in 27, Table 8.1, 227
Hadleigh (Essex) 102–3
Hall, Thomas 99
Halstow (Kent) 119, 132–3
Hampstead (Middx) 15, 79–80, 145
Hampton Court Palace 9, 14, 15
Hanway, Jonas 15
Harefield (Middx) 21, 115, 126, 142, 173, 191
Harlington (Middx) 38, 44, 73–4, 115, 139fn,
    160, 169, Plate 9
Harris, George 101, 122
Hawksmoor, Nicholas 15
Hayes (Middx)
  beershops 179, 181fn
  brickfield cottages 170, 172
  brickfields 30fn, 41, 43–4, 48, 84, 87, 248,
    253
  brickmakers 152fn, 159–62
  brick manufacturers in 93, 95, 111
  education in 200–1
  Grand Junction Canal 128, 136, 141
  missionary work in 188, 189, 200
Haynes, Henry 183
Hempsted Bros 237–8
Henderson, James 24fn, 142fn, 207, 209, 211
Heron & Rutter 66fn, 50fn, 84, 111fn, 130, 141,
    168
Heston (Middx) 26, 45, 54, 84, 93, 94, 95, 100,
    156, 159–62, 168, 179, 189, 248, 249,
    253
  brickfield cottages at 168, *169*, 173
  industrial action at 215, 220, 231

missionary work at 189
  Passingham Estate 29–30, 38, 49
  rating of brickfields 112
  schools at *199*, 200, 202
  Westbrook brickfield 54, 112, 122, 187
Heston Institution for Working Men *see*
    Westbrook Memorial
Hewett, George 98, 100
Hickman, Henry 111, 113, 131
Hill, J.C. London Brick Company 233, 240
Hiscock, Thomas 112
Hobbs, Henry 99, 115
Hoffmann kilns 31–2
Holland and Hannen 125
Holland, Henry, architect 16
Homer, Thomas, boat owner, Grand Junction
    Canal 141
Horses 3, 26, 29–30, 130–2, 140, 143, 153, 156,
    195
Houghton, John 12–13
Hounslow (Middx) 94, 124, 131, 223
Housebuilding 55–7, 60, 239–40, 242, 250–1
Hufflers 133
Hull, Smith & Co 114
Hunter, Henry 17, 76–7

Ilford (Essex) 79, 87, 145, 217, 221, 245
Import Duties Act (1932) 251–2
Industrial action *see* Strikes
Ingram, Thomas 182–3
Ingram's Patent Solid Bricks 121
Invicta brickmaking machine 101–2, 105, 242
Isleworth (Middx) 95, 100, 107–8, 160
Isleworth Brewery 180
Islington (Middx) 19, 39, 64, 73, Plate 8, 77–9,
    Table 5.1, *79*, 83, 133, 145, 159, 163,
    189, 238
Iver (Bucks) 99, 146, 231

James I, King 9–10
Jenner, Charles 15
Jopling, Joseph 106, 108, 109
Juniper, Henry 162

Kent and Essex Brickmasters' Association 122,
    225, 242–3
Kent Co-operative Brickmaking Society Ltd 31

Bricks of Victorian London

Kilns 1, 13, 15, 16, 28, 29, 34, 52, 71, 72, 75, 76, 79, 81, 106, 108, 187, 238, 243, 246
    Hoffmann kilns 31–2
    Scotch kilns 28fn, 31, 75, 121fn, 240
    see also Clamps, Brick
King, W.H. 142
King's Cross (Camden) 142, 159
King's Cross Station 59, 62, 74, 77, 122, 125, 144, 147, 238, 253
Kingsland (Hackney) 77, 83, 87, 159, Plate 10
Kingsland Basin, Regent's Canal 125, 137
Kingston (Surrey) 79, 131
Kirkaldy & Son 239
Kyezor, Henry 124, 131, 164

Lambeth (Surrey) 100, 125–6, 131fn, 223
Lambeth Palace 9
Langley (Berks) 146, 231, 232
Lea, River 133, 136, 140
Leland, John 9
Lewisham (Kent) 29, 79, 232
Limehouse (Middx) 57, 79, 125, 133
Lincoln's Inn 9
Lindsey wharf, Chelsea 139, Plate 13
London
    docks 1, 57–8, 74, 85, 122, 155
    Great Fire (1666) and rebuilding 1, 2, 7, 10, 13, 17, 22
    growth in nineteenth century 52–7
    in Middle Ages 8–10, 13
    in Roman period 7–8
    Tower of London 7, 8
London & Birmingham Railway 58–9
London & County Bank 115
London & Greenwich Railway 58, **59**
London & North Western Railway 101, 144
London & South Western Railway 146
London Brick Company 126, 132, 233, 240, **241**, 243–4, 252
London Bridge 9, 58
London, Brighton & South Coast Railway 61, 144
London Chamber of Commerce Conciliation Board 230
London, Chatham & Dover Railway 74, 104, 144, 146, 162
London County Council 80, 102, 232
London Female Bible & Domestic Mission 191–2

London Patent Brick Company 98
London, Tilbury & Southend Railway 145
Lord, W.H. 18fn, 33, 159fn, 195
Lord's Cricket ground 130
Lower Oxford Clay 11, 237, 242

Maida Hill tunnel, Regent's Canal 133
Maidstone (Kent) 132, 160, 177, 179
Malm
    brick type 14, 119, 121fn
    clay type 12, 19, 21, 38, 40
Marx, Eleanor *see* Aveling, Eleanor
Marx, Karl 151–2, 153, 226
Masters and Servants Act (1823) 215–7
Maynard, Thomas 48, 73–4, plate 9, 115, 139fn, 169
Mead, William & Co. Ltd 98–100, 126
Mecklenburg, Paul 94, 95, 97, 122
Medway, River 33, 34, 39, 64, 68, 69, Table 4.3, 74, 82, 83, 95, 132, 133, 134, 140, 144, 159, 224, 231
Merriman, J.J. 215–18
Millichamp, Henry 144
Milne, Thomas 17
Milton (Kent) 132, 160, 171, 177, 187, 192, 225
Milton Creek 49, 95, Plate 12, 133–4
Milton Hall Brick Company Ltd., Southend 249
Mission Halls 88, 189, 192, 200, 201
Missionary societies 189–92
    London City Mission 189, 191
    London Diocesan Home Mission 189–91
    Thames Church Mission 192
    Wesleyan Seamen's Mission 192
Moorfields (London) 13
Moulders 11, 24, 26, 35, 63, 69, 72, **73**, 92, 154–5, 156, 168, 172, 175, 177, 182, 184, 198, 205, 208, 210, 211, 224, 247, 249
    and piece rates 123, 182, 214, 215, 217, 218, 220, 229
    and employment contracts 215–6, **216**
Moulding gangs 11, 24, 26, 35, 68, 161, 164, **211**, 215, 217
    composition of 24, 26, 195, 196, 198, 207, 209, 212
    output of 184, 196
    wages of 109, 111, 112, 147, 152, 214, 219, 227, 228

working conditions of 153–4, 172, 175, 195, 198, 205, 207, 209

Moulding stools 106, 109
  as measure of brickfield capacity 68–70, 95fn, 101, 112, 131, 200, 248

Moulds, Brick 10, 13, 26, 33, 106, 108, Table 7.1

Murston (Kent) brickfield cottages at 170–1
  brickmaking at 32, 108, 160, 182, **250**
  missionaries at 192–3
  public houses at 179–80, **180**
  schools at 201
  strike action at 225

Myers, George 74, 124–5

Mylne, R.W., 12, Plate 1

Newell, Francis 141, 161, 179, 209–10

New Patent Brick Company of London Ltd 32, 83–4, 101–2, 115, 139fn, 169, 241–2, 246, 248

Normand, L. and Co 161

Northern & Eastern Railway Company 145

Northfleet (Kent) 29, 91, 132, 157, 160

Northfleet & Swanscombe Brickfields Co. Ltd 115

North Hyde, Heston (Middx) 26, 38, 143, 168, **169**, 179, 181, 185, 201

North London Estates Company 145

North London Freehold Land and House Co. Ltd 238

North London Railway 145–6

Northolt (Middx) 2, 30fn, 32, 38, 39, 40, 44, 48, 50, 83, 122, 139fn, 241, 246, 248
  boat owners at 141–2
  child workers at 199fn, 208
  brickmakers at 155, 159
  brick manufacturers at 92, 98, 101–2, 105
  brickfield cottages at 159, 169, 172

Norwood, Southall (Middx) 143, 160, 172, 177–8, 185, 199

Notting Hill (Middx) 94, 131, 175, 189, 223

Number-Ones 142

Oare (Kent) 132, 226

Odell Ltd 42, 48, 100–1, 105, 126, 142, 143, 166, 169, 227

Off bearer 154, 156, 168, 198, 217, 222

Oliphant, Margaret
  The Rector and the Doctor's family 76
  Zaidee 200

Omans, James 97

Ordnance Wharf, Westminster 125

Orpington (Kent) 119

Otter Dock, Grand Junction Canal **138**, 141

Otterham (Kent) 119

Paddington Arm, Grand Junction Canal 81fn, 136

Paddington Basin, Grand Junction Canal 48fn, 100–1, 125–6

Palmer's Green, Enfield (Middx) 132

Parliament, Houses of 53–4, Plate 5

Patent Waterproof & Common Brick & Tile Company 97–8

Pearse, Peter 92, 140

Peterborough (Cambs) 2, table 4.3, 117, 128, 157, 232, 237–9, 242, 243, 244

Peterborough & District Brick Manufacturers Association 242

Peters Bros 126

Peto, Samuel Morton 130, 215

Pitch-piners 134

Plowman T. & M. Table 5.1, **216**, 240, 241

Pocock, Samuel 45, 66fn, fig.5.1, 94, 114, 119, 123, 143, 169, 192, 253
  bankruptcies 101, 104
  Dawley Arms PH 179
  dock on Grand Junction Canal 140–1
  employment of children 208–9
  gravel digging 48–9, 141
  industrial relations 218

Ponders End, Enfield (Middx) 221

Pressed Brick Makers Association 241fn, 243

Primitive Methodist chapels 191, 192, 194

Public houses 73, 174, 175, 177, 178–9, 187–8, 191
  boarding of brickmakers in 172
  delivery of beer to brickfields 178
  operated by brickmakers 179, 181
  payment of wages in 181–3, 217

Pug boys 26, 154–5, 162, 195–6, 211, 217, 228

Pugmills 24–6, 33–4, 73, Plate 8, Plate 10, 106, 108, 109, 156, 196, 211
  cost of 106, Table 7.1
  horse-powered **25**, 29, Plate 10, 132, 153

Bricks of Victorian London

steam driven 107, 164, 211
Pusher-out 26, 154
Putney (Surrey) 133, 192

Queen Anne style 14
Quilter, E.F. 100

Railways 57, 58–60, 74, 136, 144–5
Ranyard, Ellen 191–2
Rates, assessment of brickfields for 111–12
Red Lion Square 13
Redgrave, Alexander 210
Reed family 153, 160, 161, 178, 195
Regent's Canal 58–9, 124
   boats on 133–4, 137, 141
   brickfields near 136
   construction of 57
   wharves on 95, 125, 137, 142
Rhodes family 28, 33, 38–9, 46, 66, 77, Table
    5.1, 83, 84–5, 92, 93, 97, 129, 131, 136,
140, 152
Richardson, Charles 70, 100, 101, 119, 125,
    137, 141
Rigby, Joseph & Charles 92, 97, 169–70, 180,
    253
Roads 15, 128, 130–2
Roberts, H. 144
Rose Farm brickfield (Isleworth) 107–8
Rosher, F. & G. 119, *120*, 125, 137, 141
Rowse, R.M. 248
Royal Albert Hall 53, 121
Royal Society for the Prevention of Cruelty to
    Animals 131–2
Rubbish *24*, 135
   as landfill 17, 50, 87–8
   as source of fuel 23, 70, 195
   return cargo on brick boats 133, 137, 139
Rutter, Daniel & Charles 31, 44, 50fn, 66fn, 68,
    84, 92, 95, 96, 111fn, 112, 131, 139,
    141–2, 215, 224, 231, 248, 253
   barges 132, 134
   brickfield cottages 168, 170
   canal boats 141–2
   employees 159, 160, 161–2, 208, 210
   Grand Junction Canal 130
   industrial relations 219, 224
   public houses 180

Sailing matches, River Thames 135–6
Salvation Army, Hadleigh Colony 102–3
Sand 3, 21 49, 99, 102, 108, 137
   deliveries to brickfields 133, 142
   use in brickfields 15, 22, 23, 26, 33, 40, 42,
    74–5, 195, 202, 239
Sand houses 22–3, 86
Schools
   attendance of brickfield children 195, 201–2,
    208–10
   behaviour of brickfield children in 197–8
   brickmakers' attitudes to 198
   charity schools 199
   National & British schools 199–201, 199
   buildings 170, 191, 200–1
   Sunday schools 192, 196, 199–200, 201
Scott, George Gilbert 32fn
Scott, Matthew 113, 114
Setter 28, 154, 155, 156, 161, ***166***, 178, 227
Sewell, Anna *Black Beauty* 131
Sewers 60, 92, 122, 164
Sheen Palace, Richmond 8
Sheerness (Kent) Table 4.3, 132, 158
Shepherds' Bush (Middx) 33, 68, 76, 78, 80, 92,
    130, 196, 229, 253
Sheppey, Isle of (Kent) 132
Shoebury (Essex) 19, 29, Table 4.3, 100, 132,
    223, 225
Shoreditch (Middx) 13, 44, 49
Silcock & Co. Ltd 115
Singlewell (Kent) 100
Sittingbourne (Kent) 19, 49, 81, 83, 104
   barges 133–4, 135
   brickfield cottages 170, 171
   brickfield workers 160, 177
   brickmakers at 32, 34, 41, 62, 68, Table 4.3,
    91, 95, 96, 98, 119, 239, 240, 243, ***250***, 252
   children's employment 203, 207, 208
   costs of brickmaking Table 8.1
   missionary work 192
   public houses 179, ***180***
   railways 144
   schools 200, 201, 202
   strikes 218, 224–6, 232
   temperance movement 181, 187
   WWI 247, 249–50
Sivers, Richard 142

Index

Skintling *see* Hacks, skintling
Skuse, George 130
Slough (Berks) 146, 184, 223, 231
    Slough Canal 146
Smeed, George 41, 62, 68, 93, 95, **96**, 97, 99,
        157, 197–8, 207, Plate 11
Smeed, Dean & Co. Ltd
    barges 132, 134–5, 146–7
    brickfield cottages 170–1, **171**
    brick manufacturing 23, 32, 68, 97, 98, 99,
        106, 108, 119, 120, 122, 132, 162, 241,
        250, 252
    children's employment 207, 210
    public houses 179
    religious views of owners 193, 194
    schools 201
    temperance movement 185, 186
    WWI 247
Smith, George *The Cry of the children from the
        brickyards of England* 204–5, **205**
Snodland (Kent) 132
South Benfleet (Essex) 132, 161
Southall (Middx) 38, 86, 245
    brickfield cottages 168–9
    brickmakers 30fn, 154, 157, 158, 161, 166,
        172
    brick manufacturers 22, 41, 67–8, 71, 92,
        93–4, 97–101, 106, 115, Table 8.1, 119,
        125, 130, Plate 3
    canal boats 141
    child workers 197
    landowners 38, 45, 51, 140
    missionary work 173, 189–90, 191
    public houses 179, 182
    railways 81, 145, 146
    schools 200, 201, 202
    strikes 216–17, 219–20, 229, 231
    temperance movement 187
    trade unions 223
    tramways 29
    women workers 209–10
    WWI 248
Southall Brick & Terracotta Co. Ltd 100
Southall Brick Company Ltd 41, 98–9, 115,
        140fn, 145, 210
Southall Brickmaking Company 106, 182, 209,
        216

Southchurch Brickfields Co. Ltd. 101
Southend-on Sea (Essex) 30, 92, 132, 225, 249
Spritsail barges *see* Barges
St Augustine's Church, Kensington 128
St Botolph's Priory, Colchester 8
St John's Church, Smith Square 14fn, 17, Plate 2
St Pancras (Middx) 85, 126, 159
St Pancras station 53, 59, 60, 77, 127
St Paul's Cathedral 7, 14–15, 17, Plate 2
St Peter's Church, Vere Street 14
Stacey, A.E. 144
Stacey, George & Sons 106
Stacey, James 141, 158, 169
Stewartby (Beds) 243–4
Stock Brickmasters' Association 252
Stoke Newington (Middx) 68, 78, Table 5.1, 79,
        83, 176–7, 215
Stone
    in London 7–10, 14, 16, 53–4, 62
    stone merchants 113, 125
    supply of 125, 127
Stow, John 13
Stratford (Essex) 221
Strikes 61, 70, 99, 122, 123, 172, 177, 213–33
Stroud family 38, 41, 78, Table 5.1, 83, 97, 122,
        130, 136, 137, 141, 152fn, 169, 176–7,
215fn, 219, 229–31
Studds, William & Joseph 48–9, 88, 97
Swale, The, (Kent) 68, **82**, 83, 132, 134, 146
Swanscombe (Kent) 115, 132
Sydenham (Kent) 74, 79, 217

Temperance movement 175–8, 184–8, 192
Temperer 26, 154, 156, 168
Terracotta 16, 53, 100, 101, 121, 125
Teynham (Kent) 27, 31, 144
Thackrah, George 162–3
Thames, River 7, 12, 16, 21, 23, 39, 48, 62,
        68, **82**, 83, 93, 95, 102, 125, 127, 130,
        132–7, 139, 141, 146, 160
    and Grand Junction Canal 57, 143
Thames Tunnel 60
Thorne, Will **222**, 222–3, 226, 228, 232
Tildesley, Samuel 67–8, 92, 94, 97, 112, 119,
        169, 190–2, 209
Tilers & Bricklayers Company 10
Tillett, Ben 221–2

Bricks of Victorian London

Tilley, George 99, 115
Tisdall, Henry 10
Tottenham (Middx) 79, 145, 221, 228
Townsend, William 114
Trade Marks 120–1
Trade unions 69, 122, 158, 213–33
    Combination Act (1824) 213
    legal representation for members 215–17,
      218, 227
    London Trades Council 213–14
    see also Gasworkers' and General Labourers'
      Union *and* Strikes
Tramroads 29–31, 102, 141, 145, 146
Trimmer family, 62, 77, 87, 141
Trimmer, James 65, 111, 199
Trimmer, Sarah 199
Trollope, Anthony *The Last chronicle of Barset*
      151–2, 162–3, 188
Truck payments 182–3

United Operative Brickmakers' Benevolent
      and Protective Society of the South of
      England 214
Upchurch (Kent) 132
Uxbridge 2, 38, 64, 81, 83, 95, 106, 114, 118,
      126, 136–7, 143, 158, 177, 184, 186, 228
Uxbridge Board of Guardians 157
Uxbridge Magistrates Court 209, 216–17
Uxbridge Road Brick Co Ltd., Southall 248

Vauxhall (Surrey) 70, 100, 125
Victoria Park, Hackney 87, 119

Walk flatter 26, 35, 198, 227
Walthamstow (Essex) 136, 145, 221
Wanstead Flats (Essex) 217, 221
Ward, William, Honduras Wharf 125
Ware, Isaac 14
Waring Bros 60, 119, 168, 210
Warner, John William 97
Warner, William 123
War Office, Whitehall 240
Washbacks 21–2, 31
Watkins, George 141
Watkins, Stephen Drayton 92, 114, 184
Watkinson, Mr. 225
Weather, effects on brick manufacture 15–16,

      18–19, 23–4, 27, 62, 70, 152, 157, 228,
      245, 248
    flooding 49–50, 84, 86, 245
    frost 152
    rain 70, 196, 214–15
Wesleyan Chapel, Sittingbourne 192
Westbourne Green, Westminster 130
Westbrook Memorial, Hounslow 192, *193*
Westbrook, Edward 54, 92, 112, 122, 137, 187fn
West Drayton (Middx) 83, 128, 253
    brickearth at 42
    brickfield cottages at 173, *174*
    brickmakers 157, 160, *165*, 184, 194
    brick manufacturers 21fn, 31, 84, 101, 104,
      106, 119, 139, 169, 231, 248
    canal boats 144
    docks 140fn, 141
    gravel digging 48
    landowners 38–9, 41, 46
    missionary work 188, 191, 192
    public houses 179–80
    railways 81, 145–6
    temperance 185–6
    trade unions 223, 226
Westminster Cathedral 239
White, Samuel 141
Whitehead, John & Co. 108
Whittaker & Co. 108, 237, 242
Whittlesea station, Great Eastern Railway 240
Whittlesey (Cambs) 244
Whymper, Frederick 178fn, 206–7
Willesden (Middx) 76, 86, 95, 130, 250
Willesden & Acton Brick Co 240, 246
Willesden Brick and Tile Co Ltd 95, 98
Willett, William 229–30
Williams, J.& S. 33, 78, 107fn
Wills & Packham 68, 119, 132, 134, 186, 218,
      247, 252
Wills, Daniel 95, Plate 12
Wolff Dryer Co. Ltd 32, 246
Woodford (Essex) 221
Woods, John 100
Woolwich (Kent) 23, 79, 158
Workhouses 73, 85, 124, 227, Plate 8
    and brickmakers 156–8, 163, 166, 175–6, 224
Workmen's Compensation Act (1897) 219
Workshop Regulation Act (1867) 203